Books on the Theatre
by George Jean Nathan

Mr. Nathan, who is the authority on the American theatre and drama for the *Encyclopædia Britannica* and the *Britannica Book of the Year,* has published the following books on the subjects:

Testament of a Critic
Art of the Night
The House of Satan
The Autobiography of an Attitude
Since Ibsen
Land of the Pilgrims' Pride
Materia Critica
Comedians All
The Popular Theatre
The Critic and the Drama
The Theatre, the Drama, the Girls
The World in Falseface
Mr. George Jean Nathan Presents
Another Book on the Theatre
The Avon Flows
Passing Judgments
The Intimate Notebooks of George Jean Nathan
The Theatre of the Moment
The Morning after the First Night
Encyclopædia of the Theatre
The Entertainment of a Nation
The Theatre Book of the Year, 1942–43
The Theatre Book of the Year, 1943–44
The Theatre Book of the Year, 1944–45
The Theatre Book of the Year, 1945–46
The Theatre Book of the Year, 1946–47
The Theatre Book of the Year, 1947–48
The Theatre Book of the Year, 1948–49

The Theatre Book of the Year

1948〰1949

The THEATRE Book

OF THE YEAR

1948 ✦ 1949

A Record and an Interpretation

BY

GEORGE JEAN NATHAN

ALFRED A. KNOPF

NEW YORK : 1949

Foreword

It NEED HARDLY again be recalled that many of our theatrical producers' pet, consoling explanation of unfavorable criticism of one of their exhibits is that it was composed by a critic suffering from dyspepsia. That the explanation long since has taken its place in the joke-books has not hindered its autoactivation. The belief that a critic beset by one malaise or another is bound to be influenced by his personal discomfort against a play which duty compels him willy-nilly to review is but one of a number of fallacies shared alike by producers, playwrights, and volunteer secular diagnosticians. The fact of the matter is that, instead of being influenced against what he has to review, the critic's indisposition influences him rather in its favor, and for a reason that even the amateur psychologist may determine.

When the critic for one cause or another finds his physical and mental vivacity not what it should be, he, like any other man, is inclined to be self-apologetic and in that mood far from contentious. He is induced by his enfeebled state to resign himself for the time being to the doctrine of *laissez-faire,* to let things slide, and to avoid anything in the way of discommoding argument. The mere consciousness of so little as a pimple on his nose has been known to humble a man's self-assurance in the presence of another man or, more particularly, woman whom otherwise he would flee as from the plague. Any critic who has been practising for any length of time knows that the less fit he feels the greater his disposition to be easy on what he reviews. He will not, of course, openly admit it — his *amour propre* is too considerable for that; but the truth remains that any such one depressed by anything short of smallpox is natu-

rally reduced to a charitableness which under other circumstances would be wholly foreign to him.

It is not only theatre criticism that has been inflicted
with the opposite conviction. Criticism in general has frequently been criticized in turn on the senseless ground of
its practitioners' health and, in some cases, even looks, as
may be amusingly noted in a recent study of the methods
of modern literary criticism, *The Armed Vision,* by one
Stanley Edgar Hyman, wherein Van Wyck Brooks is sum-
marily dismissed with the observation that he has aged and
has now a white mustache. "In what way hair on the lip,
no matter what its color, can interfere with critical judgment," Joseph Wood Krutch has added, "Mr. Hyman does
not make clear."

Drama criticism remains, however, the chief victim of
such simious prejudices and confusions. Shaw's devastat-
ingly accurate criticism of Henry Irving, it will be remembered, was attributed by numskulls to his jealousy of a rival for the affections of the fair Ellen Terry, and his
equally riddling criticism of sentimental Victorian twaddle
to the fact that he did not eat meat. And Beerbohm's objection to some of the juvenile sentiment flooding the stage
of his day was argued by his detractors to be predicated on
the circumstance that he had a bald head. Unfavorable
criticism, in short, is ever thought to have a dubious well-
spring or motive. The clichés are numberless: the critic is
a disappointed playwright; the critic employs criticism as
a derrick for his little ego; the critic is a failure who seeks
to vent his spleen on others who have succeeded; the critic
is a homely creature who dislikes an actor who is handsome; the critic is against an actress because she has won a
role coveted by an actress of whom personally he is fond;
the critic is a drunkard on the score that he enjoys a Martini before his dinner; the critic has dined well before the
show and a decent meal notoriously corrupts the brain; etc.

It is further sometimes charged against the critic that his
reviews tend toward one extreme or the other, that they
are either comprehensively laudatory or comprehensively
detractory, and that seldom if ever do they allow anything

to the middle ground. The charge is often true, but its truth is retroactively foolish. There are various plays that are completely bad, plays with no slightest redeeming qualities, and the only honest manner in which to review them is to say just that, flatly. There are, as well, plays that are wholly admirable and qualifications of their admirableness are simply the gesture of critics who wish to be arbitrarily different and thereby attract some attention to themselves. Qualifications in such cases are infinitely less symptoms of critical acumen and equity than of a desire to gain a reputation for those virtues at the expense of judgment and intelligence.

A still further charge is that the critic is prejudiced in favor of certain kinds of drama and just as prejudiced against other kinds. Again, true. But prejudice, if sound, is what gives the critic his standing. Every man, whatever his calling, acquires prejudices based on experience, so why not the critic? There are, obviously, silly prejudices as well as sound, but the former soon betray and defeat their merchants. Prejudices which are the consequence of critical education are among the most forceful weapons in the critic's arsenal. Show me a critic without prejudices and I'll show you an arrested cretin.

A third allegation is that the critic too often aims to be clever and witty instead of being straightforward and simple, and that this is deplorable. How and why it is deplorable is hard to make out. A review is intended to be read and if cleverness and wit will help it to be read, so much the better. The theory, moreover, that cleverness and wit may not be reconciled with forthright honesty is kin to one which would maintain that intelligence is best to be expressed dully and that judgment is most acceptable if recorded in glassy writing. The most valuable dramatic criticism of modern times, from Shaw to Palmer, from Montague to Howe, and from Béraud to Kerr, has been that which has been percolated through wit, humor, and literary legerdemain; the least valuable that which has been purveyed like an austere frost. Opinions long and strongly stated have a way of becoming objectionable and even slightly offensive, however valid they may be. Best to serve, they should be coated with varied brightly colored dyes. The dyes do not penetrate seriously into them; they are largely superficial; but, as with an Easter egg, they engage and tickle the attention of such children as would disdain the egg in its common, unadorned state.

We hear that the critic should efface himself in his criticism and not, as is the practice of some, employ it in part as a personal show-window. The contention is that of other critics who hope to make acceptable their own lack of any personality by decrying it in their betters. Anyone who uses criticism as a personal show-window must have the goods to display in it or soon go out of business. A good critic can no more keep his personality and all it stands for out of his criticism than he can keep it out of his speech, his politics, or his love-making. Impersonal criticism, if there can be such a thing, is like an impersonal fist fight or an impersonal marriage, and as successful.

To ask of a critic that he dismiss his personality and its various facets from his criticism is an affront both to him and to criticism itself. It is like asking the individual to convert himself into a blank and to allow the blank, like a whitewashed flat wall, to reflect what rays there may possibly be against another such wall which is the reader. Personality, far from deflecting the light, makes it seem relatively brighter and yet more comfortable on the eyes by embellishing it with shadow and color. What the objectors object to is really not any such factual personality but what is sanguinely passed off for it through the common journalistic over-use of the first person singular pronoun. The critic who dots his paragraphs with "I's" may conceivably enjoy a personality as striking as Napoleon's or General Coxey's but he does not know how to sell it. True personality does not work itself thus contrabandly into criticism; criticism naturally mirrors it.

It is also the habit to look askance at the critic who contradicts himself. Such contradiction is held to be the mark of an insecure and untrustworthy mind. It should rather be the habit to look askance at the critic who does not occa-

sionally contradict himself. Contradiction may as well be
the offspring of increased education, experience, and perception as it may be of the vacillation induced by ignorance. The critic who stubbornly adheres to original statement is sometimes like a bull-dog who gluttonously clings
to a rubber bone. There is a tide in the affairs of art as
there is in the affairs of man and, while the basic principles
may not be affected, there are ripples that glint with new
lights and these new lights now and then dim the antecedent ones. The critic who vainly is unwilling to contradict himself is accordingly in the position of a man who has
been unpleasantly punched in the eye, which thereupon
turns black, but who stoutly denies to witnesses of the contretemps both that it took place and that his eye is not its
normal color.

"Whenever either side of the scale is over-weighted,"
writes Eric Bentley in a treatise called *Theory and Theatre*,
"it is for the critic to try — by exhortation, invective, satire,
or whatever — to weight the other side. In a sense the critic's job is not to be impartial but always *to weight the other
side* (italics his), the side that needs it." This is an ap-
plaudably generous point of view and one that appeals to
every man's impulse to help the underdog, but otherwise it
would convert the critic into a mere propagandist. The
critic who would arbitrarily weight the other side, whatever it might be, would be a suspect critic indeed. The
temptation to do it is wholly understandable, and in moments of careless thinking I have not been the only one
who has succumbed to it (Mr. Bentley seems to prove that
he, among others, is like me in this regard), but such
weighting surely is no part of criticism. It is part, rather, of
critical politics. I agree that in at least one sense the critic's
job, as Mr. Bentley puts it, is not to be impartial. He should
fight for what he soberly deems right and best, and should
pitch his lance come hell or high water; and if over-weight-
ing his stand will assist his purpose, let him over-weight it
to the limit. If another critic who, though agreeing with
him, elects then to posture as playing fair by sophisticating
the virtues of the other side and thus elevate himself as a

square-shooter over the other, he is not only critically dishonest but, however cunning, a critical fraud.

There is, finally, it need scarcely be repeated, a distaste
for any man who sets himself up as a critic of other men
and their works. It is not for me to argue its justice or injustice. But the terms in which it customarily vents itself
are too often questionable. There surely must be better arguments lying around somewhere; I myself, indeed, can
think of some honeys, though I shall here wisely keep them
to myself.

A critic, for example, will be derogated because he is a
"dapper dresser," like Richard Brinsley Sheridan, Chopin,
and Disraeli; because he is self-assured and hence "pompous," like Talleyrand, Botticelli, and Wagner; or because
he does not go to a barber frequently enough, like Andrew
Jackson, General Grant, and Walt Whitman. He is dis-
countenanced by ill-natured playwrights like Moss Hart
who take to the radio to observe, acidly, that but one modern dramatic critic has ever written a successful play, to
wit, William Archer and *The Green Goddess,* only to be
informed to their embarrassment that among the large assortment who have written successful plays have been Robert de Flers, Franklin Fyles, Charles Hoyt (whose satirical
farces have clearly influenced some of Hart's plays), Herbert Farjeon, Channing Pollock, St. John Ervine, C. M. S.
McLellan, Charles Frederic Nirdlinger, Victor Mapes,
Charles Henry Meltzer, H. Granville-Barker, Frederick
Schrader, A. E. Thomas, Frederick Donaghey, Frederic
Hatton, Harry B. Smith, Pérez Galdós, Charlton Andrews,
André Obey, Thompson Buchanan, Augustin Daly, Paul
Potter, Walter Browne, George Ade, Hermann Bahr, Ash-
ley Dukes, Edmond See, Harold Brighouse, Bronson How-
ard and, along with a lot of others, G. B. Shaw.

If the critic pens sweet words about a pretty new young
actress, even one of unmistakable talent, it will be said of
him that he is a sentimental mark when it comes to the fair
sex. If he has no taste for cheap, soapbox propaganda in
drama, it will be claimed against him that he knows nothing of what is going on in the world and that his interests

are confined to the world of Broadway. If he reviews a succession of miserable plays exactly for what they are, he will
be accused by their producer of conducting a vendetta
against him, inspired by unstated but darkly implied motives. And, if by any chance he rises to any eminence in his
profession, the gossip columns will not let an opportunity
pass to make him ridiculous in one way or another and to
minimize what esteem people may conceivably have for
him.

He is, in short, a black sheep — in a pack of jackasses.

Contents

The Theatre Book of the Year

1948 ᔑᔐ 1949

Honor List

THE BEST AMERICAN PLAY:
DEATH OF A SALESMAN, by Arthur Miller

THE BEST FOREIGN PLAY:
THE MADWOMAN OF CHAILLOT, by Jean Giraudoux, the faulty adaptation notwithstanding

THE BEST MUSICAL:
SOUTH PACIFIC, by Richard Rodgers, Oscar Hammerstein II, and Joshua Logan

THE BEST REVUE:
LEND AN EAR, by Charles Gaynor

THE BEST MALE ACTING PERFORMANCE:
JOSÉ FERRER, in *The Silver Whistle*

THE BEST FEMALE ACTING PERFORMANCE:
MARGARET PHILLIPS, in *Summer And Smoke*

THE BEST STAGE DIRECTOR, DRAMATIC:
SIDNEY KINGSLEY, in *Detective Story*

THE BEST STAGE DIRECTOR, MUSICAL:
JOSHUA LOGAN, in *South Pacific*

THE BEST SCENE DESIGNER:
JO MIELZINER, in *Summer And Smoke* and *Death Of A Salesman*

THE BEST COSTUME DESIGNER:
MOTLEY, in *Anne Of The Thousand Days*

THE BEST CHOREOGRAPHER:
PAUL GODKIN, in *Ballet Ballads* (*Willie The Weeper*)

The Year's Productions

THE HABIMAH COMPANY. May 1, 1948

A repertory of four plays: THE DYBBUK, by S. Ansky; THE GOLEM, by H. Levik; ŒDIPUS REX, by Sophocles in a version by Saul Chernikhovsky; and DAVID'S CROWN, by J. Lamdan from Calderon de la Barca. Produced by Theatre Incorporated for the American Fund for Palestinian Institutions for a 6 weeks' engagement in the Broadway Theatre.

THE COMPANY

Ari Warshawer, Aaron Meskin, Shimon Finkel, Hanale Hendler, Hanna Rovina, Ianna Govinska, Aaron Kutai, Jehuda Rubinstein, Abraham Baratz, David Vardi, Shimon Bruk, Shlomo Bruk, Zvi Ben-Haim, Menachem Benyamini, Zvi Friedland, Raphael Klatzkin, Joshua Bertonov, Tamar Robins, Tmima Judelevitch, and Shoshana Duer.

Directors: 1. *Eugene Vachtangoff;* 2. *B. Varshilov;* 3. *Tyrone Guthrie;* 4. *Alexei D. Dicky.*

THE REPERTORY of the celebrated company, hailing from Palestine and employing the Hebrew tongue, consisted, as noted above, of four plays: *The Dybbuk, The Golem, Œdipus Rex,* and *David's Crown.* The first two offered no problem to dramatic understanding, since they have been seen before on the stage in English translation, and the third, of course, is a classic familiar from a number of productions to English-speaking audiences. The fourth, however, despite its non-Hebrew origin, was strange and, except for the English synopsis provided by the management, which as usual in such cases was not of much help, presented a doubled difficulty in its appraisal. I say doubled because any wholly honest estimate of the performances of even the three familiar plays is not possible if one does not to the

slightest degree understand the language. The point generally made in such junctures is that, if one knows what a
play is about and indeed has already reviewed it in a
tongue one comprehends, one should be able to judge its
performance without trouble. It pains me to differ. The
play itself provides no problem, but the performance poses
several. Let us say, in elementary illustration, that the company were to act *Hamlet,* with which critics are, or should
be, on ready terms down to the last detail. Take, as an obvious test, these lines from the often quoted and perfectly
known soliloquy:

> O, what a rogue and peasant slave am I!
> Is it not monstrous that this player here,
> But in a fiction, in a dream of passion,
> Could force so his soul to his own conceit
> That from her working all his visage wann'd,
> Tears in his eyes, distraction in 's aspect,
> A broken voice, and his whole function suiting
> With forms to his conceit? and all for nothing!

The critic of course knows that the actor is reading the
speech but, since he has no knowledge of the language in
which it is being read, how is it possible for him to tell
whether the actor is doing ably by it or botching it? How,
in other words, can he conceivably know that the actor is
not reading it in some such manner as this:

> O, watta rogue and pleasant slave am I!
> Is it not monstrauss that this player here,
> Buttin' a friction, in a dream of passion,
> Could foresaw his soul to his own conceit
> That from her waking all his visage went,
> Tears in his eyes, distraction in suspect,
> A broken vice, and his whole function seating
> With farms to his conceit? and all for nothing!

I exaggerate, granted. But the point is there just the
same. It is possible for him only to guess at the actor's reading, and guessing is hardly a critic's prerogative. All that
he can do is struggle to reconcile the actor's voice, expres-

sions and gestures with what he hopes is a proper rendering of the lines. He cannot know — and such knowledge is
all-necessary — if the actor is punctuating the speech correctly, if he is giving it the correct inflections or if, in fact,
he is not rather garbling it out of all meaning.

It is thus when I read some monolingual critic's learned
remarks on the subtle nuances of the performance of a
Habimah play in Hebrew that I am blushfully reminded of
a night years ago in Tokyo. I had been invited to attend
the performance of a program of short *Nō* dramas and,
learning the names of the particular specimens that were to
be the bill of the evening, I prepared myself by procuring
and reading the plays in the Fenollosa English translations.
Though I knew and understood probably not more than
half a dozen words in Japanese, and those identified with
matters decidedly unrelated to the *Nō* drama in whole or
in part, I subsequently prided myself, and indeed showed
off a bit, on my ability to comprehend pretty fully what I
had heard and seen on the stage. My vainglory, however,
was not to last long, though my Japanese host courteously
saw to it that it was not abashed until lunch the next day,
when he gently informed me that the program of the night
before had been suddenly changed and that the dramas I
had seen were not the ones I had prepared myself for but,
though there is some essential similarity in various of the
Nō plays, ones that dealt with subjects quite different.

Whenever a critic is confronted by a play in an incom-
prehensible language yet has heard and feels that the acting company offering it deserves his serious consideration,
he accordingly falls back, like a trick acrobat, on the word
"interesting." Or, if he feels that does not go far enough,
elaborates with such phrases as "ensemble acting perfected
by long training," "gestures of remarkable eloquence," and
"voices richly capable of running the gamut of the emotions." That he can not know whether the ensemble acting
is strictly in key with the play, whether the gestures are at
all relevant, or whether the voices are properly registered
to the business in hand apparently does not count. He has,
he thinks, not only done his duty but has slyly managed to

give the impression that he knows enough in other directions to atone for what he does not know in the really only important one.

Under the circumstances, and foregoing the usual refuge in such hollow stencils, all that I therefore am able to say about the Habimah players is that they form a highly, even extravagantly, specialized group; that they employ the emotional and florid style of acting associated with the theatre of their race, whether in a more elevated enterprise like this or in such local offshoots as the Maurice Schwartz and other companies; and that they at least bring to an acting stage too often bloodless and pale and tired an unmistakable vigor and a powerful vibration. The performances may and do seem excessive to alien eyes and ears, but it should be remembered that at least two of the plays in the repertory, being part of the dramatic literature of their people, are naturally suited to such delivery, and that the Greek classic, though a thing apart, is not less well adapted to it.

A brief recapitulation of the three Hebrew plays:

The Dybbuk, whose author's real name was Shloyme Zalmon Rappoport and which was once called *Between Two Worlds,* is, as the latter title suggests, a drama of the living and the spirit spheres. The dybbuk is a spirit that insinuates itself into a person, and the play describes the entrance of such a spirit, in the guise of the soul of the grieving young man who has lost the young woman of his heart's choice, into the latter's corpus. The spirit is finally exorcized and the young woman joins her beloved in death rather than marry the man whom her father has chosen for her.

The Golem is a paraphrase of the Frankenstein theme in which a man who fashions a gigantic creature to fight with the Jews against their enemies is compelled to destroy the monster when it gets out of hand.

David's Crown, a Hebrew adaptation from the Spanish, narrates the tale of the bloodshed that followed the disputes among the offspring of David in their quest of his throne.

The direction of the four plays, particularly of *The Dybbuk* by the talented late Russian, Vachtangoff, and *Œdipus Rex* by the Englishman, Tyrone Guthrie, seems, so far as I can tell, to be commendable, though, as I have said, my critical opinion under the exotic circumstances should not be taken too seriously. Everything, in brief, about the Habimah company may conceivably be all that it should be but, since the barrier of language stands in the way,

any express to me for difficult as quite is it
for is it as it on verdict sound really
sentence a read to readers speaking-English
.manner Hebrew the in printed this like

In conclusion, as with a phosphorescent clock or glow-worm in the daytime, one however vaguely senses that the illumination is there even if one can not see it.

HOLD IT! May 5, 1948

A musical comedy with book by Matt Brooks and Art Arthur, music by Gerald Marks, and lyrics by Sam Lerner. Produced by Sammy Lambert for 46 performances in the National Theatre.

PROGRAM

RODNEY TRENT	Bob Shawley	"DINKY" BENNETT	"Red" Buttons
MRS. SIMPKINS	Ruth Saville	PAUL	Paul Lyday
MR. SIMPKINS	Douglas Rutherford	GEORGE MONOPOLIS	
MRS. BLANDISH	Helen Wenzel		Douglas Chandler
MR. BLANDISH	Budd Rogers	PENNY	Penny Carroll
"SARGE" DENTON	Larry Douglas	MR. JENKINS	Paul Reed
BOBBY MANVILLE	Johnny Downs	JOE	Tom Bowman
HELEN	Helen Wenzel	CHARLIE BLAKE	Pat McVey
JACK	Jack Warner	HEADWAITER	Douglas Rutherford
CHUCK	Bob Evans	MRS. JOLLOP	Ruth Saville
"JUDGE" ROGERS	Kenny Buffett	O'BRIEN	Scott Lewis
SID	Sid Lawson	MARTIN	Martin Kraft
JESSICA DALE	Jet McDonald		Budd Rogers
PAMELA SCOTT	Patricia Wymore	REPORTERS	Sid Lawson
MILLIE HENDERSON	Ada Lynne		Helen Schurgot
BUDD	Budd Rogers	FELIX DEXTER	John Kane
BERNIE	Bob Bernard		

SYNOPSIS: The two acts are laid on and in the environs of the campus of Lincoln University.
Director: Robert Perry.

As I HAVE BEEN heard to remark before, the critic who is fond of boasting that, whatever the occasion, he always has an open mind is not only a refugee from the truth but in all probability has no mind at all, open or shut. There isn't one of the bevy — and that includes the best along with the worst — who hasn't any number of prejudices, some of them perfectly sound, others wholly senseless. As a member of the species, I have my full share, some, I believe, grounded in merit; some, I suspect, just as far-fetched as those of any of my colleagues, living or dead.

As a sample of the latter, I offer my prejudice against writers and composers who professionally affect diminutives of their Christian names. The prejudice is not a recently acquired one, and has long been shared by my old collaborator in critical sin, Dr. Mencken. In the years gone when we were editing magazines, it was our joint distaste for authors who reduced their baptismal tags to the bartender level that not only impelled us to delay reading their manuscripts for at least a month but that, if we finally accepted them, prevailed upon us to communicate to the barbarians our heartfelt desire that they repent and permit us to print their names undefiled. Jack London had higher financial aims than we could afford to meet in those days and accordingly did not bother our æsthetic bias. But, of all the others, Jim Tully was the sole conspicuous literatus who managed to insinuate himself in that style into our pages, and then only after he had convinced us of the Jim with a birth certificate whose authenticity he had sworn to by the Governor of Ohio, his native state, politely accompanied by two cases of Michelob.

When, therefore, I read that the authors and tunesmiths of this *Hold It!* bore such labels as Matt, Art, and Sam, the producer such a one as Sammy, and the cast such as Red, Johnny, Tom, Jack, Bob, Kenny, Sid, Budd, Tom, Pat, and Larry, I confess that I approached the show in a frame of mind not considered suitable to a member of the critical profession. And certainly not in as hospitable a mood as would have been the case had the gentlemen in question billed themselves more punctiliously as Matthew Brooks, Arthur Arthur, Samuel Lerner, and Samuel Lambert, and the members of the company under the names recorded in their families' Bibles. (Red Buttons I didn't so much mind, since nicknames and contractions are traditional among comics; I once even went so far as not to throw up in the case of one calling himself Snitz Edwards.) There was, of course, no bias against the gentlemen themselves, since I knew nothing about half of them and had had small experience of the other half. I would, in the beginning stages of their careers, have been just as prepossessed

against Billy Gilbert and Art Sullivan, Vic Herbert, Reggie
de Koven, or Osk Hammerstein.

It is a senseless attitude, as I have admitted, at least in
such instances as the latter, but there are many others that
seem to make it somewhat less irrational than I should like
to convince myself. Running over the statistics of the musical shows of the last six seasons — it might just as aptly
be twelve as six — there appears in an odd way to be some
warrant for my quirk. Among the numerous authors of the
dreary *Of V We Sing* were such as Mike, Bea, Joe, Alex,
Ned, Al, Sam, and Mel. Sam, Lou, and Hy figured among
the creators of the affliction, *Let Freedom Sing*. Dave and
Leo were among those responsible for the four-perform-
ance soupbone, *You'll See Stars*. Jack, Ray, Buddy, Dan,
Les, and Sid had a hand in the poorest of the reincarna-
tions of the *Ziegfeld Follies*. And Dan, Lou, Phil, and Don
were mixed up in that memorable junkpot, *Artists And
Models*.

To continue. A Ted, Benny, and Lou sponsored the tur-
key, *Take A Bow*. A Hi, a Bern, and a Fred were guilty of
the horrendous *The Girl From Nantucket*. A Jack, a
Johnny, a Nat, an Eddie, and a Ted all had a finger in *Nel-
lie Bly*, which died after sixteen cancerous performances; a
Joe and a Don in *The Duchess Misbehaves*, that cripple,
which died more mercifully after five; and a Jack and
Sammy in the fungus called *Toplitzky Of Notre Dame*.
And in the most recent season there have been Sammy,
Jule, Bob, Milt, Patsy, Ted, Lou, Ken, etc., occasionally to
aggravate matters. Georgie doesn't like it. The good shows,
he reflects, usually do not seem to be written by the Macs,
Guses, Sigs, Petes, and Mitchs, but by men who have enough
respect for themselves not to call themselves by the names
of racetrack touts, waiters, and helpless dogs. And if anyone tries to mortify me by departing from the topic in immediate question, to wit, the theatre, extending the inquiry to other fields, and snortingly mentioning, say, Ben
Jonson or Walt Whitman, I shall throw back at him, for
every such impeccable exception he can think of, a load of
such as Ben Hecht and Walt Mason, not to mention such

as Lew Wallace, Vicki Baum, Bram Stoker, Alec Waugh, Will Cuppy, Gene Stratton-Porter, Phil Stong, and Budd Schulberg.

Since surprises in the world are few and far between and since it is always an effective writing trick to make a reader think one is firmly committed to a certain point of view and then pleasantly fool him, I should accordingly like to report that this *Hold It!*, for all my stipulated prejudice, turns out nevertheless to be an excellent show. But, as I say, surprises are not common these days and it turns out to be far from anything of the kind. Its book is a silly concoction about some college boys who have lost their pooled financial resources and who, in the hope of recouping them, enter one of their number who has played a female role in a campus show in a screen test contest. The complications that ensue until his girl friend finally agrees to substitute for him when he is unmasked succeed only in complicating one's speculation as to how any such imbecile plot ever got by the stenographer who was hired to type it. The incidental comedy, to strain semantics to the breaking point, involves, among other equally cheerless things, a succession of antics of the kind that figured in college shows in the days when the football players wore whiskers, and when the agony abates for a moment or two someone comes on and does a tap dance or sings something about its being so nice having the girl you love close to you, which somehow does not do anything to improve matters.

THE ALCHEMIST. May 6, 1948

A revival of the comedy by Ben Jonson, with incidental music by Deems Taylor. Produced by the New York Theatre Company for 14 performances in the City Center Theatre.

PROGRAM

PROLOGUE

LOVEWIT	*Bert Thorn*	MAID	*Tyler Winn*
JEREMY	*José Ferrer*	SUBTLE	*George Coulouris*
COOK	*Stanley Carlson*	DOLL COMMON	*Nan McFarland*

THE PLAY

FACE	*José Ferrer*	ANANIAS	*Robinson Stone*
SUBTLE	*George Coulouris*	KASTRIL	*Hiram Sherman*
DOLL COMMON	*Nan McFarland*	DAME PLIANT	*Phyllis Hill*
DAPPER	*William Nichols*	PARSON	*Will Kuluva*
DRUGGER	*Ray Walston*	LOVEWIT	*Bert Thorn*
SIR EPICURE MAMMON	*Ezra Stone*	1ST OFFICER	*Stanley Carlson*
PERTINAX SURLY	*Robert Carroll*	2D OFFICER	*Leonardo Cimino*

Scene: *Lovewit's house, London.*
Director: *Morton Da Costa.*

THE IDEA that benevolence born of sympathy does not occasionally play a pretty part in conditioning many reviewers' estimates of theatrical productions must be getting something of a setback these days. Let an actor like Laughton or Garfield come on from the Hollywood mint between pictures and act for a brief spell in an experimental play for comparative chickenfeed and the admiration for his remarkable generosity, which his income tax happens conveniently to take care of, results in notices that are the envy of a lot of New York legitimate actors who are very lucky if they get even that much money a few weeks in a whole year. In turn, let a Negro actor or a Negro company give a performance which in the case of white actors would be dismissed with an "adequate," and sympathy for the underdog will frequently generate reviews that lead the public to believe that such great artists have seldom been seen on the stage since the days of Alcibiades. Or let a troupe like the Habimah appear on the local scene after surmounting all kinds of difficulties on the trip over, and compassion not only for its fortitude but for a people who have been widely persecuted gives birth to notices, particularly on the part of reviewers who do not understand anything that is going on on the stage, which sound as if they had been written by Schrafft.

A French bistro singer named Piaf arrives and, since her press-agent has sent out word that she typifies the indomitable spirit of the poor French working classes and can not afford more than one dress that cost six francs, the boys' hearts bleed for her. Katharine Cornell, because she is courageous enough to produce a Shakespeare classic that heretofore has always lost money, gets such a reception as has not been matched since Dutch Schultz came back to his circle from Canada. And José Ferrer's effort with small funds at his command to install a repertory company in the City Center Theatre softens up some of even the more callous colleagues, who, if they find that their reviews can not be comprehensively eulogistic, nevertheless pitch their millinery into the air for José the Intrepid.

I am not saying that some of the recipients of such sentimental reviews now and then do not deserve what commendation they get. What I am saying is simply that, whatever you may have dreamt to the contrary, there are numerous times when forthright criticism suffers from tender magnanimity and misleads readers through its noble, if critically equivocal, intentions. One of the chief differences between reviewing and criticism, indeed, is that the former's heart too often is located in its head.

In Ferrer's case, however, the benevolence is just so much extra parsley, and wasted. Everything considered, he has done his economical job very well and needs no handouts of good-will from me or anyone else. He and his company's production of the ribald Jonson semi-classic provides the local stage with a lot of the kind of intelligent fizz

it seldom enjoys and by and large proves a credit both to
his judgment and enterprise. As in the instance of his production of *Volpone* last season, there has been some criticism of his intermittent circusing of the script, but I can
find little objection to it. While it may offend the tradi-
tionalists, some warrant for it may be found in a close
study of various portions of the play, and it assuredly assists in getting rid of some of the library smell which they
would prefer to remain undisturbed. But, whether in the
library or on the stage, the comedy of sour humanity with
its rich gallery of gold-greedy rascals and with its picture of
Elizabethan quackery in wholesale operation remains one
of the two most bawdily biting plays of its period. The performances in the main are serviceable, and the direction
for the most part competent. A general finish may be lacking, and now and again the comic flow may consequently
seem for a while to halt, but on the whole Jonson is given
his fair day in court.

The original five acts of the play have been compressed
into two, and a prologue has been added, unnecessarily, in
the belief that the exposition stands in need of some clari-
fication. There also have been some heavy cuts in the
script. But, though the aforesaid purists may writhe in pur-
ist pain, nothing that has been done to the play violates or
diminishes its old theatrical effect. It persists as the second
feather in the cap of as intellectually amusing a dramatist
as has ever graced the English-speaking stage.

SALLY. May 6, 1948

*A revival of the musical comedy with book by Guy Bolton,
music by Jerome Kern, and lyrics by P. G. Wodehouse and
Clifford Grey. Produced by Hunt Stromberg, Jr., and William Berney for 36 performances in the Martin Beck
Theatre.*

PROGRAM

NADINA	Gloria Sullivan	SALLY	Bambi Linn
THE YOUNG WAITER	Charles Wood	THE GRAND DUKE CONSTANTINE	
THE OLD WAITER	Holger Sorenson		Willie Howard
OTIS HOOPER	Jack Goode	MRS. VISCHER VAN ALSTYN	
ROSIE	Kay Buckley		Kathryn Cameron
LILY BEDLINGTON	Bibi Osterwald	TOTO	Lucy Hillary
SHENDORF	Henry Calvin	OLGA	Andrea Mann
MICKEY SINCLAIR			
	Robert Shackleton		

SYNOPSIS: Act I. Scene 1. *Shendorf's café in Greenwich Village.*
Scene 2. *The Long Island garden of Mrs. Van Alstyn.* Act II. Scene 1.
The Church Around the Corner. Scene 2. *The kitchen of Shendorf's café.*
Scene 3. *"The Follies."* Scene 4. *Backstage.* Scene 5. *The Church Around
the Corner.*
Time: *The early Nineteen Twenties.*
Director: *Billy Gilbert.*

Nostalgia, once so warmly acceptable to readers of writings on the theatre, seems to have gone out of fashion. The current style is for the writer not only cautiously to sidestep it and loudly to deny any trace of its existence in himself but even more emphatically to decry it in others, to dismiss them as feeble-minded and in all probability with one foot already in the grave, and to proclaim blanketwise that nothing in the older days was what it has been cracked up to be and is to be compared with the remarkable glories of the present. This is supposed to indicate several things: that the writer is an open-minded, sagacious, and independent fellow upon whom memory has been allowed to play no tricks; that he is still satisfactorily young enough to appreciate the miraculous fact that the world never fails enormously to advance and improve; and that he is sufficiently wise to realize that distance generally lends an unwarranted enchantment to the view. What it rather indicates, I daresay, is that the writer is simply up to the dodge of hiding what he does not know by airily dismissing the desirability of knowing it and reassuring those of his readers whose experience is as limited as his own that they have not missed what they have missed.

This is not to say, of course, that writers of a nostalgic bent are not just as often frauds. Trading in nostalgia is no better than boycotting it. It becomes a legitimate business, however, when memory is born partly of the mind and not wholly of the emotions, or at least when recollection has been filtered through a measure of critical perception. Too frequently, though, even when it is not arbitrary, it is the offspring of an emotionalism either soberly uncontrolled or the result of temporary indisposition or alcoholic liquor. Malaise has a way of turning the thoughts backward to other days, and the bottle, it need hardly be confided, induces an agreeable melancholia wherein one basks whimsically in the moonshine of the yesterdays.

The practising, professional school of nostalgia may be illustrated by some such selection as this from a recently published book on the Edwardian period in the London theatre, *Carriages At Eleven,* by one W. Macqueen-Pope:

> The great building (Covent Garden) is aglow, its gas cressets blow in the summer breeze above its high pediment, the odd little glasshouse perched on its portico is a pool of light, every window gleams, and a rich yellow flood pours out from under its covered carriage drive. One by one, in endless procession, the carriages roll up Long Acre or up Bow Street from the Strand, cockaded coachman with rug-covered knees, cockaded footman with arms folded and white buckskin legs, sitting stiffly to attention. Inside are handsome, moustached men in tails and white waistcoats; lovely ladies in their full array of trains, low necks, and silks and satins. And on their arms, their fingers, their cor-

sages, around their necks, gleam a fortune of jewels — rubies, emeralds, sapphires, diamonds, pearls in rope and dog-collars. And on their elaborate coiffures glitter diamond tiaras, for every woman in those days was a queen and behaved accordingly . . .

Champagne popped and fizzed, pretty mouths munched sandwiches of caviar or foie gras . . . Kisses were freely given, or stolen adventurously, vows were made, hearts beat and fluttered — and always the dance went on and laughter rang everywhere . . . And still the waltzers revolved, or the lancers made them scream with delight as the strong young males lifted the dainty girls off their feet. Who cared for tomorrow? It would be as today, as yesterday. The world was rich, secure, and prosperous . . . The youths went to work unjaded, for the tonic of joy kept them alert — and there was the night to look forward to again; the girls to sleep and dream until the day failed and dusk came with the stars and the gas lamps for another round of frolic in the eighties, the nineties and the Edwardian nineteen-hundreds which seem so far away but which are so near in terms of time.

The school is compounded of equal parts half-truth and replete buncombe merchanted through a kind of travel-brochure literature. It follows closely the pattern of perfume advertisements interlarded with references to past figures and institutions. And its net effect is to induce in all but the most sentimental reader a sensation akin to having partaken of a keg of mush soaked in an apricot sauce. It isn't that its merchant is sometimes not wholly honest according to his lights, if unfortunately still in the grip of an arrested juvenility. It is simply that often what was actually a fifty-cent oil-painting is peddled in a frame embellished by a thousand dollars' worth of gilt.

But there is, as well, another kind of nostalgic writing, based on times and things that were accurately observed and upon which is impressed the bona fide romantic memory derived from such accurate observation. Distance has been tried and not found wanting; recollection is treated

to doubt and skepticism and yet survives, with all its little
silver bells still tinkling. It is not, however, always thus
buoyant; sometimes it is decidedly unwelcome and disturbing, since, while delusion may make one happy,
equally beautiful truth may depress one. Nostalgia is accordingly now and then much less agreeably wistful, as
most believe, than disagreeably incommodious. Far from
providing an escape from the present, it doubly stresses the
present. It is, in short, often as dangerous to your self-con-
tentment and pleasure as thinking of the excellent dinners
you got twenty years ago for a dollar while presently paying a ten dollar check for a considerably less satisfactory
one, or, I impertinently venture, of your yesterday's girl in
the presence of your venerable wife.

Revivals of drama do not much suffer from nostalgia,
since drama frequently has a way of recreating itself whoever acts in it. It is the musical shows that are vassals to it;
not the superior examples like *The Merry Widow* and the
like, for they can stand largely on their own, but the lesser
ones and the song and dance and girl shows. It is, of course,
too much to say that one such of the past is impossible of
entirely conciliating revival, though I have no statistics at
hand to prove it. But it is not too much to say that the
challenge is a severe one. I for one, indeed, can not think
of a single such revival in many years — and that includes
relatively very good ones like *Show Boat* — which has
wholly succeeded in exiling the original from blissful
memory. Too many factors interpose themselves, realistic
as well as purely sentimental. Such shows, in the first place,
are primarily for men in their younger and gayer years. As
the years go on and men grow older and are less given to
superficial pleasures, they are subject to a closer analytical
scrutiny, which is disastrous. When one looks back on
them, any such analysis is somehow remitted, since one
looks back not on the shows alone but coincidentally on
one's self as one was in those other days, and such remem-
brance has a way of confusing one's then rosier self with
the shows. One saw them through still relatively shining
and untroubled eyes in what was, in Kipling's phrase, a

cleaner, greener world, or at least one that, compared with the world of today, seemed to be so.

Nor is the nostalgia necessarily sentimental; a lot of hard fact supports it in various directions. The shows of the years gone, in the first place, were much more attractive in physical detail. With the enormously increased expenses — something like four or five times as great — it is next to impossible to put on a revival of one of them with anything approximating its original splendor. The enforced economy takes its toll of scenery and costumes, and the result is a stage that generally looks like a poor relation of the original production. The theatres in which the revivals are housed, furthermore, miss all the air and color and style of those that housed the same shows in the yesterdays. Aside from the still remaining Ziegfeld, where is there one to match the New Amsterdam and its golden *Frolics* roof, or Dillingham's Knickerbocker and Globe, or the Casino, or the Broadway, or the Herald Square, or their like? The Shubert, Imperial, and the Music Box are good enough in their way, but what of the others? The Adelphi has all the gayety and tone of a retired car-barn. The Century's interior looks like a provincial stock company house of fifty years ago. The Majestic and Forty-sixth Street theatres, with their steep tiers of seats back of the orchestra proper, seem more appropriate to sports events than to musicals, and the Coronet, National, and Broadhurst, along with the St. James and Martin Beck, which now and then are given over to musicals, remain essentially houses for drama. One enters them in a dramatic, not a musical show mood; when musicals are in them they seem self-conscious and a bit embarrassed, like rural churches that have been turned for the nonce into summer theatres playing such things as *The Voice Of The Turtle.*

It is thus when one sees a revue in the austere surroundings of, say, the National, that one reflects on the intrinsic geniality of a revue theatre of yesterday like the Weber and Fields Music Hall, warm with crimson and gaudy and with its cheery downstairs bar where the pretty girls gathered when the show was over and where Mock Weber, Joe's brother, held forth expansively as host and raconteur. It is thus when one braves the gales that howl down dark Fifty-ninth Street and goes to the Century that one harks back to the old New Amsterdam, its façade as brilliantly lighted as a Gilbert and Sullivan battleship, its promenade broad enough to contain Charles Belmont Davis, Diamond Jim Brady, Captain Jim Churchill and Marie Dressler walking abreast, and its auditorium deep enough to render Donald Brian's singing voice fortunately inaudible. And it is thus when one sits in one or another of the present incongruous theatres that memory turns back to Daly's, the home of *The Geisha, San Toy,* and all those other softly lovely things, to the Moorish Casino and the George Lederer shows with all their gorgeous girls, and to other such houses enveloped by the feel and aspect and very fragrance of music and dance and charming femininity.

The girls, the girls. It is always the girls that figure most prominently in any such business of recollection. That there are not just as many attractive ones today as there were then is obviously nonsense. There are plenty of them. But they do not seem to be on the music show stage. A musical with even one or two pretty girls in it these days is almost a phenomenon. What the producers seem fanatically intent upon giving us instead are female ballet dancers with legs beside which gnarled oaks look like young birches and with faces that are recognizable as such solely on the score of a large ear on either side. And not only such ballet sights but grotesque female comics, singers apparently chosen for their leather lungs, altitudinous show-girls with all the physical appeal of giraffes, chorus girls who mostly look like the inspiration for aspirin, and, above all, leading women who would have set Ziegfeld in his day to howling like a wounded coyote. In all the shows of the last three seasons, in fact, there have been but two or three principal girls of any perceptible looks in face and figure, and one of them scarcely assisted the picture with her talent for emitting from time to time a whistle so shrill that it shattered the eardrums. As to the chorus and show-girls, my count numbered only a handful out of hundreds who might have stacked up with all the many who tickled the vision, to specify but one of the affectabilities, in the past.

If this strikes the present generation as rather far-fetched, let anyone who can remember back no more than twenty years compare girl with girl now and then. Or, specifically, since this revival of *Sally* has inspired these general remarks, let anyone try to find today other girls like those when this same show was originally produced. Here, for any such comparison, are the names of just a very few on the musical stage in that 1921 period: Marilyn Miller, Adele Astaire, Louise Brown, Betty Compton, Irene Delroy, Bobby Perkins, Lily Damita, Marion Sunshine, Marion and Madeleine Fairbanks, Claire Luce, Dorothy Knapp, Constance Carpenter, Hilda Ferguson, Gladys Glad, Marion Davies, Justine Johnstone, Edna Leedom, Anastasia Reilly, Ruby Keeler, Hannah Williams, Mary Eaton, Kathryn Ray, and Beth Meakins. Or, to go back not more than ten or twelve years, Grace McDonald, June Havoc, Carmen Molina, Marcy Wescott, Ann Miller, Evelyn Laye, June Allyson, Beryl Wallace, Prudence Hayes, Della Lind, Joyce Beasley, Marissa Flores, June Clyde, Carmen Miranda, Joan Wetmore, Helena Bliss, and at least two dozen similar fragrant blossoms. Or, to go back only six or seven years or even less, Evelyn Wyckoff, Leila Ernst, Jane Ball, Sunnie O'Dea, Elaine Barry, Vera-Ellen, Marjorie Knapp, Sally Bond, Joyce Matthews, Mary Healy, Susan Miller, Irene Hilda, Diane Davis, Frances Mercer, Patricia Marshall, Ilona Massey, Mary Ganley, Mary Roche, Nan Wynn, Althea Elder, Eva Reyes, Kathleen Roche, Geraldine Stroock, Vera Zorina, Geraldine Spreckels, etc. Small wonder the eyes roll backward.

And what of the music? Aside perhaps from Richard Rodgers, where today is there anyone who consistently approaches the quality of Victor Herbert, Reginald De Koven, Franz Léhar, Emmerich Kalman, Jerome Kern, Edmund Eysler, Ivan Caryll, Sidney Jones, Lionel Monckton, Leslie Stuart, Gustave Kerker, Ludwig Englander, Paul Tietjens, Henry K. Hadley, Edward German, Paul Rubens, Ed Jacobowski, Alfred Robyn, André Messager,

George Gershwin, Vincent Youmans, and men like them? Small wonder, as well, that ears turn backward. Even the Frimls do not seem to be composing any longer, if you want to bring that up.

And where nowadays is there anything like the lush, purple, moonlit scenery of Joseph Urban, or like the old Ziegfeld numbers with all the girls sailing over your head on Springtime swings laden with fresh flowers of the fields, or the orchestras of sixty and seventy musicians, or such whole choruses of beauties as one saw in *The Wild Rose, Havana,* and many other such shows, or comedians making their entrance with parachutes, or first-night audiences like those photographed on the covers of old Empire Theatre programs dressed to the hilt and magnificently devoid of moving picture scouts and similar contemporary vermin? Or the neighboring bars with their entr'-acte huge goblets of champagne, or the toasts of the town like Lillian Russell, Edna May, Lotta Faust, Helen Hale and suchlike, or the stage-doors choked with florist messengers, or the great, gala road theatres like Philadelphia's Broad and old Forrest, Pittsburgh's Nixon, Baltimore's Academy of Music and Cleveland's Euclid Avenue, or the dazzling openings that turned Atlantic City's Apollo into Manhattan on holiday, or stages with Sousa's whole brass band booming down the final curtain?

Sentimental, my eye! Facts, gentlemen, facts! And if facts are sentimental, make the most of it.

To revert to the girls, what seems to have happened in these later years is that most of the pictorial ones have either deserted the musical for the dramatic stage or have chosen the latter in the first place. Their ample number in that quarter only attests to what I have said before: that there are quite as many of the attractive species at present as there were in the past, even if the stages on which they display themselves are different. Compare those two stages in the last half dozen or so years. In all the eighteen musicals of the 1941–1942 season, the only six fair girls were the before mentioned June Allyson, Joyce Matthews, Helena Bliss, Jane Ball, Sunnie O'Dea, and Vera-Ellen. But in that same season, the dramatic stage disclosed all kinds of such posies as Virginia Peine, Heather Angel, Margaret Callahan, Gertrude Flynn, Louise Stanley, Betsy Blair, Ruth Gilbert, Fay Wray, Eleanor Phelps, Betty Furness, Lillian Bond, Elizabeth Inglise, Jessica Tandy, Helen Craig, K. T. Stevens, Elaine Shepard, Eleanor Lynn, Frances Heflin, Jayne Cotter, Joan Newton, Judy Parrish, and Elizabeth Eustis. As well as, among others, Irene Winston, Julie Stevens, Mary Barthelmess, Phyllis Avery, Florence Sundstrom, Haila Stoddard, Helen Walker, Mary Anderson, Sally Bates, Virginia Lederer, Gertrude Musgrove, Lauren Bacall, Olive Deering, Toni Gilman, Constance Dowling, and Lesley Woods.

In the following season, 1942–1943, the twenty-two musicals purveyed only seven new girls of any prehensile quality: Marjoric Knapp, Nanette Fabray, Carol Bruce, Mary Healy, Patricia Marshall, Frances Mercer, and Ilona Massey. But the dramatic stage overflowed with a cargo consisting — to name only the more outstanding — Cecilia Callejo, June Hayford, Gwen Anderson, Gertrude Beach, Wendy Barrie, Marcella Markham, Carol Marcus, Joan Tetzel, Barbara Bel Geddes, Edna Best, Katharine Hepburn, Julie Haydon, Elizabeth Scott, Nancy Kelly, Florence Rice, Helen Trenholme, Elizabeth Fraser, Arleen Whelan, Adele Longmire, Madge Evans, Tutta Rolf, Jane Sterling, Joan Caulfield, Geraldine Fitzgerald, Phyllis Hill, and Jean Bellows.

If you are not too bored, read on. In the 1943–1944 season, there were twenty-five musicals and all that they freshly disclosed were Milada Mladova, Mary Roche, Althea Elder, Eva Reyes, Geraldine Stroock, and Vera Zorina. The dramatic stage, on the other hand, was full of girls like Virginia Gilmore, Irene Worth, Jane Huszagh, Phyllis Adams, Luciel Richards, Betty Field, Jayne Cotter, Patty Pope, Terry Holmes, Lois Wheeler, Beatrice Pearson, Gloria Hallward, Susana Garnett, Sonya Stokowski, Dolly Haas, Wini Johnson, Janet Tylor, Lois Hall, Gloria Willis, Annabella, Marguerete Lewis, Jean Gillespie, Agnes Doyle, and their pictorial equivalents. The next season, 1944–

1945, had twenty musicals and provided in the attractive department only these eight new girls: Lillian Andersen, Gloria Story, Dolores Grey, Nan Wynn, Carole Landis, Elaine Barry, Jan Clayton and Sheila Guys, a fairly good record. But glance at the dramatic stage in that same period and consider a quorum of such as Mary Sargent, Joann Dolan, Yolande Donlan, Michael Mauree, Hilda Simms, Elaine Ellis, Marguerite Clifton, Bethel Leslie, Patricia Kirkland, Irene Hervey, Helen Marcy, Joan Chandler, Mary Orr, Jane Wyatt, Marjorie Lord, Anne Jackson, Elaine Carter, Toni Eden, Phyllis Brooks, *et al.*

Now that we have gone this far, let us not stop. In the 1945–1946 season, the sixteen musicals contained just two new girls worth the connoisseur eye: Clarissa (a specialty dancer) and the colored Ruby Hill. The dramatic stage, however, busied that eye with a lot like Bonnie Nolan, Marianne Stewart, Margaret Hayes, Gloria Stroock, Adrienne Ames, Pamela Rivers, Frances Dee, Jan Sterling, Jane White, Jacqueline Dalya, Madeleine Le Beau, Frances Reid, Ottilie Kruger, June Knight, Susan Douglas, Mardi Bryant, Margaret Leighton, and so on.

Though this is getting as tiresome to me as it undoubtedly is to you, now that we have begun it, we will nevertheless finish it. The 1946–1947 season offered sixteen shows and, with them, these likelier new lookers, five in number: Leonora Corbett, Leila Ernst, Anne Jeffreys, Gloria Hamilton, and Marion Bell. The dramatic theatre on the other hand came forth with a rich supply including Gloria Humphreys, Pat McClarney, Penelope Ward (one of the most beautiful creatures the stage has uncovered in years), Jean Parker, Jane Middleton, Julie Harris, Andree Wallace, Marta Linden, Lorraine Miller, Mary Alice Moore, Ingrid Bergman, Patricia Neal, June Dayton, Joyce Heron, Temple Texas, Nina Foch, Dortha Duckworth, Betty Caulfield, *et al.* And the 1947–48 season, here estimating it to run from June first to June first, presented sixteen musicals and in all of them only these relatively exceptional feminine items: Glen Alyn, Kyle MacDonnell, and Mary Alice

Bingham, along with an unidentifiable chorus girl, probably Rhoda Johannson, in *Make Mine Manhattan*, not one of whom, except possibly the Bingham girl, was to be compared, on the dramatic stage, with Meg Mundy, June Lockhart, Tilly Losch, Marsha Hunt, Faye Emerson, Rene Ray, Ann Pearce, Neva Patterson and Jocelyn Brando, among others.

The revival of *Sally*, which has inspired this garrulity, brings the evidence in all quarters to a head. To pursue the matter of girls, anyone who bravely hopes to fill a musical show role once played by the incomparable Marilyn Miller is more than rich in optimism, and Bambi Linn is the girl in this case. Her sole contributions to the job of making her audience forget the memorable Miller are a sweet manner, a cute face, and a talent for the kind of dancing more or less associated with ballet, which in the first two instances is not, alas, quite enough and in the last altogether too much, at least for those of us who are not given to regarding as irresistibly charming the periodic spectacle of a woman gyrating like a furious egg-beater on her big toe. Further to pursue the subject, such girls in the original production as Mary Hay, Dolores, Alta King, Betty Williams, Barbara Dean, Vivian Vernon, Gladys Montgomery and Mary McDonald may not, aside from the celebrated Dolores, have been remarkable for any real beauty but they were made to seem so by the Ziegfeld magic in lights, costuming, and presentation. Those in this production, even the seemingly comely Mary Alice Bingham, may or may not be attractive off the stage, but on it they are so shabbily costumed, so badly lighted, and so crudely presented that the Ziegfeld girls, whatever they were, looked comparatively like the most beautiful creatures seen in the world since Helen of Troy. The production in general, indeed, has the appearance of a hand-me-down; nowhere in it is there the slightest trace of the brilliant and dazzling Ziegfeld prototype. Only the Jerome Kern score of that other day, here augmented with some of his songs from *Leave It To Jane* and *Oh Lady! Lady!*, and the presence of the amusing Willie Howard in Leon Errol's old role make the once captivating show still tolerable, and even at such times as they occupy the stage the dancing ghost of that fair girl of the Twenties somehow gets in the way of pleasure.

BALLET BALLADS. May 9, 1948

Three ballets with words and lyrics by John La Touche and music by Jerome Moross. Produced by the Experimental Theatre, Inc., with Nat Karson, for 69 performances in, initially, the Maxine Elliott Theatre.

PROGRAM

SUSANNA AND THE ELDERS

PARSON	*Richard Harvey*	HANDMAIDENS	*Margaret Cuddy*
SUSANNA (Dancer)	*Katherine Litz*		*Barbara Downie*
SUSANNA (Singer)	*Sheila Vogelle*	ELDER (Moe)	*Frank Seabolt*
CEDAR FROM LEBANON		ELDER (Joe)	*Robert Trout*
	Sharry Traver	ANGEL	*James R. Nygren*
LITTLE JUNIPER TREE			
	Ellen R. Albertini		

WILLIE THE WEEPER

SINGING WILLIE	*Robert Lenn*	COCAINE LIL	*Sono Osato*
DANCING WILLIE	*Paul Godkin*		

THE ECCENTRICITIES OF DAVEY CROCKETT

DAVEY CROCKETT	*Ted Lawrie*	ANN HUTCHINSON (Singer)	
SALLY ANN	*Barbara Ashley*		*Gertrude Lockway*
INDIAN CHIEF	*Lorin Barrett*	ANN HUTCHINSON (Dancer)	
BACKWOODSMAN	*Carl Luman*		*Sharry Traver*
MERMAID	*Betty Abbott*	GRACE SHERWOOD (Singer)	
COMET	*Olga Lunick*		*Arlouine Goodjonh*
BROWN BEAR	*William A. Myers*	GRACE SHERWOOD (Dancer)	
GHOST BEAR	*Robert Baird*		*Barbara Downie*
JOHN OLDHAM (Singer)		NATHANIEL TURNER (Singer)	
	William Ambler		*Arthur Friedman*
JOHN OLDHAM (Dancer)		NATHANIEL TURNER (Dancer)	
	John Castello		*Beau Cunningham*

Director: *Mary Hunter*.

THE IDEA HERE is the fusing of speech and song with dance, and it comes off interestingly in all three cases. The presentation is at once comparatively novel, witty, and engrossing and is the first production by the Experimental

Theatre that lends any authenticity to its name. While it is an outgrowth of the later day passion to do something markedly different at all costs, unlike the majority of the exertions it is motivated by an inner critical intelligence and is not the usual arbitrary change merely for change's sake. It has plan, purpose, and sound approach, whereas the greater number of the experimental didoes are little more than old, cheap, worn bonnets hopefully offered as something fresh and new by pinning a few horsefeathers on them.

Such horsefeathers appear not only in the theatre and drama but in a number of the other arts and crafts. In music, the result is tonal balderdash like Herman M. Parris' recently composed symphony depicting the reactions of a young woman about to undergo an appendectomy and regaling the ears with a hotchpotch of woodwinds, brasses, and muted strings mimicking the fair one's odyssey to and from the operating table. In literature, the consequence is novels cast in the form of newspaper headlines, laundry lists, clinical charts and thirty-page soliloquies set in upside-down type, along with others which consist in such æsthetic triumphs as dismissing grammar, syntax, punctuation, and lucidity in favor of sentences, paragraphs and whole chapters composed of meaningless words loosely strung together on the theory that meaninglessness if constantly reiterated takes on in some occult manner a considerable import and even some literary splendor. In painting, the application of thumb-tacks, slices of old patent leather shoes and dabs of mayonnaise is made to pass for a revolutionary advance over the demoded performances of such reactionaries as Rembrandt, Rubens, and the unimaginative like. In sculpture, we get marbles purveying the human anatomy in terms of walruses afflicted with elephantiasis and, in architecture, pre-fabricated houses consisting mainly of windows and with the toilet facilities and kitchen conveniently combined. And, in the drama, experimental genius takes innumerable such shapes as amplifying Expressionism with jive music, Greek choruses, Hallowe'en masks and locomotive headlights, substituting manifold short scenes for cohesive dramaturgy, converting the classics into contemporary sociological and political melodramas, and courting illusion with stages set with cardboard pianos, kitchen chairs and home-painted screens, with actors dressed in their business clothes, and with the scene illuminated by three dollars' worth of fifty-watt bulbs. When, accordingly, something like this *Ballet Ballads* comes along and gives evidence that some talent and fancy and honest skill have gone into it in place of the horsefeathers aforesaid, long dormant respect again awakens.

The ballets, devoid of all artiness, present, in *Susanna And The Elders*, choreography by Katherine Litz, the Biblical story of the virtuous Susanna and the lubricious elders through the medium of a parson's sermon at a revival meeting; in *Willie The Weeper*, choreography by Paul Godkin, the boogie-woogie dreams of a marijuana addict; and in *The Eccentricities of Davey Crockett*, choreography by Hanya Holm, the exploits of boyhood's hero in the fields of Indian fighting, amour, etc. Though the joint use of lyric speech, song and dance here and there finds the elements in some slight conflict with one another and though balletomanes may be inclined to shudder at the contamination of their sacred art by what impresses them as poisonous embellishments, the general scheme, whatever its intermittent shortcomings in immaculate design and execution, has a definite fascination and, further developed and polished, promises a substantial and invigorating addition to stage entertainment.

The Moross music, particularly for *Willie The Weeper* and *Davey Crockett,* reveals its composer as one of uncommon range and ability, and the La Touche lyrics have humor, wit, delicacy and, when called for, dramatic force. All in all, a successful adventure in a synthesis of several of the theatrical arts.

HOPE'S THE THING. May 11, 1948

Three one-act plays by Richard Harrity. Produced by Eddie Dowling under the sponsorship of the American National Theatre and Academy for 7 performances in the Playhouse.

PROGRAM

GONE TOMORROW

Mrs. Muldoon	*Peg Mayo*	Peter Muldoon	*Ralph Cullinan*
Mrs. Lacey	*Ruth Vivian*	Jerry Canavan	*Barry Macollum*
Willie	*Ken Terry*		

HOME LIFE OF A BUFFALO

Joey	*Kevin Mathews*	Molly	*Leona Powers*
Josey	*Ray Dooley*	Otto	*Vaughn Taylor*
Eddie	*Eddie Dowling*		

HOPE IS THE THING WITH FEATHERS

Doc	*E. G. Marshall*	Charlie	*Lou Gilbert*
Steve	*George Mathews*	Old Man Nelson	*Dan Reed*
Wiler	*Robert Alvin*	Joe	*Frederic Martin*
Oscar	*Philip Robinson*	A Man	*Jabez Gray*
Sweeney	*Will Geer*		

Directors: *Eddie Dowling and Joseph Kramm.*

THE BUSINESS IN HAND may be quickly finished. Of the short plays, only the last, *Hope Is The Thing With Feathers,* has any relative merit and it was reviewed in an earlier presentation in the directly previous volume of these annals. *Home Life Of A Buffalo,* dealing with a vaudeville couple who futilely hope to make a comeback in an entertainment medium that has all but disappeared, is an amateurish rehash of an already long devitalized theme, is further dulled by some painful sentimentality, has been wretchedly directed by Mr. Dowling, and owes any theatrical interest it may have solely to the appearance in it of Ray Dooley, who has returned to the stage not only with

her old comical baby act but with a newly disclosed aptitude for more serious acting after an absence of fourteen
years. *Gone Tomorrow,* about an Irish family awaiting the
demise of a well-heeled but disturbingly cynical old uncle,
is another wearisome affair and, as directed by Dowling
with its actors seated lifelessly at a table, seems to go on for
years despite its mere twenty-five minute length. Only
Hope Is The Thing With Feathers, with its whimsical humor about a group of vagabonds dozing in Central Park
and eventually arousing themselves over the possibility of
snaring a duck for much needed food, has, as noted, any
comparative juice, any directional skill (Joseph Kramm's
contribution), and any properly modulated acting. The
two other exhibits fail signally to fill out an acceptable theatre evening and induce considerable wonder at Dowling's
interest in them. They are trashy things and have no place
in the record of a producer who has given us some of the
most respected plays that our stage has had in the last
dozen years. It is a pity to observe one like him dissipate
his efforts and reputation on such paltry merchandise.

The enterprise deservedly was an instant failure.

S. S. GLENCAIRN. May 20, 1948

A revival of the group of one-act plays by Eugene O'Neill. Produced by the New York City Theatre Company for 14 performances in the City Center Theatre.

PROGRAM

MOON OF THE CARIBBEES

YANK	Richard Coogan	THE DONKEY MAN	
DRISCOLL	George Mathews		George Coulouris
OLSON	Ralph Roberts	DICK	Bobby Busch
DAVIS	Ray Walston	MAX	Mack Busch
COCKY	Kenneth Treseder	PADDY	Harry Kadison
SMITTY	Robert Carroll	BELLA	Juanita Hall
PAUL	Leonardo Cimino	PEARL	Mildred Joanne Smith
IVAN	Harold J. Stone	VIOLET	Rena Mitchell
SCOTTY	Winston Ross	SUSIE	Catherine Ayers
BIG FRANK	Stanley Carlson	THE FIRST MATE	Charles Summers

IN THE ZONE

SMITTY	Robert Carroll	IVAN	Harold J. Stone
DAVIS	Ray Walston	YANK	Richard Coogan
OLSON	Ralph Roberts	DRISCOLL	George Mathews
SCOTTY	Winston Ross	COCKY	Kenneth Treseder

BOUND EAST FOR CARDIFF

YANK	Richard Coogan	PAUL	Leonardo Cimino
DRISCOLL	George Mathews	SMITTY	Robert Carroll
COCKY	Kenneth Treseder	IVAN	Harold J. Stone
DAVIS	Ray Walston	THE CAPTAIN	Ralph Sumpter
SCOTTY	Winston Ross	THE FIRST MATE	Charles Summers
OLSON	Ralph Roberts		

THE LONG VOYAGE HOME

FAT JOE, PROPRIETOR OF A DIVE		COCKY	Kenneth Treseder
	José Ferrer	IVAN	Harold J. Stone
NICK, A CRIMP	Victor Beecroft	KATE	Phillippa Bevans
MAG, A BARMAID	Phyllis Hill	FREDA	Nan McFarland
OLSON	Ralph Roberts	TWO ROUGHS {	Robinson Stone
DRISCOLL	George Mathews		Bobby Busch

The action of the first three plays passes on the British tramp steamer, Glencairn; of the fourth, in the bar of a low dive on the London waterfront.

Director: *José Ferrer.*

THE REVIVAL of the four O'Neill short sea plays under the group title, *S. S. Glencairn,* recalls the sensation they created when originally produced thirty-three years ago. That much of the stir was induced by the advent of an undeniably promising new playwright is obvious. But I think that at least part of it was due to the picturing, for the first time on an American stage, of sailors who had been caught by first-hand observation and who resembled something like the real article.

Sailors as they had hitherto been shown in our theatre were as far from the factual as authors, painters, college boys and *grandes dames* still are. The drama, chiefly of a low melodramatic order, presented them as being perpetually on shore-leave in Chinatown and ever close at hand to trip up villains in opium dens as they were about to flee the police, all of the latter redheaded and responding to the name of McCarthy. In the musical shows, they were generally found in the chorus and were always occupied either in hitching up their breeches and simultaneously kicking out their right feet or coming on with pink-powdered bosoms bared and booming their voices into paeans to the rolling ocean waves. Vaudeville vouchsafed them either as acrobats whose climactic business was climbing on one another's shoulders and then toppling off and in unison performing a somersault, or as stooges for a sidewalk comedian in a straw hat whose duty it was dumbly to look around and killingly exclaim, " Naw, I don't see " when the comic inquired of them if they had been to sea. And burlesque never failed to depict them as creatures of wholesale amorous proclivities who, after a ditty attesting to their fabulous puissance, spent the rest of the evening either engaging in innuendoes of an unseemly nature with the aristocratic Mrs. Van Astorbilt, whose favorite hangout appeared to be the Bowery, or pinching the somewhat more democratic chorus girls' posteriors as they were making their exits.

The variations in all cases were so slight as to be negli-

gible. In only one of the melodramas do I recall a tar who
did not obediently squirt tobacco juice, show the effects of
recent alcoholic indulgence, proclaim that he could whip
the whole damn British Navy singlehanded, and rush to assist the hero when he was fallen upon by the myrmidons
of the villain. In the musical shows, the pattern seldom altered, nor did it in burlesque. Possibly now and then the
vaudeville stage would daringly go to the extreme of having the sailor ask the comedian the question instead of vice
versa, but otherwise there was no change.

The consequence of all this was that any theatregoer
who had never got nearer water than Long Branch, New
Jersey, was persuaded that the ships of the seven seas must
be manned entirely by drunks with a propensity for chorus
and acrobatic work, with a highly moral and even pugi-
listic concern for the triumph of virtue over vice, and,
somewhat paradoxically, with a comprehensive taste for
employing their thumbs and forefingers as pincers upon
the protuberant section of the female anatomy. And the
second consequence was that when O'Neill appeared with
these portrayals of sea dogs which did away with most of
the flapdoodle, which dug somewhat deeper into their characters, and which showed them as he himself as one of them
had observed them, the surprise and shock were such that
he was hailed and esteemed out of all proportion to the size
of his achievement and it was only many years later, when
he wrote such really important drama as *Strange Interlude*
and *The Iceman Cometh,* that he was disesteemed by some
of the very same hailers as a pretentious windbag and false
alarm.

The revived plays are *The Moon Of The Caribbees, In
The Zone, Bound East For Cardiff* and *The Long Voyage
Home,* and what I have written above is certainly not to
be taken as any reflection on their relative merit, or the
merit of at least three of them. The reflection is rather on
those who saw in them, and in the other short plays called
Ile, Where The Cross Is Made and *The Rope,* not merely
the promising talent that shone out of even the weakest of
them but a genius that was partly in only one of them, *The*

Moon Of The Caribbees, and that was not to fructify until long afterward.

O'Neill, indeed, sniffing the over-generous view of some of the plays, was himself not backward in criticism of it. Of *In The Zone,* for example, he truthfully declared, "It is too facile in its conventional technique, too full of clever theatrical tricks, and its long run as a successful headliner in vaudeville proves conclusively to my mind that there must be 'something rotten in Denmark.' " Of the one-act play in general, he stated, "It is an unsatisfactory form; it cannot go far enough." And of *S. S. Glencairn* as a whole, "I do not claim any originality for the general idea, as Schnitzler had already done the same thing in *Anatol.* And doubtless others."

However, small present matter. If *In The Zone* is a purely theatrical fabrication and if *The Long Voyage Home* is much less critically worthy than *Ile, Bound East For Cardiff,* like it, has at least the smell of its author's subsequent flowered dramaturgy, and the lyrical *The Moon Of The Caribbees* remains still after more than three decades one of the few deserving achievements by an American playwright in the one-act form.

The productions and performances of the plays do not always do them full service, but even half service in such a case is welcome. I, among a lot of others I am sure, would much rather have almost any kind of service in plays like them than service even *de luxe* in such as two of the recent Harrity one-acters or all six of the Noel Coward sort that lately comprised *Tonight At 8:30.*

THE VIGIL. MAY 21, 1948

A play by Ladislas Fodor. Produced by Alexander Markey in association with George Jessel for 11 performances in the Royale Theatre.

PROGRAM

VIOLET	*Louise Jones*	ESTHER	*Mary James*
MR. WOODS	*John Seymour*	LUCIUS	*Dennis King, Jr.*
JUDGE	*Edward Van Sloan*	MR. PINCHAS	*Joe E. Marks*
COURT CLERK	*Tony Dowling*	JOSEPH OF ARIMATHEA	
COURT STENOGRAPHER	*Lee Baxter*		*Lauren Gilbert*
COURTROOM GUARD	*Rand Elliot*	LADY PROCULA	*Muriel Hutchison*
PROSECUTOR	*Henry Wilcoxon*	PONTIUS PILATE	*Guy Spaull*
COUNSEL FOR DEFENSE		SAUL OF TARSUS	*Milton Parsons*
	Ian MacDonald	BEULAH	*Helen Seamon*
THE GARDENER	*Tom Fadden*	SADOC	*King Donovan*
ASSISTANT TO THE PROSECUTOR		SUSANNA	*Ann Pearce*
	Andrew George	PROF. THADDEUS	*Dan Reed*
ASSISTANT TO THE DEFENSE		MARY MAGDALENE	*Maria Palmer*
	Tom Donovan	SIMON	*Walter Palance*

SYNOPSIS: *The action takes place on the nights between Good Friday and Easter Sunday. The time is the present. Act I. A courtroom in any small town in the United States. Act II. The same. Act III. The same.* Director: *Alexander Markey.*

LADISLAS FODOR has been living in Hollywood, which accounts for the probability that he has not been doing any reading. If he had been, he would have come to know that the idea of transplanting Biblical characters to modern times, presenting them in modern dress, and identifying them with the contemporary point of view is scarcely the novelty he believed it was and that the stage for some years now has been fairly chummy with it. He would also have realized that even keeping the Biblical personages in their period but giving them modern speech and thus bringing them closer to the modern appreciation has similarly become a familiar practice. He would have known, in short, that his play, which sets the story of the Resurrection in a present day American courtroom and so hopes to drive the story into current terms, is far from being the startling innovation he imagined it to be but is simply a variant of something with which the theatre has long been acquainted.

To confine ourselves to the local theatre and not to go too far back, we have had in the last thirty-odd years plays, like the one by Wilbur Daniel Steele, which have shown us a darkened stage from which we heard the voices of what we supposed were people of our own time, only to behold when the lights at length went up that they were those of the Nazarene and the people around Him. We have had the story of Christ and Judas in modern apparel, the story of the Mother Mary in the language of today, and other stories of Scripture pictured in a contemporary light. We have had so many of these variations and paraphrases, indeed, that just about the most sensational play we could get would be one that abandoned all such hocus-pocus and gave us its story in the original undefiled Biblical form. The religious chariot races have been relegated to the past, and with them the religious lion pits, and, while I do not miss them, I still think they would be a lot more acceptable than some of these later versions of the Holy Book by our combination Charles Rann Kennedys, O. Henrys and Salvador Dalis.

With small exception, Biblical plays, whatever their nature, do not, however, find in me an enthusiastic audience. At rare intervals one with the originality and imagination of a *Family Portrait* may fascinate my sympathetic attention, but in the aggregate, even when they are not so bad, they disquiet me, probably for much the same reason that anything out of place, like, say, dimples in a heavy-weight pug, jolts my sense of the congruous. Though the theatre often has been asserted to be in its own way a church and indeed originally stemmed from the church and though in some of its loftier aspects it still is, nine-tenths of the gospel plays of modern times that have been displayed in it no more properly belong in it than even some such dramatic masterpiece as *Lear* belongs in St. Peter's. They belong in

it, moreover, to my way of thinking, less even than some of
the Miracle and Mystery plays themselves belonged in or
anywhere near it. That is, unless one considers fitting to a
House of God plays like, for example, the fifteenth century
Mary Magdalene with its sanctified Biblical figures hob-
nobbing with a Max Reinhardt character called Lechery
and with its scenes showing the miraculous birth and the
resurrection of Lazarus interrupted by low comedians turning cartwheels the while they chewed at the period equivalent of dill pickles.

Though not precisely to be described as an excessively
pious man, I nevertheless find embarrassing the spectacle of
Broadway and Hollywood hams soberly masquerading as
divinities and saints. And I find it not less disconcerting
when the language of the Bible is transmuted into a modern speech which frequently sounds much less suited to the
lips of figures out of Holy Writ than to those of the characters in *Charley's Aunt.* I am as liberal a theatregoer as has
been known in this world since Leopold of Bavaria or Diamond Jim Brady, but when I am invited to accept some
actor, whom I saw only a few months before in something
like *Strange Bedfellows,* as, say, one of the Twelve Apos-
tles, my obstreperous chuckles are likely to bring on an
usher post-haste. The Oberammergau impresarios know
their business.

There is, however, a greater reason why the average Biblical play seems to be at odds with the theatre, at least the
theatre as we presently have it. Such a play as *The Miracle,*
pure spectacle, or such a one as *The Green Pastures,* whimsical humor, are thoroughly in key with it. But it is not
that kind I refer to. The plays I mean are those which try
to straddle the drama and the pulpit and achieve only the
latter, to the displeasure of audiences who may be forgiven
for wanting for their four dollars and eighty cents something a bit different from what they can get gratis in a
church; those which sanctimoniously, yet with both eyes on
the box-office, sell Faith like a celestial hair restorer and
which belong not on a theatre stage but in a pitch tent; and
those which mistake a medium that is essentially one of

entertainment — whether light or serious, trivial or important — for an evangelical tabernacle, minus only the rear lemonade stand.

The Vigil combined the worst features of various such plays, failed to convert the ticket seller, and soon expired.

Some of the performances, notably those of Henry Wilcoxon, King Donovan and, at least in one scene, Maria Palmer, were creditable, but the direction would have deadened even a play much better. Though dramatic movement is not easily to be managed in any play laid throughout in a courtroom, Mr. Markey could think up no other course than to employ a door at stage left as his sole pivot, with the result that for two and one-half hours the stage presented a seemingly interminable succession of witnesses alternately parading in and out of it, and with the second and collateral result that, while the characters were doing it, the stage was every now and again held up and the action delayed. The playwright's old device of using the audience as the jury and of having opposing counsel intermittently step to the footlights and address it had the usual effect not only of halting the action further but of making the audience feel that it was being imposed upon by a playwright who hoped to cajole it, against its inclination, into lending itself to his vacuous argumentation. A play that does not belong in a theatre can scarcely be passed off as belonging by swindling an audience into a belief that it is part and parcel of it. Imagination, poetry and style may create a theatre of their own, whatever subjects they elect to deal with; but when plays like Fodor's have not a glimmer of those qualities and are placed upon a stage they offer the appearance of the Bible published as a yellow-back.

SEEDS IN THE WIND. MAY 25, 1948

A play by Arthur Goodman. Produced by Eunice Healey and Harald Bromley for 7 performances in the Empire Theatre.

PROGRAM

STEFAN JAKUBEC	*Tonio Selwart*	CARL	*David Burke*
TONYA	*Sidney Lumet*	FRANZ	*Michael Citro*
MARTA	*Abby Bonime*	NIKOS	*Bobby Nick*
JOSEF	*Jerry Stone*	BORIS	*Stanley Martin*
POLDI	*Teddy Rose*	KATERIN	*Mimi Strongin*
GRISCHA	*Richard Kenny*	LIZA	*Eeta Linden*
VLADI	*Donald Rose*	PHILLIPA	*Winnie-Mae Martin*
ERIC	*Kenneth Terry*	MAMINKOO	*Lee Graham*
JANI	*Jimmy Dutton*		

SYNOPSIS: Act I. Scene: *Inside the house the children built.* Act II. Scene 1. *Outside the House. The same night.* Scene 2. *Same as Act I. The next day.*

Time: *July, 1945.*

Place: *A spot in the Carpathian Mountains in Czechoslovakia.*

Director: *Paul Tripp.*

ONE OF THE CHIEF side-products of the first World War was a stock of spy plays almost large enough to choke the stages of England, France and America. One of the chief side-products of the second was an equal stock of plays so full of predicated ideologies that there was no room left in them for drama. After any war it seems that most of the playwrights interested in the subject gather in a hall and agree to write much the same kind of play. Arthur Goodman was evidently present at the last meeting. Though his exhibit views the war from a relatively fresh angle — the homeless orphan survivors of Lidice — he follows the set principle of so assiduously occupying himself with a recipé for future enduring peace in the world that he has found no time remaining for the little matter of dramatic animation. The consequence is so much talk about the desirability of children of all nations and races banding themselves together and outlawing war that his play rapidly falls into a coma, which is further promoted by his audience's reflection that children who had gone through the horrors and terrible cruelties which he describes would be less likely to think of forgiveness and tranquillity than of hateful retaliation and revenge. The coma is still further assisted theatrically by the spectacle of a stage full of youngsters so spic and span after three forsaken and desperate years on a remote mountain top that it seems that their mothers survived the Lidice holocaust with them and have solicitously installed themselves in the kids' dressing-rooms. And it is yet still further encouraged by stage direction which so botches the youngsters' efforts to win the sympathy of the audience that it waywardly suggests the director must be a man of persistent Nazi leanings who has sought thus cunningly to get even with them for their attempt at propaganda.

The plot machinery involves the intrusion into the children's hideaway of an elderly Czech soldier, the manner in which he disturbs their plans, and their eventual dispatch of him as another adult contributing to world unrest and disaster. The machinery, however, lacks both oil and sense. After its first few moments' whirr, it dies down in the static business of having the old soldier either sit or stand close to the center of the stage and of bringing to him successively one child or another to discuss matters pro and con. And it misses sense in the soldier's cajolery of them with promises of new pairs of shoes (he had been a cobbler by profession) when a sufficient number of them, despite their playwright's hope to persuade us that they have been pursuing the rugged mountain existence for several years, are observed to be fitted out with the latest thing in footwear obviously purchased just in time for the opening performance. It similarly misses sense in various dramatic directions. For one example, in the idea that it would be any more possible to achieve a philosophical homogeneity in youngsters of radically divergent nations and races than it has been in adults. For another, the paradoxical inability of the children in the play to get along without quarreling among themselves, and the necessity they feel for nominating one of their number, the eldest, to act as their dictator. The exhibit, in brief, is essentially a fantasy given a contradictory realistic treatment and hence made thematically foolish. The language in which it is couched is furthermore of a flatness and aridity that sterilize even the few realistic moments which have any faintest token of virility.

SLEEPY HOLLOW. June 3, 1948

A musical play, based on Washington Irving's Legend Of Sleepy Hollow, *with book and lyrics by Russell Maloney and Miriam Battista, music by George Lessner. Produced by Lorraine Lester for 12 performances in the St. James Theatre.*

PROGRAM

IKE	*William Ferguson*	HENDRICK	*Ward Garner*
ROELF	*Larry Robbins*	EVA	*Mary McCarty*
MRS. VAN BRUNT	*Laura Pierpont*	LUTHER	*Russell George*
MRS. VAN TASSEL	*Ruth McDevitt*	ICHABOD CRANE	*Gil Lamb*
MRS. VAN RIPPER	*Jean Handzlik*	ANNIE	*Margery Oldroyd*
WILHELMINA	*Ellen Repp*	LENA	*Peggy Ferris*
MR. VAN BRUNT	*Bert Wilcox*	NICK	*Franklin Wagner*
MR. VAN TASSEL	*Tom Hoier*	PIET	*Shaun O'Brien*
MR. VAN RIPPER	*Morley Evans*	BALT	*Ray Brakeley*
JACOB VAN TASSEL	*Bobby White*	WALT	*James Starbuck*
WILLIE VAN TWILLER		CHRIS	*John Ward*
	Walter Butterworth	BERTHA	*Margaret Ritter*
HANS VAN RIPPER	*Alan Shay*	MARGARET	*Jo Sullivan*
MARTIN VAN HORSEN		ELIZABETH	*Kaja Sumdsten*
	Richard Rhoades	JENNY	*Ann Dunbar*
STUYVELING VAN DOORN		MR. VAN HOOTEN	*Ken Foley*
	Lewis Scholle	JOOST	*John Russel*
TEENA	*Doreen Lane*	CONSCIENCE	*Ty Kearney*
HILDA	*Robin Sloan*	INDIAN	*Kenneth Remo*
GRETA	*Sylvia Lane*	COTTON MATHER	*William Mende*
BROM "BONES" VAN BRUNT		THE LADY FROM NEW HAVEN	
	Hayes Gordon		*Dorothy Bird*
KATRINA VAN TASSEL			
	Betty Jane Watson		

SYNOPSIS: *The play takes place in the Autumn of 1795 in the village of Sleepy Hollow up by the Tappan Zee on the east bank of the Hudson River. Act I. Prologue: The churchyard at the crossroads of the village. At night. Scene 1. The churchyard. The following morning. Scene 2. The river bank. The following morning. Scene 3. The schoolroom in a clearing. Later that morning. Scene 4. The kitchen of the Van Tassell house. The following Sunday morning. Scene 5. The river bank. Several days later. Scene 6. The churchyard. Sunday evening. Act II. Scene 1. The Van Tassell barn. A few days later. Scene 2. The river bank. Later that day. Scene 3. The attic room in Eva's house. That night. Scene 4.*

The kitchen of the Van Tassell house. The following night. Scene 5. *The churchyard. That night.* Scene 6. *The churchyard. The following morning.* Directors: *John O'Shaughnessy and Marc Connelly.*

THE FIRST SCENE of the evening was laid in a cemetery and though at least seven of the subsequent scenes were designated otherwise the show paid no attention to the program and didn't stir from the graveyard. While the original notion was a possibly valid one, what was done with it was a perfect example of triumphant error. Instead of working the familiar Washington Irving legend into a fluid book suitable to musical accompaniment, the usually alert Russell Maloney, together with Miriam Battista, chopped it up into ill-assorted pieces, threw it at the stage, and made it quickly talk itself to death. The sole gesture toward theatrical necessity was the incorporation into it from time to time of such doubtful jocosities as observing that the plural of papoose is papeese and causing a coyly innocent maiden to suspect that when a man alluded to her pulchritude he was referring to something naughty.

The composer, George Lessner, evidently took the plot's insistence upon ghosts literally, with the result that his tunes, announced to be in the Dutch spirit of 1785, were for the greater part wraiths of Lehár, Victor Herbert, and other old friends. Ichabod Crane, the migratory schoolmaster, was converted into a low comedian and cast in the person of a lanky mime named Lamb whose idea of comedy consisted mainly in forcing his features into a look of calflike bewilderment, loping around the stage like an anemic bloodhound sniffing a pack of Elizas and, when in desperate need of a laugh, dropping the butt of his musket on his foot and affecting a surprised look of pain.

The direction apparently persuaded itself that a lack of vitality in the materials might be camouflaged by instructing the players to comport themselves with an excess of it, and that lines devoid of all humor might be made to seem brim-full of it by having the parties thereto beam and grin as if they had swallowed Bobby Clark. It was also the direc-

tion's belief that determined smiles on the part of some of
the ladies, notably Betty Jane Watson, who played the lead,
would be instrumental in radiating great personal charm,
and that if they would only bound and bounce about the
stage as if it were a trampoline an audience would happily
regard them as overflowing with joyous youthful spirits.
Contributing additionally to the malfeasance were a dozen
or more children who, when called upon to speak lines,
were either wholly unintelligible or who offered sounds
identifiable with those of a bottle of beer poured down the
throat of a reluctant teetotaler. What slight diversion there
was in the show was provided by a saucy minx named Mary
McCarty who seemed to have let interfering direction roll
off her like water off a duckling's back; by, of all things, a
ballet dancer named Dorothy Bird with a relieving pretty
face; by David Ffolkes' attractive costuming; and by not
looking at the ordinarily accomplished Jo Mielziner's dull,
flat scenery and lighting that would not have been acceptable to the windows of Truman's old haberdashery store.
The published news that the production cost two hundred
and thirty thousand dollars, which was provided by one
hundred and three angels, seemed to argue that the man
who once made a fortune selling the Brooklyn Bridge for
a dollar and a quarter died much too soon.

Since a sense of professional duty sometimes handicaps
the critical inclination to run out on any such show, one
casts about for ways and means to pass the time while it is
endlessly pursuing its thankless business. In my case, I usually find some diversion in recalling the derivation of the
early measures of the songs and either humming to myself
what will obviously be the rest of them or anticipating the
arbitrary change for the worse which the composer will
make in one or another part of them by way of achieving a
protective suggestion of originality.

I also bemuse myself by looking at the inevitable girl in
the ballets who indulges herself in nonsensically eccentric
behavior and works her features into clownish grins in the
hope that the audience will detect in her potential talents
as a rare comédienne. When I get tired of looking at her,

which is pretty quickly, I while away the time speculating why the vocalist lovers always end their sentimental duets by filling their lungs to the bursting point and so outyelling each other that the songs' effect is less one of mutually expressed tender passion than of a pair of jealous professionals determined to minimize and abash each other's vocal gifts.

There is, too, some amusement in watching what the lesser players do when they are not figuring in the immediate action and have been left standing idly around for the nonce. If they just stand still, look like so many kitchen chairs dispossessed onto the sidewalk, and do nothing, they are not so bad. But few of them, with or without the approval of direction, do any such thing. Believing that they have to busy themselves in some manner, they either enter into imaginary rapt conversations with one another during which the girls now and then avert their faces and flirt their eyes over the audience or listen with such exaggerated intensity to the fictitious colloquies, consisting mostly of soundless mouth movements, that one gets the impression they have suddenly heard the news that their salaries have been raised a thousand dollars a week.

There are, finally, the ever-reliable program notes. The program notes have made many an intolerable show temporarily tolerable. In them one may tipsify one's senses by reading of the royal lineage of some of the chorus girls; the confidence that the star, who does not look a day over fifty, is really still a tender miss, since, though she has been on the stage for countless years, she started at the age of six; and the fact that the leading man has appeared with acclaim in a long list of great Broadway musical successes like *Hairpin Harmony, Louisiana Lady, If The Shoe Fits,* and *Hollywood Pinafore.*

THE INSECT COMEDY. June 3, 1948

A revival of the play by Josef and Karel Čapek, adapted by Owen Davis. Produced by the New York City Theatre Company for 14 performances in the City Center Theatre.

PROGRAM

PROLOGUE

THE VAGRANT	George Coulouris	THE PROFESSOR	Robinson Stone

THE BUTTERFLIES

FELIX	José Ferrer	IRIS	Phyllis Hill
	Annabelle Lyon	VICTOR	Tom Avera
YOUNG	Jane White	CLYTHIA	Rita Gam
BUTTERFLIES	Betty Low	OTAKAR	Thomas Poston
	Claire Hale		

THE MARAUDERS

CHRYSALIS	Mildred Joanne Smith	ICHNEUMON FLY	Robert Carroll
MALE BEETLE	Stanley Carlson	ITS LARVA	Chevi Colton
FEMALE BEETLE	Paula Laurence	MALE CRICKET	Ray Walston
ANOTHER MALE BEETLE		FEMALE CRICKET	Annabelle Lyon
	Bobby Busch	PARASITE	Bert Whitley

THE ANTS

BLIND ANT	Leonardo Cimino	WOUNDED MAN	Bert Whitley
1ST ENGINEER	Alexander Scourby	TELEGRAPHER	Ray Walston
2ND ENGINEER	Robert Carroll	JOURNALIST	Tom Avera
AN ANT	Sidney Walters	WAR-WORKER	Joyce Hill
ANOTHER ANT	Ted Allegretti	BOND SALESMAN	Chevi Colton
INVENTOR	Robinson Stone	A TRAITOR	George Hall
ANOTHER MESSENGER	Mack Busch	YELLOW COMMANDER	José Ferrer
QUARTERMASTER	Thomas Poston		

EPILOGUE

1ST MOTH	Jan White	1ST SNAIL	Bobby Busch
2ND MOTH	Betty Low	2ND SNAIL	Mack Busch
3RD MOTH	Claire Hale	WOOD-CUTTER	Arthur Newman
4TH MOTH	Annabelle Lyon	WOMAN	Nan McFarland

The scene is the outdoor insect world.
Director: *José Ferrer.*

How much money it costs our larger cities to establish
and operate their park zoos, I do not know; but whatever
the amount, it seems to me to be an awful waste of money.
The theory that the zoos are immensely edifying and instructive, particularly to the young, is so much gobblede-
gook. Just how an education in natural history is to be
gained by watching a monkey disport himself in a manner
which if practised by the onlooker would land him in jail
for six months or by listening to a sea lion roaring like Jan
Kiepura, I hope to have someone confidentially explain to
me, with graphs. I have in my lifetime scrutinized elephants galore and the sum total of wisdom I have gained
from the extensive study is the knowledge that they can
squirt water out of their nozzles for the distance of a city
block, which not only has not made me a nickel but has
not even got me an honorary degree from Columbia. I
have also for many years closely observed the gnu and,
though I have brought to the observation all my noted
mental faculties, you can add up my erudition in the remarkable discovery that it has curved horns, a long tail and
a face that resembles Monty Woolley's, which great information in turn has not raised either my financial or social
standing an iota.

In much the same way, I have seldom found profitable
plays that deal with the imaginary relationship of animal
life to human life. And that holds also for those about insect and fowl life. Once in a blue moon a Rostand's lyrical
line may make something like *Chantecler* tolerable in spite
of the spectacle of a lot of actors foolishly covered with
feathers and pretending to be barnyard poultry identified
with *Homo sapiens*. And once in a pair of blue moons I
run across a play script like the late Avery Hopwood's
Dogs' Heaven which, though the rest of it leaves me calm,
diverts me with a scene in which the canine paradise is
shown to be a realm consisting wholly of trees and street
hydrants. But much more often, unless Bernard Shaw gets
himself up as a lion and vengefully leaves speech to his

mortal characters, I find little more authentic entertainment in the plays than is to be had in a downstairs circus menagerie after the circus itself is over.

These plays, like, for example, the Duffey-Alexander *The Greatest Show On Earth,* which seek to parallel animal behavior with human, are for the larger part merely conventional and very bad plays which the authors hope to palm off as novel and meritorious by costuming the otherwise obvious characters as fauna. The trick may be fascinating for the first ten minutes but it thereafter becomes all too transparent, and what an audience gets for the remaining two hours is just the old, bad play momentarily relieved by one's reflection that, if the acting in it is to be listed with the rest as an art, what an eminent statesman Henry Wallace might have been if only he had dressed himself up as *Macacus inuuos.*

The use of animals, fowl or insects for dramatic purposes, except in the higher reaches of classical drama, seems to be simply the stratagem of inferior playwrights in substituting a superficial originality for their inability to achieve a profounder. The animal kingdom is much better off on the musical comedy or vaudeville stage, neither of which enters into any such nonsense as contributing mind to creatures seemingly very happy without it. There is, at least so far as I am concerned, infinitely more amusement in Ed Wynn's old horse act, in the one-time vaudeville duck named August Müller or in a Dan Leno's Drury Lane lion than in any play which figs out the old, familiar Henry Arthur Jones triangle characters as honey bears, tigers and snakes and asks me to imagine that I am getting something chock-full of fresh, new genius.

This revival of the Čapeks' play is responsible for these reprehensions. As those oldsters who saw it when it was performed here twenty-seven years ago under the title, *The World We Live In,* may recall, it again pursues the analogy business, this time between insects and human society which, as things stand today, seems pretty hard on the insects. There is some ingenuity in the treatment but once more the venerable stunt becomes recognizable before long and for the rest of the evening the effect is largely of a man performing over and over the same card trick and merely varying the accompanying patter.

Another difficulty with all such plays is that the actors, with the approval of their directors, usually seem to be under the impression that animals, fowl or insects seldom under any circumstances comport themselves with the slightest reserve but always behave as if they were the progeny of Ray Bolger and Agnes de Mille. What follows is such a physical to-do as would soon exhaust any antelope, rooster or even ant in the pink of condition. Were I a playwright and were I in a thoughtless moment to write any such play, the first thing I should do would be to instruct the director to take a week off and learn that, with few exceptions, God's theoretically lesser creatures generally conduct themselves with some measure of *sang-froid* and not invariably like a lot of tap dancers, trapeze performers, and Presidential candidates.

HOWDY, MR. ICE. JUNE 24, 1948

An ice skating show with music and lyrics by Al Stillman and Alan Moran. Produced by Sonja Henie and Arthur M. Wirtz for 10 months' performances in the Center Theatre.

PRINCIPALS

Eileen Seigh, Skippy Baxter, Freddie Trenkler, Paul Castle, John Walsh, Buster Grace, Harrison Thomson, Jimmy Sisk, Cissy Trenholm, Rudy Richards, Buck Pennington, Nola Fairbanks, Richard Craig, Jinx Clark, William Douglas, Fred Martell, Eddie Berry, John Melendez, and Frederick Werner.

Director: *Catherine Littlefield.*

THE IDEA THAT it is always necessary to see a show in order to know what it is like is akin to the idea that it is always necessary to be bitten by an alligator to know that it wasn't a mosquito. Therefore, though it may offend the punctilious, I can think of no reason why I should go to this new skating show for the purpose of writing a review of it. I may not, true, be able to anticipate certain minor details in it, but a review that goes in for minor details is wasting its and the reader's time. What the reader properly wants is one which will give him an over-all picture. The circumstance that the girls wear pale green instead of the usual bottle-green costumes in the number in which they represent hunters in the forest scene or that a skater jumps over four hurdles instead of the customary three is interesting only to the performers directly concerned, if the reviewer mentions their names. The reader is no more interested in such stuff than he would be in a review of a novel which saw fit to include the information that the hero's name at one point in the sixteenth chapter is printed in Caledonia instead of the preceding Baskerville type or that in the twenty-fifth Ebenezer, the old Negro slave, appears with only one shoe on.

Aside from such negligible items, one ice show is bound

to be so much like another that attending it for critical appraisal is the obligation solely of such as devotedly to the
same judicial end return time after time to Western movies, plays of Yorkshire life by young British dramatists, or
Italian table d'hôte dinners. There are, after all, just so
many things performers can do on skates, and the variations are scarcely more bewitching than Tin Pan Alley's in
the case of old standbys like Chopin's *Fantasie Impromptu*.
Nor does it convert old-hat into the latest Daché creation
by having a dozen skaters go through the familiar routines
in place of half a dozen. There are a lot of different things
one can do with the ice in an icebox, but not with the ice
on a stage. Novelty in the shows is confined merely to slight
variants of the skating gymnastics, some of the costumes,
and numbers which present the stereotyped glidings and
twirlings in front of different scenery. And, throughout,
the lighting remains identical season after season: purple
for the romantic numbers, pink for the solo, amber for the
nondescript, and white for the comic, with maybe a horrible mixture of all four for the spectacular finale, which
generally looks like something the Kiralfy brothers used to
throw out of their circus before it got even to Columbus,
Ohio.

If the musical accompaniments were written by composers like Lehár, Kalman, Herbert, or Fall, the senses might
be lulled into remitting the endlessly duplicated stage doings, but the chopsticks provided the shows by Broadway
one-finger virtuosi fail in any such accommodation and
only accentuate the ding-dong nature of the exhibits. If,
furthermore, someone could somehow work in a little good
revue dialogue here and there and momentarily relieve the
depressing impression of a stage full of deaf-mutes interrupted at half-hour intervals by pig squeals from the skating clown, it might help a bit. But, as the shows stand, they
offer all the variety and stimulation of sitting for three
hours before a large group of adolescent morons alternately
sliding around a floor to the accompaniment of optimisti-
cally hopeful jukebox tunes and passing off vaudeville acrobatics of an 1890 vintage as a sensational achievement

by putting them on steel runners, the meanwhile in both cases making faces like Leonardo da Vinci in the throes of a superhuman invention.

At this point, I expect some irascible reader to throw down the book in disgust and dispatch a letter to the publisher demanding how his ass of a reviewer can possibly know, if he does not see the show, that it may not contain a skater of such extraordinary skill as to make all previous skaters look like amateurs. Presuming that the skater in question does not happen to be the aforesaid reader's cousin and taking him seriously, I have the honor to reply that even were the show to offer such a marvel, I wouldn't know it and my review of it would accordingly be much less acceptable if I went to it. All skaters of any proficiency at all look much alike to me. The incredible genius which would be indicated by one who would whirl around thirty times instead of the mere commonplace twenty-nine would be lost on me, ignoramus in such matters that I am. Nor would I, I fear, be able to appreciate the phenomenal talent of one who executed an *entre-chat royal,* a *tour en l'air,* a *grand fouetté à la seconde,* and a *pas de bourrée,* that is, unless she did them all simultaneously, which is not likely. Most of those I have seen — and their number has run into the hundreds — have struck me as being extremely skilful in their idiotic way and to see one a shade more skilful would not, I suspect, make a particularly profound impression upon me. Even if I recognized the fact, I would not know how to describe and explain it to the reader and my review would thus seem all the dumber. Not attending the show consequently has its virtues in an oblique critical direction.

But say I again did attend one like this *Howdy, Mr. Ice.* What you would get would be a review exactly like those you have got from me for the last seven or eight years, and one obviously even more tiresome. All the stencils would again perforce put in an appearance: "graceful but monotonous," "expert but tedious in its repetitious rhythm," "refrigerated ennui," and the rest. There might conceivably be a good word for some of the costumes, and perhaps the mention of a pretty girl in the skating ranks might slightly relieve the critique, but, unless miracles have returned to earth, the sum and substance of it would doubtless necessarily be much the same old thing.

Under the circumstances, you may congratulate yourself that I did not go to the show and that you are spared any such review.

SUNDOWN BEACH. September 7, 1948

A play by Bessie Breuer. Produced by Louis J. Singer for 7 performances in the Belasco Theatre.

Program

Cecil	Nehemiah Persoff	Arthur Bond	Warren Stevens
Merle	Martin Balsam	Henry	Tom Avera
Hazel	Treva Frazee	Ella	Lenka Peterson
Vanilla	Jennifer Howard	Belle	Kathleen Maguire
Tourist	Ellen Mahar	Nancy	Phyllis Thaxter
Helen	Vivian Firko	Tommy	Joseph Fallon
Pop	Elmor Lehr	Ida Mae	Julie Harris
Thaddeus Long	Steven Hill	Muriel	Cloris Leachman
Otis	Don Hanmer	Major Paul Walters	
Buster	Joe Sullivan		John Sylvester
Grits	Michael Lewin	Psychiatric Captain	Ira Cirker
Nadine	Joan Copeland	Sheriff	Robert Simon
Nona	Anne Hegira	Lou	Lou Gilbert
George Washburn	Edward Binns		

SYNOPSIS: *The scene of the play is an island off the Gulf Coast of Florida in the Spring of 1945, during the last months of the war. The action takes place at "Sundown Café," near an air-force hospital for convalescent combat crews. Act I. A Saturday afternoon. Act II. Three weeks later. Act III. Three weeks later.*
Director: *Elia Kazan.*

During the summer hiatus I entertained myself, among other useless ways, by confecting and publishing a prediction of certain ingredients which would doubtless figure in the various war plays that were announced for production. One of these was the kind of booze-parlor, bedroom and bath lingo already made familiar to us in plays like *Mister Roberts, et al.* That it similarly would be justified as a more or less faithful recording of the speech of the men dealt with was granted. But that repetition would make it tiresome, that the measure of startle it had when heard from a stage for the first time would be materially diminished, and that after several more allotments of it we would embrace to our bosoms any play whose language kept its trousers buttoned was a feeling I could not suppress. Once the novelty of such four-letter words and four-word epithets had worn off — and the nap had already got a little shiny — two and one-half hours of the thing was not going to be easy to take.

The boys' passes at the girls, I hazarded, would undoubtedly also continue to figure in a number of the plays. That the passes would be as authentic as the speech went without saying. But, like the speech, they too, I ventured, would be doomed to tedium from long theatrical acquaintance. Their pattern has become as fixed as that of derby hats, and has begun to feel just as tight around the head. There is, for example, the overdone comedy pass which usually takes place in a juke-box joint or wayside tavern, which involves the usual pert minx of accommodating morals, which is conducted with a brassy give-and-take, and which culminates in a jovially triumphant slap on the lady's stern and the inebrious joint departure of the couple to convenient parts. There is, for another, the amorous approach to a tropical island belle by a GI or gob reduced to communicating his intentions through the sign language, supposed in turn to reduce the dusky beauty to coy but nevertheless acquiescent stitches and the audience to unbounded mirth. There is, furthermore, what may be called the pass *en masse,* which presents the Army, the Air Force and the Navy as composed entirely of adolescent Casanovas in passionate, if facetious, pursuit of females of all races and color. To say nothing of the occasional more solemn pass at a buddy's wife, widow, or girl couched either in the language of mad despair — "the whole world's in a rotten mess; let's seize our chance for happiness while there's still time" — or in the language of tough determination — "you're the one I want and, by God, nothing is going to stand in my way!" These and others equally senile might be expected to show up again and to make the colder blooded among us doubly chilly.

I also observed that I was very much afraid that we were to be asked to sit through a large service of the banal readjustment business. That is, plays which would again beseech our interest in the problem of reconverting the boys into civilians and fitting them into the pre-war pattern of things. The problem may be dramatically seasonable but the manner in which it would be worked out, if we were to judge from the plays we had hitherto suffered, would not be anything to root us to the spot. Nor, I feared, would matters be much different with the sister plays dealing with the mental, physical and psychological rehabilitation of boys whose experiences had unbalanced their normality. Both these plays, the latter in particular, seldom fail to offer us the GI who has become a neurotic of vast proportions, a role which provides a field-day to any young actor able to vibrate his body like a hoochie-coochie dancer and agitate his mop of hair like a simoon. Usually further in evidence is the GI who has been seriously crippled but who radiates good cheer and sunshine, not to mention the one similarly incapacitated who contrastingly goes about growling his indignation at the politicians and big business men whom he accuses of being responsible for his condition. Likewise on view would assuredly be our old friend, the wife who in her soldier-husband's absence has had improvised offspring, which hapless circumstance would again lead to the scene between her and the returned husband that was sure to stir the audience's emotions with all the furious power of a swizzle-stick. "You don't know what loneliness can do to a person, Jake; the long, lonely nights, the long, empty days. It wasn't that I don't love you, Jake, 'cause I do, I do. It was the hunger for you that made me do it, the desperate, crying hunger — and loneliness."

And we could rest assured that would not be all. There would again be the boy whose bitter disillusionment seeks relief in strong drink; the major whose four terrible, bloody years in the Quartermaster's department have unfitted him for civilian life; the scene in which the delirious aviator in the rehabilitation ward jumps out of bed and wildly proclaims his determination to rejoin his squadron; and the one in which the wife does not at first recognize her returned, greatly changed husband and, when eventually she does, falls sobbingly on his shoulder.

Though this *Sundown Beach* is about the Air Force in the late war, the fliers who figure in it are grounded by afflictions of one kind or another and the play finds itself in much the same position. One of the main reasons for its plight is the aforesaid familiarity of many of its elements. I appreciate that adroit treatment and powerful imagination may lay hold of materials as threadbare as even the oldest Pat and Mike story and convert them into something that seems as fresh as a daisy. But, though Miss Breuer has performed bits of her task with some mild ability, she misses both the competence and literary-dramatic fire that might scrape off the general mildew. The end product, accordingly, is scarcely more than a succession of theatrically obvious and poorly related case histories of incapacitated fliers and their attempts at self-readjustment which seem either to have been plucked out of or paraphrased from previous plays like *Truckline Café, Foxhole In The Parlor, Skydrift, Men To The Sea*, etc.

Miss Breuer herself serves as a first-rate critic of another facet of her play. In an interview before it opened, she allowed, "It's a cross-section which is a complete portrait of the flier. I wanted to represent every kind of man who had psychiatric wounds. from an illiterate hillbilly to the most literate intellectual . . . I didn't actually see a hillbilly. I'd like to say that I took the eye of one man, the nose of another, and the head of a third." If the lady will forgive me, that is a hell of a way to go about creating authentic character and writing a good play. To treat of an illiterate hillbilly without ever having seen a hillbilly is not likely to be overproductive of meritorious results, and arouses considerable further suspicion of her literate intellectual and other characters. Nor is sound and revealing character to be achieved by dismissing an individual as an individual and fashioning a figure with an eye, nose and particularly head borrowed from three distinct and wholly different men. What happens under such circumstances is less the complete portrait of a flier that Miss Breuer hoped for than the kind of thing other little girls fashion by cutting out sections of the manikins in the pages of women's magazines and pasting them together on pieces of cardboard. True character is not to be derived from any such syntheses. While the author contrives to make some of her people superficially convincing, one consequently gets the over-all impression that — factual case histories or not — they have had their wounds, physical, emotional, psychiatric, or what not, sterilized with greasepaint.

All this, of course, is the purely critical point of view. The layman sometimes has a way of overlooking such breaches and swallowing what he sees with a willing mouth, and one who has accepted as logical a heroine, as in *A Streetcar Named Desire,* who seeks the realization of her dream of sacrosanct love through prostitution or an ingenious and merciless swindler, as in *All My Sons,* whose brain is confounded to the point of suicide by sentimental qualms is not apt to find too much fault with characters that comport themselves less like victims of actual war psychosis than like victims of the theatrical view of it.

This theatrical view becomes clearly evident in the nature of the springboard from which Miss Breuer has elected to project herself into her theme. That springboard is the tried and true hokum of what is known in the vernacular as love. Love and sex are constantly all over the stage, and almost everything is seen through their eyes. It occasionally seems, indeed, as if the cast of characters is made up largely of Alfred Kinsey, Ella Wheeler Wilcox, Henri Bataille, Mae West, the backers of *Sailor, Beware!,* Frederic and Fanny Hatton, Al Woods, Nancy Choremi, and the stenographer who typed *The Rats Of Norway* for Keith Winter. Miss Breuer's approach to this phase of her subject matter, while doubtless impressive to some in her audience, is, however, every now and then as suspect as her approach to character. In witness whereof, consider this additional confidence in the before-mentioned interview: "It (the play) is the story of people at a certain moment of stress in time

. . . Men like these never talk to each other about their
experiences. Only to the women they love do they reveal
themselves."

With all the politesse this side of Windsor Castle, I
nonetheless privilege myself a loud hoot. Miss Breuer's
conviction that men like those her play deals with never,
unlike most men, talk to each other about their emotional
experiences indicates simply that she did not get around
enough. What they or any other men rather do not do is
talk to each other about such matters when strangers, particularly female strangers, are about. When they are alone,
they often are to be restrained from confiding to each other
only by a team of wild horses, as any male's helpless and
suffering ear can attest. The notion that most of them are
excessively taciturn about their girls, their loves, their adventures and their general amorous life is one held mainly
by ladies like Miss Breuer and deaf smoking-car porters.

The author's supplementary notion that such men as she
treats of reveal themselves only to the women they love is
equally poppycock. Any man in or out of a flier's uniform
reveals to the woman he loves not the whole and exact
truth about himself so much as that part of it which he believes will most affect and impress her. Love and truth may
go hand in hand when the parties to love have advanced
far beyond youth, but in other cases nothing so threatens
and dismays love as complete honesty, whether on the
man's side or the woman's. The difference is that when a
man is in love he lies beautifully about himself and when
not in love seeks escape and safety in blunt and entire
truth. Miss Breuer's excursions into passion, romance, frustration, infidelity, and all the other bacteria of the subject
have the air of having been made on an old-time river side-
wheeler.

The acting by the members of a group known as the Actors' Studio and the direction by Elia Kazan, who worked
on the play with them for all of eleven months, are strained
and ineffectual. Instead of achieving the orchestrated performances *à la* Moscow which was clearly the dream, the
stage presents the spectacle of an extended series of

chipped and scattered emotional duets, all made somewhat ridiculous by directing the parties thereto as if the males were so many boisterously melodramatic Theodore Kremers and the women so many ten-twenty-thirty Hedda Gablers. The whole, indeed, provides the effect of an old Keith and Proctor vaudeville bill performed by a company recruited from the Charles E. Blaney blood and thunder gallery melodramas and directed like Pawnee Bill's Wild West show.

In this, as in other productions which seek to capture a complete realism, the latter regularly suffers a blow when the characters are called upon casually to toss a lighted cigarette to the ground and then hold up the action in making certain that the theatre fire regulations are served by seeing to it, with great painstaking, that it is fully and safely extinguished.

SHOW BOAT. September 7, 1948

A revival of the musical play by Jerome Kern and Oscar Hammerstein II. Produced by Richard Rodgers and Oscar Hammerstein II for a limited engagement of 17 performances in the City Center Theatre.

PROGRAM

WINDY	George Spellman	SAL	Rita Christiani
STEVE	Fred Brookins	BARKER	Walter Russell
PETE	Gerald Prosk	FATIMA	Sylvia Myers
QUEENIE	Helen Dowdy	SPORT	Robert Fleming
PARTHY ANN HAWKS	Ruth Gates	DAHOMEY KING	La Verne French
CAPTAIN ANDY	Billy House	LANDLADY	Sara Floyd
ELLIE	Clare Alden	ETHEL	Assota Marshall
FRANK	Sammy White	MOTHER SUPERIOR	
RUBBER FACE	Gordon Alexander		Lorraine Waldman
JULIE	Carol Bruce	KIM	Danice Dodson
GAYLOR RAVENAL	Norwood Smith	JAKE	King Brill
VALLON	Fred Ardath	JIM	Selden Bennett
MAGNOLIA	Pamela Caveness	DRUNK	Walter Russell
JOE	William C. Smith	LOTTIE	Sara Dillon
BACKWOODSMAN	Howard Frank	DOLLY	Elaine Hume
JEB	Gerald Prosk	SALLY	Janet Van Derveer
SAM	La Verne French	OLD LADY ON LEVEE	Ann Lloyd

SYNOPSIS: Act I. Scene 1. *The levee at Natchez on the Mississippi. In the Eighties.* Scene 2. *Kitchen pantry of the* Cotton Blossom. *Five minutes later.* Scene 3. *Auditorium and stage of the* Cotton Blossom. *One hour later.* Scene 4. *Box-office, on foredeck. Three weeks later.* Scene 5. *Auditorium and stage during the 3rd Act of* The Parson's Bride *that night.* Scene 6. *The top deck. Later that night.* Scene 7. *The levee at Greenville. Next morning.* Act II. Scene 1. *The Midway Plaisance, Chicago World's Fair, 1893.* Scene 2. *A room on Ontario Street, 1904.* Scene 3. *Rehearsal room, Trocadero Music Hall. A few nights later.* Scene 4. *St. Agatha's Convent. About the same time.* Scene 5. *Trocadero Music Hall. Just before midnight. New Year's Eve 1905.* Scene 6. *Stern of the Show Boat, 1927.* Scene 7. *Top deck of the* Cotton Blossom. *That night.* Scene 8. *Levee at Greenville. The next night.*

Director: *Hassard Short.*

THE GRAND SHOW'S RETURN to the local scene brings us again to reflect how foolish are those critics who in recent years have objected to old-fashioned sentiment in musical comedy, which is much like objecting to sugar in pastry. Musical comedy is the pastry of the stage and sentiment is as inevitably a part of it as it is of patriotism, love, or old cuspidor heirlooms. The best musical comedies have always been found to swim in it. Sometimes it has been masked with caprices of one sort or another but its face nonetheless has been plainly recognizable, and to the shows' great profit. For when most people go to any such exhibit they go, cynical as otherwise they may possibly be, with moonlight and Chinese lanterns in their brains, and Chinese lanterns and moonlight are discommoded by gusts of chill air.

It is understandable that critics whom duty compels to review innumerable such shows itch for something different and the itch, like a mosquito bite on the coccyx, occasionally impels them to strange and ungainly postures. They do not say frankly that at least for the time being they have become tired of sentiment, but convert their tiredness of it into a derogation of it *per se*. They do not argue that it no longer has any place in musical comedy so much as they argue that it no longer has any place in their personal tastes. They do not, in short, criticize it but criticize themselves.

The public, however, pays little heed to them and goes on delighting in the old, appropriate sweetenings. In the last ten years the large majority of musical comedies that have achieved three hundred or more performances have been those which stuck basically to the tried and true confectionery, not those which have chewed it and spit it out. Once in a while a *Pal Joey* or a *Kiss Me, Kate* which hides its sentimental core in a superficial toughness may strike the trade's fancy, but when all is said and done it is the musical comedy with harps in its pocket that fills its other with cash. Through the years, moreover, it is *The Student*

Princes and the *Blossom Times* that enjoy the longest box-
office life up and down the land. And the statistics of the
theatre in New York, that hypothetically hardboiled and
wicked city, prove that of the authentic musical comedies
in the last fifty years which have passed the five hundred
performance mark all of seventeen out of nineteen have
had violins in their hearts, stars in their eyes, and roses in
their hair. Musical revues, musical shows, and the like, as
distinguished from musical comedy, often succeed on more
sophisticated levels, though one of them without any occasional relief in the shape of sentimental song would surely
find the going pretty rough. And, even in the case of the
revues, it has been such as the late Florenz Ziegfeld's *Follies,* which were as sentimental on the whole as decorated
candy boxes, that have gained lasting celebrity and that
most consistently attracted customers.

It long has been believed that unless a musical comedy,
particularly a sentimentally romantic musical comedy, has
a lot of good comedy relief it will not stand much of a
chance. The facts knock the theory into a cocked hat. The
comedy relief in *The Merry Widow* is not only propor-
tionately negligible but is doleful to boot, yet *The Merry
Widow* has enjoyed an enormous prosperity. Various other
musical comedies for more than half a century have captivated the public without more than a meagre leaven of
comedy, and that of the kind that would not evoke a titter
from even a laughing hyena. Such successes of the far past
as *Veronique, The Mocking Bird, The Waltz Dream, The
Orchid,* and *Mlle. Modiste* contained very little comedy relief, and what minor share they did contain was fairly
dampening. Such of a later period as *The New Moon, The
Desert Song, Rose Marie,* and *The Vagabond King* were in
much the same position. And such of more recent times as
Song Of Norway, Brigadoon, and *Carousel,* which was seen
again at the City Center in the following January, have
offered books which likewise have rested mainly on sentiment as opposed to humor. In most cases it has been a
general cheerfulness of spirit rather than incorporated wag-
gery that has benefited them. They have imparted in vary-

ing degree a feeling of romantic gayety rather than a gayety heavily derived from comics bumping into each other, suffering epilepsy at the sound of pulled champagne corks and cracking interpolated jokes on Yonkers, the Erie Railroad, and the Gowanus Canal.

If, in certain examples, I have included among the musical comedies offerings which have been listed as operettas, I may say that the difference between them in the Broadway theatre is often insignificant and that what is dubbed an operetta seems frequently to be just a musical comedy with three or four more songs and a chorus that is made to conceal its inability to dance by joining in them.

The critics' protest against sentiment in one and all becomes doubly ridiculous when one considers their willing acceptance of it in the drama. Plays like *Life With Father, The Glass Menagerie, The Winslow Boy, Years Ago, Edward, My Son,* etc., warmly gathered to their bosoms, are every bit as sentimental, in fact, even more so, than the musical comedies which they condescendingly have criticized for being a little too much on the honeyed side. What else, indeed, in this increasingly drab world, should such shows be? If a dramatic play about a gruff old paterfamilias, or a faded Southern belle, or a boy wrongly accused of theft, or a yokel virgin bent on a stage career, or a father ambitious for his offspring may be sentimental, what is wrong about sentiment in a musical show about pretty young girls in love, about the handsome lads they are in love with, and about moons and rainbows and far green islands and dreams?

As for me, damned if I know.

HILARITIES. September 9, 1948

A vaudeville revue with music and lyrics by Buddy Kaye, Stanley Arnold and Carl Lampl, sketches by Morey Amsterdam. Produced by Ken Robey and Stan Zucker for 14 performances in the Adelphi Theatre.

Principals

Morey Amsterdam, Betty Jane Watson, Enid Williams, Harold and Lola, Sid Stone, Raul and Eva Reyes, Connie Sawyer, the Holloway sisters, Gali Gali, Larry Douglas, George Tapps, the Calgary brothers, Al Kelly, the Herzogs, Gil Maison, Mitzi Novelle, and Gerald Austen.
Director: *Mervyn Nelson.*

WHEN IT COMES to sticking out one's neck, calling a show *Hilarities* is to risk running a dead heat with Marie Antoinette. Like prefacing a story with the remark that it is awfully funny, it has the effect of challenging an audience with the prediction that what it is to hear and see will lay it in the aisles and is more than likely to get the customer's back up and invest him with an air of defiance, much as he is made to bristle when anyone starts a conversation with a "Now listen, I'm telling you!" It is overselling goods sight unseen, and strikes the potential buyer a little like a confidently rosy prospectus on the corkscrew business in a Prohibition town. The consequence is that unless the show bearing the label is a lot better than merely good the customer's induced prejudice will make him think it is not any good at all.

The sponsors of the present exhibit, who are new to the show business, should have studied the situation before they took any such chance. They might have learned that various similarly named shows in past seasons have had a bad time of it. *Bright Lights of 1944,* for example, antagonized its trade as being so doubly dim that it extinguished itself after just four performances. *Keep 'Em Laughing* did not do anything of the sort and went down the drain before very long. *Take A Bow* fell on its face in short order,

and so did *For Your Pleasure*. And the same with still other
such promissory notes. An audience, it appears, wants to
find things out for itself and does not like to be hornswog-
gled into esteeming acrobats, tap dancers and jugglers as
the particular *Jollities of 1948* or ventriloquists, more tap
dancers and imitators of Al Jolson and Eddie Cantor as the
indubitable *Festivities* of that or any other year. Audiences,
in short, have grown up, well, anyway, a little, and the day
when you could palm off a bunch of dressed-up old vaudeville acts on them as a revue superior in wit and humor to
the exceptional Rip revues in Paris is gone, and gone with
it the time when a comedian temporarily out of a real job
could be surrounded by a dog act, a female contortionist
and a xylophone player and sold as legitimate theatre fare.

It seems to be the persistent hope of the producers of
such shows that they will be able to get away with almost
anything, however stale and dull, if only they have a master of ceremonies in the person of an even moderately
competent comedian come on at intervals and divert the
audience's attention from it. The idea may work in the
night clubs, where a gag like "The next act needs no introduction; what it needs is an act" is considered to be almost
Voltairean in the richness of its wit, at least by those who
are sufficiently snozzled, but in the theatre it may be allowed to lose some of its effect, especially after it has been
repeated in one form or another for something like an hour
and a half. The theory that a poor act may be made to seem
not only less poor than it is but even pretty excellent by
spoofing its poorness and thus presumably ingratiating it
with the spectators somehow no longer functions as the
producers fondly anticipate. Nor does the opposite technique avail when the master of ceremonies works his features into a more solemn pattern and announces that what
the lucky customers are next to behold is "that sterling artiste who has no peer in her field," when the customers duly
appreciate that the matchless artiste in question doesn't figure eight-nine-ten with others in her profession and is, to
boot, so moldy that you could get a carload of penicillin
out of her.

Vaudeville is not necessarily dead but the vaudeville acts out of which shows like *Hilarities* are manufactured find its patrons for the greater part in that condition. Some of the present items are individually commendable but collectively they run so routine and hackneyed a course that an audience's interest languishes and soon expires. It is not only novelty in the acts that is lacking; it is novelty in their presentation. The prevalent manner of presenting them, in this and in shows like it, merely heightens the evening's humdrum. What is needed is something a bit different. It should not be too difficult to think up ways and means to turn the trick. Olsen and Johnson managed it by crocheting the old acts into a kind of Steeplechase Park crazy-quilt, a device which they borrowed from the celebrated London *Crazy Gang* shows of Flanagan and Allen. And a number of more elaborate revues have successfully achieved it by concealing the obvious contours of what have been essentially vaudeville acts with choruses of pretty dancing girls, rousing ensemble numbers, processions of fashion models in front of the drop curtain, and Hit Parade songs cabbaged from Puccini. There are surely other ways as well, and maybe, let us pray, much better ones. But the sponsors of things like this *Hilarities* seem to be too lazy — or perhaps too unwisely sanguine — to try to dream them up. The result is usually a show that suggests a barker in the guise of a conférencier standing at the flap of a tent and ballyhooing in Broadway lingo the rheumatic Fatimas, spurious Siamese-twins and dyspeptic sword-swallowers on display inside.

Morey Amsterdam, who serves the current evening as general factotum, is a radio and night club comic with, I am told, a devoted following which laughs fit to bust whenever he opens his mouth. His talents are scarcely productive of any such volcanic reaction in my case, but, even if they were, I fear that the program of acts behind him would call for an entire Primrose, Dockstader and West minstrel show as an assistant master of ceremonies to put it in the money.

SMALL WONDER. September 15, 1948

A musical revue with sketches by Charles Spalding, Louis Laun, Max Wilk, and George Axelrod, music by Baldwin Bergersen and Albert Selden, and lyrics by Phyllis McGinley and Billings Brown. Produced by George Nichols III for 134 performances in the Coronet Theatre.

PRINCIPALS

Tom Ewell, Alice Pearce, Mary McCarty, Marilyn Day, Hayes Gordon, Tommy Rall, J. C. McCord, Jonathan Lucas, Alan Ross, Joan Mann, Chandler Cowles, Joan Diener, Virginia Oswald, Bill Ferguson, Jack Cassidy, Kate Friedlich, Mort Marshall, Evelyn Taylor.
    Director: *Burt Shevelove.*

THE TITLES of musical shows are generally more than plain, but this one puzzles me. Did the sponsors intend the "small" to refer to the production's modest nature? Or did they seriously mean to suggest that the show was in its way a little phenomenon? Or did it have something to do with Paul Small, the talent agent? Or was "small wonder" simply a borrowing of the familiar phrase which is usually followed by a "that"? Assuming it was the latter, I may report it is small wonder that the show is not remotely what it might be because of the obvious disabilities of the humorists and songwrights who were hired to hatch it.

These disabilities take on a particular acuteness in the efforts at satire, which is the evening's main intention, and become especially onerous in numbers in which several cowboys and a cowgirl who have discovered oil on their ranch appear in silk-fringed chaps and a diamond tiara; in which the leading comic harangues on the outmoded human corpus in this era of mechanical improvements in all other quarters; in which the business of selling democracy to foreign countries over the radio is travestied; in which various types of best sellers are lampooned; and in which a rhumba finale in a South American setting is killingly programmed as "Badaroma." I refrain from calling further attention to a bridal number to lyrics titled "Nobody Told Me" and a monologue on the catch phrases that figure in the advertising racket. There is also, I hesitate to add, an item about the trials of commuters.

The staging is the kind which hopes to relieve the conventionality of the standard solo tap number by having a girl stand to one side and banter a lyric consisting entirely of the ejaculation "show-off!", which throws a stereopticon picture of small white cottages on the backdrop during the commuter ditty, and which evokes the lazy atmosphere of a South American town by raising the curtain on the spectacle of the ensemble dozing in postures more commonly associated with expert acrobats. The music throughout sounds as if it had been composed in competition with a battery of dentists' drills. And the whole is so economically and skimpily produced that there are times when one would enthusiastically welcome the execrable but lavish taste of an old Earl Carroll revue. The costumes in particular are so cheap and frowzy that they would despoil the looks of most of the girls who wear them if the latter had any. That two of them, Marilyn Day and Mary McCarty, manage to triumph over the atrocities is about the only thing in the show, in short, that is a small wonder, though the latter's apparently growing conviction that making faces is a prime requisite of comedy scarcely assists her in the conquest.

It was doubtless the revue's title and the circumstance that the show offered little to keep my attention on the stage that caused my thoughts to emigrate and to do some wondering of an erratic nature on their own. Among the speculations which I scribbled on my program while the exhibition was apparently occupying other people with its entertainment values were a half hundred or so, most of them happily irrelevant. I wondered, for example, why it is that —

1. American actors with diction so slovenly that the mother tongue in their mouths sounds like the speech of

an immigrant Polish barber nevertheless uniformly, when it comes to the two words "record" and "poem," articulate them with high-toned precision as "re-chord" and "poh-em"?

2. The characters in American plays representing young liberals usually wear suits that look as if two extra pairs of pants came gratis with them, are given to lipping innumerable unlighted cigarettes, and reserve their political and social ideals largely for the ears of the leading ladies?

3. Playwrights swoon with ecstasy at the sound of the word "Democracy" and would sooner die of cholera than define it in any such manner as being the theory that all men are born equal, notably in intelligence and wisdom, and that, even if they are not, they are bound to achieve those qualities if guaranteed complete independence from the influence of such as possess them?

4. The maids in middle-class American stage households seem never to wear garters?

5. The moment a second-rate playwright or song writer, hitherto a failure, has a Broadway box-office hit, he feels safe in constituting himself an authority on his art and becomes condescending to even the critics who have given him good notices?

6. A published poet may mention the moon sentimentally without criticism whereas even a first-rate musical comedy lyric writer will be derided if he does so?

7. Even the member of a theatre audience who thinks some such pun as referring to the Tennessee city noted for its imbecile censorship as *non compos Memphis* is amusing feels it nevertheless incumbent upon him to shudder and dismiss it as beneath contempt?

8. Even very bad English actors never seem to be really as bad as they are?

9. Negro actresses, however otherwise beautiful, usually have feet that don't look right?

10. Middle-aged white actresses with henna'd hair, however immaculate they really may be, generally look a little soiled?

11. Whatever the nature of the stage lighting, even the smallest zipper on an actress' dress takes on the look of the Comstock lode?

12. Of all the various animals that have figured in plays, a horse has invariably looked to be the most uncomfortable and out of its element?

13. Though it was a rare season that at one time did not offer a play with a character designated as "Pablo, a peon," Pablo has not made an appearance even once in the last fifteen years?

14. The four piece orchestras which are now and then hired to play entr'-acte music at the dramatic shows are seldom instructed in the nature of the play of the evening and regale the audience with such selections as "You're The Top," "Begin The Beguine," and "Dixie" for Euripides, Ibsen, and Chekhov?

15. Lady Percy's remark to Hotspur in *Henry IV* is generally believed to refer to one of the fingers on his hand?

16. One can usually much more readily foretell the resolution of good drama than bad and the ending of a fine drama is most often apparent whereas that of a pulp mystery play is relatively surprising?

17. More critics do not appreciate that one of the differences between a first-rate and second-rate dramatist is that the former thinks out his characters whereas the latter simply feels them out?

18. Though characters in plays have drunk champagne, brandy, Bourbon, Rhine wine, juleps, applejack, Montrachet, Chianti, cocktails, Madeira, sherry, ale, beer, punch, vodka, vermouth, rum, slivovitz, absinthe, gin, saki, and almost every other tipple known to Christendom, including most of the liqueurs, there has never yet in the history of drama so far as I know been one who has drunk Scotch whisky straight?

19. Humor in criticism, however intelligent and searching, is generally looked at askance and privately deplored as corruptive of critical importance even by those who appreciate its appositeness and merit?

20. The better and worthier modern plays have seldom

been those which have taken advantage of the latest developments and improvements in modern stagecraft?

21. The vanity of the average actor is so great that he has come to regard a critic's description of his performance as "adequate" as condescending and even a bit insulting, when "adequate," were he to look up its meaning in a dictionary, means "equal to the requirement or occasion" and "fully sufficient"?

22. No actor has ever failed to make an impression in the role of a drug addict or dope fiend, even when his performance has been a caricature of realistic characterization?

23. A cold in the head is always comical on the stage, and a sneeze downright hilarious?

24. In the plays dealing with the American Revolution no soldier has ever been shown as having carnal desires, much less demonstrating them?

25. Ibsen's *Rosmersholm* is customarily staged as if it had been lighted by Strindberg?

26. There is always one supernumerary in mob scenes who spoils everything by his seeming inability to restrain himself from staring out into the audience?

27. Negro servants in plays make their exits twice as slowly as white servants?

28. Many actresses can walk down a flight of stairs naturally but few can walk up without an air of self-consciousness?

29. A man and a woman character who declare their intention of making a new world for themselves never go about the business where they are but invariably depart for other quarters, usually indeterminate?

30. The proprietor of an Italian restaurant on the stage always comports himself as if he were afflicted with a benign St. Vitus dance?

31. However elaborate a stage dinner, there never seems to be any butter on the table?

32. A baby grand piano on the stage must always have a vase of flowers and at least one silver-framed photograph on it?

33. An actor who has few assets other than a deep voice

and who reads his lines with great deliberation, even **if**
they should not be read that way, is generally credited by
the reviewers as being one of "authority"?

34. An actress known to be good-looking who plays a
role which calls for her to indulge in a makeup that makes
her look homely usually gets flattering notices from the reviewers, even if her performance isn't worth a nickel?

35. Audiences will always applaud a stage setting that
contains a large crystal chandelier?

36. Music critics who on their nights off attend Broadway musical comedies sometimes praise scores which, if
they were to hear them in a concert hall, would cause them
to throw fits?

37. Actresses famous as great personalities are chiefly
those who have had or have the manners of charwomen?

38. An actor has seldom if ever failed in the role of Napoleon Bonaparte?

39. A blonde actress is never fully satisfactory as a tra-
gédienne?

40. One rarely if ever sees in the histories of the American theatre the name of Marc Lescarbot, who wrote its first
acted play?

41. But one critic in England, David Garnett, and but
one in America, your obedient servant, has ever mentioned
in the public prints the meaning of Hamlet's "country matters" speech to Ophelia and Malvolio's comments on the
capital letters in the letter-reading scene, or has commented
on the regular omission of one of the letters?

42. A reviewer who writes extravagant praise of a young
playwright's first produced play will never confess his over-
enthusiasm when the author's subsequent plays prove he
was excessive in his view of the former's talents, but will
elaborately qualify his doubts in order to persuade his
readers that he was not a big fool in the first place?

43. In all the many plays in which a character has realistically mixed Martini cocktails there has been only a
single instance (*Town House*) where **he has** remembered
to put an olive or onion into **them?**

44. Stage money never looks in the least like anything but stage money?

45. So few authorities on the American theatre seem to know that the first musical comedy written by a man of any American blood (he was part English) was *The Fashionable Lady* (1730) and that the author was one James Ralph?

46. A highly dramatic scene, however good, in a period play which involves an actor with trousers properly several inches above his shoe tops always waywardly seems just a bit comical?

47. Even those critics who write most rapturously about J. M. Barrie feel it necessary to do some apologizing for him?

48. The word "resin" has not been pronounced correctly by an American actor in the last forty years?

49. Actresses who act Shakespeare's inflammatory temptress, Cleopatra, customarily play her with such an imperious frigidity that it is a wonder Antony did not freeze to death in bed?

50. No actor, however incompetent, who has put a putty mole on his cheek and adorned himself with a seedy frock coat and stovepipe hat has failed completely in impressing the critics that he was a pretty good Lincoln?

51. It is usually overlooked in the treatises on the beginnings of realistic staging in the American theatre that a great sensation was caused simply by Mrs. John Drew's introduction of a carpet into one of the scenes in *London Assurance*?

52. It is not known that the only two four-letter words still believed never to have been spoken on the American stage were spoken by the late Richard Bennett during the New York run of *Jarnegan*?

53. No matter how bad the ad libbing of an actor when something goes wrong on the stage, it is sure to get a hand from the audience, which regards it not only as indicating remarkably quick thinking but as a pretty high grade of wit?

54. Heroic characters may be given to pipes or cigarettes but never to cigars?

55. I waste my time recording such trivial stuff as this and gaining a reputation for frivolity when I might be boring the reader to death and earning a fine reputation by printing instead a dull essay on "The Relation of the Aristotelian Aesthetic to the Drama of Racine and Corneille"?

HEAVEN ON EARTH. September 16, 1948

A musical comedy with book and lyrics by Barry Trivers and music by Jay Gorney. Produced by Monte Proser and Ned C. Litwack for 12 performances in the Century Theatre.

Program

James Aloysius McCarthy		Lieut. Sullivan	Wynn Murray
	Peter Lind Hayes	Officer Jonesy	Dorothy Keller
Friday	Dorothy Jarnac	Officer Blandings	Betty George
Punchy	Danny Drayson	Sailor	Billy Parsons
Fannie Frobisher	Caren Marsh	H. H. Hutton	David Burns
Florabelle Frobisher		Magistrate Kennedy	Dick Bernie
	Ruth Merman	Sailor with Trumpet	
Mrs. Frobisher	Nina Varela		Steve Condos
Commissioner Frobisher		Officer O'Brien	Bert Sheldon
	Irwin Corey	Radio Engineer	Jack Russell
Officer Clabber	Claude Stroud	Slim	Remi Martel
John Bowers	Robert Dixon	Dippy	Jack Russell
Mary Brooks	Barbara Nunn	Butch	Bill Hogue
The Lovers {	June Graham		
	Richard Darcy		

SYNOPSIS: Act I. Scene 1. *Central Park. Noon.* Scene 2. *The Housing Commissioner's office. That afternoon.* Scene 3. *Central Park. That afternoon.* Scene 4. *The Hutton Home of Tomorrow. That evening.* Act II. Scene 1. *Central Park. Next Morning.* Scene 2. *A cell block in the Park Jail. That morning.* Scene 3. *Police court in the Park Jail. That morning.* Scene 4. *Fifth Avenue. Immediately afterward.* Scene 5. *Interior of Hutton home. Late that day.* Scene 6. *Central Park. Immediately afterward.*

Directors: *Eddie Dowling and John Murray Anderson.*

IF THE ANNOUNCEMENTS were to be believed, I wrote several months before the Fall season opened, the coming months would offer more musical shows than we had seen for a long time in any single year. Out of the magnanimity of my disputed heart, I presented to the producers several suggestions that possibly might help to keep a lot of them from too early deposit in the storehouse. That none of the suggestions would be followed was, of course, natural, since the only one most sponsors of such shows seem even faintly to heed is that imparted to them after their wares fail and that consists in their bankers' admonitions to take up their notes by the first of the following month, or else.

My initial recommendation, when they found either a good or even fairly good book for their shows, was that they leave it strictly alone and not labor, as they generally do, under the delusion that an audience would walk out on it unless they interrupted it from time to time with tap dancers, incongruous ballets, impersonations by the comedian of various stage and screen stars, and other such extrinsic chestnuts. Many of the most successful musicals from the days of *San Toy* to *The Merry Widow* and from *The Merry Widow* to *The Student Prince* and *Oklahoma!*, I reminded them, have permitted their books to go their ways without infecting them with vaudeville and night club acts, along with a cluster of women teetering on their great dactyls. And many of the quickest failures contrarily have been those which have deemed it necessary to horn into their stories not only with such excrescences but with such added barbiturates as pantomimic monkeyshines behind scrims, chorus chases in front of the drop curtain during scene shifts, interpolated five minute solo scenes in which the comedian gets drunk and kisses a statue of the Venus di Milo, and stretches in which the soprano is allowed free rein to agonize everybody with fierce demonstrations of her coloratura virtuosity.

Since the music for the majority of the exhibits would be acceptable chiefly to those whose musical education began with a hurdy-gurdy and ended triumphantly with a juke-box, it might, I observed, be nice of the producers to have some consideration for that portion of the audience which has progressed a bit further and not make it laugh itself sick over the customary elaborate orchestral arrangements which hope to pass off something like *The Sassafras Can-Can* for Beethoven's *Ritter Ballet*. And, while they were about it, it might, I hinted, be another good idea for them to stop reprising song numbers which even at the first hearing make an audience yearn for the sweeter melody of a jammed automobile horn. Still another fine idea, I said, would be to have the chorus girls wash their hair at least once every other week. Observing the usual bevy of young females decked out in neat and attractive costumes but with mops of hair that are plainly shampoophobes is hardly conducive to instilling a sense of passionate desire in the male customers, except possibly in the case of any barbers who may be present. And the next time I had to look at a plot's Dream Girl with her pale nylon stocking heels reinforced with sizeable rectangles of what seem to be woven porous plasters, I was, I promised, going to bring back into action my old slingshot.

These, you say, are minor matters. Perhaps. But just the same we have seen plays even as notable as Hauptmann's *The Weavers* fall completely to pieces simply because the child playing Mielchen at one point accidentally dropped her little panties, and shows as creditable as *Rainbow* go suddenly and entirely to pot because of the momentary intestinal lapse of a mule.

Unless my nose missed its old powers of divination, it furthermore struck me that the trade was beginning to lose its taste for the cyclone species of stage direction that gives shows the appearance of running madly away from themselves, which, considering the quality of many of them, indicates that they have some good critical sense. There was a day when a show so essentially slow that it had trouble lifting its feet off the stage could be put over on the gudgeons by directing it into a pace so furious that they had no time to detect its underlying snoozy nature. But that day seems to be over. A stage full of boys and girls dashing frantically around for no discernible purpose other than dashing frantically around is no longer successful in fooling an audience into thinking there is life where there is none. The *Show Boats, Carousels, Annie Get Your Guns* and *Brigadoons,* it reflects, are not any such artificial tornadoes.

The aforesaid talented nose also sniffed the fact that some of the so-called "musical satires" were going to have a particularly difficult time of it. For some years now, audiences have been bamboozled by Broadway showrights who are fascinated by the high-toned sound of the phrase but whose ability in a satirical direction has been limited to having a janitor dream he is President of the United States and in that capacity turn the White House into a rendezvous for a colored quartet masquerading as Arabs on the trail of a low comedian disguised, gratuitously, as Ernest Bevin. And the audiences, whose idea of satire is slightly different, are beginning, unless all signs fail, to scratch themselves. A public that has lately further enriched Bernard Shaw's already copious bank account is no longer likely to be taken in by satire labels on musical beer steins that contain nothing more satirical than tap water. It expects satire to consist in something a little more than an opening song number in which the chorus rhymes Petrillo with get Quillo, a feeble ribbing of the conventional, feeble music show book, and a female madcap who comes on, opens her mouth in a broad, toothy smile, and does not identify herself as Eleanor Roosevelt.

Among the producers who expectedly dismissed the remarks as simply another instance of critical sauciness, and with the usual minimum of sense, were the gentlemen responsible for everything connected with this instantaneous two hundred and seventy thousand dollar failure, *Heaven On Earth*. It does not, true, contain all the elements mentioned, but it makes up for those few it has omitted with many others even more goose-pimply. It tries, for example, to conceal the fact that it has nothing else by dosing its stage with a parcel of comics and, since the comics are mainly of an inferior brand, not only accentuates the nothing else but loses the else as the evening plods its jogtrot course, thus indicating the weakness of a theatrical philosophy which holds that, whereas one dreary clown is numbing, four or five dreary ones operating in unison will constitute a circus. Whenever anyone sings a song the directors bring on either a female toe dancer to twirl an irrelevant accompaniment or several dancers of both sexes to exercise their limbs in the background. One of the comedians, Peter Lind Hayes, offers not only the usual imitations of screen actors but, for extra measure, one of a punchdrunk prize fighter which we had believed was done for back in the era of Harry Watson, Jr., and his skit about Philadelphia Jack O'Brien. Another of the comics, David Burns, appears in the old flamboyant gambler's costume that we believed also had passed from the stage with the death of Pete Dailey. Claude Stroud, a third droll in the part of an Irish policeman, when asked if he has a fairy godmother, replies with the gag out of *One Of The Finest* (*circa* 1898), "Well, I got a sergeant I'm not sure of," thereupon coyly placing his nightstick to his lips. A fourth wag, the pint-size Irwin Corey, is of the explosive pidgin-English mixed with Yiddish school, sprays saliva upon his vis-à-vis, and at intervals hops atop a table further to galvanize his art. All seek to heighten their humorous flavor with red noses or coats three sizes too big for them, and with trousers uniformly ten inches too short. There is also a fifth comic not clearly identified in the program who executes a clog dance during which he periodically hoists his baggy breeches by the crotch, which we had imagined disappeared from the burlesque stage when Sliding Billy Watson himself got tired of it.

In the first book on the theatre I ever wrote — the year was 1915 — I included in a chapter on musical shows the standard song cues of that and the preceding twenty-five years. Some of them were the following:

1. "How *much* do you love me?"
2. "Yes, but there's only one girl in the world for me!"
3. "Yes, but there's only one town in the world for me!"
4. "Yes, but there's only one street in the world for me!"
5. "You are so near and yet so far."
6. Any allusion to a rose.
7. Any allusion to the moon.
8. Any allusion to the stars.
9. Any allusion to ale.
10. "It seems only yesterday."

11. "Those were the days — youth and Spring and the highroad!"

12. "Home is where the heart is."

13. "Wine! What a comrade in times of despair and sorrow!"

14. "Do you remember that waltz we heard on that wonderful moonlit night in Venice?"

15. "Will you marry me?"

16. Any allusion to gypsies, particularly a female gypsy.

17. "The girlies: how I love them all!"

18. Any allusion to a white girl named Mary.

19. Any allusion to a colored girl named Mandy.

20. "Well, anything can happen."

21. "But one can always dream."

22. "Remember the words of the wise old owl."

23. "I wonder how many girls you've told that to."

24. Any allusion to a bench in a park or a ride around a park.

25. Any reference to wedding bells.

26. "Hail!" (It matters not in the least to whom.)

Here, after the many years, the cues and the songs are again in evidence, as may be gathered from numbers called "In The Back Of A Hack," "Anything Can Happen," "So Near And Yet So Far," "Don't Forget To Dream," "Bench In The Park," "Home Is Where The Heart Is," "Wedding In The Park," etc.

The sickly sweet book of the show has to do with a benevolent vagabond who tries to find a home for a homeless young couple who wish to marry and sounds as if it had been concocted by someone simultaneously reading *Finian's Rainbow* and Saroyan's *Sweeney In The Trees* while seated in a bathtub filled with glucose. Much of the music sounds in turn as if it had been composed on an indignant fish horn. The settings and costumes, by the erstwhile imaginative Raoul Pene Du Bois, are fairly hideous; and the stage direction by the Messrs. Dowling and Anderson harks back to the period when all that was deemed necessary for a successful musical show by their prototypes was a green park bench, one blue and one pink gelatine slide, a scene in which the leading lady would appear in an elaborate wedding gown, a comedian who blew cigar smoke into another comedian's face, a topical song (here it is "What's The Matter With Our City?"), and a joke about Steve Brodie.

On this occasion, they remembered to include everything but, puzzlingly enough, the joke.

MAGDALENA. September 20, 1948

A "musical adventure" with music by Heitor Villa-Lobos, book by Homer Curran and Frederick Hazlitt Brennan, lyrics by Robert Wright and George Forrest. Produced by Homer Curran and Edwin Lester for 88 performances in the Ziegfeld Theatre.

PROGRAM

PADRE JOSEF	Gerhard Pechner	ZOGGIE	John Schickling
MANUEL	Peter Fields	DANSEUSE	Lorraine Miller
SOLIS	Melva Niles	TERESA	Irra Petina
RAMON	Henry Reese	THE OLD ONE	Gene Curtsinger
MARIA	Dorothy Sarnoff	CHICO	Patrick Kirk
PEDRO	John Raitt	JUAN	Leonard Morganthaler
MAJOR BLANCO	Ferdinand Hilt	CONCHITA	Betty Brusher
DOCTOR LOPEZ	Carl Milletaire	MAJOR DOMO	Roy Raymond
GENERAL CARABANA	Hugo Haas	BAILADORA	Marie Groscup
CHANTEUSE	Betty Huff	BAILADOR	Matt Mattox
CIGARETTE GIRL	Christine Matsios		

SYNOPSIS: Act I. Scene 1. *The courtyard of Padre Josef's chapel near the Magdalena River.* Scene 2. *A private dining room in the Little Black Mouse Café in Paris. Two weeks later.* Scene 3. *The boat landing at the Muzo Village. Ten days later.* Scene 4. *At the Shrine of the Madonna. The same evening.* Act II. Scene 1. *At the Singing Tree. A few hours later.* Scene 2. *The kitchen of General Carbana's hacienda. The next afternoon.* Scene 3. *Terrace of the General's hacienda. That evening.* Scene 4. *The floor of a canyon near the General's hacienda. A few minutes later.*
Director: *Jules Dassin.*

As sure as death and taxes is equally grim criticism of musical show books. That most of the latter are pretty grisly and that the criticism of them is fair is, alas, true. But, though it certainly would be convivial to get books much better, if and when everything else about a show is satisfactory I think it makes little difference. Of course, I impart the thought in the strictest confidence and trust the reader not to tell anyone else about it, since if it got around that I had made any such subversive statement people who hitherto may have had some slight respect for my opinions might begin to look at me with suspicion. But, all the same, between you and me I repeat in a loud stage-whisper that a book which is somewhat wormy is not too seriously disturbing if the rest of the evening is savory enough. There is considerable hypocrisy in this current critical attitude toward the books of these entertainments. As I have only too affably agreed, the majority of them are scarcely anything to embarrass the reputations of Wagner, Wette, Hofmannsthal, Gilbert, and such boys and girls. But, measly as many of them are, some of those which have been superiorly relegated to the dump, and not without justice, have not been any sillier and duller than the librettos of *Lakmé*, *Manru*, and *The Magic Flute* which haven't been especially harassed as equivalent horrors.

Do not, however, let all this mislead you into imagining for a moment that I am going to enter into any Chestertonian argument over the book of this *Magdalena*. That is, unless someone squares off and contends that its love story of a jungle belle converted to the Faith and a fellow Indian captivated by the machine age in the form of a gasoline bus is a *Rosenkavalier* with tropical fern leaves. It is goosey stuff and away with it, yet even so it is not so very much worse than the books of long esteemed sub-classics like *The Beggar Student*, *The Bohemian Girl*, and *The Gypsy Baron*, which are the sort of thing that could not hold the ear of anybody over twelve save he constituted himself a volitional half-wit. But, as I have said, what matter? The man who goes to a musical exhibit, whether musical comedy or operetta, primarily for the sake of its book is like the one who takes out a pretty girl for the sake of listening to her talk. The one who on the other hand does not give a continental whether the gypsy chieftain turns out to be the Doge of Venice in disguise or whether La Passionata, the masked dancing girl and toast of Seville, is or is not eventually revealed to be little Sally Meyerkraus of Akron, Ohio, and marries Amontillado Trocadero, the bull-fighter, or her old childhood sweetheart from Dayton — any such man carries his good sense in the right pocket and starts off with the odds all in his favor. That is, as noted, if there are enough compensations in other directions.

In *Magdalena,* there fortunately are. In the first place, there is the Villa-Lobos music, which has the advantage of having been composed by someone whose experiences in the tonal art have not been limited, as often seems to be the Broadway case, to the saxophone or harmonica. This fact, obviously, will make a lot of theatregoers pretty mad, since the score is not what they customarily describe as "tuneful" and does not contain the kind of songs beloved of adult bobby-soxers, disc jockeys, night club dance bands, and folk in general who admire a melody only if it is as catchy as the mumps. But to those whose instruction has gone a bit beyond Count Basie, the Whiffenpoof song, and the Bing Crosby platters, the Brazilian's experiments in color, rhythm, harmony, modulation and instrumentation are fascinating and provide a welcome relief from the tin-pannery which simultaneously inspires in some people a tapping of feet and in their neighbors a tapping of foreheads.

There are also the prodigal settings and costumes, by Howard Bay and Irene Sharaff respectively, which not only thaw the eye but which provide an equally happy respite from the frugal cheesecloth strips, pasteboard flats and cotton chic which batter the vision in so many of today's shows. There is, further, the choreography by Jack Cole, which fills the stage with movement somewhat more acceptable than the stock chorus and ballet routines and with a grace more that of fluent human bodies than of the usual piano-legged spinning-wheels and kangaroos in tarlatan. And, finally, there is a good company in good singing form, even if the girls are not anything to drive one crazy.

Above all and everything, however, Villa-Lobos remains the hero of the evening. In this, his first work for the musical theatre, the unflagging composer of more than fifteen hundred symphonies, concertos, suites, operas, songs, piano pieces for youngsters and, it appears, almost everything else but solos for the bagpipe, proves himself to be not the usual condescender to the lighter form of stage entertainment but an independent and honest craftsman. His score, which stems here and there from primitive folk sources, remains true to itself and resists any temptation to court cheap popularity with the kind of tunes venerated in proportion to their adaptability to blasts from puckered lips or droning noises from tightened. In it, there is little compromise, and, even if there were, the probity of the orchestrations, involving a multiplicity of such pixilated South American percussion instruments as the recoreco, pio, matraca, chucalho de metal, and something that gives off a sound like an iron hoop thrown violently into a tin bathtub, would sufficiently conceal it from the popular ear.

The abundant presentation as a whole has been condemned and even ridiculed as old-fashioned by some of the streamline maniacs, who are not happy unless musicals of whatever sort are patterned after modern toilet plumbing and performed by a company trained less in the arts than in a gymnasium. It may, in a sense, be old-fashioned but so, for that matter, are Offenbach's *The Grand Duchess* and homemade cheesecake and, when it comes to me, I'll take them.

A STORY FOR STRANGERS. SEPTEMBER 21, 1948

A fantasy by Marc Connelly. Produced by Dwight Deere Wiman for 7 performances in the Royale Theatre.

PROGRAM

NEWT FENDER	*Joseph Sweeney*	POLICEMEN	*Richard McMurray* / *Victor Parber*
AUDREY	*Joann Dolan*		
GEORGE HUBINDER	*Paul Huber*	ST. ELMO OTTLEY	*John McGovern*
A. J. KISSLE	*Frank Tweddell*	MRS. PATOON	*Grace Valentine*
MR. MERCER	*Edward Nannary*	MAYOR ORRIN SULLY	*Tom Hoier*
SOPHIE WHITING	*Jane Hoffman*	VINCENT GATLING	
HECTOR WHITING	*George Cotton*		*Joseph. L. Graham*
NORMAN HUNT	*James Dobson*	DUNBAR STOTE	*Lauren Gilbert*
BESSIE	*Joan Gray*		

SYNOPSIS: *The action takes place in Huntsville, Michigan, in 1934. Part I. Scene 1. A barbershop, September fourteenth. Scene 2. A porch, the previous July. Scene 3. An office, the same day. Scene 4. A stable, the same day. Part II. Scene 1. The barbershop, September fourteenth. Scene 2. The porch, September eighth. Scene 3. The stable, the same afternoon. Scene 4. The barbershop, September fourteenth.*

Director: *Marc Connelly.*

THE AMERICAN AUDIENCE in the aggregate asks that the theatre merely satisfy the imagination it already has rather than stimulate it to new and unaccustomed flights. It is for this reason that fantasy, except on the more elementary levels, is seldom successful with it. The fantasy it is capable of assimilating and willing to accept is strictly limited to that with toy wings, in other words, that of someone like Barrie, which amounts mainly to fanciful child's-play in knee pants. Let a writer permit his imagination to soar beyond the ghostly patter of baby feet, dreams in which downcast slaveys envision themselves as Cinderellas wooed by handsome princes, or magic woods in which the characters learn what they might have been, and by and large he will be bound for disaster. For the fantasy which with very few exceptions flourishes on our stage is the rudimentary fantasy of gauze curtains, off-stage flutes, and penny valentines in four dollar boxes. That which goes even a little farther in its journey through the mists to the stars, that which combines fancy with wit and wit with poetic invention, most often is doomed.

From the now distant day of Eleanor Gates' experimental *The Poor Little Rich Girl* to the later day of Margaret Curtis' admirable *A Highland Fling,* the story has been the same. What the public cherishes is not any such freshness of inspiration, not any such amalgam of vivacious imagery and humor, but rather, at the highest, Maeterlinckian kindergarten charades about blue birds symbolic of happiness which are ever accommodatingly to be found close to one's own fireside; in the middle ground, adaptations of Continental plays in which impoverished artists fall asleep and dream horrible dreams about being married to rich women; and, at rock bottom, exhibits about sedate college professors who fall in love with circus equestriennes but conclude, after much wandering about in Expressionist settings, that they are safer off with students' ponies than with lady acrobats' horses. For one *Liliom* that exceptionally manages to win the public's favor, fantasies like *My Heart's In The Highlands,* delicately lovely and gently musical, hence must fail of popular approval. Even classics like *The Tempest,* indeed, must rest for their appeal chiefly on college boys and girls and others sedulously education bent, and must seek to coax a wider trade with artifices like trick revolving stages, name ballet dancers as Ariels, and wags of the Abbott and Costello school in the roles of Trinculo and Stephano, not to mention well-known ex-prize fighters as Calibans.

The hard row that fantasy has to hoe is indicated in the fact that of the recorded fifty-six plays which have accomplished runs of five hundred or more performances on the New York stage in the last fifty years but one, *The Green Pastures,* was to be described as a fantasy, and even there the description misses strict accuracy. *Harvey* and *Blithe Spirit,* which have figured in the list, are fantasies only in relatively small detail and are rather to be designated as

whimsical comedies. Fully nine-tenths of the real fantasies
produced in the period were failures. To be generally prosperous, fantasy is most safely to be made into musical comedy like, for example, *One Touch Of Venus* or *I Married
An Angel,* and its mild volitations made digestible through
interruptions of song and dance.

Genuine fantasy is, however, no facile accomplishment
and only too often the blame is shared with the audience
by the playwright. "One of the intellectual amusements of
my school-days," wrote William Archer in 1897, "was to
make a formless scrabble of ink on a piece of paper and,
while the ink was still wet, to fold the paper together.
When reopened, it exhibited a hideous blot, to which,
however, its sheer symmetry imparted a semblance of design, so that the eye of imagination could find in it a but-
terfly, or a dragon, or a spread-eagle, or some other bi-
pinnate and fantastic object." Any number of the fantasies
attempted by our ambitious but imperfectly equipped
playwrights resemble that folded paper and its design.
There is nothing of value and sense in them save what the
childishly eager eye fools itself into imagining it discerns.

Mr. Connelly's play is just another such smear. A mixture of fantasy, parable, and old Winchell Smith rustic hokum, it borrows the familiar talking horse idea and, with
an added and confusing mixture of dramatic styles, hopes
to indicate how the miracle of the equine conversational-
ist transforms the hypocrites and knaves of a small town
into creatures with hearts as golden and tender as Wiener
schnitz'ls. The proceedings open with the spectacle of the
moral transformation and then resort to flashbacks picturing the genesis of the wholesale conversion, each accompanied by a narrator in the person of one or another member of the cast standing in the dark whose only apparent
reason for being is to distract the audience's attention from
the noise made by the scene shifters. To make matters even
less sprightly, the author drags in a copious dose of mythol-
ogy about centaurs, etc., to pave the way for the sudden
linguistic gifts of the horse and, to make them considerably
less sprightly still, ends his garbled doings with a preach-

ment to the effect that animals are wiser than human beings and feel sorry for their stupidity, which is at least a
new view of the mental and philosophical powers of,
among others, the jackass. The play is mostly bleak exposition, is rooted to a single spot until a few minutes before
its conclusion, and gives the impression of a man starting
to tell a story, interrupting himself for the benefit of newly
arrived listeners, and constantly starting it all over again.

The author's stage direction causes the actors to read
their lines in a dead monotone and to stand around like
figures in an ecclesiastical minstrel show, generally facing
the audience with such grave intentness that one expects
them at any moment to break into "Rocked In The Cradle
Of The Deep." The directorial staples include the species
of hearty greeting wherein males lift ladies off their feet
and wherein the ladies clasped in embrace gleefully kick
their legs backwards, the abrupt activity of the electrical
switchboard and the amber radiance accompanying the
miracle, the town trollop made to speak with the regula-
tion Ann Thomas brassy-squeak, the Hi Holler coaching
of the chubby yokel dim-wit, the comedy of the man in the
barbershop with lather on his face, the Socony oiliness of
the villain and, not to mention other things, a folksy quality imparted by having the Michigan characters talk like
'way down Easters.

GRANDMA'S DIARY. September 22, 1948

A "satirical comedy" by Albert Wineman Barker. Produced by the American Theatre Group for 5 performances in the Henry Miller Theatre.

Program

HARRISON	*Augustus Smith*	CARY	*George Neise*
PETER	*Herbert Evers*	BORIS	*Leonard Elliott*
ALICE	*Eileen Prince*	GAINES	*Robert E. Griffin*
LINDA	*Gertrude Rozan*		

SYNOPSIS: *Seventeen hours of Spring in the penthouse of Linda Perdue in New York City. The time is now. Act I. Later afternoon. Act II. That night. Act III. The next morning.*
Director: *Albert Wineman Barker.*

FOR MANY YEARS now, my departure after the first act from a play that is obviously worthless has variously entertained and outraged some of my good friends on the newspapers. They can not, it seems, understand how anyone, even a critic of almost forty-five years' professional experience, can possibly tell the quality of a play after seeing only one-third or half of it. If you were to ask them if it is impossible for them to judge a baseball pitcher who has given nine successive bases on balls in a single inning, or a prize fighter who has been knocked down three times for counts of eight in the first round, or a newspaper whose salary checks have bounced for successive weeks, they would hardly pause for a reply. But they appear to regard the theatre as so excessively mysterious that, even if a play's first hour reveals it to be an unmistakable catastrophe, it may nevertheless suddenly thereafter bloom like a rose and turn out in the end to be something of a masterwork. It is a pretty idea, but my optimism is not of such bulk. I am willing to be convinced, but thus far in nigh half a century no proof, alas, has been forthcoming.

Abandon such low references to baseball players, fighters and honoraria and regard more relevantly the novel. You have dined satisfactorily, have installed yourself in a comfortable chair, have settled back in it, have casually picked up a book to pass what you hope will be a pleasant evening, and open the covers. The first thing that engages your eyes is the sentence, "One fine morning in May a fine carriage stopped before Madame Selini's door, and from it descended a handsome, aristocratic gentleman, evidently of the old school." You groan, but let things take their course and read on: "He was ushered into a handsomely furnished room where, in a few minutes, he was joined by Madame Selini herself. Sir Oswald bowed with stately courtesy and quaint, old-fashioned grace. 'Have you been so fortunate, madame, as to find that which I am in search of?' he inquired. 'I think you will be pleased, Sir Oswald; nay, I am sure you will,' answered the lady. 'I have a lady waiting to see you now who will prove, I should say, a treasure!' "

At this point, if your education in belles-lettres has progressed further than Upton Sinclair and kindergarten, you instruct your handsome and aristocratic manservant to seize the book gingerly with his thumb and forefinger, to bear it with courtly grace from the premises, and to deposit it in the most convenient jardiniere, while you yourself hop out of your chair, grab your hat and coat, and seek relief in the nearest tap-room. You know perfectly well that any such novel — you muse that the author was Bertha M. Clay — could not conceivably improve as it went on and that if you were charitable enough to continue in its presence you would duly encounter such added bilge as "Madame quitted the room with gliding, subtle grace and then Sir Oswald, in his courtly fashion, placed a chair for Miss Hastings . . . an elegant, well-dressed lady with a quiet grace and dignity that seemed natural to her; there was not the slightest trace of awkwardness or *mauvaise honte* in her manner . . . 'My dear madame,' said Sir Oswald, 'can you imagine what a wild vine is — a vine that has never been cultivated or pruned but allowed to grow wild in all

its natural beauty and strength, to cling where it would, to
trail on the ground and to twine 'round forest trees? Such
an vine is a fit type for my niece!' "

You know perfectly well, in brief, that, if anything in
this wide world begins and continues for a while in any
such vein and manner, there is not the remotest likelihood
that it will soon or late overwhelm you with an improvement so remarkable that it will knock you out of your seat.
And in exactly the same way you know that a play like this
Grandma's Diary, which begins with lines like "No woman
forgets a husband very easily — unless he's living with her
all the time," "I think you have a splendid brain — for a
woman," and "Every time I look at you I could hiccup,"
can not imaginably get to be any better even if it runs until three o'clock the next morning. Especially and particularly since the characters have no more life than the antique and moribund plot of the husband who tires of his
wife, takes up with another woman, becomes fed up with
her, and returns to his mate, whom he suddenly observes
to be not only a rare being but one much more beautiful
and desirable than he had thought. And, more especially
and particularly, since the acting, direction and everything
else are perceived after about fifteen minutes to be frightening.

Not so long ago my old and valued friend, the usually
levelheaded and soundly critical Walter Prichard Eaton,
published an appeal for the decentralization of our theatre,
now confined largely to Broadway, and for the institution
of independent municipal and state theatres in other parts
of the country. Only by such means, he argued, is the future of our drama, presently threatened, to be safeguarded.
In support of his contention, he specified the necessity for
wide opportunity of production if young playwrights are
to be encouraged, an opportunity which so often is closed
to them under the current restricted theatre dispensation.
And in support and proof of the opportunities which they
once enjoyed when the theatre was far-flung he offered several points. I record them, with comment.

1. "If Eugene O'Neill had not had the Provincetown

Players to put on his early dramas of the sea, he might have waited indefinitely for recognition."

The fact is that the very first play O'Neill ever submitted to a Broadway producer, *Beyond The Horizon,* was snapped up instantly and produced not long afterward. The producer in question, incidentally, had not seen any of the short sea plays done by the Provincetowners.

2. "Recognition of Shaw came in America because a young actor, Arnold Daly, could afford to experiment with *Candida* in a tiny theatre."

The fact is that recognition of Shaw came in America because an older, established Broadway actor, Richard Mansfield, sometime before had produced *The Devil's Disciple* in a large theatre.

3. "There must be an equivalent of the old-time road companies and the old-time stock companies . . . where playwrights can see their work produced."

The fact is that the old-time road companies and the old-time stock companies stuck for the most part to plays and playwrights already well-known, established, and popularly successful. Seldom did they afford an unknown playwright an opportunity and, on the rare occasions when they did, the plays were the kind that most of even the inferior producers on Broadway today would hesitate to sponsor. I lived through years of those early stock companies and if ever they put on a play by a new playwright that was worth looking at, I must have been in hospital when they did it. The plays I did see were mostly such tried and true old stuff as *All The Comforts Of Home, Jim The Penman, Richelieu, East Lynne, Sweet Lavender, Captain Swift,* and the like, with maybe an occasional production of *The Rivals,* or one of Pinero's so-called problem plays, or perhaps Robertson's *Caste.* The old-time road companies, when they did not confine themselves to popular Broadway plays, went in mainly for such standbys as *Uncle Tom's Cabin, Sis Hopkins,* and *Way Down East.* An O'Neill, Kelly, Hellman, Williams, Anderson, Miller, or any other new playwright like any one of them would not have stood a chance for a hearing in that period.

4. "When Baker (Prof. G. P.) began (his playwriting course at Harvard) in 1907, there were two hundred plays a year produced in New York."

The fact is that in 1907 the productions in the New York English-speaking theatre, aside from programs of Arnold Daly one-acters and Ben Greet classical repertory, numbered not two hundred but a meagre ninety-seven, all of thirty-seven of which were musical shows.

5. "There were (in the same year) hundreds of road companies."

The fact is that there were considerably less than hundreds, and that many of those there were duplicated the same Broadway play.

6. "A theatre which does not present a constant body of new plays, reflecting the age, is only half alive."

The fact is that in 1907, that golden year in Mr. Eaton's view, only twenty of the ninety-seven productions could by any stretch of the imagination have been said to fit into his stipulated catalogue, and most of the twenty were without any critical merit. Forty years later, in the allegedly sterile year 1947, twenty-nine plays out of a total production, dramatic and musical, of sixty-eight, exclusive, as in the first instance, of revivals of the classics, fitted into his catalogue, though, also as in the first instance, merit in the majority of them was lacking.

But what I am really getting at is this common belief that young playwrights have immense difficulty in obtaining a hearing in our contemporary theatre and sufficient opportunities for production. The trouble, I think, lies the other way 'round. All kinds of young playwrights with no talent, whether present or potential, get chances which they in no wise deserve, and so damage the theatre rather than help it. There may possibly be a few who merit opportunities and do not get them, though I do not know who they may be even after a wide reading of manuscripts; but there are innumerable others not worth a farthing who, like this Barker, year upon year get their day in court and duly and fitly fall flat. This is, in fact, the third hearing that Barker has been granted and in all three he has proved that the generosity of the Broadway theatre has been ill-advised. During the last recorded season and up to this point in the present one, that theatre and its direct local tributaries have afforded productions to all of forty-five of the newer and younger playwrights, both solo and in collaboration. Of the forty-five, a grand total of thirty-eight indicated no competence whatsoever and would better have been denied the opportunity to prove it. Of the remaining seven, just one demonstrated some skill and promise, while six were only middling. The small summer theatres in the adjacent terrain provided an additional hearing to at least a dozen young 'uns, but one of whom showed any talent more notable than that of a second-rate amateur.

TOWN HOUSE. September 23, 1948

A comedy by Gertrude Tonkonogy, based on the stories by John Cheever. Produced by Max Gordon for 12 performances in the National Theatre.

Program

Lucille Tremaine	*June Duprez*	Mrs. Osgood	*Margaret Dale*
Jack Tremaine	*James Monks*	Katherine Levy	
Pete Murray	*Hiram Sherman*		*Elizabeth Dewing*
Esther Murray	*Mary Wickes*	Vince Barber	*Henry Jones*
Ramona Murray	*Roberta Field*	Putnam Phelps	*Edwin Jerome*
Carol Hyler	*Peggy French*	A Man	*Klock Ryder*
Larry Hyler	*Reed Brown, Jr.*	A Woman	*Vera Fuller Mellish*

SYNOPSIS: Act I. *A Spring evening.* Act II. Scene 1. *A few weeks later.* Scene 2. *Several days later.* Act III. *Again a few days later.*
Director: *George S. Kaufman.*

T HERE HAS BEEN no slicker director of local commercial comedy than George S. Kaufman. In the matter of pace, lift, wisecrack and the other requisites of the humble species he usually has proved himself to be expert. But he has been operating in the field for so long and his technique so seldom changes that his handiwork suffers from his audiences' advance recognition of and familiarity with it. In this respect he is like the slit evening skirt duly anticipated in the case of radio, night club and vaudeville blues singers. It may have style but the style is well-known simonpure Broadway, and out of yesterday's shop window.

The technique in question has two particular idioms. The first is an alternation of leisurely with quick-step tempo, often in the same scene; and the second is the medication of dialogue, wherever possible, with gag flourishes. In illustration, were Mr. Kaufman one day waywardly to be entrusted with the direction of, say, *Romeo And Juliet,* his established method — to sample a single speech — would probably result in something like the following:

Romeo: He jests at scars that never felt a wound.

But soft! what light through yonder window breaks? (*Sees Juliet above at window.*) And watta break!

It is the east and Juliet is the sun, to say nothing of the *Times, Herald-Tribune* and *Staats Zeitung;*

Arise, fair sun, and kill the envious moon,

Who is already sick and pale with grief

That thou her maid art far more fair and warmer than she.

Be not her maid, since she is envious;

Her vestal livery is but sick and green

And none but fools do wear it; cast it off. (*Aside*) That's good casting, eh, Max?

(*He interrupts his apostrophe momentarily to hop-skip backwards, bend down, and pluck a rose. The thorn pricks his finger and draws blood, a drop of which falls on his arm.*)

Out, God damned spot! out, I say! (*Aside*) One more out to go.

Here's the smell of the blood still:

All the cleaning fluids of Arabia and Walgreen will not

Sweeten this little sleeve.

(*Returning to Juliet*)

See, how she leans her cheek upon her hand!

O, that I were a glove upon that hand,

That I might touch that cheek, not to mention certain others.

(*He crosses rapidly to left for no reason, re-crosses rapidly to right for the same reason, and resumes.*)

The master's hand is visible in every detail of the Tonkonogy script. Played on two levels picturing the lower and upper floors of a Donald Oenslager mansion which three markedly different couples have taken over on a co-operative basis, a comedy itself without the slightest life has been plied with the director's vitamins in such wholesale doses

that the corpse intermittently sits up again and issues a
squeak, though to no perceptible avail. For what it all
amounts to is nothing but a long, dry succession of episodes
in which the couples one after the other take stock of their
troubles, quarrel, decide to give up the co-operative plan,
and finally for some reason not at all clear discover that
they can not get along without one another (there is, I
take it, a parable on international relations intended here)
and settle down together in mutual peace and contentment.

Laying hold of the script, Kaufman has gone to work
like a circus roustabout. Doors are employed for such rapid
entrances and exits as have not been surpassed since the
Byrne brothers converted the stage of their *Eight Bells* into
something indistinguishable from Harrigan and Hart's
The Mulligan Guard's Ball, which in turn could not be
distinguished from the bar adjoining the Palais Royal on
an opening night. Stairways are made to present the effect
of the combined treadmills of *Ben Hur, The County Fair,
The Whip,* and *In Old Kentucky.* Gags follow one another
so quickly, and determinedly, that Milton Berle seems in
comparison to be a Dreiser. "If I'm to clean the sidewalk,
how should I dress?" asks Miss Tonkonogy's young snob.
"Black tie and overalls," cracks Mr. Kaufman. "You
shouldn't always be mixing drinks," protests one of Miss
Tonkonogy's wives to her husband as he prepares the bottles and shaker. "All right, I'll drink 'em straight," snaps
back Mr. Kaufman. "I'm going upstairs to take a bath,"
says one of Miss T.'s male characters. "On Mondays?" sur-
prisedly exclaims Mr. K. "How do I look standing in front
of this fireplace?" inquires a Tonkonogy husband. "You'd
look better lying down and skinned," retorts his wife with
Mr. K.'s help. One of Miss T.'s characters mentions a very
large package of goods. "They should have thrown in Chinatown," adds Mr. K. At regular intervals someone is instructed to mention Klein's dress shop, Bergdorf-Goodman,
Park Commissioner Moses, Guy Lombardo, or something
or somebody in order to lend the doings a topical sauce. In
the hope that the show might one day go on the road, there

is also included a reference to the Belvedere Hotel in Baltimore. Mr. Kaufman, in a word, does not miss a trick, except making a play appear out of the thin air, since, for all his dexterity with the pea, what persists in occupying the stage is the empty shell. He has in the end, it seems, simply swindled himself.

Most of the acting company holds up fairly well under the frantic circumstances, which involve so much clambering up and tumbling down one stage level to the other, so many blackouts and such labored parallel dramaturgy that the spectator himself is soon exhausted. Contributing to his exhaustion in other directions, and contributing generously, are the director's apparent belief that fashionable young society folk act as if they had been brought up by the late Lawrance D'Orsay, the author's apparent belief that a publisher would finance a two million dollar magazine just to rid his residential district of a couple of disagreeable neighbors, one of them the prospective editor, and the spectator's very definite realization that physical and vocal hullabaloo alone never yet has constituted entertainment, outside perhaps of a freshman cane rush or a political convention, and then only with the assistance of strong drink.

TIME FOR ELIZABETH. September 27, 1948

A comedy by Norman Krasna and Groucho Marx. Produced by Russell Lewis and Howard Young for 8 performances in the Fulton Theatre.

PROGRAM

MR. ROBINSON	Kenneth Patterson	MR. MCPHERSON	Leonard Mudie
WALTER P. SCHAEFFER		KAY DAVIS	Katherine Alexander
	Russell Hicks	ANNE DAVIS	Ottilie Kruger
MISS GREENE	Eleanor Lawson	RICHARD COBURN	Dick Hogan
ED DAVIS	Otto Kruger	MR. JASPER	Harlan Briggs
HARRISON OGLETHORPE		GEORGE ZWILLING	Edward Clark
	John Arthur	AMY ZWILLING	Theresa Lyon
LILY SCHAEFFER	Leila Bliss	VIVIAN MORGAN	Sheila Bromley

SYNOPSIS: Act I. *Office of Ed Davis, Vice-President and General Manager of the Snowdrift Washing Machine Company. Early December, 6 p.m.* Act II. Scene 1. *The living room of an apartment in the Oceanview Arms, Florida. Two weeks later.* Scene 2. *The same. Six weeks later.* Act III. Scene 1. *The same. Four days later.* Scene 2. *The same. Three months later.*

Director: *Norman Krasna.*

I VENERATE GROUCHO MARX as a comic second only to Bobby Clark, Ed Wynn and Kissin' Jim Folsom, since he is one of the few clowns who has been able to make me laugh with the look of his face alone and before uttering a sound. In my classical book, those ferocious black eyebrows, those panther-glaring eyeballs and that obscene black mustache, all screwed up into the semblance of a lascivious Tom cat on the capricious snoop for a canary, are the stuff on which dreams are made. But when the exemplary fellow tries his hand at playwriting, as he here has in collaboration with Norman Krasna, I pronounce the curse of Cain upon him, rip off his epaulets, and excommunicate him from my society. His and Krasna's little number is, forsooth, not just a turkey but the whole Ottoman Empire. Starting out with the possibly available, if not too vernal, idea that retirement from business and a life of quiet and ease are not what popular theory cracks them up to be, the partners have unwritten the kind of comedy that would not be too funny even if Groucho himself, assisted by such other geniuses as Smith and Dale, Professor Lamberti and Beatrice Lillie, were to take over the acting of it. To cast as the chief purveyor of its doubtful humors any such straight actor as Kruger, whatever his competences may conceivably be in another direction, is like casting Groucho as Siegfried.

I shall not bother you with details of the occasion beyond pointing out that, though the temperature of its Florida scene is announced to be eighty-five degrees Fahrenheit, the characters ravenously relish corned beef and cabbage and revel in hot baths; that the jokes follow such patterns as observing that cornstarch pudding was probably intended for hanging wall-paper; that stamping character consists in having a man pronounce "genuine" as "genuwine"; and that the hero seriously accepts as a revelation hitherto unheard of a moss-eared quotation from Omar Khayyám. After two acts I departed the premises, went home, and relieved myself by chuckling over the recollection of Groucho as a ship's officer presiding over an accident on deck and peremptorily commanding the group of young women gathered about to go to their staterooms at once, with the hoarse whisper that he'd be down in a minute.

Krasna's stage direction was the opposite of Kaufman's and seemed to be bent upon rendering the script even more lifeless than it was, with the result that the stage at times appeared to be a large couch with the actors trying to go to sleep on it. Among the latter, Russell Hicks, exercising his independence, played the business tycoon as if the role were a tin thunder-sheet, and Miss Alexander the retired hero's wife with such visible concern for the proper disposition of her limbs when in a sitting posture that she seemed haunted by the fear of an intruding tabloid camera man. Leonard Mudie, in the bit part of a philosophical employee, got a round of applause for being not altogether unlike a human being who had somehow sneaked into the proceedings; Leila Bliss acted the wife of the tycoon with such an excess of grandeur that one imagined she had mistaken the play for *L'Aiglon;* Ottilie Kruger, as the hero's daughter, at least looked pretty; Theresa Lyon was convincing as a fat, lazy housewife; Sheila Bromley played the siren with the staple dispensation of arch smiles and caudal vibrations; and Harlan Briggs a Florida old-timer much as if the state were governed by Lottie Blair Parker.

The play, I was told, was of course not without one of those fabricated happy endings of which, in general, C. E. Montague once wrote, "For this is the happy ending dearest to the lover of the 'wholesome' play: that known causes should not have their known effects; above all, that in last acts any leopards which gain the playgoer's regard should be left rigged out in snowy, curly lamb's wool, and nice Ethiopians go off at the end as blonds with straight, tow-colored hair."

EDWARD, MY SON. September 29, 1948

A play by Robert Morley and Noel Langley. Produced by Gilbert Miller and Henry Sherek for the rest of the season's performances in the Martin Beck Theatre.

Program

Arnold Holt	*Robert Morley*	Eileen Perry	*Leueen MacGrath*
Evelyn Holt	*Peggy Ashcroft*	Prothero	*Victor Beecroft*
Larry Parker	*Ian Hunter*	Burton	*Godfrey Kenton*
Harry Soames	*Torin Thatcher*	Summers	*Waldo Sturrey*
Dr. Waxman	*Dayton Lumis*	Phyllis Maxwell	
Cunningham	*Waldo Sturrey*		*Dorothy Beattie*
Ellerby	*Godfrey Kenton*	Betty Fowler	*Patricia Hicks*
Hanray	*D. A. Clarke-Smith*		

SYNOPSIS: Prologue: *In the Theatre.* Act I. Scene 1. *Arnold's flat in Brighton, 1919.* Scene 2. *The same. 1924.* Scene 3. *The same. A few weeks later.* Scene 4. *The Headmaster's study, Graingarry School. 1930.* Act II. Scene 1. *Offices of Arnold Holt & Co. 1934.* Scene 2. *Eileen Perry's flat. 1935.* Scene 3. *A hotel room in Alassio, next day.* Act III. Scene 1. *Lord Holt's house in Charles Street, London. 1938.* Scene 2. *The same. 1941.* Scene 3. *The same. 1948.*

Director: *Peter Ashmore.*

SINCE, like *The Winslow Boy,* this *Edward, My Son* deals with a father's persistent devotion and loyalty to his male offspring in the face of the latter's adversities, it would be a remarkably original critic who would refrain from alluding to it as *The Holt Boy* and, as I do not wish to show off and make it not unanimous, I shall string along with the rank and file. The resemblance of the one play to the other, however, ends there. *The Winslow Boy,* for all the glare of its machinery, was at least written with some slight respect for the adult ear; *Edward, My Son* on the other hand is written largely for an ear still in diapers. Regard, for example, such shopworn teething-rings as "It's just that he makes me rather uncomfortable. I don't know why. Perhaps it's just that I've an idea I've met him somewhere before or seen his picture or something but can't place it." Or "Only one day it would be nice to take a holiday again like other people." Or, "Now listen, Harry, you've got to get hold of yourself. Talking like that won't get you anywhere . . . besides, it's not true." Or "Larry's in love with you; I think you're in love with him; I think that's why you want a divorce.". . . "You must be *mad!*" Or "When Greek meets Greek they always open a restaurant." Or "You wore a blue dress with a flower at the waist." . . . "Fancy you remembering that!" Or "What is her objection to America?". . . "I think it's the Americans." Multiply these by a hundred and you have a fruity idea of the importation's flavor.

I have mentioned the visibility of *The Winslow Boy's* machinery. In this case it is not only visible but steps right up and hits you in the face. If I give only one example take my word that there are dozens, and all equally flagrant. Arnold Holt, the protagonist, comes before the curtain on one of several occasions and addresses the audience: "Well, ladies and gentlemen, that's how it started; not a very original beginning to a love story, and I'm afraid it doesn't have a very original end. But it was a love story, illicit, discreditable, often unsatisfactory. But there were moments when we two together managed to touch the stars. Absurd, ridiculous, middle-aged nonsense. . . . What I wanted to say to you at this stage was this. I'm not apologizing in advance for the next scene, it's there because I want you to see it as part of the whole picture, but do believe me that it's not there because I fancy myself as any sort of a middle-aged Don Juan." If that is not machinery and toy machinery at that, you can have my baby's walking bunny. Moreover, if audiences are willing to accept any such actor explanation and apology in lieu of a dramatist's achievement, the day will come when a play may be dispensed with altogether and its place taken merely by an actor's two hour descriptive speeches. Moreover still, if actors are going to come out and do the destructive criticism of such plays for the critics, we boys are going to be out of jobs, and I don't like the country for long.

That Robert Morley, assisted by his crony Noel Langley, concocted the exhibit as a star vehicle for himself may explain a lot of things, including such shameless box-office hokum as has not been seen hereabout since they fastened a plastic tail to an out-of-work burlesque chorus girl and sold her to the Atlantic City boardwalk yokels as a mermaid at a fifty cent admission charge. If Morley has overlooked anything to fatten his role, the late Creston Clarke, who so hammed up for himself simple plays like *The Last Of His Race* and *The Power That Governs* that they looked like *Quo Vadis* with Clarke playing even the lions, lived in vain.

Morley bequeaths himself a field day. He peddles touching father-love like campaign buttons. He bends men to his will by secretly buying up mortgages on their lives and, when they confess they are beaten, magnanimously reprieves them. He pleasures himself as a great captain of industry and as an irresistible sexual magnet. He is a fellow of such charm that he completely captivates and outwits a fair young creature intent upon snaring his son with imminent progeny. He goes in for the hokum of gradually ageing makeup (the play spans twenty-nine years) which always impresses audiences as being less greasepaint and false hair than extraordinary histrionic virtuosity. He preserves the stage and the audience's attention mainly for himself by keeping the son, whom the audience is aching to see, off stage and by dropping the scene curtains just as he is about to appear. He makes cute between-scenes speeches. He neglects nothing to rivet the attention to Morley short of coming down into the auditorium and selling Crackerjack. He has himself a grander time, in brief, than anyone has had since at the age of six I acted all eighteen roles in *The Desperado Of The Plains,* including that of Chawawatee, the Indian squaw beloved of Pecos Sam, for the edification of my younger brother and the milkman in the loft of the family stable.

What such commercial clamjamfry would be like without its present largely expert acting company is not, as critics are always fond of saying, hard to imagine. It would be like just what it is with such a company. Acting such as that of Morley and some of his associates, meritorious as it is, can not convert a sow's ear into a silk purse. The best it can do is to employ the ear as wallet and fill it with the money of those who can not distinguish between a talented performance and a talentless play. Since, fortunately for the management if not for the health of the drama, such theatregoers are numberless, it was to be expected that this British father-love counterpart of the old mother-love gumbo would richly impress audiences and pay good returns. Only one thing was missing from the general picture: the placard *Next Week: "East Lynne."*

I have mentioned the expertness of most of the acting. I should explain, perhaps, that the expertness is mainly technical and that, like so much technically devised acting, it sometimes misses the warmth and conviction of acting less calculated, precise, and exact. One admires its proficiency much as one does that of a fine trapeze performer, a painstaking essayist or a tirelessly trained dog, yet one's emotional reactions are the same. The tricks are too readily penetrated by the experienced critical eye. The effect, it may be said, is that of a perfected and smoothly working machine, commendable in every respect but not to be described as particularly stirring. Morley, for example, has so mastered the various facets of his craft that he is able to project every detail of the role of the scoundrelly father who would sacrifice anything or anybody for the sake of his worthless son, save only the rather important one of making one believe that he feels what he is doing and is not demanding that his audience feel it for him and in his stead. He acts his emotion from the outside in rather than from the inside out. He talks emotion without seemingly experiencing it; like a paid mourner, he indulges in all the appropriate postures and tears but it remains at best but a superficially plausible performance. And so with Miss Ashcroft as the mother.

Better are some of the subsidiary players who have not yet trained themselves out of all inner sensibility, in particular Torin Thatcher, as an early business partner whom

Holt selfishly discards, and Ian Hunter, as the stenciled Cayley Drummle nobly and silently in love with the heroine. Leueen MacGrath, who has an abundance of the looks which usually persuade the younger critics and more susceptible older ones that a great deal of histrionic ability must inevitably accompany them, is nevertheless impressive as Holt's mistress, which leaves me standing where you place me; D. A. Clarke-Smith, as the headmaster of the school that decides to expel young Holt and who is made to reconsider by the father, is convincing despite the conventional inclination to picture irresolution through blubbering speech; and Patricia Hicks welcomely acts the young woman with child by Holt's son without the usual director's insistence that, regardless of the lines, she comport herself in view of the imminent bastard as if she were playing Marguerite in Scene 1, Act IV of *Faust* to the Siebel of Westbrook Pegler.

PRIVATE LIVES. OCTOBER 4, 1948

A revival of the comedy by Noel Coward. Produced by John C. Wilson for the rest of the season's performances in the Plymouth Theatre.

PROGRAM

SIBYL CHASE *Barbara Baxley*	AMANDA PRYNNE	
ELYOT CHASE *Donald Cook*		*Tallulah Bankhead*
VICTOR PRYNNE *William Langford*	LOUISE	*Therese Quadri*

SYNOPSIS: Act I. *The Terrace of a hotel in France. A summer evening.* Act II. *Amanda's flat in Paris. A few days later. Evening.* Act III. *The same. The next morning.*

Director: *Martin Manulis*

TALLULAH BANKHEAD, who forty years ago would have been billed in vaudeville, like Bonita, Elsie Janis and the Hupfschlägel Brothers' trained pup Frieda, as "That Personality Kid," here displays herself in full eruption. Obviously directed by Olsen and Johnson, who somehow do not receive the due program credit, she does almost everything to the Coward play but swing out over the house on a trapeze and toss her garters to the audience, which would not have been too bad another idea. For the truth is that her capers help to seltzerize a comedy which otherwise would be bubbleless and dated. While a better job than its author has generally contrived, it nevertheless needs all her horsing to screen what once was peculiarly revered as a wit worthy of Congreve and Wilde and is now less peculiarly recognized as a cross between that of Mrs. Pat Campbell and a borrowed dress suit.

A second view of the seventeen year old play throws into bold relief both Coward's characteristic faults and occasional merits. To his minor credit are the trick of successfully passing off the foam for the champagne, now and then a sense of the comic value of a smartly chosen word, and an ability in ellipsis, with its mild surprise, where he appreciates his inability amusingly to support and sustain more extended treatment of a scene. His chief delinquency is his unintentional artificiality. He usually impresses one as believing that his people are drawn pretty closely from life, yet they stubbornly turn out in his hands and through his idiosyncrasies of thought to be either caricatures of caricatures or phonograph-wired manikins, all bearing an approximate resemblance to Coward himself. He thus much less traces the society of his period, as his admirers maintain, than a segment of it as he imagines it would be if it were constituted of various manifestations of himself. His comedies are accordingly not reflections of an era but reflections of and on Coward, in an automatically distorted mirror, and their final effect is of a topical song scored for a bass and rendered in tenor.

The late James Agate defined the Coward technique from the particular to the general as beginning with some perfectly serious theme, stripping it of its seriousness, and finally making a long nose at it. "They were nothing, sir, be they addressed to what they may!" he quoted Dr. Johnson as replying to a clergyman who had asked whether it was not a fact that Dodd's sermons were addressed to the passions. And then, referring to one of Coward's plays, noted that it is nothing whether it be addressed to our sense of the past, our feeling that *Bitter Sweet* should have a coda, or the author's hankering after a new genre. Though only one example of Coward's work was in immediate mind, the criticism seems in many respects to be apt in a somewhat more inclusive view. In most of the plays a sense of the past is contrarily evoked in one by the all too obvious and rupturous strain on the part of Coward to be excessively modern, which gives his work the color of a forced and painstaking withdrawal from yesterday, like a ready-made short skirt that has been let out to satisfy the "new look." In most of the plays, too, there is the transparent pathological fear of normality and honest sentiment and the furious gesture at airy scorn, like a small boy's protective swipe at another small boy when the latter catches him in the act of talking to a pretty little girl. And in most of them, as well, there is patently the intransigent determination to achieve something startlingly new, even at the expense of considered sense, like a woman who adds a stuffed parrot to an otherwise old but attractive and perfectly serviceable hat in the hope of making it seem of the ultra-mode.

All this is not to say that Coward has not a skill of sorts. He has. It is the skill, however, not of a dramatic artist but of a clever vaudevillian. It knows its audience; it wears the right spangles; its animal act in which lap dogs, cats and donkeys go through the motions of human beings is nimble hanky-panky; and it makes money. It also enjoys the surface glitter of a mica trove, and is as valuable. It is often, in a word, what is called "good theatre" by such people as believe good drama is a violation of the phrase.

To the immediate sample of the Coward art, which deals after the old German two-couples-in, two-couples-out dramaturgical comedy formula with a divorced pair who on the eve of their honeymoons with others rediscover each other to the old French comedy reunion result, and which is related in the usual Coward cattish dialogue consisting in an adolescently impish mockery of decency, respectability, masculinity and the feminine virtues, Miss Bankhead brings, as noted, the shrewdest sort of acting criticism. Which is to say, the application of a farcical treatment bordering on burlesque to the comedy's insecurity in the hope of making it pass for something approximating lively theatrical pastime. Her technique in the joust is a relevant mixture of that of Mae West, George Robey, Eva Tanguay, and General George Patton. If a line is flat, she distracts attention from it by throwing herself onto a couch and lifting her legs into the air in such wise that the audience may catch a glimpse of her bottom. If another strikes her as being badly in need of some missing intelligence, she struts across the stage like a rooster, wheels sharply, and fixes the audience with an eye that seems to say, "My God, all *you* have to do is listen to it; I have to *speak* it!" When she rightly feels that a little pace will help matters, she makes a headlong tackle of her leading man's neck and winds herself about him like a clerk wrapping up a bundle in the Christmas rush. There is not a moment when she isn't hurrying first-aid to the script and giving it copious injections of strychnine, cod liver oil, monkey gland extract and Crosse and Blackwell's chow-chow. It seems, true, an awful lot of trouble to go to in order to give some life to a play that might better be left dead, but, after all, a girl must eat.

Cook does ably by the part of the husband originally played by Coward, but casting any such masculine actor in a role essentially effeminate in speech, thought and act makes what otherwise might be aberrantly amusing sound rather dirty and unpleasant. Barbara Baxley manages the young woman deserted on her honeymoon very well indeed for a novice, though as the young man deserted by Miss Bankhead on his, William Langford, whose body and voice seem to be encased in a strait-jacket, performs in the more usual novice manner.

SUMMER AND SMOKE. OCTOBER 6, 1948

A play by Tennessee Williams, with incidental music by Paul Bowles. Produced by Margo Jones for 100 performances in the Music Box.

PROGRAM

ALMA AS A CHILD *Arlene McQuade*	ALMA WINEMILLER
JOHN AS A CHILD *Donald Hastings*	*Margaret Phillips*
REV. WINEMILLER	ROSA GONZALES *Monica Boyar*
Raymond Van Sickle	NELLIE EWELL *Anne Jackson*
MRS. WINEMILLER	ROGER DOREMUS *Earl Montgomery*
Marga Ann Deighton	MRS. BASSETT *Betty Greene Little*
JOHN BUCHANAN, JR. *Tod Andrews*	VERNON *Spencer James*
A GIRL *Hildy Parks*	ROSEMARY *Ellen James*
DUSTY *William Layton*	PAPA GONZALES *Sid Cassel*
DR. BUCHANAN *Ralph Theadore*	MR. KRAMER *Ray Walston*

SYNOPSIS: Prologue: *"Early Sorrows."* Part One: *a Summer.* Part Two: *a Winter.*

The entire action of the play takes place in Glorious Hill, Mississippi.

Time: *Turn of the century through 1916.*

Director: *Margo Jones.*

W E ARE NOW being entertained by the criticism that since Williams' play is essentially much the same play as his *The Glass Menagerie* and *A Streetcar Named Desire,* which were pronounced pearls of uncommon price, it is not much good. There are some things I experience little headache in figuring out but this is not one of them, and I am puzzled. If something is like something else which has been regarded as tiptop, I can not see why it becomes no good just because it resembles that virtuous other something. Perhaps I am stupid.

It is perfectly true that this latest offering has features in common with Williams' other plays, *Streetcar* in particular. As in them, and to some extent as in his *Battle of Angels* which expired in Boston before reaching New York, we again have the neurotic young Southern female, the conflict with members of a family, the rebellion against fateful circumstance, and the eventual despair and defeat. The preoccupation with sex which so infects his exhibits, along with his juvenile belief in the profound drama invariably associated with fallen women, is also present. He seems to be unable to free himself from such bewitchments. The deranged Dixie damsel or a slight variant of her shows up regularly not only in his work for the stage but even when he offers things like *Portrait Of A Madonna* over the radio. And sex obsesses him in a more wholesale and agonized manner than ever it has occupied humorously the French farce writers. He suggests a very moral youngster who has sneaked a look at Defoe's *Moll Flanders*, has been inordinately wobbled by what little he has understood of it, and has used his piece of chalk not to scribble vulgarly on any back fence but on his nice, clean, black Sunday school suit. He additionally in this newest item again runs to fragmentary treatment with its Mielziner tricks of scenery and lighting, and with the previous filagree of ghostly off-stage music. The dramatic effect, because of the frequent gradual dimouts or quicker blackouts, is once more of a story read by an oil lamp which has not been sufficiently refilled, which flickers fitfully, and which from time to time goes out. And the metaphor likewise describes the playwriting.

There is still further even repetition of theme. Now again it is the frustrated young woman who loses her dream at the fists of reality and has her end in despondency or worse, just as it was with the daughter in *The Glass Menagerie* and the sister in *Streetcar* and the girl in *Battle Of Angels* and the woman in the radio show. And there are, as well, the fancy figures of speech to hide a mistiness of ideology, the canapés of questionable symbolism, and the general air of a half-written play expanded, for good or ill, by a stage director. So much allowed. But, though the final result of this *Summer And Smoke* is quite as unsatisfactory as that of his previous plays, the fact that it in some ways resembles them is no more soundly to be held against it than the equally undeniable fact that a number of

Strindberg's plays closely resemble one another is to be
held against them. Any such attitude is unfair and foolish. It is box-office criticism, and that is the business not of
critics but of ticket buyers, if they happen to feel that way
about things.

Since I get in free of charge, it is properly expected of
me by the management that I abstain from such a leaning
and employ myself in a somewhat stricter and more elevated direction. Thus serving the producer, I will confide
to Margo Jones that the play's principal weaknesses are
mainly the same weaknesses which have afflicted most of its
author's plays. The first is his debatable character drawing;
the second is his adolescent point of view; and the third is
the ultimate impression that, though he obviously starts
off with complete honesty, his still limited resources impel
him in the end to purely theatrical fabrication. Though in
this play, for one example, his portrait of the frigid min-
ister's daughter come to a pass with a fleshly lover (change
the sexes, add a bigger dose of religion, and you have the
same old Hall Caine-Henry Arthur Jones-Robert Hichens
stuff) is convincing for some of the distance, it then plainly
begins to take worried stock of its icy monotony, throws
honesty overboard, and tries desperately to jounce the audience with the venerable hokum of the heroine's cynical
finish in prostitution. It is, of course, not entirely impossible that a puritanical woman might suddenly turn trollop, but surely not such a one as Williams depicts. Or, for
another example, take the aforesaid earthy lover. Though
the spiritual is supposed eventually to triumph over the
physical in him, the author pictures him nevertheless in
the end as succumbing eagerly to matrimony with the
young daughter of a harlot who apparently has inherited
some of her mother's anatomical fervor. Add to all this
some dilettante symbolism in the shape of a fountain called
Eternity and something about drinking its waters and you
have the feeling that Williams in turn had the feeling that
his script lacked "depth" and industriously squirted the al-
legorical ketchup into it.

In the window of even the smallest, humblest grocery

store there is some article or other that catches the eye and fetches one, and so with this dusty, minor play. It has its few moments of canned dramatic interest and now and then a fleeting glint of writing, though scarcely in such school-girl indulgences as "I feel like a water-lily on a Chinese lagoon." But over-all, unless I am blind to its author's argued genius, it amounts only, I think, to a victory of theatrical sateen over dramatic satin.

Mielziner's setting and lighting are again so expert, contributive and effective that it has struck some it might be more auspicious if he wrote Williams' plays for him and let Williams take a chance with the lights and scenery. The acting company, with Margaret Phillips and Tod Andrews independently excellent in the principal roles, is a good one. Miss Jones' direction, however, challenges the script sorely by, among other things, often seating the leading characters, the heroine in particular, downstage and having them fixedly address the audience, which gives the play the static flavor of a series of lectures.

It is more or less known that in the preparation of a novel Sinclair Lewis not only works out extended genealogical charts of his characters but further supplies himself with copious notes on their possibly inherited or acquired processes of thought and tastes in food, drink, ointments, underwear, if any, women, and what not else. The consequence is that, whatever opinion otherwise one may or may not have of the novels in their entirety, the characters in them with small exception stand as authentically revealed as if they had just stepped out of the bath. It is only on the occasions when he has chosen to neglect or forget his ample notes and records that, as in the case of a *Kingsblood Royal,* they have failed in complete conviction. It is also more or less known that Eugene O'Neill goes even farther than Lewis and in the preparation of a play does not content himself merely with such genealogical charts, etc., but writes what amount to complete life histories of his characters, including their diseases since adolescent mumps and measles, their old girls, and the prison terms served by their great-great-grandfathers.

It is on the other hand the mark of many of our playwrights, and especially of some of the newer and younger ones who have been selected for the critics' particular enthusiasm, that they seem to know so little of their characters beyond the purely superficial that the latter expose themselves as no more than paper figures cut out with dull, if occasionally polished, scissors. The result is a parade of characters often scarcely more material than those of musical comedy and operetta. As in those forms of entertainment, they appear to have been born coincidentally with their first entrances; there is nothing behind them; we are simply told who and what they are and are asked to accept total strangers as intimate acquaintances. They are, in brief, so many antecedentless Topsys maneuvered by plainly visible strings.

One of the most palpable of these strings is so-called type casting, the resort of playwrights who, unable to achieve character internally, seek to mask their inability with ready-made externals. First impressions are handily substituted for final impressions. Hazlitt's philosophy of human beings is conveniently juggled out of sense in terms of actors. "First impressions," said he, "are often the truest . . . A man's look is the work of years; it is stamped on his countenance by the events of his whole life . . . There is . . . something in a person's appearance at first sight which we do not like and that gives us an odd twinge, but which is overlooked in a multiplicity of other circumstances, till the mask is taken off and we see this lurking character verified in the plainest manner in the sequel." An actor's face, good or evil, which is deemed pictorially appropriate to a role is thus made to take the place of inner character, and the lines in that face are made to pass muster for more searching and revelatory lines of dialogue. Instead of a living creature what we get is an articulate mummy, presently crumbling to dust.

Other illusory artifices are equally recognizable. A familiar one is the stratagem of establishing character not in and of itself but through the observations of others, that is, the interpretation of character by proxies. Another is recourse to the easy melodramatic formula of evolving character, or what is made to seem it, through action, which is to say, character in terms of extrinsic motivation. A third is a figure's description of and comment on himself, which may be defined as personal topography in terms of a travel folder. And still a fourth is the employment of a makeup box in lieu of an inkwell.

Two of the new, younger playwrights who have been especially favored by the critics are this Tennessee Williams and Richard Harrity. That each has virtues is to be allowed, but sound character drawing, at least thus far, is scarcely one of them. Of the two, Williams is the more adept in the legerdemain of concealing his weakness and fooling the less perceptive into seeing things that are not there. His bag of tricks includes what may be described as a scrim treatment of character, that is, the hiding of any real delineation behind pseudo-poetical gauze which blurs his audience's vision. This, augmented with soft, off-stage music, cajoles an audience into imagining that it actually sees a character that is only vaguely suggested to it. What one is reminded of is the icing on the cardboard cakes which sidestreet merchants display in their shop windows: dummy pastries with plausible surfaces. The moment Williams leaves off such duplicity and tries his hand at more realistic portraiture his shortcomings become apparent. What we then see is character in mere melodramatic outline, and painted in the harsh crimson hues of drunkenness, lust, vindictiveness, acrimony, etc., or in the harshly contrasting lavender of hearts and flowers. When his aim is tragedy, what results is a threnody on a zither; when his aim is fanciful serio-comedy, what results largely suggests Saroyan in a second-hand Prince Albert.

There is, moreover, occasionally such confusion in Williams' character drawing that his characters seem individually from time to time to be different people at severe odds with themselves. An illustration in addition to those already offered is to be had in the instance of his heroine in *A Streetcar Named Desire*. Motivated mainly from without rather than within, the figure is pulled this way and

that according to the demands of the plot and becomes so
psychologically, pathologically and logically muddled that
she gives the effect of three totally different women housed
in the same body. The author's possible apology that the
character is a case history derived from research is not dramatically extenuating. A case history has to be deftly fitted
in with the characters who are not case histories. In this instance, it is merely paraded among them, with the parading
now and then interrupted by some distracting flights of
poesy and bits of melodrama. Even as an alleged case history, the character is wide open to psychiatric doubt. It is,
for example, debatable that a woman revolted by the spectacle of homosexuality would find moral sanctuary in promiscuous prostitution with its possible occasional depar-
tures from sexual normality, or that one of even her degree
of mentality would seek real love through a purge of mud,
or that her avid quest of illusion would impel her search
into so absurdly antagonistic a channel. Her final insanity
is surely a poor blanket to cover up any such patchwork,
and her ultimate tragedy an anti-climax.

Richard Harrity, endorsed chiefly on the score of his
short play, *Hope Is The Thing With Feathers,* indicates
something of an aptitude for types, but the types incline
much more toward vaudeville than toward authentic character. They are, in the play named, personified gags. They
give the impression of a group of minstrels with Harrity as
their interlocutor: vagabonds on park benches lacking only
tambourines and bones. That they are amusing is to be
granted, but they are amusing not as characters so much
as well-handled performers. In neither of his two other
short plays, the sum of his produced work thus far, is there
any increased evidence of ability. The one called *Gone Tomorrow* offers only blurry photostats of the stereotyped
characters in the lesser Irish comedy-drama; and the second, *Home Life Of A Buffalo,* only copies of long stage-
familiar vaudevillians.

That character, despite Aristotle's perplexities, is the
most difficult achievement in dramatic composition need
hardly be restated. Few of our contemporary native play-

wrights have proved themselves able to master it. Count off O'Neill, Kelly, Hellman, van Druten and one or two others and you have called the roll. Some of the rest have succeeded in dissembling the task and in beguiling audiences and even many of the critics into accepting the counterfeits as the real thing, but that they are merely haberdashers of dickeys who sell unsubstantial false-fronts for the complete shirt is plain to anyone who submits them to the test of a triplicate critical mirror. Their feints then quickly betray themselves. Among these is, first, the sham of giving a hollow character some bulk by making him the repository of the playwright's independent sociological, political, theological or merely amatory doctrines, which are frequently not only equally hollow but which are arbitrarily stuffed into him with a pile-driver, the sheer noise of which, like a riveting machine operating on a vacuum, rattles the auditor's head out of any sharp, analytical attention. Secondly, there is the fobbing off of manikins as characters of some depth by overloading them with rapid mechanical plot complications, often melodramatic, which hoodwink a dizzied audience into believing that the action proceeds from the character instead of from the tricky playwright.

Thirdly, there is the device of attrition whereby a character nonentity is made to seem of some eventual size and importance by bringing him into conflict with other character nonentities who slowly grind themselves into a superlative nothingness, leaving him lord of the empty scene. Fourthly, there is what may be called the rebel ruse. This consists in lending a character of obvious inconsequence an air of consequence by causing him to oppose the accepted comfortable thought of the moment, represented by the other characters, and carefully casting the role with an actor admired personally by the rank and file of theatregoers. And, fifthly, there is the snare of comedy interruption, which glosses over deficiencies in character plumbing and character appraisal with an intermittently laid on humor calculated to jostle criticism off the scent.

LOVE LIFE. October 7, 1948

A "vaudeville" with book and lyrics by Alan Jay Lerner, music by Kurt Weill. Produced by Cheryl Crawford for the rest of the season's performances in the Forty-sixth Street Theatre.

P R I N C I P A L S

Nanette Fabray, Ray Middleton, David Thomas, Gene Tobin, Cheryl Archer, Johnny Stewart, Elly Ardelty, Jay Marshall, Johnny Thompson, Lyle Bettger, Victor Clarke, Larry Robbins, David Collyer, Arthur Partington, Barbara McCutcheon, Holly Harris, Carolyn Maye, Sylvia Stahlman.

Director: *Eliza Kazan.*

THE ATTEMPT at something novel in the way of a musical show takes the shape of a liberal paraphrase of Thornton Wilder's *The Skin Of Our Teeth* which presents in the persons of a timeless and ageless couple a picture of married and family life against the changing American background from the year 1791 to the present. It combines in the telling such diverse media as vaudeville, circus, straight drama, satirical revue and allegory, embroiders the design with dance, ballet, pantomime, choral singing, etc., and resorts to nigh everything else except the motion pictures, foghorns and whirling platforms used by Piscator in *Hoppla, Wir Leben!* in the days when he was running wild in Berlin. Though, as in various other such strivings for a new form, originality again fails to include a first act finale without the routine quarrel of the lovers and their temporary parting, what threatens to be chaos resolves itself into a fairly distinguishable pattern, and the sum is a fresh and often pleasantly diverting show.

As Lerner first conceived the book, my guess is that he saw it as a much more direct and orderly affair. Doubtless a little fearful lest the story be too serious for the musical stage, he evidently seized upon the notion of annexing the vaudeville tail to it. While the scheme is both imaginative and, despite its seeming eccentricity, valid enough and while for the greater part it serves well his purpose, there are several periods in the evening when it seems to be out of joint and a little uncomfortable. The introduction of a trapeze performer, for one example, in a scene that has no more connection with a trapeze performer than it has with *Timon of Athens* has a tendency to make one slightly suspicious of the entire enterprise, as does, for another, the opening scene in which, for no faintest reason that anyone can figure out, a magician, after introducing the two principal characters, proceeds to perform the levitation trick with the man and the sawing-a-woman-in-half act with his future wife. The show as a whole, however, nevertheless somehow manages peculiarly to hang together, like the apparently solid, separate steel rings which, when tossed at one another by a prestidigitator, puzzlingly join themselves into a chain.

Weill's score — some of his arrangements and orchestrations are nicely contrived — offers several fetching songs, among them, "Here I'll Stay," "Green-Up Time," "I Remember It Well," "This Is The Life," and a ballad, "Love Song," though once again, in view of their derivative nature, one can hum them, after hearing the first few measures, without many slips. But, even so, it is pleasant to be among old acquaintances, just as it was in the case of his *Knickerbocker Holiday's* "September Song," a close relative of Drdla's "Souvenir," several of his numbers in *Street Scene,* which were descendants of Puccini, his *Johnny Johnson's* "To Love You And To Lose You," which was in part a sister to Dresser's "Come Tell Me," and so on.

Materially assisting the evening are Michael Kidd's choreography, which in the "Green-Up Time" number comes close to being as exciting a dance spectacle as the local stage has seen recently; the performances of Nanette Fabray and Ray Middleton as the couple whose contentment over the ages is invaded by the forces of industrialism, women's rights and such other hypothetical symptoms of progress; and the direction of Elia Kazan, which succeeds in infusing

the show with pace and vitality without resort to the
George Abbott four-alarm technique. Of considerably less
assistance is a stage inhabited largely by ladies so deficient
in physical charm that to all intents and purposes it suggests less one housing a musical show, or what such a show
should fully be, than a stock company playing *Tortilla
Flat*. That the ladies are talented is not to be gainsaid, but
one has a right to wish that when one buys an expensive
box of candy it not be formidably wrapped in burlap and
have at least a few pretty ribbons on it. Nor is the romantic
mood which the show ultimately hopes for much helped by
such a number as that in which the women appear in old-
fashioned long underwear, which makes even the less un-
lovely of them look like gnarled sacks of corn husks, and
by lyrics which have to do with women's depilatory exerci-
tations.

WHERE'S CHARLEY? October 11, 1948

A musical comedy, based on Brandon Thomas' Charley's Aunt, *with adaptation by George Abbott, music and lyrics by Frank Loesser. Produced by Cy Feuer and Ernest H. Martin in association with Gwen Rickard for the rest of the season's performances in the St. James Theatre.*

Program

Brassett	John Lynds	Mr. Spettigue	Horace Cooper
Jack Chesney	Byron Palmer	A Professor	Jack Friend
Charley Wykeham	Ray Bolger	Donna Lucia D'Alvadorez	
Kitty Verdun	Doretta Morrow		Jane Lawrence
Amy Spettigue		Photographer	James Lane
	Allyn Ann McLerie	Patricia	Marie Foster
Wilkinson	Edgar Kent	Reggie	Douglas Deane
Sir Francis Chesney			
	Paul England		

SYNOPSIS: Act I. Scene 1. *A room at Oxford University.* Scene 2. *A street.* Scene 3. *The garden.* Scene 4. *Where the nuts come from.* Act II. Scene 1. *The garden.* Scene 2. *A street.* Scene 3. *Where the ladies go.* Scene 4. *A garden path.* Scene 5. *The ballroom.*

Director: *George Abbott.*

THE MUSICAL VERSION of Brandon Thomas' inexhaustible old heifer takes us back to the period when the spectacle of a man in a woman's dress was a guaranteed laugh producer second only to the jokes about Hetty Green, the Mona Lisa, and the Smith Brothers' whiskers. Times have changed and it may no longer be as acceptable as it once was, but, shameful as the confession is, it did seem awfully funny then. I recall, indeed, that when as a youngster I first saw Etienne Girardot in those scandalous white ladies' pantaloons — it was sometime back in the happy dark ages — I made such a scene that my duenna, a proper woman, blushed so furiously at my conduct that I thought for the moment she had come down with the scarlatina. What is more, a little later when I had arrived at the mature age of

ten and had become worldly and sophisticated, I nevertheless and in spite of myself found the spectacle still comical
and no end embarrassed the male retainer employed to accompany me when on pleasure bent — also a lofty and very
circumspect creature — by howling with mirth at similarly
clad comedians like Neil Burgess in *The County Fair* and
H. A. Du Souchet in *My Friend From India.* It is occasionally argued that the most sophisticated men are, after all,
the readiest gulls and in my case it must have been true,
since even at the age of eleven, when the world had become an open book to me, I continued to be immensely
entertained by those two biddies, the Russell Brothers, and,
a bit later, no less by George Monroe. But, now that the
years have descended upon me and I have lost much of my
youthful culture and wisdom, I seem no longer to respond
to the business as I once did. At my present advanced age
I have actually got to the point, I freely admit, where I like
women's clothes to be occupied by women, good-looking
preferred. Maybe I have become blasé. Maybe that early
succession of comics in skirts followed by four years of college shows with the football team in chorus girl costumes,
followed in turn by the endless sight of female impersonators like Julian Eltinge, Karyl Norman, *et al.,* and again
followed by epicene exhibits like *Pleasure Man* — all interlarded with intermittent revivals of *Charley's Aunt* —
maybe it has all taken its toll of me.

I don't know, but whatever the reason I can not any
more work up much of the old fervor for the humor of a
male disguised as a female and having a time of it trying to
accommodate himself to a skirt that flies up and hits him in
the nose whenever he sits down. Nor is the ceiling longer
in danger of cracking with my guffaws when the skirt thus
elevated reveals him to be clad in lace-edged white petti-
coat and bloomers. Though all around me I may hear people laughing fit to kill, these erstwhile hospitable features
do not move a muscle. In some ways they haven't changed.
They still beam and crackle, if you must know the worst,
when a clown delicately with thumb and forefinger pulls
out the seat of his breeches and then suddenly lets go of it

and causes a torpedo in his belly-pad to explode. And they still react handsomely in the presence of some other such gross souvenir of the 1890's as a comedian's shrill whistle of admiration upon beholding a statuesque blonde and the entrance on the gallop of a cop who, quickly surveying the situation, seizes him and kisses him on both cheeks. I am, in other words, in some respects evidently a fellow of impeachable taste. But I have at least progressed sufficiently in the higher æsthetic not to make a holy show of myself when a wag in furbelows, as in this *Where's Charley?*, happens into a ladies' retiring room and is innocently accepted, to his doubtful dismay, at his masquerade value. That day in my life is past.

It is for such reasons that the present exhibit fails to find me a receptive customer. Ray Bolger, the star, is diverting when he goes into his old dance routine; Allyn McLerie and the lovely Doretta Morrow are agreeable girls to have around; the ensemble is slightly more attractive than some others which have lately acted like cinders on the eye; and one or two of Balanchine's choreographic numbers are fair enough. But, low as my tastes may be, I am no longer amused by, among other things, a comedian who backs out of a room, bumps into a statue or picture and bows an apology, or who pours tea into a top hat which a guest has left on a chair and then adds cream and sugar. The butler who drops whatever he may be carrying when startled and the song number in which the cast stands at the footlights and describes a parade or horse race presumably going on in the audience also neglect to stimulate me. And so it is that with any such show whose humors center mainly on a man garbed in women's apparel I would rather take one like *Love Life* or *Magdalena* which keeps it pants on.

THE LEADING LADY. OCTOBER 18, 1948

A play by Ruth Gordon. Produced by Victor Samrock and William Fields for 8 performances in the National Theatre.

PROGRAM

MAUDIE	*Margot Stevenson*	STOATSIE	*Guy Spaull*
CLYDE	*James MacColl*	GERALD	*Ian Keith*
CLARA	*Elizabeth Dewing*	GAY	*Ruth Gordon*
ANNIE	*Margaret Barker*	HARRY	*Wesley Addy*
LESTER	*Harry Worth*	BENJY	*John Carradine*
IDA	*Sonia Sorel*	MRS.	*Laura Pierpont*
WILLIAMS	*Mildred Dunnock*	OLD CARTER	*William J. Kelly*
CLARISSA	*Brooke Byron*	MRS. GILSON	*Ethel Griffies*
TREM	*Ossie Davis*	EUGENE	*Douglas Watson*
EVERETT	*Emory Richardson*	MR. BECKWITH	*Harry Sheppard*

SYNOPSIS: Act I. *The 30th of December, 1899. Midnight.* Act II. *October, 1901. Late afternoon.* Act III. *January, 1902. Early afternoon.*
    The play takes place in the home of Gerald and Gay Marriott, 60 West 27th Street, New York City.
    Director: *Garson Kanin.*

PLAYS ABOUT THE THEATRE and its people, of which this is another, seem to have averaged but a single creditable one out of every dozen, though now and then one among the other eleven may have made money at the undiscriminating box-office. For each commendable *The Royal Family* there has been a long parade of inferior merchandise like *The French Touch, Return Engagement, Heart Of A City, The Walking Gentleman, Stage Door,* and *Curtain Call.* And for every amusing *The Play's The Thing* we have been delivered a lot of herrings like *The Fabulous Invalid, My Dear Children, On Stage, Wonder Boy, Censored,* and *Straw Hat.* For each only fair *Theatre, No Time For Comedy* or *The Butter And Egg Man,* indeed, we have been fed enough rubbish like *Tell Me Pretty Maiden, The Little Spitfire, I Must Love Someone, Sure Fire,* and *The Comic* to choke us.

Since the days of *Trelawney Of The Wells* there has existed a legend that plays dealing with the theatre are not interesting to audiences and are headed for failure. Like most theatre legends, it has been and is generally true only when the plays are bad plays which would fail if they treated of any other subject under the sun. The really good plays have most often succeeded, though there have been, as noted, very few of them. The great majority have been as marked at birth as equally poor plays about dowdy little Cinderellas who have turned up in last acts dressed like Mrs. Stuyvesant Fish, prostitutes who have been redeemed and exalted by pure love, prosecuting attorneys who have suddenly been overcome by the recognition of the accused as their own mothers, and other such flapdoodle.

The fault of most of the theatre plays which have failed has been their adherence to and constant reduplication of the types they have dealt with. The actress heroines, for example, have usually been shown either as creatures of so temperamental a constitution that they have apparently employed their maids solely as targets for thrown footwear or as airy beings whose amorous activities would seem to have left not more than a few nights a year for their professional. Their husbands, in such cases as they have entertained matrimony, have similarly followed a standardized pattern. Either they have been actors whose equal temperament has made wedlock indistinguishable from the battle of Chickamauga or they have been non-professionals of a more or less puritanical and prosaic nature who have not been able to appreciate their actress-wives' artistic or amatory foibles, with the result that the latter have either with sentimental understanding taken tender leave of them or with sarcastic denunciation of the poor worms have flounced off with more bohemian and accommodating male companions.

The other types have been not less predictable. The actress' chum and confidante has customarily been the brash, breezy minor actress of liberal morals, always given to crossing her legs several inches above the deadline and impressing the wistfully skeptical heroine with her pragmatic philosophy of life, expressed in a vernacular never heard on land, sea or anywhere else but hypothetically part and parcel of everyday backstage speech. The actor hero, theatregoers will readily recall, usually seems to have spent all his savings on silk dressing gowns and is the only man on earth who is able to tie his bow tie without looking in a mirror and while debonairely carrying on a conversation. His chief occupations are laboriously trying to keep up an appearance of youth despite his advancing years, reclining on a divan and nonchalantly indulging in colloquies over the telephone with one or more female infatuates, confiding to his valet such matters as the ordinary human being would not tell his priest, laying unction to his vanity in a ducal condescension toward importuning creditors, and failing to notice the whimsical critical smile of his wife.

There is, too, the stereotyped gentle old stage-doorman, generally cast with a broken-down, elderly and slightly rheumatic actor who has not had a job for fifteen years and may be had for the minimum salary. And the retired actress now grown plump who has married a man from Altoona, Pa., and has contentedly settled down, and who makes the heroine speculate for a fleeting moment if a career, however brilliant, is worth it all. And, certainly, the producer or manager, often with a Yiddish accent but named Mountbatten or such so as not to offend the racially sensitive, who either explosively remonstrates with the heroine on her contemplated marriage to the scion of wealth and fashion or who affectionately tries to wheedle her into doing his hard-headed theatrical will.

These are only a few samples of the character nursery and do not include that other chronic friend, the young playwright full of high resolve and dreams who is disillusioned either by the practical nature of the theatre or by the representation thereof in the person of an actress whom hitherto he had worshipped from afar. Or the actress' mother, a ferocious old harridan with her eye set solely on her daughter's career and financial gain, who is customarily employed for comedy purposes. Or the director of high temperamental voltage who alternately cajoles and berates the star. Nor are the plots of the plays much more original. One concerning an actress like, for instance, Charlotte Cushman, who led a life not markedly dissimilar to the average woman's, or an actor like Forbes-Robertson, who was as normal as Calvin Coolidge, or a producer like Charles Frohman, who was as temperamental as an eiderdown blanket, would be so revolutionary that it would cause us to celebrate the occasion with a big bonfire of nine-tenths of all the theatre plays in the Samuel T. French catalogue.

Though Miss Gordon has departed from the character and plot formulæ at least to some extent and though she is to be congratulated for doing so, she still adheres sufficiently to the expected. Her ground-plan, acceptable enough, is the American theatre at the turn of the century and a married acting couple who are among its leading lights. The wife is so completely under the spell and influence of her mate that, when he dies, she is lost and unable to pursue her career. The embellishment of the ground-plan, however, resorts to so much that has come to be orthodox that the play seems to be largely the same old-fashioned thing. The actor-husband, for example, is the overly temperamental and imperious actor out of many such old novels as *The Impostor* and more plays than Molnár or Sacha Guitry can probably remember. The elderly actress with her cynical view of the business, the gentle old actor happily resigned to whatever befalls, the saucy young novice ready to dispense her charms wherever they will bring in returns, the older playwright given to an ironic attitude and the eager young one enamoured of the star actress, the disillusioned, sharp-tongued maid who presides over the star's household, the husband who, with the usual glass of champagne in his hand, collapses from a heart attack after a violent diatribe, and the solicitous auctioneer who comes to dispose of the impoverished actress' effects — all are again *in statu quo*. Standing toasts are offered for little reason other than to make a pretty stage picture. Effective period scenery by Donald Oenslager, attractive period costumes by Mainbocher, and allusions to Frohman, Belasco, Joe Jefferson, Nat Goodwin, Maxine Elliott, Clyde Fitch, Delmonico's, Bustanoby's, the Holland House and other figures and haunts of the era are substituted for any intrinsic, real dramatic atmosphere. And the last act wins the cake for showing not only the rubber-stamp scene in which the faithful old servant takes sad leave of his destitute mistress but enough other moist leave-takings on the part of other characters to stock the entire Henry Arthur Jones library.

One or two episodes, such as that in which the actress salves the vanity of her actor-husband by reading into a newspaper review of their joint performance unwritten tributes to him, are likeable. But such devices, among others, as having the young playwright arrange for his beloved actress' comeback by writing a play based on her own unhappy life — "How does it end?," she archly inquires as the curtain is about to fall. "This way," he replies, gathering her in his arms — such devices are as musty as the motion picture, *A Double Life,* which Miss Gordon wrote in collaboration with Garson Kanin, which earned great kudos for its originality in the Hollywood art area, and which, in its story of a Shakespearean actor influenced by his Othello role to murderous off-stage impulses, had been duplicated at least thirty-five years before in the Italian play, *Sirocco,* by Pordes Milo, done into English a few years later by H. C. M. Hardinge and Matheson Lang under the title, *Carnival,* and produced in London and New York.

The exhibit further indicates its author's unfamiliarity with the period in which she has laid it. Marie Tempest is referred as Maria. Maude Adams, the recluse, is portrayed as a chipper party girl. The play, *The World And His Wife,* is mentioned in the 1901 act; it was not produced and seen until 1908. *Florodora* is announced to have had twenty touring companies in 1901. The show was produced in New York in November 1900, and what touring companies there were did not flower so soon. *Candida* was first professionally produced in New York in December 1903; it is to be doubted if it would have been the subject of rapt discussion among actors several years earlier. The term "tear-jerker," unless I am mistaken, was invented by H. L. Mencken in 1912 and its use early in 1902 seems premature. And so on.

The acting company was moderately competent, though Miss Gordon's well known and irritating mannerisms in voice and carriage scarcely assisted the acceptance of a portrait of a celebrated actress of the period of even Julie Opp, Bertha Galland and Adelaide Prince.

Garson Kanin, who managed the stage direction, deplored in an interview the many drama critics who choose always to be witty at the expense of the plays they review. Out of sheer curiosity I should like to ask him two questions. Just where, first, has he encountered all these witty critics? I have been reading play reviews, including some of my own, for a long time now and I have been unable to detect much more wit in the great bulk of them than would fill a thimble, with plenty room left in it for even a fairly good Ambrose Bierce quip. Not only must Mr. Kanin have a very peculiar taste in wit but he must be of the opinion that the genuinely witty criticism of a Shaw or Beerbohm, Walkley or Agate, has been damaging to the drama, whereas the solemn dulness of that of some reviewer for a whistle-stop gazette is of prodigious help and encouragement. One of the characters in Miss Gordon's play is a dramatic critic who is the repository of the author's wit, such as it is. Since he is the only really interesting and entertaining character in the play, I should like, secondly, to inquire of Mr. Kanin how he feels about him. If Mr. Kanin is consistent, he should dislike him no end and should have persuaded his wife either to eliminate him from her script or rewrite him in the vein of one of his admired and respected dullards like the late J. Ranken Towse, whose reviews had all the ésprit of iced tea. Miss Gordon's play would have been much better if more of even the wit which Mr. Kanin seems to discover in the critics had found its way into it. As it stands, it is an overly talkative, humorless, dawdling and down-hill transaction planned with a deep affection for the theatre but with its blueprint badly smudged.

It is to be hoped that Mr. Kanin will properly relish this review, since it hasn't the faintest touch of wit in it.

MY ROMANCE. OCTOBER 19, 1948

A musical play, based on Edward Sheldon's Romance, *with book and lyrics by Rowland Leigh, music by Sigmund Romberg. Produced by the Shuberts for 95 performances in, initially, the Shubert Theatre.*

PROGRAM

BISHOP ARMSTRONG (Tom)	VLADIMIR LUCCACHEVITCH
Lawrence Brooks	Nat Burns
SUZETTE ARMSTRONG Joan Shepard	MISS JOYCE Natalie Norman
ALICE Marion Bradley	BERTIE WESSEL Lawrence Weber
HARRY ARMSTRONG	GEORGIANNA CURTRIGHT
William Berrian	Verna Epperly
MISS POTHERTON	MARGARET FEARS Mary Jane Sloan
Hildegarde Halliday	LAWRENCE RILEY Andy Aprea
CORNELIUS VAN TUYL	THYRA WINSLOW Lou Maddox
Melville Ruick	DEWITT BODEEN Donald Crocker
SUSAN VAN TUYL Hazel Dawn, Jr.	ROSELLA Allegra Varron
PERCIVAL HAWTHORNE-HILLARY	MME. MARGUERITA CAVALLINI
Tom Bate	(Rita) Anne Jeffreys
MRS. DEWITT Barbara Patton	CHARLOTTE ARMSTRONG
VERONICA DEWITT Gail Adams	Madeleine Holmes
OCTAVIA FOTHERINGHAM	TOSATTI Tito Coral
Luella Gear	1ST MAID Edith Lane
SIR FREDERICK PUTNAM Rex Evans	2ND MAID Patricia Boyer
LADY PUTNAM Doris Patston	PAGE BOY Norval Tormsen
RUPERT CHANDLER Melton Moore	

SYNOPSIS: *Bishop Armstrong's library in the rectory attached to St. Giles Church, New York City. The present. Act I. Home of Cornelius Van Tuyl, New York City, 1898. Act II. Rectory, St. Giles Church. Six weeks later. Act III. Mme. Cavallini's suite at Brevoort House. Four hours later.*

Director: *Rowland Leigh.*

IN THE THEATRE, whatever its mutations, one may be certain of at least one thing: that the wrong men will always be falling in love with actresses, opera singers, circus equestriennes, and waitresses in inns, preferably in Baden or the Tyrol. In the 1913 Sheldon play from which the present show has been derived it is again an opera singer and the

swain is a man of the cloth; and, as in most of the other
versions, the ill-assorted pair are doomed to heartbreak and
eventual wistful parting. On this occasion, Sigmund Romberg has once more been called in to supply the twain's
tide and ebb with the mesmeric molasses which passes in
his case for music, and he supplies it in the same abundant
doses with which he sugared such other variants of the
theme as *The Student Prince* and *Blossom Time.*

I have written before of Mr. Romberg, as of some other
of our music show composers, that one's chief entertainment in listening to him consists, after the first few bars of
his melodies, in confidently humming to one's self the rest
of them, since his compositional reproductivity is on a par
with that of a schizophrenic mosquito's. And one's secondary entertainment derives from his attempt now and
then momentarily to fool one by borrowing not exactly the
tune one anticipates but one or a combination of tunes
slightly different. The sum and substance, however, remain largely the same, even if he occasionally calls on the
brasses and percussion instruments to raise such a racket
that one can not hear one's private tonal exercises. But,
despite the camouflaging din which he presently raises, it
is not altogether impossible to wrap one's lips around his
obvious pluckings from a large variety of melodies by Plan-
quette (*The Chimes Of Normandy*), Lehár (*The Land Of
Smiles*), Coward (*Bitter Sweet*), Oscar Straus (*The Chocolate Soldier*), and others.

The show provides still some extra entertainment. So
antique is it that not only can one thus hum in advance
the Romberg score but with little more trouble mumble in
advance most of Rowland Leigh's additions to the already
familiar Sheldon dialogue which seldom miss a chance to
echo the clichés of shows of the species. Mr. Leigh's comedy interpolations are not less painful and include, among
several dozen others, such titbits as "I am at a loss what to
say" — "Why not say goodbye?"; "My next husband will
have to have one foot in the grave and the other in Tif-
fany's"; and "High notes are always accompanied by low
morals." As to the Sheldon dialogue, a liberal portion of

which is retained, one muses at the high reputation once enjoyed in our theatre by a playwright who could write such drool as the Italian opera singer's description of her first love: "A young man come join our serenata — Beppo, 'is name vas — Beppo Aquilone. 'E vas 'ansome an' 'e 'ad nize voice — oh, ver' light, but steel simpatica. Ve stan' together vhen ve sing an' 'ave — I dunno — vone, two duet. An' so it go for two, t'ree week an' 'e say noding much, but every time 'e smile an' look at me my 'eart is full vit great beeg vishes an' I feel like everyt'ing in all de vorld is new an' born again. An' so vone evening 'e come vit me to my leetle room — and den 'e tell me dat 'e love me — an' all night long 'e 'old me close an' keess me — an' I feel 'is 'ot breat' like a fire upon my face — an' de beating of 'is 'ot 'eart, it come like strong blows 'ere against my own. An' den 'e sleep. But I — I do not sleep. I lie still an' quiet an' in my mind I have vone t'ought — 'Is dis vhat people mean vhen dey say — *Love*?' " Along with more in the same rich vein and the conclusion, "An' den 'e sigh an' put 'is 'ead 'ere — on my shoulder — like a leetle baby dat is tired an' go to sleep again. An' oh! I put my arm about 'im an' I smile an' t'ink, 'For Love I vaited all night long, an' vit de day — *it come!*' "

The stage direction is the kind which, when someone pulls the cork of a champagne bottle, instructs a stagehand in the wings to set off what sounds like a cannon. Anne Jeffreys and Lawrence Brooks sing the leading roles proficiently, though their acting both in the matter of the former's calisthenics and the latter's unrelieved pious rigidity is scarcely conducive to promoting the desired romantic mood of the show. While Hazel Dawn, daughter of *The Pink Lady's* remembered star, is a personable ingénue and while one or two of the other ladies in the company may be looked at without a feeling of alarm, it seems that whoever picked out the rest of the ensemble, judging from their looks and figures, must not only have been blind but unversed in Braille.

Waxing solemn recently, H. I. Phillips, the humorist, issued the following protest:

What has become of the old-time musical comedy that was musical and a comedy? What has happened to the idea that laughter should not only be permitted in the theatre, but encouraged? With few exceptions, the musicals of the last half dozen seasons, and especially of this one, have been so lacking in laughs and all-around rollicking fun that only by digging back through your memories could you realize that once upon a time people left musical shows . . . chuckling over the comedy scenes. This column is convinced that producers follow a new creed:

1. If it's real funny something is wrong with it.

2. Any part calling for a good comedian must be regarded with deep suspicion.

3. Always remember in writing, accepting or producing a musical show that the audience is never happier than when dedicating a new funeral parlor.

Where the great Broadway showman of yesterday put special emphasis on amusing the customers it is amazing how many producers of today have been sinking their dough into musicals with "No Laughter Permitted" written all over them.

Though, like Mr. Phillips, I relish good comedy as much as any other citizen, I fear that he has dedicated his indignation to error when he imagines that most of the better old-time musical comedies were replete with laughter and that "the great Broadway showman of yesterday put special emphasis on [thus] amusing the customers." There were, true, musical comedies in the older days that rested largely on the talents of such comedians as Francis Wilson, De Wolf Hopper, Sam Bernard, Joe Cawthorn, Jimmie Powers, Frank Daniels, Eddie Foy, Jeff De Angelis, *et al.*, and a lot of them were not very funny at that. But there were many, many more — and some of them figure as memory's treasures — which did not rely upon laughter for their pleasure and acceptance, and which, as I pointed out in an earlier chapter, had a minimum of comedy, sometimes, indeed, almost imperceptible. As examples of a few out of many, I cite again such as *The Arcadians, The*

Geisha, San Toy, Florodora, It Happened In Nordland, The Fortune Teller, The Little Duchess, and *Dolly Varden.* Or *The Wild Rose, The Highwayman, The Country Girl, The School Girl, The Silver Slipper,* and *The Mocking Bird.* Or, again, *Three Little Maids, Red Feather, The Two Roses, Woodland, Miss Dolly Dollars, The Dollar Princess, Veronique,* and *The Little Cherub.* Or, still again, *My Lady's Maid, The Belle Of Mayfair, The Little Michus, The Orchid, Miss Hook Of Holland, The Waltz Dream, Mlle. Modiste,* and *Havana.* If cataloguing were not as wearisome to the reader's eye as it is to the writer's hand, it would be easy to expand.

Yet even were Mr. Phillips' point of view sound — and his point of view is shared by numerous old codgers — I believe that he is still in error in the matter of the present musical shows. Have the musicals of the last half dozen seasons, as he argues, been so lacking in laughs? Critical merit not figuring the one way or the other, Eddie Cantor's *Banjo Eyes,* Ray Bolger's *By Jupiter!,* Bobby Clark's *Star And Garter,* Ethel Merman's *Something For The Boys,* and also *One Touch Of Venus* were surely not altogether on the grim side. What, too, of Bobby Clark's *Mexican Hayride* and *As The Girls Go,* of *Bloomer Girl,* of Mitzi Green's *Billion Dollar Baby,* and of the revues like *Call Me Mister, Lend An Ear,* and *Make Mine Manhattan?* Was *Annie Get Your Gun* a funeral parlor, or *Beggar's Holiday,* or *High Button Shoes,* or Beatrice Lillie's *Inside U.S.A.,* or *Love Life,* or *Kiss Me Kate?*

What is wrong with so much musical comedy is not its alleged minimum of humor but its tendency, as in the case of this *My Romance,* to encroach upon the field of drama at the expense of its old gayety and free-for-all flavor. It seems, indeed, as if our musical comedy is becoming more and more dramatic as our drama becomes more and more musical comedy. Shows are being either derived from dramatic plays or written in terms closely approximating straight plays. It is not that some of them aren't worthy; it is rather that, worthy as they are, they have lost much of the welcome old freedom, ease and happy abandon. A show

like *Magdalena,* poor as its book is, is nevertheless much
more dramatic than a straight play like *Time For Elizabeth* or *A Story For Strangers* or *Summer And Smoke,*
which last utilizes such musical show attributes as music,
electrical fireworks, and even something that resembles a
Spanish hoochie-coochie dance. The music aside, derivative
shows like *Street Scene, Porgy And Bess, The Chocolate
Soldier, Carousel, Oklahoma!,* etc., admirable as some of
them may be, remain largely and essentially the straight
fare they originally were. And many such other derived
shows as *Louisiana Lady, Under The Counter, Sadie
Thompson, The Firebrand Of Florence,* etc., not only do
not add anything to the plays from which they stemmed
but subtract from them. Surely the show under immediate
notice is a case in point.

To return to the wonderful old laugh shows which Mr.
Phillips misses, I take the liberty of repeating for his pleasure a literal description of a perfectly typical one, *Molly O,*
produced thirty-odd years ago and the work of two of the
foremost musical comedy writers of the period, Harry B.
and Robert B. Smith.

The first act curtain's rise disclosed "The O'Malley Villa,
Newport," with a view of the Bay of Naples on the backdrop. Entered Freddy Sands, described in the program as
"a little brother of the rich" and obviously a Newporter to
the manor born. Thus, accordingly, Freddy to a lady of
fashion: "I'm the only guy around here, kid, who knows
(*indicating a sizeable beer glass with his hands*) where to
get a tall one!" Freddy then pretended that his walking
stick was a musical instrument and drolly fingered it. This
done, he stepped to the footlights and sang a lyric pertinent
to Newport about a girl named Anna from Savannah who
met a man from Havana. Entered subsequently a young
miss and her young man. The latter beseeched a kiss. "But
kisses," pouted the young miss, "are intoxicating." To
which her young man retorted, "Then let's get soused."
Followed a duet, "Marry Me And See," in which the young
man urged the young miss to fly away with him and nest
like a turtle dove with true love under skies fair above.

There now appeared Dan O'Malley, considerately described in the program as an Irishman, whose wife, Prunella O'Malley, had social aspirations. Mrs. O'Malley, we were informed, was called Prunella because her husband had been instrumental in forming the prune trust. Mr. O'Malley had been forced by his spouse to dress up and was in comic distress because his patent leather shoes pinched his corns, to which now and again he dolorously alluded. (Later, Mr. O'Malley sneaked off and reappeared in a pair of carpet slippers, amusing the audience greatly.) Freddy now again entered and indulged in a colloquy with Mr. O'Malley, the three most hilarious points in which were a query as to how Mr. O'Malley kept peas from rolling off his knife, a suggestion as to the noiseless eating of soup, and an allusion to Kankakee. Freddy then referred facetiously to Mrs. O'Malley's diamonds as "ice," a witticism interrupted by the entrance of the tenor in the uniform of a huzzar who, pausing only to bestow a contumelious look upon Freddy, burst into song on the ease with which a man may tell the right little girl when the right little girl comes along.

The huzzar, it presently developed, was to marry Molly, the niece of the opulent O'Malley's, who, after a jolly quip to the effect that kisses are not round but elliptical (pronounced a-lip-tickle so that we might get it), approached the footlights and sang that love is an art to warm the heart oh Cupid's dart. The irresistible Freddy, once Molly had finished, now grasped the huzzar by the hand and tearfully congratulated him on his coming marriage, which he referred to as an execution. This accomplished, Freddy came down and, walking back and forth at the footlights, sang about the girl who wins my heart she must not be too stout I know what I'm about she must have a figure which is de rigueur. O'Malley and Mrs. O'Malley thereupon re-entered. "When you married me," observed Mrs. O'Malley, "I thought you were well off." "When I married you," retorted Mr. O'Malley, "I was way off!" Then a quip about the marriage knot being a noose, another about Eve and the figleaf — and Freddy, who had exited but in some in-

scrutable manner had again insinuated himself into the
scene along with the huzzar, alluded to the latter's forthcoming wedding and playfully allowed that he would be at
the ringside.

"Do you drink anything?" inquired the huzzar.

"Yes, anything," replied Freddy.

After an interval, Josette, described as "a Viennese artiste," appeared with a bunch of flowers.

"What are those flowers?" Freddy asked.

"Zay are ze wild flowers," answered Josette.

Freddy reached for them.

"Oh, *non, non, non*," cried Josette in her native Viennese tongue, "You moost not touch zem!"

"Ah, I see," retorted Freddy, "that's what makes 'em
wild!"

Josette's young man now came on and the trio executed
a ditty called "One Way Of Doing It," in which were described different ways to woo a woman. Between the verses
and the chorus the trio illustrated the lyric with stage business. For example, Freddy pretended to enter a jewelry
shop with Josette, the while the latter's young man pretended to be the clerk.

"That's a nice necklace, dearie," said Freddy to Josette;
"put it on; you can have it." Then, to the clerk, "How
much is it?"

"Fourteen," replied the clerk.

Freddy proceeded to count out fourteen dollars.

"Fourteen *thousand*," said the clerk. Whereupon Freddy
simulated a faint.

After another verse, the trio put their heads close together and burlesqued grand opera, during which Freddy,
his back turned, suddenly reversed to kiss Josette and, her
place meanwhile having been taken by the young man,
much to his dismay kissed the latter instead.

The huzzar now discovered that Molly believed he was
marrying her for her money and, his pride stung to the
quick, confided his decision to leave his bride immediately
the ceremony was performed. A messenger boy presently
delivered a telegram to him which he had sent to himself

and the huzzar, bringing his palm sharply up in salute of the messenger boy, tore open the envelope. Farewell, farewell, I must away at crack of day, he sang to Molly, and the curtain came down.

I shall not go into details of the second act. A few memoranda will serve. "Why, where have you bean?" asked Freddy. "Bean?" said Mr. O'Malley. "I've bean in Boston." "Do you know Michelangelo?" he inquired. "Mike," rejoined Mr. O'Malley, "old Mike Angelo? An' sure I know Mike. Me and him used to work on the railroad together."

Mrs. O'Malley then entered wearing a small black mask and Mr. O'Malley, utterly deceived, mistook her for a beauteous Spanish señorita and proceeded to flirt with her. "Sacramento fandango?" he began, archly. "Chianti spaghetti," returned Mrs. O'Malley, coquettishly. When Mrs. O'Malley subsequently unmasked and roundly berated Mr. O'Malley for cutting up with a strange woman, Mr. O'Malley blandly assured her that he knew who it was all the time.

Freddy appeared a little later and, observing Mr. O'Malley in a grotesque costume with which he had adorned himself for the grand ball, inquired, "What do you represent?"

"I'm a Spanish humidor," replied Mr. O'Malley.

"You mean toreador!" exclaimed Freddy.

"Well, it's all the same to me," said Mr. O'Malley. "What's a toreador?"

"A toreador," explained Freddy, "is a Spanish bullfighter."

"Well," said Mr. O'Malley, "I feel like a Spanish onion."

Mr. O'Malley then asked Freddy what a toreador does.

"A toreador," Freddy told him, "is a man who throws the bull."

"Well," replied Mr. O'Malley, "I've thrown a lot of bull myself."

"But a toreador throws the bull in the arena," protested Freddy.

"Well," said Mr. O'Malley, "I had some f-arena for breakfast."

LIFE WITH MOTHER. October 20, 1948

A play by Howard Lindsay and Russel Crouse, based on the writings of Clarence Day. Produced by Oscar Serlin for the rest of the season's performances in the Empire Theatre.

Program

Father	Howard Lindsay	Hazel Willoughby	Jo Anne Paul
Whitney	David Frank	Bessie Fuller Logan	
Harlan	Robert Wade		Gladys Hurlbut
John	Robert Antoine	Mrs. Willoughby	Amy Douglass
Margaret	Dorothy Bernard	Clyde Miller	Robert Emhardt
Clarence	John Drew Devereaux	Cousin Cora	Ruth Hammond
Michael	Michael Smith	Kathleen	Marguerite Morrissey
Vinnie	Dorothy Stickney	Dr. Humphreys	A. H. Van Buren
Bridget	Mary Diveny		

SYNOPSIS: Act I. Scene: *The living-room of the Day country home at Harrison, N. Y.* Act II. Scene 1. *The same. Saturday afternoon.* Scene 2. *The same. Just before twilight.* Act. III. Scene 1. *The morning-room of the Day house on Madison Avenue in New York City. A few days later.* Scene 2. *The same. Late that afternoon.*

Time: *The 1880's.*

Director: *Guthrie McClintic.*

The pleasures of *Life With Father* resulted directly from a recollection of similar happenings in one's own family. Those of this sequel, *Life With Mother,* result indirectly from a recollection of happenings in the Day family in the previous play. There may possibly be a better way quickly to suggest and criticize the nature of this second picture of the Day household but I can not think of one, and I have scratched my brains now for a full half-minute. In other words, the entertainment one gets in this case is not altogether unlike that which one used to get from a return visit to a favorite stock company or, as also in the bygone years, to the Rogers Brothers in such successive musical shows as *The Rogers Brothers In Harvard,*

The Rogers Brothers In Wall Street, etc. It is not that Howard Lindsay, Dorothy Stickney, and some others are again seen in their former roles, since the story this time is a bit changed, as it was in the past instances. It is rather that not only are the principals the same but that their acting personalities are the same, that the plays are of an essential body and flavor, and that the whole therefore affects one like a non-alcoholic and agreeable hangover. If anyone at this point argues that I have dragged in the old stock companies by the tail, that the points of similarity are altogether too far-fetched, and that the plays they presented were basically not in the least alike, I ask the more venerable of my clients to recall, for just a few examples, the several old standbys dealing with Richelieu, *Divorçons* and its carbon copies and, surely, such comedies as *The Professor's Love Story* and *A Bachelor's Romance.*

There are, however, many things much the same and some of them are and have been no worse for it, as, for instance, smoked brook trout, the Ziegfeld *Follies,* and kissing. Like the last named, which is perhaps more relevant to the issue, this *Life With Mother* may not be entirely as enjoyable as it was when we had a crush on it nine years ago under its maiden name, and mature reflection may smile a little at its affectations of eager youth, but it is still nevertheless acceptable as a good friend. It is pleasant to be with it and to think of old times, even if it occasionally seems to be trying awfully hard to rekindle the former warm affection. The strain on its part to re-create the old love does not at times make for comfort and there are moments when the old girl lingers a little too long and emphatically on pictures in the *Life With Father* album. Yet one is not unwilling to suspend impatience and to accept the situation with good grace, and the evening hence profits from one's acquiescent wistfulness.

Father Day, in the person of Mr. Lindsay, seems to have sneaked off to a lot of burlesque shows in the intervening years and now to have absorbed some of the low comedians' tricks, while Mother Day, in the person of Miss Stickney, has more circumspectly stayed at home and remained her charming former self. And two or three of the other familiar characters have evidently accompanied Father on his Mutual Wheel jaunts. But it has not done too much damage and, though their guardian director, Mr. McClintic, has not seen fit to reprimand and correct them, they still provide a very amiable few hours.

The audiences' reaction to the play seems to be much like my own. For example, though a new set of scenery has been supplied by Donald Oenslager for one of the acts, it is the old Stewart Chaney set salvaged from the previous play for another, showing the Days' house in New York, which nightly draws the loudest applause.

The plot, if anything so sketchy may be called that, here deals with Mother's failure to have received an engagement ring from Father in the rush of his courtship and her efforts to retrieve the one he had earlier given to a girl whom he subsequently jilted in her favor. The most amusing scenes are those in which a small son of the family, hitherto suppressed, resolutely recites an interminable school-learned poem while the household is embroiled in a heated discussion of the value of the stock of the Chesapeake and Ohio railroad; in which Father is confronted by his youthful love, now grown fat but still coy and flirtatious; and in which the hay, grain and feed merchant recently married to Cousin Cora and hilariously acted by Robert Emhardt drives Father to distraction with his omniscience in the matter of food, drink, tobacco, gardening, arboriculture, and every other subject that happens to come up.

The particular skill of the playwrights lies paradoxically in creating a sentimental atmosphere with an avoidance of sentiment, or at least with only the slightest, indirect emphasis on it. At but two points in the play is there a more direct approach and even then it is knitted with humor.

MINNIE AND MR. WILLIAMS. October 27, 1948

A fantasy by Richard Hughes. Produced by John Gassner and David Dietz for 5 performances in the Morosco Theatre.

PROGRAM

THE REVEREND JOHN WILLIAMS		GLADYS	*Elizabeth Ross*
	Eddie Dowling	OWAIN FLATFISH	
MINNIE	*Josephine Hull*		*Clarence Derwent*
SCRAGGY EVAN	*Gwilym Williams*	MRS. JONES BAKEHOUSE	*Grace Mills*
TIMOTHY YSGAIRNOLWEN		MR. GAS JONES	*Geoffrey Lumb*
	Paul Anderson	MRS. RESURRECTION JONES	
MARI JONES	*Lee Wilcox*		*Gwyneth Hughes*

SYNOPSIS: *The action takes place in the kitchen of the Williams' cottage in a Welsh village at the turn of the century. Act I. Scene 1. About nine o'clock of a September evening. Scene 2. Next morning. Act II. Immediately after. Act III. A year later.*

Director: *Eddie Dowling.*

TWENTY-SIX YEARS AGO, the Welsh Richard Hughes wrote a fantasy, called *A Comedy Of Good And Evil,* about a small child who, despite her innocent appearance, was an emissary of the Devil. For some reason that one hundred Madame Blavatskys in congress assembled could not divine, its local producers elected cheesily to rename it *Minnie And Mr. Williams.* And the tot, for another reason two hundred Annie Besants inspired by copious draughts of hooch could not intuit, was then cast with an actress visibly in her twenties who, though of limited stature, no more properly suggested what she was supposed to than Ernest Truex would Butch Jenkins. In such situations it is the custom of some producers to argue that the thing simply had to be done, since, they say, it is impossible to find a youngster capable of handling any such ticklish part. They are correct in at least one particular. It is impossible to find the youngster by sitting on their rumbles in their offices, with the doors permanently marked "Out For Lunch." If once in a while they were to get up, go out, and look around they might solve the problem. They might, for example, find a wonderful little kid named Sibyl Stocking, who gave such an excellent performance not long ago in *The Bees And The Flowers.* Or one like Joan Lazer, who was so good last season in *Me And Molly.* Or others quite as talented. The discovery of unusually equipped little girls has never been too difficult for producers who have made it their business to find them. In the past we have seen any number of them, such as the remarkable Fugaczy child who gave a sensational account of herself in a formidable role in *Revolt;* the tiny Joan McSweeny in *Solitaire* whose performance prompted Carl Van Doren when the curtain fell to declare that she was the only woman he ever loved; Amelia Romano who startled critics and audiences at the age of eight and went on in her early teens to even more acclaim in *Plumes In The Dust* and, to abbreviate a considerable list, the twelve year old Jacqueline Horner who gained wide notice a few years ago in *Swan Song.*

I am by no means reflecting on Elizabeth Ross, who was picked instead to play the role. She is a skilful actress and did as well by it as any other such young actress probably could. It was not her fault that she was too adult for it and so made the play further ridiculous. The most adroitly mimicked youngling voice, manner and bearing never can make us believe that the one merchanting them is other than what she actually is. Producers' theory to the contrary has provided us with some of the most waywardly amusing occasions in our theatre. There was the time, for example, when Mrs. Fiske, then forty-seven, ventured to display herself as a sixteen year old chick in the early portion of Edward Sheldon's *The High Road.* And the other time when Blanche Walsh, also in her forties, tried to persuade us, in *Redemption,* that she was a tender Russian maiden of seventeen or thereabout. And the still other time when one of the several passionate young Tondeleyos in *White Cargo* was cast with a lady who the very next year became a grandmother. If politeness were not what it is, even juicier memoranda might be added.

It is all very well to talk, with Coleridge, about the voluntary remission of judgment which is supposed to make us believe in anything, however absurd, if only we do not sufficiently put our minds to it. My own powers in that direction from long and commanding experience have indeed been so richly developed that I am able to believe for a split-second that there may be some second-rate lyrical quality in such of Tennessee Williams' highly regarded dialogue as "I thanked God for you, because you seemed to be gentle, a cleft in the rock of the world that I could hide in." But, though I have mastered the art to even that extent, I remain still so backward that to me an actress generally looks her age, or something pretty close to it, and that, heave and perspire as I will, I find it hard to accept as Little Eva one who should be playing Eliza.

Coming to the play itself, Mr. Hughes says that he was impelled to write it because "the notion of entertaining a devil unawares had a new twist." It is to be feared that Mr. Hughes in his day did not get around much. Entertaining a devil unawares had already been the pastime of Continental playwrights like Molnár and English like Chesterton. And, unfortunately for the virginity of his theme, it has in the intervening years also been the familiar diversion of numerous stage practitioners like Benn Levy, Eugene Vale, *et al*. That, however, is a detail and of no critical importance. More important is what he and his local editors and revisers have made of the conceit.

That Hughes has a prose style of merit, along with some imagination and sensitivity, is not news to readers of his fiction, and at least a trace of that style is discernible in his play. But it is one thing to have a gift for fiction and another to have a gift for drama, and the latter he seems to have been denied. Nor have his local masseurs been able to help him. The result is a parable, about a Baby Snooks with hair ribbons in the semblance of horns who scampers about a stage spouting feeble Chesterton paradoxes, which may be called a play only in that some people hitherto recognized as actors are engaged in it and read its lines in costume from an elevated platform set with a piece of scenery. And not only is it a play largely in name only but one which seems to have gone home after its first act. Following that act what occupies the stage is simply a dramatic vacuum in which the initial act's lines and business are endlessly repeated until shortly before closing time, when an actor designated as a guardian angel appears and makes matters a little flatter by entering into a debate with Baby Snooks on good and evil which sounds like a rewrite of an old morality play by a young Harvard cynic. That the little she-devil, after a brave show of defiance, is thereupon converted to pious rectitude, perhaps you need not be informed.

Contributing to the play's immediate failure was stage direction which permitted a lot of gratuitous loud off-stage singing to make much of the dialogue unintelligible; so much hopping, jumping, whirling and twirling by the Devil's little advocate that she seemed rather to be an advocate of Agnes de Mille; and enough stale infernal red-lighting and holy white-lighting to suffice a half-dozen *Faust* road companies. Josephine Hull and Eddie Dowling were illstarred in the production, which was sponsored by, of all people, that otherwise sagacious dramatic critic, John Gassner. If I myself were ever to horn into the business, it would probably be just my luck to revive *Grandma's Diary*.

In a statement from his home in Merionethshire, Wales, Mr. Hughes, in reply to an inquiry as to just what his confused play was intended to mean, said, "Someone once asked a famous dancer what her dance meant. She answered, 'If I could put it into words, why should I go to the trouble of dancing it?'" If Mr. Hughes really knows what his bewildered play means, which seems to be doubtful, that is scarcely a convincing rejoinder, since dancing often properly has no meaning, in the precise sense of the word, and is addressed simply to the eye's relish of grace, as some music is to the ear's of sweet and meaningless melody. The dancer who made the answer was as questionable a mentality as Mr. Hughes is in this instance. She might as well have argued that, since Rembrandt had no difficulty

in explaining what his paintings meant, if explanations
were needed, there was no reason why he should have gone
to the trouble of painting them, or that, since Beethoven
could describe what his symphonies meant, he was a fool to
have gone to all the bother of composing them.

Mr. Hughes' subsequent evasion is not less transparent.
"I can't pretend in a plain statement to tell you what the
play means," he declared, "for if I could there would be no
need for the play." Required reading for Mr. Hughes in
this respect should be, among a lot of other things, Shaw's
prefaces to his plays. "But," he presently relented, "I can
give you a few ideas about it." The sum total of the few
ideas is as follows: "The subtitle of the (revised) play is *A
Comedy Of Good And Evil,* and that is what it is; Good
and Evil, the funny side people are usually solemn about."
While that is an explanation of the treatment, it still side-
steps the issue and tells us no more about what he is driving at than we knew before, which was nothing.

But let us be patient. "A dramatist has no right to order
his audience to think . . . but if I can make you think
about the problem of Good and Evil by making you laugh,
why shouldn't I try? So I treat certain notions about that
pair of philosophical twin notions as comic." Here we still
engage double-talk that attempts to conceal any answer to
the first question: what is the play about? We further are
edified by the argument that a dramatist has no right to order his audience to think, which would be surprising news
to some pretty good ones from Æschylus and Sophocles to
Shaw and Pirandello, as also by the notion that we may be
persuaded to think only through laughter, which similarly
would be news to some other very fair dramatists like
Porto-Riche, Giacosa and Galsworthy, among others.

"I have also been asked many questions of detail," continued Mr. Hughes, still not answering the main question.
"What became of Minnie's leg when it was all over? Why
should an angel have double-jointed toes? Why was Mr.
Williams so set against going to Bangor? What was the
golden-haired young Gladys really after?" Then — "Those
are questions for you to answer, for you to imagine your

own answers," he explained, still not explaining anything and keeping his score one hundred per cent.

It is plain, in short, that not only are we completely in the dark as to what meaning, if any, Mr. Hughes' play has, but that Mr. Hughes is in the same situation that we are.

SET MY PEOPLE FREE. November 3, 1948

A play by Dorothy Heyward. Produced by the Theatre Guild for 30 performances in the Hudson Theatre.

Program

George	Canada Lee	Cuppy	Theodore Hines
Rose	Mildred Joanne Smith	Belleisle	Harry Bolden
Denmark	Juano Hernandez	Lot	Louis Sharp
Captain Wilson	Blaine Cordner	Jemmy	George Dosher
Phyllis	Marion Scanlon	Sinah	Musa Williams
Eliza	Gail Gladstone	Blanche	Urylee Leonardos
Gullah Jack	Leigh Whipper	Peter Poyas	Earl Sydnor
Trader Henri	Somer Alberg	Jessie Blackwood	
Morris Brown	Frank Wilson		Thomas Anderson
Patrolman	Tyler Carpenter	Ned Bennett	Earl Jones
The Mauma	Bertha T. Powell	Rolla Bennett	William Marshall
Pompey	Alonzo Bosan	Monday Gell	Charles McRae
Tina	Edith Atuka-Reid	Perault Prioleau	John Bouie
Aneas	William Warfield	Mingo Harth	Eric Burroughs
Pharaoh	William McDaniel	Blind Philip	Harold Des Verney
Benbow	Wanza L. King	Frank Ferguson	Richard Silver
Rachel	Fredye Marshall	First Drummer	Samuel Brown
Adam	Merritt Smith	Second Drummer	Moses Mianns

SYNOPSIS: Act I. Scene 1. *Breakfast room in the house of Captain Wilson, Charleston, S. C., year 1810, evening. Scene 2. A room in the slave quarters of Trader Henri, night. Scene 3. African church in Cow Alley, evening. Act II. Scene 1. A room in Denmark Vesey's house, April, 1822 (twelve years later than Act I). Scene 2. Breakfast room in the house of Captain Wilson, April, 1822, night. Scene 3. A room in Denmark Vesey's house. Scene 4. Wadmalaw Island, early May, night. Act II. Scene 1. Breakfast room in the house of Captain Wilson, June 16, before dawn. Scene 2. A room in Denmark Vesey's house, June 16, an hour before midnight. Scene 3. George Wilson's cabin.*

Director: *Martin Ritt.*

WITH NO GREEDY, illaudable wish to snatch the laurel from my colleague, Brooks Atkinson, for his virtuoso criticism of a recent operetta: "The music is not as good as it sounds," I yet remark about this *Set My People Free* that it is not as interesting as it is. Should anyone accordingly be tempted to doubt my modesty and insist upon proudly promoting me over my colleague, I had perhaps better explain. The play is an interesting one to anybody seeing it for the first time, but when one has seen it in one form or another a number of times, as some of us have, it is not as interesting as it might be. Plays equally based on historical fact which have dealt with a Negro's urge to free his people from oppression, injustice, or something or other have been no rarity on our stage. In recent years alone we have had several, among them *Our Lan'*, *Henri Christophe* and *Haiti*. Though the situations they have treated and the plots through which they have related them may have been somewhat different, the themes and resolution have been essentially much alike. And so it is with this Heyward offering.

The Negro who now is beset by the passion to liberate his brothers is Denmark Vesey, a slave, who in the early 1800's contrived to buy himself from his overlord and organized his former fellow slaves into a rebellion against the whites. Betrayed by one of his followers, who preferred to remain loyal to his master, Vesey's plan went awry, yet his faith remained and he proclaimed that ultimately his dream would be crowned with glory. While the setting and documentary aspect of the story thus take on a superficially divergent color, it will nevertheless be observed that at bottom the play is like others we have engaged. Though the treatment in this case is slightly more able than it has been on some previous occasions and though it is poor criticism which would maintain that simply because plots are basically alike a play is not what it ought to be, the fact remains that when it comes to Negro plays the similarity is somehow peculiarly accentuated and the plays as a consequence appear to be largely not only aural but visual echoes of one another. I realize that this has an unfair sound and I admit that it is unfair, but just the same I think most theatregoers will agree to its practical truth.

The precise reasons I do not know. My guess for what it is worth, however, is that so many Negro actors' perform-

ances are of a physical and emotional identity, so many of
the plays seek color through the old recourse to chorals
and frenzied rituals, and so much of the stage direction is
of the same general nature that even if the plays varied
markedly the impression would at least partly remain that
they were sisters under their skins. It is the same with Negro musical shows. Entertaining as some of them are, most
of them after a while seem to be fundamentally as alike as
two black-eyed peas in a pod. Let what stories they may
have be as different as they will and the shows yet appear
to be largely duplications. The comedy, whatever the material, has the air of being identical; the dancing follows a
set pattern; the mood of one show resembles that of the
others; and the net effect is much the same. If there have
been more than one or two Negro musicals as distinct from
other Negro musicals as many white musicals, however
poor, have been from one another, I am not fortunate
enough to have seen them.

It is on these grounds that I have become a bit tired of
such plays and shows, at any rate as a theatregoer if not
necessarily as a reviewer. In my professional capacity I can
take them in my stride, much in the impersonal manner of
a dutiful and upright doctor going the rounds. But in a
personal capacity I no longer attend them with much pleas-
urable anticipation and often feel that if I were a volunteer theatre customer I should think for some time before
laying out my money for most of them.

I know that this admission will be received with noticeable sarcasm by those who argue that the critic and the
man are one and the same and are as indissoluble as Rom-
ulus and Remus or frankfurters and sauerkraut. But,
while it is true a great deal of the time, it is not always true.
There are, for example, a number of things for which I
have small personal taste yet for which I nevertheless entertain a proper measure of critical respect, among them
the drama of Racine and sweetbreads *à la Reine,* the music of Schönberg and electric razors, the novels of Stanislaw
Przybyszewski and tuba players, and the acting of Lynn

Fontanne and French poodles. And, conversely, there are
some things which fetch me personally, eccentrically constituted as I am, but which do not get by my critical alter
ego, like, for instance, the celebrated old burlesque show
spittoon skit, California Riesling, ketchup on lettuce, and
absurd mystery plays like *The Ouija Board* and *Trick For
Trick*. There is, in short, no more honest reason why the
personal self of a man should always and invariably be in
agreement with his critical self than why a vegetarian sur-
geon should shudder at carving a side of roast beef.

So, even while admitting the several merits of this *Set
My People Free*, I still record the fact that it had a very
drowsy effect upon me. I have too often now viewed that
scene in the Negro church with the congregation working
itself up into paroxysms. I have now heard too many tom-
toms beating in the jungle night and seen too many Negroes wildly beating their bare chests and jumping up and
down in ritual ecstasy. I have already too many times
looked at that dark room in the Negro cabin and seen the
palpitant fugitive being hidden by the respected Negro
woman and heard his relieved "This is the last place they'd
ever think of looking for me." Too often, as well, I have
been faced with that scene in which the owner of the plan-
tation brings home his young bride and in which the Negroes awkwardly come forward to welcome her. And too
much I have had of conjur doctors, Negroes piously quoting from the Bible, brusque white overseers, slaves named
Pompey and Aneas, unctuous Negro preachers with a keen
eye for the collection plate, and loud choral singing behind
the curtain to distract the audience from the pandemonium
of the scene shifters. And, mammy, I am fed up.

Juano Hernandez, Canada Lee and Mildred Smith have
the leading parts. Hernandez's main contribution to the
role of the insurrectionist is a powerfully expanded chest;
Lee gives his features a picnic in that of the tormented,
loyal slave; and the last named, gently convincing as the
slave's wife, provides the evening with its only affecting
performance.

The staging is but fair to middling and, among other things, shows the servitors in the Southern mansion wearing in the dreadful heat of summer the same heavy, formal attire which they have worn in the cold season. The settings by Ralph Alswang, however, are creditable.

BRAVO! November 11, 1948

A comedy by Edna Ferber and George S. Kaufman. Produced by Max Gordon for 44 performances in the Lyceum Theatre.

PROGRAM

Vilna Prager	Janet Fox	Stephanie	Zolya Talma
Rudy	Oliver Cliff	Anna Zinsser	Elena Karam
Martin Link	Edgar Stehli	Lisa Kemper	Christiane Grautoff
Zoltan Lazko	Oscar Homolka	Jeffrey Crandall	Frank Conroy
Rosa Rucker	Lili Darvas	Sophie Marelle	Fritzi Scheff
Lew Gilbert	Morton Havel	Wallace	King Calder
Jimmy Flint	Arthur Havel	Black	George Cotton
Kurt Heger	Kevin McCarthy	Jane Velvet	Jean Carson

SYNOPSIS: Act I. December. Act II. February. Act III. April.
Scene: An old brownstone house in the West Sixties, New York.
Director: George S. Kaufman.

The ADVANCE out-of-town reports on the play were so fiercely grim that, having often after long experience become rather cynical in such cases, I went to the New York opening in a somewhat optimistic mood and learned, as sometimes in the past, that it was not entirely ill-founded. That rewriting had been done during the try-out period and even directly afterward was more or less apparent, but there was not enough of it to keep one from speculating why it is that plays which are condemned outright on the road frequently, when we get a look at them, are discovered to be not without some commendable qualities.

The reason is not altogether elusive. Plays like this are designed primarily for metropolitan showing and find themselves astray in other surroundings. The people they deal with are people with whom many New Yorkers are familiar yet who are recognized very faintly, if at all, in the thitherward communities. The humor, as well, is what for want of a more exact phrase may be termed New York humor and depends largely for its acceptance on acquaintance with persons, places, manners, language and eccentricities of conduct which are peculiar — and peculiar is surely the word — to the American metropolis. To expect an audience in even such a city as Boston to respond to something as intimately Manhattan, despite an appearance of more general scope, as various elements and flavors in a play like this is to believe that that audience in its personal constitution is identical in cosmopolitanism, attitude and idiosyncrasy with a New York one, a belief that would take some believing. I am not reflecting on the Boston or any other out-of-town audience any more than I am vouching for any superiority in the New York audience; I simply argue the difference between them. While a New York audience may possibly not like the play any better than such a road one, which turned out to be true in this instance, the reasons for the dislike are not always the same.

That the play, about a group of Central European theatrical refugees trying to get a foothold in America, has its serious shortcomings, no one, least of all I, will contradict. Its dramaturgy here and there is patchy; it does not follow any perceptible direct line; and it intermittently goes off on rather incommodious tangents. But it has so much incidental honest sympathetic charm, so much droll observation of character and so much understanding humor that, in my case, it makes on the whole for agreeable alternately touching and comical diversion. And two better performances than Oscar Homolka's and Lili Darvas' as the displaced Molnár-like playwright and his inamorata whom for years he has been too busy to find time to marry, I have not seen since the season started.

They say that plays are not written but rewritten. They do not but should also say that, when they are rewritten — and at the last moment, as to a degree this one has been — plays are not only rehearsed but re-rehearsed. *Bravo!* has not been re-rehearsed enough, with the consequence that some of its rewritten last act finds its actors stumbling all over themselves and many of its points garbled. It is further evident that a little additional rewriting might have helped not only that final act but the preceding acts. Nev-

ertheless, even as it stands, the play entertains me a deal
more than many another theoretically more polished one.
Its characters in the main are freshly drawn; there is no
dusty air, so common to many of these plays about theatre
folk, in a larger portion of the dialogue; and the humor, to
use a now moribund adjective of the early Twenties, is
civilized. It may not, in the strict critical sense, be a good
play — and just for the sake of professional standing let it
so be recorded in these annals — but, good or not, it contains much of the stuff on which good plays are made.

Some nine years ago, Dorothy Thompson in *Another
Sun* also collaborated on a play, and a bad one, about Central European theatrical refugees who sought to establish
themselves in this country. But where the present playwrights have regarded their characters with ironic humor,
the previous writers elected to regard theirs with such sentimental solemnity and with such radio commentator hysteria that their exhibit died an almost instant death, un-
mourned. It may be entertaining, which her play was not,
to recall Miss Thompson's wrath over her brain-child's failure, which she expatiated on in a magazine treatise, "The
Theatre: A Comment On America."

It seemed to be Miss Thompson's conviction at the time
(1940) that the theatre was in a terrible way and surely
doomed because it was given to diversion and because, accordingly, it was not making its customers "realize the
war." Since her own attempt to make its customers realize
the war went awry after only eleven performances, one was
to be forgiven for suspecting that her gloom conceivably
hinted at an axe in the woodpile, particularly since she did
not seem to know that in the directly previous seasons no
less than twenty-nine plays intent upon making the customers realize the war saw production. Nor did she seem
to know what she was talking about when she argued collaterally that "we can't face the fact of death in our theatre." In the same seasons, we had faced the fact of death in
exactly seventy-two different plays.

Only in the German theatre before Hitler could Dorothy find "that which great works of creative art produce

for us — an illuminating experience." For "anyone who
has seen . . . Moissi's ghost-haunted Hamlet or Kortner's
Richard III has never been quite the same person since."
Well, I have seen them both and Moissi's ghost-haunted
Hamlet did not stack up one-two-three with either John
Barrymore's or Maurice Evans' in our own theatre. And as
for Kortner's Richard (Kortner, incidentally, to get back
to the axe in the woodpile, was Dorothy's collaborator on
Another Sun), it was pure and unadulterated ham and, in
that respect, not materially superior to our own Walter
Hampden's, which, in the classic words of the late Ring
Lardner, is going some. Further, as for these great works of
creative art, didn't Dorothy know that in the half-dozen
previous seasons our theatre had shown all kinds of productions of Shakespeare, to say nothing of Ibsen, Strindberg, Chekhov, Sheridan, Shaw, *et al*? And, just by the way,
it had also generously shown such typical German pre-war
exhibits, so admired by Dorothy, as Max Reinhardt's *The
Eternal Road* and Piscator's *King Lear, War and Peace* and
Nathan the Wise, along with Bruckner's *Danton's Death,*
Zweig's *Jeremiah,* and the refugee revue called *Reunion in
New York,* one and all of them, by general critical and popular agreement, in production pretty dreadful.

But one could not stop Dorothy. "The theatre demeaned
to the purpose of a *Hellzapoppin* is, however, only a reflection of our whole bourgeois world," she argued. Just one
theatre out of all New York's fifty or more was demeaned
to the purpose of *Hellzapoppin,* a swell show; the old German theatre of which Dorothy is such a rapt partisan had
its relative counterpart in the famous Max and Moritz
hanswurst shows, making old Germany an equally bourgeois world; *Hellzapoppin* itself was a derivative of the
London Palladium's *Crazy Gang* shows, making England
an equally bourgeois world; the *Crazy Gang* shows were a
derivative of the celebrated old Marinetti Milan vaudeville
shows, making Italy in the past an equally bourgeois world;
the Milan shows were a derivative of the Goldoni buffooneries, making eighteenth century south Europe an equally
bourgeois world; and the Goldoni buffooneries were a de-

rivative of the ancient Roman improvised sannio rough-
houses, making everybody bourgeois.

Dorothy had more ideas. There was, it seemed, no
mother-love in our theatre. Dorothy observed derisively
that she had encountered it only in the movie *Dumbo,*
"and Disney had to make the mother an elephant in order
to make her human." Dorothy should have looked around
more. She would have had her fill of mother-love in the
preceding two or three theatrical years in all sorts of plays
ranging from Euripides' *The Trojan Women* to the Hey-
wards' *Mamba's Daughters* and from the German Brecht's
Mother to the Czech Čapek's *The Mother,* as well as in a
dozen native dramas like *Family Portrait, Morning Star,*
etc.

But what agitated Dorothy most greatly, even above her
lament that love isn't love in our theatre, at least the way
they make it in such of her favorite French movies as *The
Baker's Wife,* was the fear that we, unlike the English
whose theatre "realized the war" for *them,* would go to pot
unless our own theatre similarly realized it for us. It might
have interested our heroine to know that, as her lines were
being written, nine-tenths of the English theatres, far from
realizing the war for their customers, were lightly entertaining them with plays and shows like *Blithe Spirit, Dancing Years, Get A Load Of This, Why Not Tonight?, Big,
Top, The Land Of Smiles, Happidrome, Baby Mine, Quiet
Weekend, Fine And Dandy, Full Swing, No Orchids For
Miss Blandish,* and *The Man Who Came To Dinner.*

Incidentally, I wondered if Dorothy stopped thinking of
the changed woman she is since she saw Moissi and Kortner long enough to get around to that mere musical show,
This Is The Army?

AS THE GIRLS GO. November 13, 1948

A musical show with book by William Roos, music by Jimmy McHugh, and lyrics by Harold Adamson. Produced by Michael Todd for the rest of the season's performances in the Winter Garden.

Program

Waldo Wellington *Bobby Clark*	Miss Swenson *Cavada Humphrey*
Lucille Thompson Wellington	Butler *Curt Stafford*
Irene Rich	Floyd Robinson *Douglas Luther*
Kenny Wellington *Bill Callahan*	Diane *Mildred Hughes*
Mickey Wellington	Photographer *Kenneth Spaulding*
Betty Lou Barto	Ross Miller *Jack Russell*
Tommy Wellington	Daphne *Dorothea Pinto*
Donny Harris	Photographer *William Reedy*
Guard *John Sheehan*	Blinky Joe *Dick Dana*
Kathy Robinson	Darlene *Rosemary Williamson*
Betty Jane Watson	Secretary *Ruth Thomas*
Barber *Hobart Cavanaugh*	President of Potomac College
White House Visitor	*Douglas Luther*
John Brophy	Premiere Danseuse *Kathryn Lee*

The scenes of the two acts are laid in and in the environs of the White House, Washington, D.C.
Director: *Howard Bay.*

About a week before the show opened in New York, I met a man who had seen it during its preliminary engagement in Boston. I inquired of him what it was like. "Thank God," he replied, "it's like a 1920 show and not one of these 1948 affairs!" Though I suspected that I knew what he meant, I asked him to explain. "It may," he said, "have some things wrong with it, the so-called book for instance, but it's got girls, whole lots of girls, like the old shows had and not just the skimpy handful we get in most shows today, and with me that's one hell of a point in its favor."

I understood the connoisseur perfectly. A musical show — he obviously was not referring to operetta or the higher grade musical comedy — is properly a girl show and not, as it so often has come to be, one that places its emphasis elsewhere. Nor should it be one that offers only ten or a dozen girls chosen less for their decorativeness and tantalization than for their virtuosity as ballet and jive dancers or their talent in low comedy sketches and other such deplorably irrelevant directions. As things stand, there is often little to look at these days but the scenery, and with the cut-out cardboard kind in wide economical practice, even that has many a time been denied us. My acquaintance's comment accordingly reminded me of an illustrious Frenchman whom I invited to accompany me several years ago to one such exhibit. Half-way through the first act his impatience got the better of him. *"Mon Dieu,"* he exclaimed scornfully, waving a hand at the stage, *"men!"*

If these "men" shows have many other points to recommend them, the absence of attractive girls does not too acutely matter. But they all too seldom have. In such junctures the girls are a vitally necessary and welcome drug. Just as, when all things are said and done, there is nothing on a stage more pleasant to the eye than a pretty girl in a white dress, so in even an otherwise dull show is there nothing so relieving as a number of pretty girls in dresses of almost any color, except perhaps purple. And, when they are pretty enough, it does not in the least count if, like the tackle on a onetime University of Pennsylvania football team, they can do anything else or not.

The tackle, a junior in the Arts department of the university, was a wonder in all respects save one: he never spoke a word to the other men on the team. This bothered the new coach who, eager to establish the desired *esprit d'corps,* approached him on the subject. "Why don't you be friendly like the other guys and mix with them?" he demanded of the two-hundred and fifty pound recruit from the neighboring coal mine country. "Me no speak English," was the reply.

If, to repeat, the girls are sufficiently comely and hence proficiently tackle our libidos, it is of no importance whether other attributes, except possibly the ability to dance a few elementary steps and sing a few notes not too far off key, are or are not within their equipment.

In the present voluptuous show there are no less than forty-two of the distractions, a sufficient proportion of them surprisingly comfortable on the vision and, as if that were not enough to carbonate my quoted acquaintance, there is also Bobby Clark to ogle them with a cannibal relish and vicariously to cuddle them. About this Bobby's art little remains after all these happy years to be said. That, diminutive as he is, he stands head and shoulders above most of his competitors has for some time now been clear. Though he may repeat himself show in and show out, though his capers with cane, cigar butt and painted-on spectacles do not much vary, and though his lascivious leer and goatish hop and skip are just as lascivious and just as goatish as they were three decades ago, no matter. He is as ageless as the slapstick itself and, like it, the seemingly inexhaustible font of low and gaudy humor.

One look at Bobby and the smell of rosemary permeates every nook and cranny of the house. In recollection's eye one again is a youngster playing hookey at all the old burlesque shows there ever were. There, in Bobby's shadow, are the beloved August Beerheister and Heinie Hopslinger, the former in pants capacious enough to house Jumbo and with head adorned by a miniature pancake hat; the latter, to the dismay of genealogical purists, in a Hibernian makeup. There, on the stage with Bobby, are Mrs. Vanderastor of Hoboken, "a society queen," with her imperious command to the waiter to fetch her a bottle of "Moe and Chandin brute," along with Count de Nosewiper, a howling swell in azure "full dress evening swallowtails" who rescues Mrs. Vanderastor from the lubricious attentions of the Messrs. Beerheister and Hopslinger, elegantly requests the privilege of paying for the champagne wine, and replenishes his empty pockets by reaching under the table and appropriating Mrs. Vanderastor's diamond garter. There, too, are the comedians of hobo aspect, Prince Oswald and Dudley Dustswinger, both in breeches of untold width sustained by a single rope suspender, and both in hardly immaculate undershirts. Prince Oswald is bedecked with a frowzy stovepipe hat, Mr. Dustswinger with a rococo felt number garnished with holes. Prince Oswald, the taller of the twain, takes out a banjo, seats himself, and crosses his long legs high above his ears. Mr. Dustswinger, fiddle to chin, stands beside his chair. The lights are lowered and they proceed to render the venerable sob-siphon from *Cavalleria Rusticana*, Mr. Dustswinger drawing out to its full every soulful note and employing the return trip of the bow to push the stovepipe hat off his fellow-maestro's head.

It subsequently develops that Prince Oswald is possessed of a consuming thirst and a craving for alcoholic liquor. But he has only two cents. "Hello, Sam," he says to the bartender — the scene is "the Palace Mansion of the Count de Nosewiper in Camembert, France" — "I'll betcha two cents I kin drink a glassa whiskey quickern you kin." The wager is laid. Prince Oswald pours himself a huge beaker and the great contest is on. The bartender, his name is Mick E. Finn, tosses off his small glass at a gulp. Prince Oswald continues drinking slowly until the last drop is gone. "You lose!" cries the bartender. "Well, kin youse beat that!" exclaims the Prince, imparting a large wink to the audience.

Enters now Comrade Dustswinger with a jug. "Fill this up," he bids the bartender. The latter fills the jug. Dustswinger starts to make off without paying. "Here you, gimme back that jug if you ain't goin' to pay," commands the bartender, taking the jug rudely from Mr. Dustswinger and emptying it of its contents. "But kin I have the jug back?" questions Mr. Dustswinger humbly. The bartender gruffly thrusts it into Mr. Dustswinger's hands. Whereupon our friend, with a ludicrous nudge at the audience, takes out a hammer, breaks open the jug, extracts a sponge, and treats himself to a fine tipple.

It is now again Prince Oswald's moment and, coming confidentially down to the footlight trough, he whispers to the audience how he used to love his beautiful schoolteacher, how he brought her a little peach as a present one day, how she took him on her lap and thanked him, how he next brought her a big apple and how she took him on her lap and this time not only thanked him but kissed him — and how he began saving up to buy her a watermelon.

It is all there again behind and around Bobby: the *grande dame* who suggests her lofty social status in a wholesale and not entirely discriminate use of "whoms" and who lorgnettes the presuming comedian into a humiliated silence by proclaiming that he is "beneath content"; the comic who smears shaving lather over another's face, neck and ears, pokes some of it for good measure into his eyes, and then licks it all off; the wag who in making his lordly adieux trips over the mat and lands on his bumper; the judge who uses his gavel as a drumstick and, when summoning the court to order, raps out a rat-a-tat-rat-a-tat on the bench and in his ardor falling off it; and all the kid-wonderful rest. Bobby, in short, is our foremost catalytic agent in the matter of youth and age. Bobby, in shorter short, is tops.

So what if the rest of *As The Girls Go,* which deals with the peccadilloes of the husband of the first woman President of the United States, is not so yummy? We can't have everything in this world and Bobby and forty-two girls are at least a lot more than we usually get, even if some of us are not as titillated by the titillation of the latter's often extreme décolletage as Mr. Todd evidently prays we will be.

FOR HEAVEN'S SAKE, MOTHER!
NOVEMBER 16, 1948

A comedy by Julie Berns. Produced by David Kay for 7 performances in the Belasco Theatre.

PROGRAM

HENRY WHEELER	*St. Clair Bayfield*	DEEDEE WARREN	*Peggy Romano*
BOB LAWRENCE	*Alfred Garr*	SUSAN BERESFORD	*Marian Russell*
DICK LAWRENCE	*Robert White*	EMILY BLAND	*Jean Pugsley*
LUCINDA LAWRENCE	*Nancy Carroll*	MILTON RUBIN	*Richy Shawn*
EDWARD LAWRENCE		JOE KENEAGHAN	*Ted Plummer*
	Herschel Bentley	MRS. RUBIN	*Molly Picon*
LAVINIA	*Jacqueline Andre*	SARA LOUISE	*Margaret Draper*
JACK WARREN	*Stiano Braggiotti*		

SYNOPSIS: Act I. Scene 1. *Late August. Noon.* Scene 2. *November, three months later.* Scene 3. *Christmas Eve. Late afternoon.* Act II. Scene 1. *Three days later. Afternoon.* Scene 2. *The following September. Morning.*

Time: *The present.*
Place: *The Larchmont home of the Edward Lawrences.*
Director: *Julie Berns.*

THOUGH IT HAS BEEN bruited of my memory that it is so retentive that elephants themselves have been known from time to time to consult me, I can not recall just how many plays I have seen in which the principal woman character, eager to preserve an appearance of youth, is beset by the problem not only of her rapidly growing up children but of the marriage of one of them and the appalling imminence of a grandchild. It must, however, have been at least two dozen or more. Now comes this still another and I can say one thing with certainty and that is that my memory is nevertheless good enough confidently to report that it is by far the worst of the lot. Since this, along with the statement that the acting and direction are as wretched as the play, is all that I shall write about the occasion, and since the theatre in which it is housed has recently been acquired by the Messrs. Shubert, it may be meet to consider a lengthy protest which Mr. J. J. Shubert, on behalf of his firm, lately dispatched to the publishers of the New York newspapers. I quote from it verbatim in essential part:

"As owners and lessees of the majority of the legitimate theatres in New York, we wish to place before you a request for relief from an intolerable situation which has grown up steadily over the years and which might easily spell financial disaster for the legitimate theatre in New York. This season in particular, we are threatened with adverse conditions still more unfavorable than those which have prevailed in the recent past. Back of this unfortunate situation is the lack of attractions to fill even the few legitimate theatres still left in this city. There are very few productions to replace those that have failed. The condition of which we complain makes it very difficult for producers to get further money to make new shows. Just within the last month there have been nine new productions, all forced to close immediately owing to the adverse criticism in the newspapers. This situation can only be remedied by the publishers of the New York dailies. As the owner of an important newspaper, you have it in your power to help the legitimate theatre business.

"Our dilemma is the ever growing power which has been assumed by the drama reviewers, *who now have in their hands the very life of our business.* It is doubtful that you intended to confer such power on so small a group of men. This is not a protest against any particular critic; it is a protest against a practice which has grown to a condition fast destroying our business, to say nothing of forcing the entire legitimate theatre in New York to dwindle in importance.

"When a play is condemned outright, after an opening performance, the public's reaction is not to attend. The theatre becomes dark and remains so for weeks or months until we get some other production. Before a new play can be furnished to replace the closed one, there is almost invariably a long period of delay pending preparation and a long period of unemployment for those who depend on the theatre for a livelihood.

"The theatre is the only private enterprise selected for this kind of treatment by the press. We are not a public utility. We are not 'touchy' about legitimate criticism. We realize the majority of plays are not and cannot be outstanding hits. But the average show should not be condemned entirely. It must have some merit or else it wouldn't have been produced. If the critics persist in condemning plays, producers will be unable to get financial assistance. The critic tries to make himself important by wisecrack headlines. When he reviews a play he does not say what is good and what is bad. It was always our impression that it was a critic's duty to say something descriptive of the contents of a play. I do not think you gentlemen who control our destinies are truly cognizant of the present state of affairs. There was a time when critics did criticize fairly, but this does not prevail any more.

"We are in a lawful business. You accept our advertising, as you would that of any other lawful business, and the mere fact that you accept our advertising is proof that you consider us legitimate and first-class. You do not attack the product of any other advertiser. Only the entertainment field is singled out for this type of treatment.

"The methods that have been used by the critics, particularly in the past twenty years, have done more to destroy the legitimate theatre than any other factor. I think it is appropriate for the publisher to recognize this condition that exists as a matter of fair practice of one business man to another.

"The substantial investment which goes into each theatre is always at stake, because you have delegated to your critic the power to use your newspaper as an instrument of destruction whenever his whim leads him to that direction. The practice of true journalism does not call for vesting so great a power in one man's hands, particularly when he pits his own opinion against that of the audience. So frequently the entire audience enthusiastically receives a play opening night, and the producer has every reason to believe that he has satisfied the public, only to find that the critic stands out alone and disagrees. This is due to the practice of permitting and encouraging the critic to voice his own personal preference and give way to his own particular whim concerning a performance. He ignores the ovation that many plays receive from the audience and sacrifices everything in favor of an opportunity to give vent to some wisecrack or quip against some particular feature of the play. Not infrequently the critic leaves the theatre long before the final closing, presumably to meet a deadline. He cannot judge an entire play if he only witnesses a part. Perhaps if he remained and observed the acclaim and plaudits of the audience so many plays receive, it would temper his own usually hostile judgment and lead him to add to his report the reception and response of the paying customers. In the final analysis it is for the general public, and not the critics, for whom plays are produced. However, the customary review is written from the personal viewpoint of the critic who completely loses sight of the fact the show might still have a great appeal to the average playgoer. That is the type of criticism which we cannot combat.

"You should therefore be able to recognize that we cannot remain in business where millions of dollars are at stake if the type of dramatic criticism is to continue which whittles away hundreds of thousands of dollars of investment with the publishing of each adverse criticism."

Though the force of Mr. Shubert's protest, as of his concern over the unbearable losses suffered by his firm due to the kind of criticism he objects to, was somewhat weakened by the published news a few days later that he and his company had purchased four theatres for a sum in excess of three million dollars, his arguments nevertheless bear looking into. With some of them, any fair-minded person must sympathize. It is true, for example, that generally condemnatory newspaper reviews often spell the doom of a newly produced play, with consequent loss of the considerable amount of money invested in it. A loss to

the owner of the theatre in which it has been booked also
results. This is naturally and properly deplored by any
good business man. It is also true that the public often
follows the reviews, sometimes foolishly, since they are at
times badly at fault and unjust. It is further true that there
are times when new productions to fill the void left by the
failures are lacking and that the consequence is temporarily vacant theatres. And it is true that empty theatres are
undesirable. So far, there is much to be said for Mr. Shubert's contention.

There are, as well, additional sound arguments which he
might have brought forth had he thought of them, but
these can not under the direct circumstances concern us.
Many of the arguments he has brought forth on the other
hand are poor ones, and these do concern us, these and several errors in fact.

That the reviewers possess the over-all power which Mr.
Shubert contends is nonsense. If they did, the condemnation by most of them of a play like *Summer And Smoke*
would have caused its prompt withdrawal, yet it played for
more than three months thereafter, which certainly indicates a public sufficiently independent of the reviewers'
opinions. *The Respectful Prostitute* was a success in the
face of a majority of adverse reviews; and so was *Love Life;*
and so was *Where's Charley?;* and so was *The Madwoman
Of Chaillot;* and so to a degree, despite a number of unfavorable notices, was *Small Wonder.* Last season *The Telephone* and *The Medium, Allegro, For Love Or Money,
Strange Bedfellows, Me And Molly,* and some others managed very well without the reviewers' general favor. And it
has been the same in other recent seasons. All the enthusiastic reviews of *Ballet Ballads* and *The Traitor* could not
contrarily bring them prosperity.

"The theatre is the only private enterprise selected for
this kind of treatment by the press," says Mr. Shubert.
What of book publishers and the newspaper literary critics? What of the motion pictures, radio and television and
the newspaper commentators on them? What of baseball,
prize-fighting, and other organized sports?

"The average show should not be condemned entirely.
It must have some merit or else it wouldn't have been produced," continues Mr. Shubert. The average show in this
season has not had some merit and its production clearly
indicates that the person or persons responsible for it were
at least on this occasion completely mistaken. Would Mr.
Shubert seriously contend that such duds as *The Vigil,
Jenny Kissed Me, Seeds In The Wind, The Shop At Sly
Corner, Sleepy Hollow, Leaf And Bough, Hilarities, All
For Love, Heaven On Earth, A Story For Strangers, Grandma's Diary, Anybody Home, Time For Elizabeth,* or *For
Heaven's Sake, Mother!,* for example, had such merit, even
though one or two of the reviewers in all save two cases
seemed generously inclined to detect it? Mr. Shubert is
surely too experienced in the theatre, even as a business
man, honestly to believe any such bosh. How, furthermore,
can a critic say what is good and bad in a play when there
is nothing good to speak about? As to the "critic's duty to
say something descriptive of the contents of a play," Mr.
Shubert is right. But what daily newspaper critic does not
usually say it? What daily newspaper critic, further, does
not usually say it at such length that one sometimes gets the
impression he is thereby simply and desperately filling up
space for want of something else about the play to occupy
him? The recording of plots has indeed been carried to
such extremes that much reviewing has been a trial to the
reader. And as for the critic's effort "to make himself important by wisecrack headlines," when has a critic ever
gained importance through recourse to vaudeville jokes?
However, even granting the wisecracks — a term currently
used miscellaneously to describe everything from a remark
by Wilde or Shaw to one by Joe E. Lewis or Milton Berle
— what is the objection to brightening a review of a dull
play by any means whatever? The dull play deserves no respect and the critic who would treat it seriously would be
an ass.

"There was a time," proceeds Mr. Shubert, "when critics did criticize fairly, but this does not prevail any more."
Though Mr. Shubert in an interview published in one of

the Washington newspapers not long ago paid me the compliment of excepting me from the general run of reviewers and accordingly calls for my admiration, he should be reminded that, in the time he speaks of, his firm barred from its theatres no less than four or five of the fair critics to whom he alludes. (I did not consider at least two of them to be fair, but he apparently does.)

"You accept our advertising . . . [but] you do not attack the product of any other advertisers." As I have asked before, doesn't Mr. Shubert read the reviews of books and moving pictures, much more heavily advertised than plays?

Mr. Shubert refers to the newspapers as powerful instruments of destruction. Has he not meditated that eighty-four per cent of them could not defeat Roosevelt, seventy-two per cent could not defeat Truman, ninety-six per cent could not kill the gigantic sales of *Forever Amber*, and ninety-seven per cent could not keep the public from *Abie's Irish Rose* and *Tobacco Road*?

The audience's enthusiastic reception of a play on the opening night, as Mr. Shubert perfectly well knows, often means absolutely nothing. Such receptions are a regular occurrence, and are arbitrary and mechanical. Not one play or show in thirty fails to find its audience, composed largely of friends of the actors, playwright, costumer, scene designer and management, politely vociferous in approval. The critic who would be fooled by any such bogus response, presuming he were willing to be fooled, would be an ass even greater than the one who would treat a dull play or show with affected respect. As for the critic's leaving an obviously impossible play or show before it is over, I refer the reader to the paragraphs on *Grandma's Diary* in a preceding chapter.

The notion, furthermore, that the critic is "usually hostile" is absurd. The average critic does not go to the theatre determined to be disappointed; he goes always in the fond hope that he may have a good time. If he didn't, he would quickly tire of his job and look elsewhere for a livelihood. For this you have my solemn word as one of the breed, and after forty-three years in hopeful practice.

"The customary review," says Mr. Shubert, "is written from the personal viewpoint of the critic who completely loses sight of the fact the show might still have a great appeal to the average playgoer." How, we may ask Mr. Shubert, can the critic possibly divine if a show might have a great appeal to the average playgoer? If producers can not be sure of that appeal, and the records sufficiently prove that they can not, how expect a critic to exceed them in the art of soothsaying? The only fair procedure for any reviewer is to express his personal viewpoint and let things rest there. If he were able to tell that a play or show, despite his personal opinion of it, would nevertheless in all probability enchant the public he would be a phenomenon and worth at least five hundred thousand dollars a year to any producer in an advisory capacity. Can Mr. Shubert foresee the great public appeal of a show? If he can, his estimable brother Lee should take him to task for the periodic failures he has produced.

Finally, Mr. Shubert's idea that "hundreds of thousands of dollars of investment are whittled away with the publishing of each adverse criticism" would mean that, if one of the daily reviewers lambasted a play which all the others lavishly praised, the single adverse review would bring about a loss of the great sum of money he mentions, an idea that every record in existence blows up as folly. Few of the productions that have made fortunes have ever been unanimously endorsed by the reviewers; there has usually been some minority opinion to the contrary.

Mr. Shubert's complaint, as I observed at the beginning, is understandable from his point of view, which is the making of profits, and I certainly am not criticizing him for it. If I were in his shoes, I should think and feel about things much the way he does. But, though I am not a daily newspaper reviewer and therefore not within the scope of his protest, I also do not happen to be in his shoes. The shoes I am in are those of one who views the theatre as something a little higher and better and more important than a mere mart of trade and, while the view true enough does not cost me, as it sometimes costs him, money, I neverthe-

less somehow can not see the virtue of demanding that reviewers, dumb as they occasionally doubtless are, be forced
into equivoque and dishonesty in their effort, sometimes
grantedly blind, to provide that theatre with some artistic
standing and glory.

GOODBYE, MY FANCY. November 17, 1948

A play by Fay Kanin. Produced by Michael Kanin in association with Richard Aldrich and Richard Myers for the rest of the season's performances in, initially, the Morosco Theatre.

Program

Ginny Merrill	*Bethel Leslie*	Agatha Reed	*Madeleine Carroll*
Amelia	*Sally Hester*	Ellen Griswold	
Clarisse	*Gerrianne Raphael*		*Lulu Mae Hubbard*
Mary Nell	*Mary Malone*	Prof. Birdeshaw	*Lillian Foster*
Miss Shackleford		Carol	*Betty Lou Holland*
	Eda Heinemann	Jo	*Lenore Garland*
Janitors {	*Andrew George*	Dr. Pitt	*George Mitchell*
	John Ware	James Merrill	*Conrad Nagel*
Telephone Man	*Tom Donovan*	Prof. Dingley	*Ralph Bunker*
Susan	*Patty Pope*	Matt Cole	*Sam Wanamaker*
Grace Woods	*Shirley Booth*	Claude Griswold	*Joseph Boland*

SYNOPSIS: Act I. *Friday morning.* Act II. Scene 1. *Saturday afternoon.* Scene 2. *Saturday evening.* Act III. *Sunday afternoon.*

Scene: *The entire action of the play takes place over Commencement weekend in early June, 1948, in a dormitory of Good Hope College for Women in Good Hope, Mass.*

Director: *Sam Wanamaker.*

ONE IS TO BE FORGIVEN for approaching with some skepticism a play by a Hollywood scenario writer starring a Hollywood moving picture actress, and it was in such an agnostic mood that I went to the Morosco Theatre. Though the play did not succeed in abashing my advance qualms, the screen actress, Madeleine Carroll, spanked them where it hurt most, since her performance was not only a thoroughly proficient but an uncommonly charming one. She has an admirable stage presence, authoritative without the least suggestion of the spurious self-assurance of various other film actresses who have condescendingly lent their art to the drama; she has an easy and pleasant speaking voice; she indicates little trace of that constriction of physical

movement imposed upon a player by the camera; and, if
anyone is interested in such matters, she is extremely good-
looking in a normal and non-Hollywood way.

The play, which tells the story of a Congresswoman who
returns to her old college and an old love affair only to be
disappointed in both, has its points of facile entertainment,
but it is full of the dishonest devices that make for good
theatre at the expense of sound drama, good theatre being
defined as a shrewd mixture of sentiment and gags embroidered with the semblance of a serious theme. The
theme in this case is the alleged corruption of our institutions of learning by the subservience of what should be
their guiding spirits to the realistically business-minded
boards of trustees. Without going into its merits or demer-
its, one may none the less question the skill with which the
playwright administers her medicine. Her dramatic pivot
in support of her viewpoint is the refusal of the president
of the college to show to the senior girl students a documentary film on the horrors of war, his reason being that it
might disturb the equanimity of those trustees who are to
be counted on to supply the college with the financial
means necessary to function and who happen to be in war
industries of one kind or another. So far, possibly so good.
But while she magnanimously permits the president to observe that you can not keep a college going unless the
money is obtained to keep it going, she somehow does not
permit him to observe that there isn't much sense in arguing corruption of either himself or his college in terms of
depriving the aforesaid young girls — all with but one exception pictured as dreadful imbeciles — of any such film
and contending that, were they allowed to see it, the nin-
compoops would be impressed to the point of concerning
themselves profoundly with the exorcism of all wars.

It is permissible, of course, for the drama to employ a
relatively trivial springboard from which to jump into the
depths of a theme — it has been done, and ably, by superior playwrights — but if and when such a springboard is
used its springs must be a little more substantial, surely,
than those which the present playwright has supplied it.

The weakness not only of those springs but of her play's attempt to be more than it really is becomes additionally perceptible in her heroine's rejection of the president's suit even when finally and independently he decides to risk his position by abandoning compromise and showing the film — greater men than he have sometimes hesitated in what for them have been critical situations — and in her acceptance instead of the suit of a more immaculate liberal brain in the person of a *Life* photographer with whom she had had an affair while serving abroad as a war correspondent. As to her personal choice of lovers I have no critical privilege of objection, but, when I am asked enthusiastically to sympathize with the selection on the score of the lady's argued great cultural, philosophical and other cerebral gifts, I may be excused for responding to Miss Kanin's play with an even more substantial laugh than she generates with her more deliberate gags, some of them funny enough. Such, for example, as the remark of one of her characters that *"Life* photographers are never happier than when they catch you picking your nose."

The average casual theatregoer, however, will not be too conscious of Miss Kanin's mental incongruities, since, as has been noted, she has coated them with enough glib showmanship to make them digestible as an evening's entertainment. Though her words on reactionaries and academic freedom may not persuade the few, her inserted wheezes will cajole the many. Though her arguments may seem to the minority to be disingenuous, the placing of them in the pretty mouth of a very personable young woman makes them not only acceptable but even intellectually remarkable to the majority of theatregoers, among whom I had momentary difficulty under the distracting circumstances in not numbering myself. When she solemnly presents as fresh and revolutionary such platitude (I quote her press-agent spokesman) as "Without personal honesty and a willingness to stand up and fight for what we believe in as well as a willingness to face the hard facts of the world we live in, we are lost both as individuals and as a race" — when she has at us with such copy-book truism, some of us may wince but many more will doubtless receive it as something of a revelation. It is fortunate for her Hollywood self-esteem that more people still go to the theatre with their brains, if any, in their funny-bones than go with them where Nature hopefully imagined it had placed them. Her play thus best succeeds when she does not exercise her cogitative talents but her humorous, which have some relative authenticity.

In addition to Miss Carroll's, there are creditable performances by Shirley Booth in the standard role of the Congresswoman's cynical secretary, Bethel Leslie as the only senior in the college visibly not a moron, and Lillian Foster as a sex hygiene professor miserably recovering from her first flirtation with schnapps. Wanamaker's direction is alternately good and bad. He paces the exposition with such arbitrary and immoderate speed that the girl students seem to be members of a George Abbott college musical comedy chorus and too obviously looks to his own audience effect as the *Life* photographer love interest by utilizing the old William Gillette trick of having the other actors hustle and bustle about the while he pursues his personal performance with a disdainful coolness and patrician calm. Much of his handling of the stage when he himself is not on it is satisfactory and his direction of Miss Carroll especially congenial.

LIGHT UP THE SKY. NOVEMBER 18, 1948

A comedy by Moss Hart. Produced by Joseph M. Hyman and Bernard Hart for the rest of the season's performances in the Royale Theatre.

PROGRAM

MISS LOWELL	Jane Middleton	SVEN	S. Oakland
CARLETON FITZGERALD		IRENE LIVINGSTON	Virginia Field
	Glenn Anders	TYLER RAYBURN	Bartlett Robinson
FRANCES BLACK	Audrey Christie	A SHRINER	John D. Seymour
OWEN TURNER	Philip Ober	WILLIAM H. GALLEGHER	
STELLA LIVINGSTON	Phyllis Povah		Donald McClelland
PETER SLOAN	Barry Nelson	A PLAINCLOTHES MAN	
SIDNEY BLACK	Sam Levene		Ronald Alexander

SYNOPSIS: *Act I. The living room of Irene Livingston's Ritz-Carlton Hotel suite at Boston, Mass. Time: 5:30 p.m. Act II. The same. Time: 12:30 a.m. Act III. The same. Time: 3:30 a.m.*

Director: *Moss Hart.*

IF A REVIEWER were to write of Mr. Hart as in even this road-revised and toned-down play he has written of a number of painly recognizable New York theatre people, that worthy, judging by his past performances, would so seethe with indignation that you could boil a fifty-pound salmon on him. I speak from intimate personal acquaintance with his ire, which has erupted with such gusto on the one or two occasions when I have timidly ventured to reflect on the magnitude of his genius that one would have thought I had defied Jehovah Himself. Yet what I wrote of him was the purest Rouennaise sauce compared with what he sees fit to remark about his well-known and, despite his cagey disclaimers, scarcely disguised characters, some of whom, report has it, even figure among his buddies.

As a playwright, Mr. Hart of course has a perfect right to do what he has done. Playwrights have been doing much the same thing ever since Aristophanes more than twenty-three centuries ago in *The Frogs* did to Euripides and others what shouldn't happen to a dog. Nor is the questionable taste which he displays properly a consideration of criticism, since questionable taste has also been displayed in similar directions by such creditable dramatists as Wycherley and Sheridan, among various others. Yet further, the thinness of disguise practised by him is no more criticizable, since it is not any thinner than that of Shaw in his ridicule of his fellow-critics in *Fanny's First Play*. The difference, however, is the difference between the banana peel and the broken leg. Where the eminent others made us laugh at their characters' slips and prattfalls, Hart — as did Leo Trevor in *Dr. Johnson* — bids us laugh at his characters' fractured limbs. And the worst of it — human nature being as despicable as it is — is that we do.

Our apology in such a situation is that, since he does not really call his characters by name, we can get away with our amusement and still preserve the punctilio. But we are charlatans. Lew Fields used to explain that the reason people laughed so heartily when he poked his finger into Joe Weber's eye was that they knew it did not in the least actually hurt him. When Hart sticks his finger into one of his victims' eyes the eye is injured and drips blood, yet, like jitney Neros, we nevertheless every now and then bounderishly chuckle. It is something of a commentary on both Hart and us, and also very probably on changed times and changed morals. But down at bottom, pain or no pain, it is the nasty quirk in all our natures that impels us willynilly to find amusement in others' discomfiture, even indeed when those others are our friends. Lamentable as it may be, let a friend sit on and wreck his hat, or rip his breeches, or tumble on his rear, or have a waiter spill hot soup on him, or step on a pasture muffin, or be besmirched by a dog, and our mirth knows small bounds. Similarly, so odious are we, that let a crony get the barber's itch, or swell from poison ivy, or deposit his corpus on a tack, or be sprayed by a polecat, and one would think the show was provided by Bobby Clark. And it is much the same if our friend at his age contracts mumps or the measles, loses his

money on bogus gold-mine stocks, is vouchsafed a Mickey
Finn, or is caught *in flagrante delicto* with a lady of color.
There is apparently nothing that can be done about it. We
are lice.

To give him his due, Hart doubtless appreciates all this
just as well as we ourselves do and I, for one, though I do
not commend him for doing what he has done, on the
other hand can not without hypocrisy condemn him for doing it. So I stick to business and fairly report that his play
has some very funny stuff in it along with its forced and
spurious, and that I guffawed at much of it like any other
cad.

What the exhibit in essence amounts to is a comic valentine of the show business and, like a comic valentine, it is
crude and pretty vulgar. Its thread of story is simply a variant of the many plays in which a fraternal group of people
turn acrimonious under catastrophe of one kind or another
and, when the sun again shines, return to cheer and good-
will. Hart's former collaborator, George Kaufman, wrote a
basically not altogether dissimilar and better play all of
twenty-three years ago in *The Butter And Egg Man,* to
which at several points this later specimen bears a resemblance. But, as I have said, the current paraphrase has some
high and saucy sport in it, and most of the performances,
notably those of Phyllis Povah as the stage mother, Audrey
Christie as the brassy wife of the producer, Glenn Anders
as the epicene director, Virginia Field as the temperamental star, and Barry Nelson as the idealistic novice playwright, are all they should be.

The underlying weakness of the play is its author's inability to reinforce his often malicious comment on his
characters with the wit that might shade malice into sharp
critical appraisal. His humor, furthermore, is uneven and
teeters between some genuinely hilarious barbs and such
lines as "She'll develop a cough that'll make Camille's
sound like hay fever." And his characters range from the
freshly observed and freshly drawn to, however factually
portrayed, the long familiar and stencilled star actress with

her tantrums and miscellaneous use of "darling," her dumb, stuffy businessman husband, and the elderly playwright who has gone through the mill and lounges about the stage with an inner smile at the other characters' perturbations.

THE YOUNG AND FAIR. November 22, 1948

A play by N. Richard Nash. Produced by Vinton Freedley in association with Richard Krakeur for 40 performances in, initially, the Fulton Theatre.

PROGRAM

EMMY FOSTER	*Frieda Altman*	MARY LOUISE	*Patricia Bouchard*
FRANCES MORRITT		SYLVIA	*Peggy O'Connor*
	Mercedes McCambridge	SALLY	*Ann Sorg*
PATTY MORRITT	*Patricia Kirkland*	HELEN	*Vicki Carlson*
SARA CANTRY	*Frances Starr*	GLORIA	*Rita Gam*
LAURA CANTRY	*Betty Morrissey*	SUE	*Ann Murphy*
LEE BARRON	*Lois Wheeler*	MATHILDA	*Elaine Bradford*
SELMA KEENEY	*Lenka Peterson*	BOOTS McGREGOR	*Sally Moffet*
NANCY GEAR	*Julie Harris*	GEORGETTA	*Mary Lou Phelan*
MIL CHEAVER	*Frances Freeman*	PAULINE	*Lee Truhill*
DRUCILLA ELDRIDGE	*Doe Avedon*	CAROL	*Bette Stanley*

SYNOPSIS: Act I. Scene 1. *Miss Cantry's office in Fairchild Hall. An afternoon in late September.* Scene 2. *A bedroom in Fairchild Hall. Immediately following.* Scene 3. *The lounge in Fairchild Hall. Friday afternoon, a week later.* Act II. Scene 1. *The office. The following afternoon.* Scene 2. *The bedroom. Immediately after.* Scene 3. *The office. Later, the same afternoon.* Act III. Scene 1. *The bedroom. An hour later.* Scene 2. *The office. A half hour later.*

The action of the play takes place in the Brook Valley Academy, a girls' Junior College not far from Boston.

Time: *The present.*

Director: *Harold Clurman.*

IF THERE is a really good reason why plays with only women in the cast should not be entirely satisfactory, I confess that I do not know what it is; but that they are not, even when some other things about them may be, seems to be the fact. Plays composed solely of men have managed, despite the absence of representatives of the fair sex, to be fully acceptable, yet let one forego the presence of any trousers and there is always something about it that seems to be lacking. As I say, I can not figure out just why. I ap-

preciate that this is an admission scarcely calculated to preserve any colossal esteem for a critic, since apparently the
only way such a rooster may guarantee veneration for himself is to conceal his ignorance in whatever direction by
slyly camouflaging it with superficially plausible paradox
or distracting wit, neither of which fools his self-respect for
a moment. If there is one thing I do not like, it is to fool
myself — though there have been, I fear, occasions — so I
shall not resort here to any such bourgeois imposture, let
my repute in the community suffer as it will. I shall simply
throw myself on the mercy of the court and make a few
wild guesses.

The essence of drama, as every school-boy knows, is conflict. That there may not be conflict between women as
well as men, certainly nobody is going to deny. That there
may not also be emotion, a second necessity of drama, in
conflict between the darlings will likewise hardly be disputed. But that conflict and emotion which are sexless miss
a lot of dramatic vitality is pretty difficult to disprove. In
plays that deal only with men, such sex conflict is not in-
dispensable, since men's problems may be independent of
women and yet important and interesting enough to constitute lively drama. But most of the problems of women
can not be wholly divorced from the male sex and still provide exciting dramatic material. A stage occupied only by
females, let them talk about men all they will and even
show the consequences of having dealt with the low creatures, somehow always stubbornly suggests an only half-
written and incomplete play.

Anita Loos once remarked that there is nothing much
duller than two women alone in the same room — unless
one of them is sufficiently witty. Obviously agreeing, Clare
Boothe, when she wrote the manless *The Women*, safeguarded the box-office by concocting a play in which she
looked at women through bitterly cynical eyes, stripped
them of all femininity, presented them as so many hardboiled longshoremen in skirts, and criticized them with a
ferocious irony. That the road is rocky for any play dealing
entirely with more normal girls was demonstrated by the

fact that the one and only more normal one she introduced into her caveat was the single character the critics voted unconvincing and that the majority of theatregoers sneezed at.

You will argue, naturally, that all this is simply a man's point of view, but you will, I think, be mistaken. Women seem to have found other pantsless plays quite as disappointing as men have, and such as *Nine To Five, Nine Girls, Girls In Uniform*, etc., have failed not merely because they were poor, since plays just as poor, God knows, have prospered, but rather and undoubtedly because they were not — or at least did not seem to be — plays.

The latest of the all-petticoat experiments is this *The Young And Fair.* What the author has tried to do is sensationally to knit the story of the dilemmas and compromises of a girls' junior college in Massachusetts into a dramatic sock, but his knitting is so tangled, stitch-dropped and so often self-interrupted that all that develops is the little toe. Moreover, his pack of females are so intensely and melodramatically confused not only in themselves but in the dramaturgy that it is doubtful whether his particular all-women problems could have been any more convincingly resolved even had he introduced the whole Harvard male faculty abetted by the football team.

The play, which comes to life only for a short time in its third act, is a crazy-quilt that reminds one of the old Amelia Bingham vaudeville act called, with no respect for the adjectives, *Great Moments From Great Plays.* There is, in paraphrase, the moment from *The Children's Hour* in which the malevolent girl impugns the honor of one of the teachers and, in this instance, her sister. There is the echo of the moment in *Loyalties* in which a character's Jewish blood is held over him as a social threat. There is another from *Bright Boy* about the dictator-minded student and the student wrongly accused by him of theft. There is still another paraphrased from *The Druid Circle* in which the honor of the college is at stake and in which the professor is brought by his realization of his position to resign. There is yet again the moment from the recent *Goodbye, My Fancy* in which the forces of compromise and honesty are brought face to face. And so on. All these are tossed haphazardly into a stew further peppered with melodramatic condiments relating to Fascism, appeasement, anti-Semitism, psychiatry, kleptomania, etc., and are boiled at such length that the taste disappears. That the author is intensely sincere in his indignations is plain, but too much sincerity in such cases is as bad for drama as too little. Passion for the honorable and just is a noble thing, but Mr. Nash's is so excessive that it blinds him to the dramatic purpose he has in hand.

Clurman's direction is successful in keeping the three-level stage in motion, but less successful in controlling the play's melodrama within plausible limits, a fault often noticeable in directors who served their apprenticeship with the old Group Theatre. The better performances are those of Frances Starr, Lois Wheeler, Doe Avedon, and Julie Harris, though the audience's enthusiastic response to the last named's portrayal of hysteria brought one to reflect on the acclaim always accorded any actress who is provided with a scene in which she may display the symptoms of hydrophobia crossed with those of epilepsy and orchestrated for percussive shrieks and screeches.

THE SILVER WHISTLE. November 24, 1948

A play by Robert E. McEnroe. Produced by the Theatre Guild for the rest of the season's performances in the Biltmore Theatre.

Program

Mr. Beebe	*William Lynn*	Oliver Erwenter	*José Ferrer*
Mrs. Hanmer	*Doro Merande*	Emmett	*George Mathews*
Miss Hoadley	*Frances Brandt*	Father Shay	*Charles Hart*
Miss Tripp	*Eleanor Wilson*	Mr. Beach	*Edward Platt*
Reverend Watson	*Robert Carroll*	Mr. Reddy	*Charles Kuhn*
Mrs. Sampler	*Kathleen Comegys*	Policeman	*Chase Soltez*
Mrs. Gross	*Jane Marbury*	Bishop	*Franklin Fox*
Mr. Cherry	*Burton Mallory*		

SYNOPSIS: *The entire action of the play takes place in the garden of a church adjoining an Old People's Home. Act I. Scene 1. Afternoon. Scene 2. Evening of the same day. Act II. Evening of the next day. Act III. Morning of the following day.*

Director: *Paul Crabtree.*

I AM NOW TOO ELDERLY and too far gone in an admiration for the unspeakably unromantic physical comforts of life to perform the job with the proper sympathy, but I recommend to some younger and more soulful man the composition of a treatise on the genus hobo, particularly as it has figured on the American stage. It should prove to be a piquant tome, and in return for the author's blood, sweat and tears I shall be hospitable to the receipt of a free, suitably inscribed copy, and maybe even to a perusal of it. The volume should constitute at least one picture of audiences' tastes since the early 1880's, as well as a picture of an odd facet of our theatre during that period.

The idea infected me while looking at Mr. McEnroe's conception of the tramp, a species of human which has been almost as great a favorite on our stage as its counterpart, the tzigany or gypsy, has been on the Central European.

The tramp from almost his very beginnings as a stage character has obediently subscribed to two articles in the American credo: first, that he is always more blithesome, however gloomy the circumstances, than any Astor or Rockefeller, particularly if he hasn't had anything to eat for a week; and, secondly, that combined with his buoyancy is a philosophical outlook not materially less profound than that of Hegel or Kant. The only slight departure from the second article is when he figures in musical comedy or burlesque, at which times his philosophical attributes less resemble those of the aforesaid metaphysicians than those of Bertrand Russell and Dr. Alfred Kinsey. McEnroe's hobo combines not only the two articles but the slight departure, and adds to them for extra measure a capacity for quoting verse that would be envied by Bartlett.

The first stage tramp I ever saw — I was a tot at the time — enjoyed not quite so expansive an equipment, though he did possess the demanded *joie de vivre* and at least a measure of the Kinsey attitude toward the ladies. His impersonator was Walter Jones; the show was the extravaganza *1492;* and it was this same Jones who a few years earlier in *The Pulse Of New York* had introduced the coxey character to American audiences. I remember him well. Clad in innumerable holes sparsely bordered by snitches of rags, his act, far from embracing any affinity with even such a minor philosopher as Thoreau or any remotest acquaintance with the poets, consisted mainly in an appreciative, mouth-watering appraisal of the beauties who paraded the stage and in the periodic dropping of a lighted cigar butt into his perforated garment, the wriggling of his anatomy, and the extrication of the butt from an aperture in the seat of his pants. It was exquisite.

Jones' art had an immediate and thorough influence on burlesque, and before you could catch your breath dozens of comics not only copied the great man but went so far as to improve upon his impersonation by dropping into their ensembles, along with the cigar butts, pieces of ice, cervelat wursts, and even small mince pies.

The dramatic stage, contemptuous of such bourgeois humor, was not long in purveying its own more refined concepts of the genus bum, and it soon flowered with a rich and remarkable assortment. Chief among the collection and with melodrama his habitat was the easy-going tramp, ostensibly interested mainly in clog dancing, who at the climactic moment suddenly transformed his beaming countenance into a solemn and imperious one, whipped out two formidable pistols, and proclaimed himself to be a member of the United States Secret Service. And second to him was the somewhat droopier specimen who slouched into the back-yard of a house, could not take his eyes off the golden-haired little girl playing there, lifted her tenderly upon his knee and wistfully recounted to her the story of a bad, bad man who had deserted his family some years before, and who was disclosed in the last act, with forgiveness all around, to be the Enoch Arden himself. Further variations of the genus followed in due course. There was the François Villon type, given to the brimming cup and the recitation of rhyme; the gentle, philosophic type which brought sunshine and love of life to a congress of depressed and despairing folk; the type which was viewed with alarm by all the reputable citizens in the cast but which gained their good-will by rescuing the child of one of them from some danger or other; and the lazy ne'er-do-well species which was the repository of homely wisdoms and which snapped back into action in the final act and straightened out the mortgage on the old widow's home, showed up the Mayor as a crook, and then took its hand-waving departure through the garden gate with the pack again on its back and with a song on its lips.

Though the breed does not appear so regularly on our stages as it used to, samples nevertheless have intermittently not been lacking, especially in some of the plays about Negroes and in revivals of foreign plays like *The Lower Depths*. Until José Ferrer's Oliver Erwenter it had, however, been almost seven years since Victor Kilian drifted his native, tattered, meditative way into *Solitaire*. Taking them all in all, these stage bindle stiffs, save when they become too serious, are indeed a luscious lot and Ferrer is one of the best of them. They are the gay offspring of Locke's beloved vagabond and the older wardrobe mistresses of burlesque, and life after eight-thirty p.m. has been the happier for them.

McEnroe's play is another in the line of those whose vagabonds visit their dreamy wisdom, poetry quotations (in this instance mainly Omar Khayyám), and invincible cheeriness upon the inmates of an old people's home, the usual eccentrically assorted parcel. Some of the scenes are exuberantly ribald and humorous and make for appetizing entertainment, but there are others which seem to have been trumped up to give the general pattern that arbitrary variety which is deemed necessary, often foolishly, to hold an audience's interest. The impression left by the whole, despite its hilarious periods, is of one of the pat old boarding-house plays into whose rattled midst came a stranger with a philosophy new to the residents, who reacted to it benignly either in part or wholesale.

Among the amusing performances, aside from Ferrer's, are those of Doro Merande as a cynical ancient and Frances Brandt as a frowzy stew right out of Belcher's sketchbook.

RED GLOVES. December 4, 1948

A play by Jean-Paul Sartre, adapted by Daniel Taradash. Produced by Jean Dalrymple for 113 performances in the Mansfield Theatre.

Program

Reich	J. Anthony La Penna	Marochek	Jessie White
Johanna	Anna Karen	Kirtz	Martin Kingsley
Loutec	Guy Thomajan	Hoederer	Charles Boyer
Munster	Horace McMahon	The Prince	Francis Compton
Hugo	John Dall	Karsky	Royal Beal
Jessica	Joan Tetzel		

SYNOPSIS: *The action of the play takes place in a country in Middle Europe. Prologue: Johanna's flat, early Spring, 1945. Act I. A room in a villa in Hoederer's courtyard. Spring, 1943. Act II. Hoederer's quarters in an old palace. A few days later. Act III. The same. The following morning. Epilogue: Johanna's flat.*
Director: *Jed Harris.*

T HAT Jean-Paul Sartre has an enterprising and lively mind is clear, but anyone who has closely sniffed him and his plays can not resist the feeling that there is a lot of the opportunist in its enterprise and that its liveliness embraces a very vivacious interest in the long green. He is, it would seem, less the simon-pure artistic conscience his disciples would have us believe than a doubtfully equipped playwright with a snappy instinct as to ways and means to circus himself to profitable commercial ends, which like some of his French colleagues he is not averse to regarding with considerable fervor. When Jean Dalrymple approached him about doing his *Les Mains Sales* in America and pointed out to him, somewhat hesitantly and even a bit fearfully, that not only would its excessive length have to be drastically curtailed but that some other changes would have to be made in it if it hoped to fetch American audiences, he was not long, she informs me, in making reply. "Do what you want with it," he said; "do anything short of fooling with its political ideology to make it a box-office success." I dislike to ring in Shaw again, but try to imagine even a playwright confessedly as agog over money as he is having any such attitude toward one of his scripts.

Since thus addressing himself to his American producer, Sartre evidently re-read the many American tributes to his remarkable artistic integrity, concluded that if Americans felt that way about him he would be brother to the cuckoo not to keep the ball rolling, and duly put on a big show in a Paris court contending that his play, retitled *Red Gloves*, had been defiled by arch-foes of the good, the true and the beautiful and had been altered without his permission until it was no longer the immaculate work he had conceived. The show, excellent as it was, suffered somewhat, however, from his subsequent admission that he had not read the American version.

It seemed to be our friend's chief complaint that, whereas his play, he protested, was neither pro-Communist nor anti-Communist, the American adapter had made it definitely anti, a thought which grossly revolted his sensibilities. Well, I have now not only seen the American adaptation but have read carefully the original and, while paying my warmest respects to Sartre as an accomplished press-agent, it pains me to report to him that his play has not been in the least thematically changed; that its adapter has even improved it a little in some, if not all, of the cutting and in the tightening of one or two portions of it; that it still could stand a heap of improvement whether by an adapter or by Sartre himself; and that if both in its original and adapted form it does not seem to be inclined to Communist sympathy either Sartre or I do not know what we are talking about. Sartre is not, we are informed, a Communist, but if he thinks he has written a play neither pro nor anti he is a very confused man. What most likely happened is that he appreciated, as John Gunther has reported, that almost every other person you meet in France nowadays is a Communist; that, with a weather eye to the box-office, he tried to please both pros and antis; and that in his trick balancing act he fell off the tight-rope and landed in the sawdust with a red bottom.

Far from being turned into an unmistakably anti-Communist play, as he alleged he feared, the local presentation has unintentionally been turned into a considerably more pro-Communist one than the French original. The ideology, true enough, has not been tampered with. But when you cast a Communist spokesman with a popular, handsome, charming, personally winning and very able stage and screen star like Charles Boyer and then cast his opponent with an unattractive and very bad juvenile actor of psychopathic murder roles in Hollywood Class-B pictures, it does not take even a half-competent pollster to tell you where the sympathy of the larger portion of the average audience will go.

These, however, are not strictly critical matters. Strictly critical is the fact that, while the play pretends among other things to ponder the problem as to whether the assassination of its Communist leader was actually induced by pure political logic or by outraged romantic emotion, the latter question seems to have been dragged in by the tail at the last moment. And even more strictly critical are the facts that the exhibit talks itself out of all drama and suspense, that in an effort to capture that suspense it plays so much hide-and-seek with the potential killer's revolver that it resembles a not particularly bright parlor game, and that all in all it is melodramatic claptrap. Some of the local cutting is furthermore responsible for reducing the heroine's psychological ration and making her, the wife of the Red leader's antagonist, appear and reappear on the scene with the unreasonable and ridiculous rapidity of a French farce character. Nor certainly are matters helped by casting the role, which calls for its incumbent solemnly to offer her woman's soul and passionate person to the leader, with a sweet little number who has the look of having just stepped out of *Junior Miss*. The editing may additionally be questioned for modifying the sex relationship of the pair, for abbreviating some of the impulses which drive the idealist, and for some unnecessary skimping in one or two other particulars.

In this play as in his others, however and nonetheless, Sartre manages always to seem on the point of a profundity that never materializes. He gives the impression of a man rushing toward an ocean of thought, plunging in, and emerging all dry, like one of the chorus girls who used to descend into the old Hippodrome tank. His reliance upon melodrama for facile effect provides the further picture of a man poised perilously on a high window ledge, to the acquiescent palpitation of the onlookers below, and who finally makes the jump only to land in a net.

The present production, which unfairly represents Sartre mainly in the qualification of the sex aspect noted above and in the shifting of stage emphasis from the young idealist to the Communist chief, owes what minor interest it has theatrically to Boyer's performance. Even were the play much better, the casting and acting of the two other principal roles would, as indicated, botch it. Jed Harris, in these and several additional quarters, has slipped badly as a director.

ANNE OF THE THOUSAND DAYS
DECEMBER 8, 1948

A play by Maxwell Anderson. Produced by the Play-wrights Company and Leland Heyward for the rest of the season's performances in the Shubert Theatre.

PROGRAM

ANNE BOLEYN	Joyce Redman	SIR THOMAS MORE	Russell Gaige
HENRY	Rex Harrison	THOMAS CROMWELL	
CARDINAL WOLSEY	Percy Waram		Wendell K. Phillips
THOMAS BOLEYN	Charles Francis	BISHOP FISHER	Harry Irvine
SERVANT	Ludlow Maury	PRIOR HOUGHTON	Cecil Clovelly
HENRY NORRIS	Allan Stevenson	A MESSENGER	Harry Selby
MARK SMEATON	John Merivale	BAILIFF	Fred Ayres Cotton
DUKE OF NORFOLK	John Williams	BAILIFF	Harold McGee
PERCY, EARL OF NORTHUMBERLAND		CLERK	Terence Anderson
	Robert Duke		Richard Leone
ELIZABETH BOLEYN	Viola Keats	SINGERS	Frank Myers
SERVING WOMAN	Kathleen Bolton		Donald Conrad
MARY BOLEYN	Louise Platt		Harold McGee
MADGE SHELTON	Margaret Garland	MUSICIANS	Malcolm Wells
JANE SEYMOUR	Monica Lang		Charles Ellis

The play, in two acts, takes place in England between the years 1526 and 1536.

Director: *H. C. Potter.*

AMBITION IS ONE of the most overestimated attributes listed in the copy-books. It has led infinitely more to tragedy than to triumph. Unless predicated not only on competence and talent but on something approximating genius, it is the augury of disappointment, grief, and defeat. It is modesty's sleeping-pill; humility's thrombosis. It is frequently responsible for more poor work, particularly in the drama, than passivity, the acceptance of the knowledge of personal limitations, and the doing of only that which is within one's self-recognized range.

No playwright in the American theatre is ridden by greater ambition than Mr. Anderson. It is of such magnitude, indeed, that it impels him to tasks that Shakespeare himself not always found easy. But nothing deters him, come hell, high water, or critics. That he is a competent and even talented dramatist few will dispute; but that he misses completely the genius to surmount the problems he poses for himself is only too evident to anyone who has sat upon his works. These, as in the present instance, sometimes have various endorsable qualities. They have a degree of literary facility, some imagination, a periodic pungence, and a certain flair for dramaturgy. But they sometimes, too, fly beyond their reach and, for all their determination, descend with broken, or at least injured, wings.

Much less pretentious than some of its author's previous historical efforts, this *Anne Of The Thousand Days,* a free retelling of the tale of Henry VIII and the Boleyn of his passion, is a better performance than any of his earlier essays in the chronicle form. Though it runs a diminuendo course and here and there merely flickers where it should blaze, it has its points of relative merit. The blank verse is simple and not as obtrusive as it has been on some occasions; there is less sense of heavy striving than heretofore; the story line is fairly direct; and, though surely not in its soliloquies, one of which is downright embarrassing, there is a measure of dramatic tang. There is also some intelligent humor. Let Sartre stand where he may, the play furthermore leaves no doubt, all fellow-travelers will be delighted to know, that Mr. Anderson is pro-sex. Not since the times of Aaron Burr, the Oneida Community and Tristan Bernard, nor for that matter even then, has the sport of kings been treated more explicitly. Comrade Anderson not only calls a spade a spade, though he may gild it with Elizabethan locution, but he shovels it with a mighty muscle. It is all, however, properly in the picture and, while one is able to detect the playwright's self-conscious relish in ruffling the morally sensitive, there is no slightest valid objection.

Taking liberties with the previously accepted view of Anne, the play presents her as an imperiously determined

woman almost Strindbergian in the ferocity of her hate
and love and relates her unyielding struggle with the lust-
ful but love-bound Henry to gain the title of his Queen. It
follows the monarch's break with Rome and his institution of the Church of England, his dismissal of Katherine
under Anne's resolute insistence, the birth of a girl child
instead of the son upon whom his dream is set, his eventual
dismissal in turn of Anne, her trial for adultery, her execution in the Tower, and his royal eye turned newly to Jane
Seymour. The story moves fluently under Anderson's pen
for half its distance but in its later passages intermittently
stutters.

The production's unit set, designed by Jo Mielziner, contributes, despite excellent lighting, to visual monotony,
and the voices of the two leading players, Joyce Redman
and Rex Harrison, are often of a like dramatic inflexibil-
ity which, with the set, sometimes gives the play a feeling
of sameness that is not in the script. And the direction,
handicapped by the set, periodically furthers the impression. Harrison, aside from the deficiency noted, presents a
striking Henry, deftly managing the character's bluster
crossed with humor and its strength infected by a softened
heart. Miss Redman's Anne has moments of stature, but
only moments, since her limitations as an heroic actress become increasingly obvious as the play proceeds. She is best
in the quieter passages; when the action mounts her passion takes the form of shrieks and her physical positiveness
that of comporting herself as if she believed the play to be
The Taming Of The Shrew and that Kate could best indicate her stubborn hauteur by walking about as if she
were balancing a book on her head.

The sex element in the play, accepted without blush,
causes one to reflect on the great changes that have come
over our audiences since the turn of the century. A consideration of the lines and situations in various plays during that period which dumfounded their ears or eyes, or
both, may under the present circumstances be instructive.
In the early years of the Nineteen Hundreds the scene in
the short Grand Guignol play, *Vitriol,* which showed a

man slowly dropping the searing chemical onto the fair face of the mistress who had betrayed him, brought screams from the women in the house. In those same years, Asch's *God Of Vengeance* startled audiences with its scene in which the operator of a brothel was suddenly confronted by the fact that his own daughter had become a harlot. And since that time there were other plays which contained elements which upset the equanimity of the customers. But among them all were a dozen that probably more greatly than any of the others presented items which jolted audiences out of their composure and which may be listed historically as the period's leading shockers.

The twelve were the following:

Sapho, by Clyde Fitch, based on the novel by Alphonse Daudet and a French play similarly derived from it. Produced in the early weeks of 1900, it shivered the audience morality of that era with an episode in which Olga Nethersole, in the role of a notorious demi-mondaine, glued herself passionately to the lips of her lover, played by Hamilton Revelle, for a full minute and a half and, exhausted by the frenzy of her own kiss, to say nothing of by the reciprocity of its recipient, was lifted by the latter into his arms and carried up a winding staircase to esoteric quarters. The exhibit was condemned as obscene and was closed by the police a month after its opening. The trial, however, resulted in Miss Nethersole's acquittal and the play was again put on display the month following.

A Wife Without A Smile, by Arthur Wing Pinero. Produced in 1904, it contained a scene wherein the members of a house-party whimsically attached a doll at the end of a string to the ceiling beneath the boudoir of a couple whose potential amorous course they were curious to follow. In due time the doll began dancing violently to the satisfied hilarity of the guests below and to the acute embarrassment of the audience. Though even the latter had difficulty concealing its mirth over the ribald situation, the shock implicit in the dramatic device was such that indignant word-of-mouth kept trade away and the play was doomed to early failure — and this for all the circumstance that, except for the single scene in question, it was a polite comedy with nothing in it to give offense to the most sedate.

Mrs. Warren's Profession, by George Bernard Shaw. Produced toward the end of 1905, with Arnold Daly and Mary Shaw in the leading roles, the play, which dealt with the female operator of a chain of houses of ill-repute, hit audiences' sensibilities with bombshell force and not only audiences' but New York's professional moralists'. The two chief players were arrested at the behest of Anthony Comstock on charges of producing an immoral exhibit but were acquitted. Nevertheless, the clergy and newspapers continued to pursue the attack. What caused particular shock was the forgiveness by the brothel keeper's daughter, brought up in ignorance of her mother's profession, of the latter's activities, along with a situation in which a clergyman who had been one of the mother's lovers was thought possibly to be the girl's father. One of the lines that rasped the audiences' moral sense particularly was Mrs. Warren's "Do you think that I was such a fool as to let other people trade in my good looks by employing me as a shopgirl, a barmaid or a waitress, when I could trade in them myself and get all the profits instead of starvation wages. . . ?"

The Nigger, by Edward Sheldon. Produced in December 1909, the drama, nearly forty years before Sinclair Lewis' *Kingsblood Royal,* treated of Negro blood in a man supposedly white and of his love for a woman of pure Caucasian strain. The theme at that time was theatrically sensational and induced qualms in an audience. The scene in which the protagonist confided to the heroine that he was a Negro brought gasps from the spectators, and more gasps still when with wild passion he declared that he could not let her go and when in a paroxysm of nervous terror she tried to run for the door only to have him reach it first and block her way. Adding to the general shock was dialogue presenting the South's hospitable attitude toward lynching.

The City, by Clyde Fitch. Produced in the same month of the same year, it became an over-night sensation on the score that in it for the first time on an American stage was heard the expletive, "God damn." The sudden and unexpected sound of the phrase fell upon the audience's ears like a blast of nitroglycerine. About the same time, the word "rape" was first heard from a stage in a play by William Hurlbut called *New York,* but the effect was nothing like that of the words in question. *The City* was otherwise without startle, dealing with the supposedly corrupting influence of the metropolis as against the virtuous influence of the small town. But the "God damn" heatedly shouted by one character at another in a climactic scene made it the aghast talk of the moment.

Damaged Goods, by Eugene Brieux. A translation from the French, the play was first shown here in 1913 and forthwith gave birth to outraged protestations. Its theme was society's suppression of any reference to venereal disease and, unlike Ibsen's *Ghosts,* it did not hesitate to call things by name. The theme was related through the plot of a young man who on the eve of his wedding learned that he was a victim of syphilis, the first sound of which taboo word struck the unused audience ear with the impact of a piledriver. The progress of the plot, with the young man's disregard of the physician's warning and his marriage after treatment by a quack, horrified the audience, let alone those who got wind of the matter by hearsay. But times change, and twenty-four years later the play was revived to general apathy.

Rain, by John Colton and Clemence Randolph from the story by W. Somerset Maugham. Produced in 1922, it dealt with Sadie Thompson, a prostitute come to the South Seas port of Pago Pago, her encounter with the Rev. Alfred Davidson, a missionary, his initial move to redeem her, and her sexual attraction which ripped off his mask of piety and betrayed him as a hypocrite. Some of the dialogue in which the story was related was such a mixture of sex and profanity that the ears of audiences turned red, a color which in this instance turned that of the box-office into a rich green. Samples of Sadie's lines: "You're a liar! Who in Christ's name do you think you are? You lay off me!". . . "You dirty two-faced mutt; you psalm-singing son-of-a- — "

. . . And, in the case of Davidson, his strange dreams of the mountains of Nebraska, subsequently interpreted by another character as being "hills, rounded, smooth, curiously like a woman's breasts." But above all it was the scene wherein the prostitute was at the very point of redemption when Davidson's carnal emotions impelled him to follow her to her room that stunned audiences.

What Price Glory?, by Maxwell Anderson and Laurence Stallings. Produced in 1924, the exhibit, which treated of war unheroically and unsentimentally, so scandalized audiences with its free use of salty lingo and profanity and with its general air of ribaldry, let alone its disillusioned approach to its subject matter, that it became the most talked about play of its day. The dialogue was reflected in some such line as "Who gives a damn for this lousy, stinking little town but the poor French bastards who live here?", and the blunt sex element in the free-and-easy approach to Charmaine, the daughter of an inn-keeper, by the buddies, Quirt and Flagg. One scene in particular that discomposed audiences with its nonchalance was that in which Flagg, hearing Charmaine's father through an interpreter charge a Marine with his daughter's seduction and his demand for monetary balm, acknowledged to himself the old man's healthy grounds for suspicion and started to bargain with him when suddenly he observed Quirt looking altogether too innocent. Asking the father to identify the seducer, the old man pointed to Quirt, who to Flagg's delighted relief was ordered by the Captain to marry the girl and, besides, fork over two-thirds of his pay to her.

The Captive, by Edouard Bourdet. Translated from the French and produced in 1926, it had to do with the hitherto taboo theme of perversion in women and revolted so many, despite the fact that it was tactfully written, that it was not long before the company presenting it was placed under arrest for contributing to the community's moral contamination and was released only when the management declared its intention of withdrawing the play from the stage. The scenes which were most instrumental in shock were one wherein a degenerate woman friend plied the young heroine with temptation, one wherein the latter tried desperately to escape submission through marriage to a childhood sweetheart, and a final one in which she found that she could not overcome the woman's evil fascination and deserted her husband to return to the pervert's thralldom.

The Front Page, by Ben Hecht and Charles MacArthur. Produced in 1928, the indecorum of the Chicago newspaper farce-comedy proved hilarious to audiences, who took everything in their easy stride until just before its final curtain was about to fall. At that juncture the authors delivered a line of dialogue which, while it lifted the hilarity no end, nevertheless coincidentally struck the audience in so surprised a spot that the laughter was accompanied by a considerable jolt. The scene was as follows. Hildy Johnson, a reporter who had just performed a sensational journalistic feat, declared to his editor's disgust his intention of abandoning the newspaper game and going off to New York with his recently acquired bride. Burns, the editor, made a touching farewell speech, presented Johnson with his gold time-piece as a gift, and Johnson gleefully departed. No sooner had he gone, however, than Burns grabbed the 'phone, called the police, and instructed them to arrest him at the train's first stop and return him to Chicago. The police wanted to know why. "The son-of-a-bitch stole my watch!" yelled Burns. (In *Rain* the "bitch" had been cautiously slurred.)

The Children's Hour, by Lillian Hellman. Produced in the last months of 1934, the play, which dealt with a malevolent child in a school for girls, blistered audiences not only with an echo of the theme of *The Captive* but with a driving melodramatic approach to it that in at least one episode nigh knocked the breath out of its auditors. The scene in point was one in which the evil and vengeful brat told what she alleged she had seen through the keyhole of the room occupied by two of the teachers. The subsequent cross-examination of the child, her persistence in blackening the name of the teachers by repeating what she declared was common gossip among the other little girls in the school, and the desperation of the accused women in their effort to show up the foulminded little informer held the audience in a vise-like grip. And, when the curtain to the second act fell on the brat's lying shrieks that she had actually seen what previously she said she had seen, the emotions of the auditors were drained dry.

A New Life, by Elmer Rice. In a failure by Gustav Eckstein titled *Christmas Eve,* produced for six performances in late December, 1939, there was a scene in which the cries of a woman giving birth to a child were heard from off-stage. Though the episode had a measure of shock, it did not approach that of another such in this *A New Life,* produced four years later. The scene in the Rice play which jarred audiences to the point of distress was a painfully realistic hospital picture of childbirth accompanied by all the tortured moans and screams of the mother, a role played by the author's actress-wife, Betty Field. So disturbing to the impressibilities of many women was the episode that they were forced to leave the theatre before the rest of the play was done. As a result, the offering expired after a relatively brief engagement.

All things considered, it is accordingly food for the psychologist that when a play like *Mister Roberts* came along early in 1948 with sailor dialogue that had not been equalled for frankness and with several scenes that piled vulgar detail on vulgar detail audiences' sophistication had become such that there was not the faintest blush; and that when this *Anne Of The Thousand Days* followed it with such sex allusions as had previously been forgiven only in Shakespeare nary a cheek colored.

LEND AN EAR. December 16, 1948

A revue with music, lyrics, and sketches by Charles Gaynor.
Produced by William R. Katzell, Franklin Gilbert and
William Eythe for the rest of the season's performances in,
initially, the National Theatre.

PRINCIPALS

William Eythe, Yvonne Adair, Anne Renee Anderson, Dorothy Babbs,
Carol Channing, Larry Stewart, Gloria Hamilton, Al Checco, Robert
Dixon, Nancy Franklin, Bob Herget, Beverly Hosier, Tommy Morton,
Gene Nelson, Lee Stacy, Jeanine Smith, Arthur Maxwell, George Hall,
Antoinette Guhlke, Jenny Lou Law, Bob Scheerer.
Director: *Hal Gerson.*

I suggest that some public benefactor offer a grand prize
of two million dollars to the critic who succeeds in writing
a review of a revue which will not be much the same old
routine thing, which will have a little real fizz in it, and
which will not bore the reader, who has been bored by
such reviews for years, out of his wits. The awarder need
not worry; his money will be safe; it isn't likely that anyone
will collar it. Knowing the hopelessness of going after the
prize, I shall not even enter myself in the contest, since I
have in my time reviewed hundreds of such shows and,
sweat as I would, have doubtless been just as guilty of dulness as all the rest.

There is high and sufficient reason why writing about a
revue is not an inspiring job and why any attempt to describe one of them in a manner fascinating, or even clearly
intelligible, to the reader is as difficult, if the show is a
good one, as trying to describe the taste of celery or the
smell of watermelon. When the show is bad, the business is
easy, since you may simply set down the evening's statistics
and let them speak for themselves, which, however, is also
scarcely a way calculated to win the two million dollars.
But when the revue has merits in the departments of song,

dance, girls, imagination, wit, humor and over-all atmosphere you find yourself mostly up against it, since mere statistics in such a case would not give the flavor of the show, since nothing is harder than making equally funny on the printed page what is funny on the stage, since you can not very well sing a song in type, and since if there is any fully accurate way to convey a girl's sex appeal in print without being arrested I do not know it.

It is for these reasons — and they are only a few out of many — that the reviews of the better revues always uniformly provide about as unstimulating reading as lists of cocktail recipés, advertisements of electrical vigor belts, or the ghost-written and antiseptic autobiographies of former *Follies* beauties. And it is for these same reasons, duly recognized by the reviewers, that the latter are helplessly driven to the concoction of the deadly literature that spreads its pall over the public prints whenever one of the exhibits challenges their resources. What you get on such occasions — and you get it from me along with all the others — is accordingly either laundry-list criticism detailing in humdrum fashion the various elements of the show or a rash of candied adjectives which provide a no more illuminating picture of it than the reader had before he picked up the paper. "The songs, particularly the one called 'Love Is Like A Mallard Duck,' " you read, "are delightfully witty and ingratiatingly melodious." Just where does that get you? The music publishers will not permit a reviewer to quote the lyrics, so you have to take the delightful wit for granted, and to be informed merely that the songs are ingratiatingly melodious is not going to help you much more than telling you that the Batard Montrachet I had with supper after the show tasted delicious.

Or you read that the sketch called *Hollywood Intermezzo* about a movie director's passionate affair with a sea otter was so hilarious it laid the audience in the aisles. Again, just where does that lay you? Since the sketch, if it is really amusing, probably depends less upon the lines than upon the comedian's comical getup, pantomime and naughty acrobatics, since describing humorous pantomime satisfactorily is a job that has hamstrung Diaghileff, to say nothing of even Max Beerbohm, and since naughty acrobatics if satisfactorily described would unhappily jump the paper's circulation far beyond its available newsprint supply, any hope of doing justice to the sketch that a reviewer might entertain must inevitably go scooting.

Nor is that all. If you can tell me any smart way in which to suggest the gayety of a bright revue without sounding like a man who has had too many drinks and is trying to describe the jolly time he had drinking them, I'll give you twenty per cent of the two million dollars in the dim event I should ever win it. And if you will confide to me the manner in which an especially intricate and complex soft shoe dance can be reported without seeming to be a description of a performer suffering from a combination of paralysis agitans, chorea, and plain damn foolishness, I'll give you thirty.

At this point you are doubtless saying to yourself that, if a revue presents such problems, why doesn't a musical comedy present them as well. It does, as most of the reviews you read surely attest. But, even so, the task is not quite so baffling. The musical comedy has a more or less direct story line, whereas the revue has none, or at best a mere thread which does not make much sense. It also has some form and coherence, and the girls fit more or less into its general pattern. In addition, the music, if the show makes any pretence to critical virtue, has some degree of musicianship and body and is not just the rhythmical turkey-feed or foot-tapping virus that the revue score usually is. And, if the soft shoe dance figures in it, you can very comfortably forget it. What is more, you can cheat. You can, as a certain reviewer whom I shall cautiously refrain from mentioning by name has sometimes done, embroider your review with touching reminiscence; with some learned and impressive remarks on the psychology of humor; with observations on the derivative sources of some of the better songs (always piquing to the reader); with saucy reflections on the identity of the coloratura soprano and internal otitis; and, for sure-fire, with a comparison of the chorus nosegays with those of George Lederer's and Ziegfeld's day. Which last is a device most frequently denied the reviewer in the case of a revue, since, with the possible exception of the girl put into the show by the chief backer's nephew, and more often not even then, a revue's scant quota of girls is selected less for what is still known in more reactionary circles as oomph than for an ability to hoof and clog, to hide in lavatories in the blackout sketches, and to lend imparadised voices to the "hoorays" which terminate the finale song numbers.

It is thus that in the instance of the present revue I mercifully, if choicelessly, spare you the kind of review you will read elsewhere and report simply that the show in larger part is a fresh, lively and amusing one with some delightful performers in it, that it miraculously contains in the persons of Dorothy Babbs, Antoinette Guhlke and Yvonne Adair three unusually attractive girls, and that it provides still another ground for rejoicing in the passing of the day when American producers concluded that what was wrong with their revues was that they lacked a Parisian atmosphere. Having arrived at the conclusion, it was their habit promptly to set about correcting the lack by dressing up the ticket-takers in the lobbies like Austrian artillery majors, inserting numbers into the shows in which the smaller chorus girls, most of them visibly of Irish and Polish extraction, sang "We Wee-wees Always Say Oui-Oui," to an accompaniment of savage winks at the audience, incorporating a tableau in which a female in white striptights lay prostrate at the feet of a fierce chorus boy whose face, arms and torso were smeared with lamp-black (it usually bore some such slightly enigmatic title as "Primitive Virtue"), and putting a sign over the door leading to the men's room reading *Pour les Messieurs*. This successfully accomplished, they naturally became much put out when subsequently the reviewers saw fit to express certain doubts as to the entire authenticity of the French atmosphere and delivered themselves of uncalled for smartcracks about a revue named *Passetemps Parisiens* whose chief features were a team of German acrobats, an American vaudeville

trained seal, a cockney skit cabbaged from the London
Nine O'Clock Revue, and a spectacular finale called "The
Apotheosis Of Baseball."

Not less suspect than the French atmosphere, however,
were those reviewers of the time who made mock of it in
the belief that French atmosphere was something quite different and immeasurably more exciting. For if the Parisian
atmosphere evoked by the local producers was approximately as Gallic as *sauerbraten,* the Parisian atmosphere
evoked by their French counterparts was as Gallic as *sauerbraten mit preiselbeeren.* Legend, of course, had exercised
its sweet will upon the parochial critics and had conjured
up for them the usual visions of beautiful women, their
skirts up around their ears, prancing on table-tops the
while gay boulevardiers quaffed champagne from their
satin slippers; of handsome lieutenants of Cuirassiers
lounging lasciviously on rear divans, puffing languidly at
cigarettes filled with opium, and making negligée eyes at
all the ladies; of revue stages so witty that Congreve and
Sheridan tossed enviously in their tombs; of wenches so
devilish and agitating that no French octogenarian had
need of Steinach; of melodies as soft and insinuating as
amorous eels; and of a general air of gayety and abandon
the like of which one could find nowhere else on the
planet. Legend, ever careless, had not seen fit to impart to
them the unlegendary truth that the French atmosphere of
such revue theatres as the Folies Bergère, Olympia, Cigale,
Marigny and Moulin Rouge consisted mainly rather of a
dozen dirty jokes, two dozen chorus girls in the altogether
and almost as dirty, a saucy animadversion on Briand, and
a rear promenade in which street-walkers ogled for trade
and in which one might drop a sou in a slot and weigh
one's self. But legend dies hard and lost upon the reviewers
was the fact that there was infinitely more of the hypothetical French atmosphere in a Ziegfeld *Follies* or, for that matter, in the Winter Garden or Earl Carroll revues than ever
one encountered in its supposed diocese, save alone when
the matchless Rip was in operation.

That the producers of our shows in later years have rid

themselves of the old nonsense and that, were they to indulge in it, the present-day more traveled reviewers would laugh them out of countenance is one of the most encouraging symptoms of an improved revue theatre. Some of the later shows may not be too good but, good or not, they are at least unaffectedly American, and that is a very large and very intelligent point in their favor.

MAKE WAY FOR LUCIA. December 22, 1948

A comedy, based on the E. F. Benson stories, by John van Druten. Produced by the Theatre Guild for 29 performances in the Cort Theatre.

Program

Major Benjamin Flint		Mr. Wyse	Ivan Simpson
	Philip Tonge	Mrs. Wyse	Essex Dane
Grosvenor	Cherry Hardy	Rev. Kenneth Bartlett	
Miss Mapp	Catherine Willard		Guy Spaull
Georgie Pillson	Cyril Ritchard	Mrs. Bartlett	Doreen Lang
Mrs. Emmeline Lucas (Lucia)		Godiva Plaistow	Viola Roache
	Isabel Jeans	Signor Cortese	Kurt Kasznar

SYNOPSIS: Act I. Scene 1. *Morning. July.* Scene 2. *Morning. Four weeks later.* Act II. Scene 1. *Afternoon. Two weeks later.* Scene 2. *Afternoon. Ten days later.* Scene 3. *Evening. A week later.* Act III. Scene 1. *Morning. The next day.* Scene 2. *Evening. The same day.*

The action takes place in the drawing room of a house in Tilling, a small town in the South of England. The period is around 1912, during the summer months.

Director: *John van Druten.*

My first acquaintance with E. F. Benson resulted from stealing out of the family bookcase, at the age of eleven, the novel called *Dodo.* It was a popular item in that remote epoch and my larceny was prompted by overhearing my parents discuss it. I do not remember much about the book except that it was a harmless picture of smart society which had achieved a vogue on the score of the alleged scandalous resemblance of its heroine to a well-known, high-toned English lady of the period whose identity, despite an early proficiency in eavesdropping, remained Greek to me. Though the records indicate that Benson was a very profuse literatus and confected all sorts of later works, my first acquaintance with him was my last, and his canon is a blank spot, for better or worse, in my cultural education. I thus have no means of knowing just

how much of his *Lucia* stories, upon which Mr. van Druten's comedy is founded, figures in the play. I might, of
course, were I possessed of a sense of greater responsibility,
go back and read the stories but, since I am told that there
were a half dozen of the *Lucia* novels, the idea does not appeal to me, and you will have to be content with my view
of the play as a thing independent of them. I have noted
in the papers that the story line follows closely that in one
of the books and that some of the dialogue has been culled
from one or another of them. I pass on the information for
what it may be worth, but, as I say, I do not know at first-
hand and, since I have read in the same papers so many
things which I have subsequently observed in the identical
papers were apparently based on guess-work, I shall, as I
have said, report simply on the van Druten comedy as if
Benson had never existed.

Mr. van Druten almost always treats what he writes with
taste, literary delicacy, and an easy and insinuating humor,
and these qualities are again demonstrated in this recount-
ing of the battle between two women for social supremacy
in a small town in southern England in the early years of
the century. But the play itself, which is stretched to the
snapping point, remains as mild as a semi-tropical Spring,
though scarcely as warming and with much the same
drowsy effect. Playwrights, including van Druten, have
managed to sustain stories fundamentally as tenuous as this,
but in the present instance the trick does not materialize,
and after the first three-quarters of an hour there is some
perceptible hard breathing and puffing to keep things going. Not only dialogue but episodes have the same tone
and repeat themselves, and the play seems frequently to be
killing its own time. A scene that has some liveliness is followed by one that has the appearance of having been
worked in as a treadmill, getting nowhere, until the next
lively scene comes along. And in the end one feels, like a
character in one of Priestley's spiral-time plays, that not
only has one been there before but that the comedy has
been there too, and that one has played all its scenes several times over.

Some pleasant acting helps flickeringly to gloss over the repetitive nature of the exhibit and to make the evening seem a little less static than it factually is. Isabel Jeans, dressed to the nose in handsome Lucinda Ballard period costumes, plays the role of the dilettante young widow who triumphs over her rival with a visible wealth of assurance that in less graceful hands might rid such a performance of any appeal and, except for a tendency now and then to indulge in the mechanics of stage charm and to repeat her devices in registering the emotions provided her by the playwright, manages the part agreeably. As her defeated rival, Catherine Willard, though a bit too literal and straightforward for a comedy so unsubstantial, handles with some address a role that has the set-up aspect of a bowling alley. Cyril Ritchard offers another of the *fleur de pois* characterizations at which he is so expert and, again bringing much of the quality which he has brought to Congreve, adds to the occasion's humors, as does Philip Tonge in the part of a blundering, bogusly licentious suitor for the widow's hand. His drunken scene, however, is alcoholism in its standardized stage pattern, full of the prescriptive tangled legs and speech, which reflects the inebriated human off-stage only in the reluctant observation that maybe he has imbibed too freely. The audience and the critics, however, followed principle and seemed to be deeply affected by Mr. Tonge's singular virtuosity. It appears to be that way always, whether in the case of an actor or actress, and especially actress. Nothing more impresses the average critic than one portraying a creature in her cups. That it is almost impossible for her to fail in the depiction of a sot, that the job is one of the easiest to bring off in the whole histrionic catalogue, and that it ranks on a par with the nonsense which Shaw exposed so clearly in Irving's performance of the creaking old gaffer in *Waterloo,* the critic seemingly can not persuade himself to believe. Let an actress, however otherwise inferior, come on the stage with dishevelled hair, speak as if she had a blotter in her mouth, and steady herself on the back of a chair once in a while and most critics will write of her, particularly if she remembers to pick up her drink with trembling hands and spill a little of it on her dress, as if she were an extraordinary artiste. And if she subsequently plods up a flight of stairs holding unsteadily to the banister, they will be so overcome by her genius that their reviews of her will quiver with awe.

JENNY KISSED ME. DECEMBER 23, 1948

A comedy by Jean Kerr. Produced by Michael Ellis, James Russo and Alexander H. Cohen in association with Clarence M. Shapiro for 20 performances in the Hudson Theatre.

PROGRAM

FATHER MOYNIHAN	*Leo G. Carroll*	HARRY	*Jean Jordan*
MICHAEL SAUNDERS	*Alan Baxter*	JO	*Winnie Mae-Martin*
MRS. DEAZY	*Frances Bavier*	OWEN PARKSIDE	*Brennan Moore*
SISTER MARY OF THE ANGELS		JENNY	*Pamela Rivers*
	Sara Taft	A GIRL	*Camilla de Witt*
SHIRLEY TIRABOSSI	*Bonnie Alden*	ANOTHER GIRL	*Dorothy King*
MISS STEARNS	*Ruth Saville*	MR. PARKSIDE	*William A. Lee*
MARY DELANEY	*Bette Howe*		

Time: *The present.*
Place: *The living room of St. Matthew's Rectory.* Act I. *An afternoon in the Fall.* Act II. Scene 1. *Five weeks later. Afternoon.* Scene 2. *The following night, shortly after midnight.* Act III. *The next morning.*
Director: *James Russo.*

PLOT: A young female orphan comes unwanted and unwelcome into a household but in the end captives one and all with her arch and winning ways. The final curtain shows her not in the arms of the young man who had been planned for her but in those of a somewhat older and more desirable one to whom she has lost her heart. Correct. Still another version of J. Hartley Manners' *Peg o' My Heart,* and nowhere nearly so proficient and entertaining as the original, which of course was also hokum but much more expert hokum than the poll-parrots have been able to manage. Why they want to produce these pale, amateur copies when the original is available is one of the two or three hundred things about the theatre that I do not understand. The only explanation is the hope of selling the transcripts to the movies, which is a poor hope since the movies do not seem to be buying any plays these days. *Peg* must still have a lot of life in it, because when it was done in various stock theatres in the previous summer audiences revelled in it and it uniformly did a turnaway business. I saw one of the productions and confess that I was astonished at the seeming longevity of the play's humor and even charm. With a few minor changes, I am sure that, if wisely cast, it would still amuse audiences infinitely more than any such cheap, poorly acted imitation as this. It is, as remarked, compounded of what is known on the Rialto as "hoke," but the difference between its and that of its copies is the difference between a comradely slap on the back from an old friend and one from a fresh young table-hopper.

I am, I confess, prejudiced in favor of *Peg* as against this latest paraphrase for a possibly understandable, if uncritical, reason. It provides, unlike Miss Kerr's version, an opportunity for the appearance in it of a dog, and it was a dog in the person of my own wire-hair Maxim who so handsomely adorned it in one of its summer presentations. I duly appreciate that since I have thus been connected commercially with the theatre, if in only one instance, it is nevertheless obvious that anyone who derives even the slightest monetary revenue from the object of his criticism can not be fair-minded, impartial and honest, and I not only plead guilty to the charge but confide that I am still acting as trustee of the two dollars which Maxim received as an honorarium for her week's histrionic efforts.

Freely admitting, therefore, that prejudice, combined with those two dollars, may make me a questionable critic of Maxim's performance, I wish notwithstanding to offer my opinion that Maxim was little short of magnificent in the role of Peg's pet and reached heights in its interpretation that Duse, Bernhardt and such other girls, with all their resources, could not begin to scale. I ask you, did Bernhardt, for instance, even at the summit of her career ever hold an audience breathless by sneaking up on her leading man from the rear and nipping him in the seat of his pants? If you have the impertinence to answer yes, I forthwith denounce you as one who never laid eyes on Bernhardt and who lives merely by hearsay. Well, Maxim, I boast, did what Bernhardt didn't, and not only brought down the

house but the leading man. Did Duse, I further demand
of you, even with all her superb talent ever succeed in captivating an audience solely by wagging her tail? No! It was
Ann Pennington. And Pennington spoiled it all by singing. Maxim, being a born artiste, appreciated Stanislavski's
dictum that singing while wagging the tail grievously distracts an audience's attention from the main business in
hand and astutely refrained, though some barks may have
been mistaken for singing by any admirers of Billie Holiday who may have been present.

The average dog that enters upon an acting career conducts its art after a stereotyped and recognizable pattern.
From the moment it comes on the stage to the moment it
exits it spends the time either fixing the audience with a
bored and cynical eye or looking as if at any minute it
might embarrassingly misbehave itself, particularly if the
scene be an outdoor one. Not my Maxim, however. Not
only did Maxim, pursuant to the strict rules of the acting
art, not once so much as glance in the direction of the audience, thus cleverly establishing her artiste's humility by
implying she didn't believe anybody had paid out money
to see her, but she behaved with such rare restraint that I
thought she must be someone else's dog.

Maxim's name in the pedigree books is Lady Maxi-
milian, after which bit of bragging I should like to point
out another facet of her uncommon virtuosity. The role
which she played in *Peg*, as all know who recall it from the
days when Laurette Taylor was its star, is that of a boy dog
called Michael. But Maxim's protean genius is such that
she was able to conceal her sex to so convincing an extent
that the audiences' puzzlement became audible and resulted in the management's decision to award a set of
dishes on Saturday night to the person who guessed it
correctly.

Not since the heyday of female impersonators has such a
tribute been paid to a performer.

Some of Maxim's scenes, if I say it myself, were brilliant.
In the play, there is an episode in which Peg is told by a
fashionable and snooty woman that her beloved pet can

not remain in the house, though the woman herself also has a dog that is not only freely allowed the run of the establishment but is an ignominious mutt. Surveying the mutt, Maxim managed to achieve a look of aristocratic disdain which, while perhaps not precisely in key with the demands of the script, since Peg's pet is supposed to be of inferior social status, nevertheless lent the script an added satirical value that even the author himself would have en-enthusiastically approved.

Topping this, Maxim subsequently permitted a tear to drop from her eye as if in sympathy for the cruel way in which her mistress, Peg, was being treated. I overheard one bounderish critic in the audience contend that the tear was accidentally induced by a moth that had flown into Maxim's eye, but any such explanation was unthinkable. It was pure acting art. Furthermore, there is a touching scene in the play involving Peg, who at the time is carrying her pet in her arms. During this scene Maxim proved her genius triply. Unlike such lesser actresses as the late Mrs. Fiske who, when called upon to express woe, turned her back on the audience and faked her melancholy by lowering her head and wobbling it, Maxim drooped her head in full view of the audience and let out some wonderfully realistic whines. If ever I saw sheer artistry, this was it. Stanislavski would have proposed marriage to Maxim on the spot.

Needless to say, Maxim has been flooded with another offer. But I am not certain that I will advise her to accept it. She is such a happy little dog as things have been with her that I hesitate to expose her to the trials of an actress' life and to the idiosyncrasies of dramatic criticism as it presently is practised amongst us. Maxim, being a good dog, also has some concern for me, I am sure, and would not want to damage my own professional career by casting suspicion on my reviews of her performances. As she said to me after her engagement in *Peg* was over, "Master George, I like my home too much, and one day I'd like to have babies. So the hell with trying to make a fool out of Elisabeth Bergner."

OH, MR. MEADOWBROOK! December 26, 1948

A comedy by Ronald Telfer and Pauline Jamerson. Produced by John Yorke for 41 performances in the Golden Theatre.

PROGRAM

CONSTANCE VYE	NESTA MADRIGALE
Grace McTarnahan	Vicki Cummings
HARLAND VYE — Harry Ellerbe	JAMES HOWELLS — Morton L. Stevens
SOPHIE MACDONALD — Sylvia Field	
JAPHET MEADOWBROOK	
Ernest Truex	

SYNOPSIS: *The action takes place in the Vyes' living-room in Connecticut. Act I. A Friday afternoon, in early summer. About 4:30 o'clock. Act II. The next afternoon. About 3:30 o'clock. Act III. Early the next morning.*

Director: *Harry Ellerbe.*

THIS *Oh, Mr. Meadowbrook!* is the kind of play that used to be reviewed by saucy critics simply with the *Oh.* I would not, of course, think of descending to any such low practice, but it doesn't seem to be such a bad idea at that.

It doesn't seem to be such a bad idea for three collaterally good reasons. The first is the play's apparent belief that *double entendre* of the ferocious species which figured in the Wilson Collison-Al Woods sex farces of a quarter of a century ago may still be full of amusement provided only it be indulged in every two minutes instead of the every three in the past. The second is its equally apparent belief that there may still be something enormously hilarious in the spectacle of an inexperienced and timid male besieged by several highly experienced and predatory females determined upon his anatomical acquiescence provided only a pint-size comedian with balloon eyeballs be cast in the role. And the third is its similarly apparent belief that if the first two are incorporated into a stage set representing a bedroom the whole will be irresistible provided only no slightest comprehensible reason for the women's eager pursuit of the virgin imbecile is assigned by the playwright.

THE VICTORS. December 26, 1948

A play by Jean-Paul Sartre, adapted by Thornton Wilder. Produced by New Stages, Inc., for 31 performances in the New Stages Theatre.

Program

François	*Larry Robinson*	Dubois	*Joseph Silver*
Sorbier	*Ernest Stone*	Jean	*John Larkin*
Canoris	*Boris Tumarin*	Clochet	*Leon Janney*
Lucie	*Florida Friebus*	Landrieu	*Jim Boles*
Guard	*Sid Walters*	Pellerin	*Arnold Robertson*
Henri	*Alexander Scourby*	Guard	*Robert Davis*

SYNOPSIS: Act I. Scene 1. *An attic of a schoolhouse in a village in southern France.* Scene 2. *A classroom in the same building.* Act II. Scene 1. *The attic.* Scene 2. *The classroom.*

The time is the summer of the invasion, when the Resistance Forces were taking small villages in advance of the Allied Armies.

Director: *Mary Hunter.*

Here, once again, Sartre reverts to what is essentially Grand Guignol melodrama and seeks to have it accepted for something dramatically superior by tinting it with what his admirers, despite uncomfortable evidence to the contrary, persist in describing as his "deeply probing social, political, and moral conscience." The probing in this particular instance yet again has to do with the Existentialist worry over man's obligations to his fellow-men and responsibilities to himself. The profundity of the probing, however, still again enjoys all the depth of an occulist in the digging for a cinder on the eye's outer surface. Sartre has nothing to say that has not been said often before, and very much better. His second-hand — indeed, third-hand — mind has never more plainly undressed itself. His arguments resemble those of a bookworm schoolboy debater echoing an ill-digested Voltaire and Kafka and of another heatedly replying with the concepts of the village cynic.

Originally called *Mort Sans Sepulture* (*The Unburied
Dead*), the play treats of a French underground group
placed under arrest by the Vichy military and of the efforts
of the latter to force from their prisoners the hiding place
of the Maquis' leader. Despite the sadistic tortures visited
upon the prisoners, they refuse to tell and in the end are
dispatched by their tormentors when the latter find it necessary to make a quick departure. Aside from the injec-
tion of the marked-down philosophical haberdashery mentioned, there is nothing in the play but the old formula of
helplessness-at-bay given the equally old shock treatment of
countless thrillers in the little theatre of horrors in the Rue
Chaptal, of such local melodramas of years ago as Charles
Klein's *The Third Degree,* and of the Hollywood gangster
motion pictures. Sartre, who seems to rely upon sensationalism of one sort or another as a meal-ticket, this time en-
deavors to make certain he will not miss by tripling and
even quadrupling the Guignol in the matter of atrocities
and piles torture upon torture. These, however, are as
nothing compared with that suffered by an audience
through the author's immoderate garrulity.

At least once or twice in every decade we are entertained
by the emergence of a playwright who, for a reason impen-
etrable to the more practised critics, is accepted by the public, along with the less practised critics, as a dramatist of
importance and who, until he is caught onto, basks in the
glow of miscellaneous esteem. Sartre is the latest. There is,
however, one thing to be said for him: he seems to realize
and appreciate his mountebankery and to derive a lot of
personal fun out of his bamboozling the susceptibles. In a
recent published interview, he was, for example, asked to
define just what his doctrine of Existentialism is. "It is," he
answered with charming frankness, "the means whereby I
make a living." I have no doubt that one of these days he
will similarly embarrass those who venerate the quality of
his drama by making a like reply to an interviewer who
questions him about his plays.

As little as I may admire those plays, I confess that I have
considerable admiration for a man who, like him, has the

cleverness, ingenuity and, above all, the sardonic humor
prosperously to swindle so many gulls without their knowing it. I have heard from people who know him well, that,
whatever the nature of his literary and dramatic abilities,
he is an intelligent and amusing companion, and I can
readily believe it. It takes a great deal of wit and skill to
pull off the jobs that Sartre has; no ordinary man could
possibly do it. It also takes a mind, albeit of peculiar cast.
And Sartre deserves all the credit in that line that a critic
of humanity, if not of drama, can give him. He is his decade's foremost theatrical confidence man, which in view of
the strong competition is no mean achievement. And, as
such, he will have his proud niche in the history of the
modern stage.

It is possible, of course, that I am allowing him qualities
which he does not really possess but simply with a pleasant
amiability pretends to. If, however, underneath it all he
actually conducts his profession with seriousness, and evidence in that direction is not lacking, he is a master at self-
deception. His fecundity in such directions as philosophy,
politics, sociology, the novel, the short story, the cinema
and the drama is that of a rabbit, yet he seems to operate
under the delusion that his reproductions are not rabbits
but lions and tigers, whereas even the rabbits he factually
delivers himself of are of the mechanical toy variety, stuffed
with the sawdust of borrowed ideas.

As to the acting and staging of the present play, which,
as with *Les Mains Sales,* resorts for extra sensationalism to
the use of some verbal forbidden fruit, it is perhaps better
that the tombstone of the entire enterprise be left further
uninscribed.

THE MADWOMAN OF CHAILLOT
DECEMBER 27, 1948

A play by Jean Giraudoux, adapted by Maurice Valency. Produced by Alfred de Liagre, Jr., for the rest of the season's performances in the Belasco Theatre.

PROGRAM

THE WAITER	Ralph Smiley	THE BROKER	Jonathan Harris
THE LITTLE MAN	Harold Grau	THE STREET JUGGLER	John Beahan
THE PROSPECTOR	Vladimir Sokoloff	DR. JADIN	Sandro Giglio
THE PRESIDENT	Clarence Derwent	COUNTESS AURELIA	Martita Hunt
THE BARON	Le Roi Operti	THE DOORMAN	William Chambers
THERESE	Patricia Courtley	THE POLICEMAN	Ralph Roberts
THE STREET SINGER	Eugene Cibelli	PIERRE	Alan Shayne
THE FLOWER GIRL		THE SERGEANT	Richard Sanders
	Millicent Brower	THE SEWERMAN	James Westerfield
THE RAGPICKER	John Carradine	MME. CONSTANCE	
PAULETTE	Barbara Pond		Estelle Winwood
THE DEAF MUTE	Martin Kosleck	MLLE. GABRIELLE	Nydia Westman
IRMA	Leora Dana	MME. JOSEPHINE	Doris Rich
THE SHOE-LACE PEDDLER			
	Maurice Brenner		

SYNOPSIS: Act I. The *Café* terrace of *Chez Francis*. Act II. The *Countess' cellar, 21 Rue de Chaillot.*
Director: *Alfred de Liagre, Jr.*

The Madwoman Of Chaillot as the late Giraudoux wrote it is an infinitely better play than you would suspect from the one purveyed under the same name in the adaptation of Maurice Valency. If you are a steady customer of these critical performances you will remember that more than a year before I published some fragrant words on the original and promised that, were it adroitly adapted and imaginatively cast, it would provide an extremely valuable and jolly evening in the theatre.

Should you have forgotten what I wrote, which, alas, is not altogether improbable in the present confused state of civilization, I take the liberty of recalling it to you in small part. That Giraudoux was an uncommonly inventive, witty and skilful dramatist, I observed, is evident to American audiences who some seasons ago had so much pleasure from his *Amphitryon 38,* let alone to those who are familiar with other of his plays like *Undine, Siegfried, Intermezzo,* and *The Trojan War Will Not Take Place.* In none of these has he worked with greater sparkle, sharper point and better effect than in this *La Folle.* From first to last it is juiced with a broad but trenchant humor, a smart fancy, and an imagination that with a pretty cunning brews poetry from caricature. I then went on to tell the play's story and allowed, unnecessarily, that trying to impart the idea of a good play by sketching its plot is as unsatisfactory and even as ridiculous as trying to convey the quality of a good piece of music by whistling it. It could do no more than hint at what the play intrinsically was like: an intellectual fantasy which filters profundity through a satirical grin and which gets across its theme — the curse of those materialists who would banish charm and beauty from the world — without once edging its foot toward the loud pedal or making the slightest soapbox noise.

I proceeded, somewhat bumptiously, to suggest the proper casting of the play now that Laurette Taylor, who had planned to act its leading role, was gone and now that gone with her were some others ideally suited to its other roles. And while peddling advice, which no one had asked for, I urged the translator-adapter, whoever he might be, to exercise all his talent in seeing to it that the dialogue did not lose its expansive flourish, that the action in the second act did not droop, that the bubble and gusto of the Giraudoux script did not evaporate, and that, above all, the warm tone of the whole would not suffer a chill. If all this were well attended to, I oracularized, you would get an evening in the theatre that would entertain you in entertainment's very highest sense.

Well, here you are and if you are disappointed you can not blame me. I did my damnedest. The play you now see still has a degree of the Giraudoux flavor; it here and there preserves a little of his humor and spirit; and if you do not know the original you will not know what you are missing and maybe will sufficiently enjoy yourself. But you have my word for it that it is not by a very long distance the gala occasion it might have been.

In the first place, Valency's adaptation was originally conceived as a vehicle for Grace George, of all inappropriate actresses, and to the infinite weakening of the play was politessed to suit her scarcely robustious technique and personality. Martita Hunt, who presently occupies its leading role, is an actress of a different chop, but the thinness of the treatment, along with the ill-advised direction, is still perceptible for all her efforts to thicken it. The adaptation prepared by Paul Bowles for Miss Taylor, whose ribald conception of the role was partly insinuated into it, was better but was too hurriedly executed and too sketchy, though it succeeded in capturing more of the original tone than Valency's. Secondly, the casting of the other principal roles is routine; it misses the desirable novelty and surprise; and, though the actors and actresses perform dutifully, the impression is old-hat. Because Clarence Derwent was so good as a swindler in *Topaze,* which this play in one of its lesser phases resembles, he has been cast again as a swindler. Because Estelle Winwood has given a good account of herself in some eccentric roles, she is again cast as an eccentric. And so on. It is all as foreseeable when the curtain goes up as the reiterant casting of an old-time stock company in its second season. Thirdly, the translation-adaptation frequently has a frosty air of classroom precision. It seems to be a bit afraid of the original script's boozy effusiveness and sometimes is suggestive of a college professor — I am informed that Valency is a pedagogue of sorts — who is slightly at sea in his effort to be one of the boys. It is, true, faithful in its fashion, but the fashion, if Cynara must know, is here far from rakish and definitely ascetic.

Giraudoux's central character is a frowzy old baggage out of the Paris of another and better day who is given to absurd personal adornment and who, though touched in the head, contrives a plan successfully to rid her world of the crooked, grasping and evil men who already have made it intolerable and who would make it uglier still and more hopeless. Her particular cronies are three other relics as loony as she but who, like her, in the end seem to have been just a little more sensible, for all their derangement, than others theoretically more rational. Around the women, the older harridan in particular, swarms a symbolic cavalcade of pompous knaves and rascals out to get all they can by one means or another and who ultimately collide with the old girl's prejudice to keep her section of Paris what it was in a more decent time. Through a series of shenanigans that in comparison make Smith and Dale look like the Brothers Karamazov, she gets the whole crew of them into the cellar of her house and, persuading them that a subterranean passage is full of the precious oil which they have been led to believe is under the city's soil, sends them one by one to their doom. And, as the final curtain falls, there cross the stage the withered and miserable ghosts of all such fools who have sacrificed for earthly gain the really valuable and beautiful things which might have made their lives better and richer and happier.

Any such skeletonized recital can not, as remarked, give any real idea of the play. It does not suggest, for example, that the plot is projected through an enveloping and inveigling humor, that all kinds of little imaginative touches brightly set off the character drawing, that the theme is developed with ironic indirection partly through the fate of a mere vagrant cat, that the rogues and scoundrels are handled with a grotesque and killing buffoonery, and various other such attributes. It does not suggest, further, the manner in which Giraudoux has sifted a whimsical wisdom through burlesque gauze, or the tenderness he has managed to knit into the crazy-quilt of his demented women, or the hilarious extravagance of his charlatans and impostors, or — and this is all-important — the way in which he manages to force home his ultimate point with no slightest flexing of his dramatic muscles. It does not suggest, in sum, in short, and to repeat, that one of the most effective modern plays with a social message gets that message over the footlights without, as almost all the other plays with similar messages have done, so much as once lifting its voice or making a face like a pamphleteer and without sending an audience out of the theatre wishing that it had gone instead to a good hula-hula show.

Very little of these qualities remains in the de Liagre projection of the play. Miss Hunt, imported from England, either by personal choice or because of direction performs the role of the madwoman of the title not with the called for robust humor but largely in the manner of a repertory company tragedy queen. John Carradine, in the part of the rag-picker originated in the Paris production by Louis Jouvet, also seems to be under the impression that Shakespeare had a hand in the evening and makes matters worse by alternately intoning and declaiming what properly are low comedy lines. The swindlers in the persons of the Messrs. Derwent, Operti and Sokoloff miss completely the fantastic air of exaggerated suavity and pompous W. C. Fields elegance which the roles demand; Miss Winwood offers stridency in place of tenderness and thus deletes the character of Constance, the madwoman of Passy, of its dramatic point; and most of the others are similarly guilty of botching things. Only Doris Rich, with her rough Mae West approach to the role of the madwoman of La Concorde, and Leora Dana, as the gentle love interest, fit anywhere nearly into the Giraudoux frame. The fault, obviously, is to be laid mainly to the de Liagre staging, which additionally deadens the script with so fixed and static a disposition of the actors that the stage frequently intimates that Madame Tussaud served him as a co-director.

DON'T LISTEN, LADIES. December 28, 1948

A comedy by Sacha Guitry, translated and adapted by Stephen Powys. Produced by Lee Ephraim and Jack Buchanan for 15 performances in the Booth Theatre.

Program

Daniel Bachelet	Jack Buchanan	Blandinet	Ian Lubbock
Henriette	Joan Seton	Julie Bille-En-Bois	Ivy St. Helier
Madeleine	Moira Lister	Valentine	Adele Dixon
Baron De Characnay		A Porter	Bartlett Mullins
	Hugh Miller	Michel Aubrion	Austin Trevor

SYNOPSIS: The action of the play takes place at Daniel Bachelet's antique shop in Paris. Act I. Monday morning. Act II. Friday afternoon. (The curtain will be lowered during Act II to denote the passage of time from Friday afternoon to the following Monday.)

Director: *Willard Stoker.*

It has been said of Sacha Guitry that the volume of his plays, which have run to the imposing figure of a hundred-odd, is to be accounted for in the demands of his successive inamoratas and wives that he supply acting vehicles for them or bear the consequences. True or not, his various ladies and spouses seem to have displayed themselves regularly on his stage and, such is the quality of justice, often to considerable advantage. But whether married or momentarily at liberty, the antic Frenchman for more than thirty years now has done his ample share in enlivening the Paris theatre. I have seen scores of his plays and, with few exceptions, have been most pleasantly entertained by them, since they almost always contain a cultivated drollery and a merrily impudent point of view, not to mention a very fair brand of light comedy invention.

Many of his comedies have the air of being dramatized witty supper table conversations induced by desirable feminine companions and plenty of champagne. If they seem to be superficial, the superficiality gives the impression of

being so only because any greater depth would spoil the
party. But under the superficiality one detects an observation and understanding beyond the froth and, at times,
something that comes pretty close to being as sharp and
lively a comprehension of men and women in their more
romantic biological manifestations as the French boule-
vard theatre has provided.

The plays when exported are not always fortunate.
Translation and adaptation are often as difficult as the
translating and adapting of purely American comedies like
The College Widow and *Is Zat So?* to foreign stages. The
volatile fibre and tone and the turn of phrase of a Guitry
script elude the transplanter, save he be of unusual cosmopolitanism and literary dexterity, and what emerges is
much like a corked bottle of sparkling Vouvray, flat and a
bit vinegary. It accordingly was inevitable that an English
roué of my acquaintance should once descend so low as to
describe the typically poor adaptation of one whose central character was a silly old maid who imagined that men
were wild to achieve her favors as "a Sucha Guilty version
of a goose with delusions of gander, a pungent pun however punctiliously deemed punishable by pundits and
punjabs," God henceforth have mercy on Anglo-American
relations.

The present Guitry exhibit is, however, no case in point.
One of his poorer efforts, it is a dull and dated business
about marital jealousy, made duller and worse dated by
decayed epigrams on the female sex, which would remain
just as dull and dated were it to have been translated and
adapted by a genius, which Stephen Powys is not.

As in many better Guitry comedies, the basic formula is
again the sex triangle or, if Sacha happens at the moment
to be of a more acutely sexual frame of mind in respect to
himself, quadrangle. The role he elects for himself is customarily that of a slightly world-weary and cynical post-
graduate of the school of active biology still craved, despite
his considerate allusions to himself as a middle-aged and
settled man of forty-five (or, if generously over-critical,
forty-six), by his present and past wives and fiancées, let

alone by all his former mistresses. It is his especial pleasure to preside over the desperate efforts of these ladies in the cast to renew amorous relations with him and either to discourage them from their dreams with fillets of pessimistic philosophy or resignedly to accept their importunities with reluctant lapses into a sentiment which embraces recollections of one-time affairs or honeymoons at Deauville, Monte Carlo or on the Riviera when the moon turned the sea to silver, when the smell of jasmine permeated their little bedroom, and when Spring kissed away the clouds.

Whether calling himself Daniel Bachelet, Marcel Chambertin, Jean-Pierre or what not, it is Sacha of whom Guitry always writes, and whether the ladies be named Madeleine, Valentine, Julie Bille-en-Bois, Angèle, Marie-Jeanne or anything else their single ambition, for all an occasional unfaithfulness or two, is either to regain the person of the matchless Sacha or to convince him, after they have taken up with other men, that he is the only one they ever truly loved. It must be a wonderful life and I sorely envy him. Here, poor worm, I still sit in my late years writing vicariously of such delights when I might have been a playwright and, like Sacha, had the time of my life glorifying myself night after night for more than three whole decades as a wit, beauty, and lover testified by innumerable exquisite young actresses as having seldom been surpassed in the history of the modern world. I am a big fool.

To see such a role impersonated, as in this *Don't Listen, Ladies,* by a chill, clipped-tongued Englishman like Buchanan is to see comedy unintentionally piled upon comedy. And to hear any such starched cucumber pretending to be concerned solely with the sex life is shaking realism by the tail. I appreciate that I am expected to suspend judgment in such a case as in others, but the spectacle of Englishmen posing in French plays as creatures of a volcanic libido is always too much for me, and I have to laugh in the wrong places.

THE RAPE OF LUCRETIA. December 29, 1948

A music drama with score by Benjamin Britten and libretto, based on André Obey's Le Viol de Lucrèce, *by Ronald Duncan. Produced by Marjorie and Sherman Ewing and Giovanni Cardelli for 23 performances in the Ziegfeld Theatre.*

PROGRAM

THE MALE CHORUS	*Edward Kane*	LUCIA	*Marguerite Piazza*
THE FEMALE CHORUS		ROMAN WOMAN	*Lidija Franklin*
	Brenda Lewis	TWO ETRUSCAN	*Lucas Hoving*
COLLATINUS	*Holger Sorensen*	SOLDIERS	*Kazimir Kokic*
JUNIUS	*Emilee Renan*	ROMAN MAN	*Robert Pagent*
TARQUINIUS	*George Tozzi*	ROMAN YOUTH	*Stanley Simmons*
LUCRETIA	*Kitty Carlisle*	A PROSTITUTE	*Bunty Kelley*
BIANCA	*Vivian Bauer*		

SYNOPSIS: Time: *Rome 509* B.C. Act I. Scene 1. *The General's tent in the camp outside Rome.* Scene 2. *Lucretia's house in Rome, the same evening.* Act II. Scene 1. *Lucretia's bedroom, that night.* Scene 2. *Lucretia's house, the next morning.*

Director: *Agnes de Mille.*

FOR SOME TIME now I have been toying with the notion that many of Tin Pan Alley's most popular song products are those the rhythm of which is orchestrated to one or another of the movements of the jaws in the chewing of gum. These are three in number: the blue *dolente* movement, the light *allegro di molto* movement, and the movement following the accidental swallowing of the wad and the attempts at regurgitation. A study of the favorite tunes of juke-box, radio, dance hall and suchlike addicts will, I think, substantiate the theory in greater part. In my heroic pursuit of scientific truth, I have conducted considerable clinical research in the matter and have experimented with various appropriate specimens of the younger generation, along with a herd of adults of equally arrested development, and the results would seem further to prove the beauty of the hypothesis. I accordingly have come to the conclusion that, though the song writers may not be conscious of the fact, it is the gum chewing which they themselves so actively indulge in that has automatically influenced their compositions to the large prosperity they often enjoy, since those compositions naturally accommodate themselves to the jowl vibrations of the legion of their fellow chicle munchers.

Consider the size of the market.

It is estimated that one out of every three Americans is addicted to gum chewing in those parts of the country where the product is available, which is almost everywhere, and that in the very few where it is not all of three out of three exercise their maxillary bones on such substitutes as prairie grass, corn silk, straw, tar, candle wax, corks out of old bottles and, in the more barbaric outposts, even canapés of manure. The result of the wholesale jaw movement is a nation which presents the aspect of an old colossal Grade-B silent movie, with a cast running into millions of violently active mouths out of which comes nothing resembling human sound.

Exact statistics on the amount of gum masticated by the American people are only obliquely available, but the best figures at hand show that the industry turns out a sufficient yearly supply to keep the average native jaw in operation for something like seven hours in every working day. As one small indication, we have the report of a researcher for the *New York Times Magazine,* John Stanton, who not long ago announced that a Times Square street corner yielded three thousand nine hundred gobs, that on the sidewalks in front of a centrally located New York department store were counted all of eleven thousand, and that a New York theatre has employed two inside charwomen and one outside man to clean its seats, its lobby and its pavement of gnawed remainders.

That the habit has developed to an inordinate degree calls for no research, however, on the part of anyone who has had daily experience scraping off sidewalk deposits from his shoes, chair deposits from the seat of his trousers, and strap wads in subways and buses from his hands. At an Army training camp in New Jersey during the last war, four privates had to be assigned every day to clean the grounds of openly and surreptitiously chewed souvenirs. And I have the assurance of one of the heads of one of the largest metropolitan department stores, obviously patronized for the most part by women, that one of its most trying problems is the dislodging after closing time of something like four thousand moist chunks from under counter ledges, escalator steps and railings, elevator floors and, more than anywhere else, the sides and bottoms of bargain tables.

The tapping of the feet to tunes, without which their wide acceptance would be doubtful, is, in my theory, simply a reflex of the jawbone movements, or in cases where the tappee is not a gum chewer, a kind of substitute. It plainly follows the composition of the tune, does not precede it. The tunes that sell millions of copies are written not with the feet in mind but, intentionally or by chance, with the jaws. If intentionally, the composers will, of course, deny it; their regard for their genius precludes any such admission. If unintentionally, they will dismiss the theory as poppycock, and very insulting to their art. But there it is, nonetheless, and in all its æsthetic splendor.

These ruminations again affected me while listening to Britten's score and while reflecting on the absurdity of installing it in a musical comedy theatre with any hope of finding a Broadway audience for it. Any such commercial audience is mainly, at least in spirit, a gum chewing one and devoted above all else in music to melody, or what passes for it. Give it anything which aspires to some real musicianship and which indicates a degree of sound craftsmanship, as in this case, and it expresses its discomfort in all the visible tokens of boredom. Though Britten here is surely very far from his best and though he seems to have held himself in check in the interests of the verbal effect of Duncan's libretto, several of his numbers like tenor aria describing the ride of Tarquinius to Rome, the flower duet in the second act, and the women's linen trio are of some merit and the whole has a clear technical and experimental interest. Regarded from any sharp critical level, the score in its main flow may here and there be thin to the point of emaciation and of an intellectual chill, with a minimum of emotional content; it may fail in thematic march and growth; but even when least satisfactory it intimates that in it are a noticeable gift for imagery and mood and a musical conscience.

The libretto, on the other hand, a retelling of the legend told and retold by poets and dramatists from Livy to Shakespeare and beyond, is pretentious, overly verbose, and altogether rather deadly. It is asking much to ask anyone to write music of any sort to such lines, for instance, as "With the prodigious liberality of self-coined obsequious flattery." Nor are lines to the literal effect that some officers went back to Rome the night before to observe if their mates stayed virtuously at home or that one of the wives who lay stripped in bed with an Arab told her husband she had only been having a massage conducive either to the beauties of the tonal art or to anything resembling poetic elevation. And, surely, little can be said for a wit that takes such pooped and juvenile shapes as observing that virtue in women is merely lack of opportunity or that women are all whores by nature.

The singing varies from the competent to the only faintly adequate. The décor by the British artist, John Piper, is strikingly picturesque in the setting for Lucretia's home but somewhat messy in the backdrops and in the case of the camp outside Rome. Agnes de Mille's staging, except for her fond employment of extras who are intermittently introduced to contort their bodies to no dramatic purpose, may generously be described as serviceable.

KISS ME, KATE. December 30, 1948

A musical comedy with book by Bella and Samuel Spewack, songs and lyrics by Cole Porter. Produced by Arnold Saint Subber and Lemuel Ayers for the rest of the season's performances in the Century Theatre.

Program

Fred Graham	Alfred Drake	Bill Calhoun	Harold Lang
Harry Trevor	Thomas Hoier	First Man	Harry Clark
Lois Lane	Lisa Kirk	Second Man	Jack Diamond
Ralph	Don Mayo	Stage Doorman	Bill Lilling
Lilli Vanessi	Patricia Morison	Harrison Howell	Denis Green
Hattie	Annabelle Hill	Specialty Dancers {	Fred Davis
Paul	Lorenzo Fuller		Eddie Sledge

Taming of the Shrew Players

Bianca (Lois Lane)	Lisa Kirk	Katharine (Lilli Vanessi)
Baptista (Harry Trevor)		Patricia Morison
	Thomas Hoier	Petruchio (Fred Graham)
Gremio (First Suitor)	Edwin Clay	Alfred Drake
Hortensio (Second Suitor)		Haberdasher	John Castello
	Charles Wood	Tailor	Marc Breaux
Lucentio (Bill Calhoun)		
	Harold Lang	

SYNOPSIS: Act I. Scene 1. *Stage of Ford Theatre, Baltimore.* Scene 2. *The corridor backstage.* Scene 3. *Dressing-rooms, Fred Graham and Lilli Vanessi.* Scene 4. *Padua.* Scene 5. *Street scene, Padua.* Scene 6. *Backstage.* Scene 7. *Fred and Lilli's dressing-rooms.* Scene 8. *Exterior church.* Act II. Scene 1. *Theatre alley.* Scene 2. *Before the curtain.* Scene 3. *Petruchio's house.* Scene 4. *The corridor backstage.* Scene 5. *Fred and Lilli's dressing-rooms.* Scene 6. *The corridor backstage.* Scene 7. *Backstage.* Scene 8. *Baptista's home.*
Director: *John C. Wilson.*

ONE OF THE inconvenient things about this critical job is writing a highly laudatory review of a musical show. Now and then your friends may agree with your opinion of it, but more often enough of them will fiddle around with the conversation for a while and then suddenly give you a look and demand to know what you saw in it that they, for the life of them, could not. It isn't so hard to understand at that. If there is anything in this world that depends more upon how dinner went, your immediate mood, the comfortableness of your collar, and the desirability of the lady sitting next to you, I do not know of it. For, when all is said and done, the musical show is to the theatre something in the nature of a party and, as everybody knows, there never yet has been a party at which everyone enjoyed himself equally. Or, if there has been, I seem somehow not to have been there.

There is also another inconvenient thing about this job and that is writing a highly belittling review of a show, in which event a similar number of your friends who found it greatly to their liking will give you the kind of look they customarily reserve for a garbage-can. But this does not concern me at the moment, since it is not that sort of show I am talking about. The show I am talking about is this *Kiss Me, Kate,* which is a good one. Being a man given to moderation in all things, except maybe a dozen or so, I can not go into the hysterical spasms over it that most of my colleagues, emotional boys, did. When it comes to their adjectives like "terrific," "extraordinarily fine," "magnificent," and "unexcelled," I prefer to hold them for something like the *Nibelungen Ring,* lest I have none left. I would rather use such as "bright," "fresh," "entertaining," and "attractive," which, true enough, are not any too remarkable for their novelty but which at least seem to me to make some sense.

It is, in short, an enjoyable show with some edifying features in it. The book, of the play-within-a-play species, which has to do with an actor and his divorced actress wife who are appearing in *The Taming Of The Shrew* and who parallel Petruchio and Katharine in their personal conduct, is a lively mixture of Shakespeare and Jean Bedini. Porter's tunes and several of his lyrics are considerably above his later level. The settings and costumes by Lemuel Ayers are ingenious and nice to look at. Alfred Drake is a valuable performer, Liza Kirk a valuable accomplice, and

Patricia Morison thoroughly delightful. Furthermore, anyone who says that she is not one of the most savory samples
of womanhood seen hereabout in some time may prepare
to fight me. All of which should be enough to satisfy almost
anyone, even if I still believe that the adjective fits thrown
by my confrères would possibly be more suited to a show
like *Tristan And Isolde* or, apparently, if we accept a recent advertisement in, of all publications, the *Saturday Review Of Literature,* the cheese business. "Cheese fanciers,"
it stated, "have switched to Phil Alpert's cheeses of all nations because they are tantalizing, thrilling, and terrific."

But what I have written probably will not satisfy some of
my friends, which again will not be unusual. What many
of them will object to is my "lack of proper enthusiasm"
and others of them my "never-grown-up, childish interest
in musical shows and pretty girls." It seems, whatever I say,
that I can not please them. While having a bit of supper
after the opening, ten or twelve of the creatures came to
my table. "How did you like it?" asked one. "Very pleasant
show," I replied. Whereupon he eyed me as if I had the
pox, grunted "Pleasant, hell! It's superb!", disgustedly
turned on his heel, and moved away. "What did you think
of it?" inquired another. "Good stuff," I said. "Nuts to
you," he inelegantly declared. "Good? It's wonderful!"
"What's your opinion?" several others wanted to know. "I
liked it a lot," I told them. "You did?", they returned with
pained features. "*We* didn't!" And then went on for five
minutes speculating how a man of my alleged intelligence
could find amusement in such things.

You can, in a word, sometimes influence a person to
change his tastes and prejudices in literature, politics, the-
ology, food, drink, women, and pet goats but you can do
little about him in the matter of shows of this kind. And
that holds for professional critics as well as laymen. My old
friend, James Agate, critic for the London *Sunday Times,*
was surely one of the best in his day, yet the musical show
generally had a pestilential effect on him. A collection of
his reviews sounds like a Sartre play. He would groan for
days in advance over having to see one and for weeks after-

ward over having seen it. It seemed to matter little to him whether the show was good or bad; all, or at least almost all, were poison to him; and his published agonies rivalled a catalogue of the more painful and hideous diseases, both native and exotic. "I must plump for the strong impulse and instinctive mind of the author," he would write. "Nobody else has so firm and assured a drive in the matter of witlessness." Or such tributes as "lambent innocuousness," "if musical comedy soars it must only be into the illimitable inane," and "though I stayed to the bitter end, honesty compels me to state that I missed a little of the beginning and therefore can not tell how bitter that may have been." Or "it reduces me to a fakir-like state of insensibility," "the caterwauling of seasick tabbies," "humiliating and obscene," and, all too inclusively, "the critics sit in dumb despair, like Hottentots, and at each other stare," to which he quoted a footnote: "A beautiful figure of German literature: the Hottentots remarkable for staring at each other — God knows why."

The musical show, in a word, is like the other fellow's wife or sweetheart. For one man who shares his taste, there are always those who wonder what he can see in her. Some of the wisest men I know relish such shows; some of the wisest I know can not abide them. But what matter? It is of no slightest importance. Yet I should like to have caught Agate holding hands with Patricia Morison in a dark corner at the Ivy. I wouldn't have settled with the old boy for less than ten rounds of drinks.

THE SMILE OF THE WORLD
January 12, 1949

*A play by Garson Kanin. Produced by the Playwrights'
Company for 5 performances in the Lyceum Theatre.*

PROGRAM

Josef Boros	*Boris Marshalov*	Sam Fenn	*Warren Stevens*
Mrs. Boros	*Elizabeth Dewing*	Justice Reuben Boulting	
Petey	*Sam Jackson*		*Otto Kruger*
Evelyn	*Ruby Dee*	Stewart	*Ossie Davis*
Sara Boulting	*Ruth Gordon*	Alice Widmayer	*Laura Pierpont*

SYNOPSIS: Act I. *October, 1923.* Act II. *A few months later.* Act III. *A week later. Afternoon.*

Scene: *The home of Justice Reuben Boulting on the outskirts of Washington, D.C.*

Director: *Garson Kanin.*

THE KANINS, Garson and Fay, would have it read, "Life, liberalism, and the pursuit of huffiness." Let either of them write a play and you may count on it that the hero will be a young liberal irritably opposed to what he calls the forces of reaction, even though he does not always seem to know exactly what he is talking about. But, know it or not, he is usually as bloodthirsty for a changed order as he is hostile to such cankers as men over forty with more than ten dollars in their custom-made pockets, women who prefer to marry fellows of some position, security and reserve rather than the kind who would idealistically talk their ears off in romantic cold water flats, and a world full of the odious ease, comfort, well-being, and sixty-cent lunches of the Coolidge era as against the glorious and inspiring chaos of today and, doubtless, tomorrow.

That both Kanins have done time in Hollywood may or may not have something to do with their enthusiasm for the altered order, since it is well known that the disgusting backsliders of Hollywood have degraded big dreamers like

them with offensive wads of capital, intolerable physical
luxuries, and other such gross evidences of reaction. But,
whatever the reason and motive, they seem to believe that
they have been ordained to bring a new light and truth
into the cosmos while all other people, except maybe some
who are movie writers, are sitting lazily and indifferently
on their afterparts.

It is not, surely, that I am against liberalism, at least
when and if it makes some sense, which is not always. I am
myself mentally a liberal of sorts, if physically a reactionary. I am, in short, sympathetic to the rational aspects of
liberalism and unsympathetic to others which would arbitrarily upset the applecart with all its sweet pippins, install
a sour gooseberry stand in its place, and in the process give
me an unwelcome bellyache. But either way I am tired of
this all too common theatrical hawking of idealism for possible box-office boodle and doubly tired of it when its
mouthpieces, as in these Kanin plays, offer only their youth
and boudoir potentialities as substitutes for some intelligence, logic, and philosophical horse-sense.

The latest play by the Garson of the clan is this *The
Smile Of The World*. In his previous *Born Yesterday*,
which was otherwise a jolly comedy, the liberal mastermind was, to the whimsical misgiving of many, an editorial
writer for the *New Republic*. In Fay's *Goodbye, My Fancy*,
which Garson's present play here and there resembles, the
liberal great brain, to the equal skepticism of many, was a
photographer for *Life*. And in *The Smile Of The World*
the liberal cerebral phenomenon is a legal bellboy to a Supreme Court justice, so, say what you will, Garson is im-
proving.

Once again, as in the other Kanin exhibits, the liberal's
passion for human decency and the rights of his fellow-
men somehow does not restrain him from horning in on
one of them and stealing his wife, fiancée or sweetheart,
the ethics of course being that anything is fair and honorable provided the other man, particularly if he happens to
be a mere Supreme Court justice, college president or vulgar business man, does not happen to have the same socio-

logical point of view that you have. In this particular case
it is his boss' wife with whom, between lofty speeches for a
finer and more upright deal, the hero has a secret affair and
is instrumental in making desert her husband. It seems
that the latter, who has been married to the lady for all of
twenty years and, remarkably, is not quite so amorously ef-
fervescent toward her as he once was, has rendered a decision on free speech which displeases the young hero, which
combination of outrages justifies in both his and Mr. Kanin's eyes the moral issues involved. And when in the end
the wife, illuminated by a spiritually redeemed white spot-
light, packs her bags and departs and when the young liberal follows suit, all three — wife, liberal, and Kanin —
expect of an audience that it will melt with a profuse
sympathy.

Mr. Kanin, you will recall from an earlier chapter, has
expressed himself as deploring criticism that is witty at the
expense of forthright judgment. He should admire this review. Once again there is not an iota of wit in it. It is forthright in its judgment that his play — aside from a brief
Hervieu-like scene in which the Justice discusses the marital relationship with his wife and a tardy, last minute benevolence toward the jurist — is grandiose twaddle.

The leading roles were acted by Otto Kruger, as the judicial villain; Warren Stevens, as the heroic liberal; and
Ruth Gordon, as the wife. Miss Gordon again revealed herself as so possessed of studied and become indelible mannerisms that I think she made a mistake in showing herself
so shortly after her appearance in the luckless *The Leading
Lady*. Those unvarying personal tricks and affectations
have a way of making one character seem much like another and, engaging them in such quick succession, some
spectators were likely to find themselves wondering if the
Supreme Court Justice had not married the widow of a
drunken ham actor of the early Nineteen Hundreds. Similarly mannered actresses have been careful not to display
themselves more than once in a season. Those who have
done so, if my records are trustworthy, have often regretted

it. The others, especially Stevens, performed satisfactorily.

Among the playwright's touching contributions to human wisdom, it may finally be noted, was the theory that, if only a man will go back for a short visit to the small town in which he was born and look again at the scenes of his boyhood, he will be sure to alter the wrong course he has taken in later life. Also the thesis that, if a man departs from the point of view he held as a youngster, it signifies that he has lost his intellectual balance. And, in another direction, our sympathies were once again beseeched for the wife who, following the principle of plays without number, always seems to elect the most critical and worried moment in her husband's professional life to bring up the subject of the durability of his love for her, which she doubts to the extent of a twenty-minute impassioned discourse because he has forgotten to kiss her.

Speaking to an interviewer for the daily press about the inconclusive nature of his play, Mr. Kanin pontificated as follows: "The drama has undergone so many changes over the period of years that I have an idea the various formulæ are becoming exhausted. Perhaps the next form in the theatre will be a four-act play only three of which will be performed. Audiences are at the saturation point of seeing the problem solved. I wonder if there isn't a play to present the question in a stimulating enough way to let the audience work out its own solution? I think there is a very rewarding chunk of theatre that is willing not to solve all problems. In this play we indicate an unwritten fourth act. The problem is not conventionally or finally resolved."

Mr. Kanin's education in, or memory of, drama is plainly as remiss as his notion that his play is something of an innovation in this respect. He has apparently forgotten or never heard of Ibsen or of the many other playwrights who have permitted audiences to work out their own solutions to the problems that were posed. Nor is his clairvoyance as to the possibility of "a very rewarding chunk of theatre that is willing not to solve all problems" too remarkable, since the reward has been clearly in evidence for the last fifty years. It would fill a page to name the playwrights who have shared handsomely in it, but maybe the mention of only a few like Hauptmann, Galsworthy, Brieux, and Shaw will serve.

ALONG FIFTH AVENUE. January 13, 1949

A revue with sketches by Charles Sherman and Nat Hiken, songs by Gordon Jenkins, lyrics by Tom Adair, and additional tunes and lyrics by Richard Stutz and Milton Pascal. Produced by Arthur Lesser for the rest of the season's performances in, initially, the Broadhurst Theatre.

Principals

Nancy Walker, Hank Ladd, Carol Bruce, Donald Richards, Jackie Gleason, Viola Essen, Johnny Coy, Virginia Gorski, Joyce Matthews, Dick Bernie, Judyth Burroughs, Zachary Solov, Lee Krieger, Wallace Seibert. Director: *Charles Friedman.*

I HAVE COMPLAINED in a foregoing chapter of the trial imposed upon a critic by the form of entertainment known as the revue and of the difficulty in composing an appraisal of one which will not be largely an echo of countless previous such reviews, statistics-ridden, dully literal, and painful to any reader not given to an admiration for railroad timetables, basketball scores, treatises on sectional population growths, and kindred depressing literature. And here I am confronted again by still another. Since I can not very well repeat the escape stratagem which I practised in the case of the directly antecedent revue and expect the reader to continue to be so impressed by it that he will help the sales of this book by his word-of-mouth enthusiasm, I shall have to mess around as best I can, aided somewhat, however, in this circumstance by the fact that the show is a conveniently poor one.

In substantiation of my opinion of it, I may point out that one of its big comedy moments consists in the projection of a custard pie into a comedian's face; that one of its more inventive numbers offers a shop-window in which the manikins come to life; that the finale to its first act is the South American rhumba number which already this season has figured in *Where's Charley?*, *Small Wonder,* and

Lend An Ear, and that the number is not in any way up to
the others; that it imitates, and badly, the *Make Mine
Manhattan* scenic device of different New York localities;
and that its star is Miss Nancy Walker, a lady whose come-
dic gifts lie chiefly in making herself look as hideous as
seems humanly possible. Should you still remain uncon-
vinced, I may add that the show contains a sketch, laid at
a perfume counter, whose humor consists in spraying a
male customer with what is described as an aphrodisiacal
scent and having him pursued by another of homosexual
tendencies; an elaborate blues item based on the novel conceit that a total stranger may be very lonely in New York;
a number in which boys and girls appear in skating costumes and relevantly perform a clog dance; and the sketch
in which the comedian playing a detective mistakes the
starchy butler for the corpse of the murder victim.

The relief from such material is meagre. It amounts to a
trio of fairly amusing songs, one a travesty of the sentimental torch species and having to do with a dream boy named
Irving, the second Jackie Gleason's recital of his reasons
for joining the French Foreign Legion, and the third a
pleasant little item involving a small colored child named
Judyth Burroughs; one or two funny jokes by Hank Ladd;
and Carol Bruce. Describing the typical music hall vocalist, Huysmans wrote: "To match the sounds which issued
from her throat the singer had four gestures: one hand on
her heart, the other down by her thigh — right arm in
front, left arm behind — the same action reversed, both
hands stretched out towards the public. She bawled the
verses left and right alternately, opening and shutting her
eyes according as the rasping melody was doleful or trivial.
From the back rows . . . her mouth, wide open for the
last verse, had all the blackness of a cavern." The description, admirable as it generally is, does not, happily, fit this
Miss Bruce. An attractive and tasteful young woman, she
yields herself to a minimum of the Huysmans objections
and sings her songs, here not much good, simply and
fetchingly.

I forgot to mention that, among the other less inspiring

elements of the exhibit, are a ballet dancer who periodically enters into the proceedings and hurls herself madly about the stage with possibly more technical ability than grace and beauty; a tap dancer, male, who makes such agonized faces while executing his art that he seems to be suffering the more extreme varieties of old Hindu tortures; a bevy of dancing women mostly with calves the size of Munich washbowls; the sketch in which the comedian in the guise of a hospital patient makes passes at the nurse; the baritone in the open-neck shirt who renders a sentimental ditty as if it were a speech by Earl Browder; an allusion to *A Streetcar Named Desire* as *Desire Under A Streetcar;* and a scene in which Miss Walker drinks poison in the belief that it is whiskey and for fifteen minutes thereafter indulges herself in pantomime less suggestive of the consequences of toxinfection than of close association with a vaudeville troupe of particularly objectionable acrobats.

In conclusion, it might at least a little have profited the evening if there had been a rehearsal of the pronunciation of the "avenue" of the show's title. The sounds that emanated from the company's mouths ranged from "avenyou" to "avenoo," from "avnyo" to "avnhue," from "avonoo" to "avhenyou," and from "avownhu" to something that had the ring of "avinwoo."

THE SHOP AT SLY CORNER. January 18, 1949

A murder melodrama by Edward Percy. Produced by Gant Gaither for 7 performances in the Booth Theatre.

PROGRAM

ARCHIE FELLOWES	*Jay Robinson*	MRS. CATT	*Una O'Connor*
DESCIUS HEISS	*Boris Karloff*	ROBERT GRAHAM	*Philip Saville*
MARGARET HEISS	*Mary McLeod*	CORDER MORRIS	*Emmett Rogers*
JOAN DEAL	*Jane Lloyd-Jones*	STEVE HUBBARD	*Alfred Hyslop*
MATHILDE HEISS	*Ethel Griffies*	JOHN ELLIOT	*Reginald Mason*

SYNOPSIS: *The action of the play takes place in a room at the back of a London shop. Act I. A Friday evening in August. Act II. A Sunday evening. The following winter. Act III. The following Tuesday morning.*

Director: *Margaret Perry.*

IN THE PLAYS of the now remote past, fireplaces and other household hotspots were employed for the burning of manuscripts by Scandinavian characters, old love letters and Bibles by English, incriminating state papers by French and, in the case of the more homespun American variety, for the congenial warming of the human hindquarters. Those relatively innocent days, alas, are no more. The fireplace and its likes have become increasingly morbid and sinister. Let the curtain rise and the audience observe one of them and it promptly anticipates the worst, particularly if the play happens to be of British origin. The fireplace or oven, it then knows from experience, will be utilized either for the secret disposition of the bodies of murdered friends and relatives or the heating of pokers with which to test the feigned blindness of heroes and, if not the one or the other, for a purpose equally removed from its more normal business as a bringer of comfort from the cold or a medium for the baking of delicious popovers and the roasting of fragrant beefs and chickens.

There was a time not so very long ago when even in

some English plays grates and their mantels still served happily as resting places for the modish elbows of lords, dukes and earls or, if the latter were seated, which was seldom, as stations before which in languid elegance they magnanimously forgave their wives their transgressions, which seemingly had always occurred either in Cairo or at the Pig and Whistle in Sussex, or wistfully counselled their pretty young wards to marry only for love, supporting their advice with sighful but punctiliously chivalrous reflections on the mistakes they themselves had made. The idea that a fireplace might ever be used to a less genteel end was almost as unthinkable to the audiences as the idea that any Englishman with a touch of gray in his hair and over six feet tall was not a superb actor. But, as I have said, things have changed and the English playwright who would use any such erstwhile scrupulous source of heat for anything less than a crematorium for a done-in employer, blackmailer, sister-in-law or nephew has become a rare bird.

Mr. Percy, who surely revealed himself as no such feathered phenomenon in *Ladies In Retirement,* has managed, however, to chirp momentarily like one in this case. Though he leads everyone to expect that his fireplace, which is a false front for an electric furnace for the melting down of stolen gold, will be whirled around to melt down the cadaver of a murdered extortioner, he for some reason or another that the audience can not make out abstains. Which, while it may be morally applaudable, does not do the box-office any good, since it is a bad thing to disappoint customers, evil-minded as they may be, and since a little foul excitement of any kind would help to relieve the pervading humdrum of his drowsy and dreary play.

That the latter ran for two whole years in London has been made something of by those local commentators who always jump at any such opportunity to prove that the English revel in rubbish which would not stand a chance in our own theatre. The English, true enough, now and then seem to have very peculiar tastes in such matters but not much more peculiar than ours, which often gives their commentators a similar jolly opportunity to make a nose at us. If it comes to me, however, I do not see how we can well ridicule the English for liking such piffpoof as this *Shop At Sly Corner* when our audiences appear to esteem such equivalent junk, to name only one specimen, as *The Respectful Prostitute.*

Boris Karloff's presence in the local cast as the murderer did not help things. My colleagues were of the opinion that perhaps it was because he was shown, as in the ill-fated *The Linden Tree,* as fundamentally a family-loving man and because what audiences wanted him to be was an out-and-out skunk. That may be true of movie audiences but I do not think it has anything to do with the theatre kind. What that kind wants, regardless of whether Karloff is an ogre or an angel, is an interesting play, whatever the heft of its critical quality, and Karloff has had the misfortune to appear in two that were far from interesting. Even had he dutifully murdered two dozen people in each of them, set fire to a block of orphanages and chased a herd of Frankenstein monsters for three acts, both he and the plays would have failed just the same.

The fact that this was the eighty-second failure out of a total of eighty-nine plays in the murder, mystery and detective catalogue in the period of the last fourteen seasons makes one again speculate on the reasons for the wholesale theatrical collapse of the great majority of such exhibits. The most recent statistics on fictions of the species show that their popularity among readers is so considerable that, in the field of the twenty-five cent pocket-size reprints, they lead all other types of stories with yearly sales of more than thirty-five million copies. The large popularity of publications like *Ellery Queen's Mystery Magazine,* which sells for thirty-five cents, is similarly attested to by the sales figures. Yet, though at least one-half of the plays in point were no worse than one-half of the stories that found wide acceptance, they failed signally to attract audiences and in the aggregate lost hundreds of thousands of dollars. Why?

The reason, I think, is not one of merit or lack of it but purely of economics. Even a successful mystery book published at a cost to the buyer of two dollars, two and one-half dollars or three dollars seldom achieves a sale greater than ten thousand copies. Assuming that the price of a theatre ticket for even a good mystery play were — to strike an average — two and one-half dollars, ten thousand customers would fill a theatre of an average seating capacity of eight hundred and eighty for not more than about eleven weeks, or less than three months. Any such brief run would mean financial loss and failure, the possible sale of the motion picture rights not figuring in the argument, since it is theatrical fiasco that is being discussed. And, further, if only ten thousand people are seemingly willing to lay out two and one-half dollars for a mystery book, how can one reasonably figure that even that many will be willing to pay a minimum of four dollars and eighty cents for the equivalent in play form?

LEAF AND BOUGH. January 21, 1949

A play by Joseph Hayes. Produced by Charles P. Heidt for 3 performances in the Cort Theatre.

Program

Bert Warren	*Anthony Ross*	Glenn Campbell	
Myra Warren	*Dorothy Elder*		*Charlton Heston*
Attie Warren	*Louise Buckley*	Mark Campbell	*Richard Hart*
Mary Warren	*Mary Linn Beller*	Nan Warren	*Coleen Gray*
Grandpa Nelson	*William Jeffrey*	Harlan Adams	*Jared Reed*
Laura Campbell	*Alice Reinheart*	Dr. Vincent Cullen	
Frederick Campbell			*Tom McElhany*
	David White		

SYNOPSIS: *The action takes place in and around a small town in the Middle West, the kitchen of the Warren farmhouse in the country; the living room of the Campbell home in the town; and the top of Sycamore Hill. Act I. Begins on an evening in Autumn. Act II. Begins next morning. Act III. Begins next day.*
Director: *Rouben Mamoulian.*

Unlike the fireplace and other such hotboxes, the stack of beer crates covered with painted burlap which passes handsomely on the stage for a hilltop has been used mostly for a single and more or less guileless purpose, which is to say, love. While a hilltop has been known off the stage to be productive of such less romantic consequences as a bad cold in the head, a turned ankle, ivy poisoning and ripped breeches, on the stage — on the few occasions when witches are not cavorting on it — it is regularly dedicated to fancy speeches about the moon, the stars and the wonderful smell of growing things and to handholding, kissing and other manifestations of the amorous impulse, sometimes fairly acute.

Another such hilltop has now showed up in Mr. Hayes' play and it serves as per schedule. The boy, of the kind known as a dreamer because he likes to listen to the phonograph, and the farm girl, who is also presented as having a soul because she goes about with the rapt, wide-eyed look more commonly identified with imbecility, once again climb up the burlap decked crates, orate about the wind in the sycamore trees, etc., and duly find themselves infected by the tender passion. A brother of the dreamer, a low fellow on the score of his taking a drink now and then, makes some trouble for them, but in the end — as if you had to be told — all turns out hearts and flowers.

Mr. Hayes, whose first play this is, writes consistently in purple ink, platitude, and theatrical stencils. There is much talk about the flight of wild geese to the South and other such symbolic staples; the young dreamer, alone on the stage, smells wistfully at a rose in recollection of his loved one; the difference between the girl's and the boy's families' social status is indicated by the former's address of her maternal parent as "mom" and the latter's of his as "mother"; and atmosphere for the lighter dramatic moments is evoked with an off-stage hurdy-gurdy and for the heavier with off-stage eerie wails of no discernible relation to the immediate proceedings. The characters, as lifeless as senescent rubber, are out of the dramatic storehouse of years long gone: the eccentric old grandfather, the spinster aunt who bemoans the fact that she did not seize the one chance for romance which years ago was offered to her; the mean-spirited farmer husband and father and his patient drudge of a wife; the small town doctor given to philosophical reflections on life; the frustrated wife married to a drunkard who meditates on the rosier days of her youth, now gone beyond recall; the young sport with his talk about "knocking off the dames" and his cynical credo that all women are alike in the dark; the small girl child who reads aloud, to the embarrassment of her elder sister, a love poem which the latter's swain has inscribed to her; and the fumbling oaf who grew up with the young heroine and hopes that she will in time see through her city suitor, cast him off, and marry him as she always was meant to do.

Dramaturgically, the play, which all too apparently has been influenced by the work of Tennessee Williams but much more closely by virtue of its bush-league quality,

along with its beer crate species of elevation, suggests Tennessee Mountain Landis, repeats over and over again the
materials made perfectly plain in its first twenty minutes
and is so washed under by the inundation of verbiage that
criticism most sympathetic to its ambitious young author
can not detect any value in even its riparian rights. There
is a total absence of selectivity, true character observation
and imaginative plan. It is all, however unwittingly, as
pretentious as a beribboned, elaborately lithographed hat-
box containing a piece of dollar millinery.

The acting, with one or two exceptions, is of the kind often dismissed as identical with that of the old-time road
stock companies, which is pretty hard on those companies
since a number of them were scarcely of the base order that
the younger reviewers, who were not born then, seem to be
so certain in believing. Alice Reinheart, whom I remember as a strikingly incompetent actress back in the years of
Papavert, gives a really valid and touching picture of the
frivolous town wife still holding pathetically to the rem-
nants of her youth; and Coleen Gray, recruited from Hollywood, except for the irritating mechanical fixed smile
practised by film actresses as a substitute for charm and for
gestures of the constrained, semi-paralytic type common to
many of the young ladies brought up before the cameras,
plays the girl as simply and unaffectedly as her lines will
permit. Richard Hart, as the boy beset by his love of her,
acts, however, as if his role were half a school examination
paper and half a patient waiting nervously in the ante-
room of a doctor of venereal diseases, and the rest are no
better and here and there much worse. Rouben Mamoulian, working in an idiotically over-elaborate and complex
stage set by Carl Kent showing the interiors of the farm
and town houses and rolling to either side now and then to
display the hilltop, has kept the actors moving but has been
unable to perform the same service for the dialogue, characters and play, all of which are bogus.

ALL FOR LOVE. January 22, 1949

A revue with music and lyrics by Allan Roberts and Lester Lee, sketches by Max Shulman, Ted Luce, and Grace and Paul Hartman. Produced by Sammy Lambert and Anthony B. Farrell for a forced number of statistically meaningless performances in the Mark Hellinger Theatre.

PRINCIPALS

Paul and Grace Hartman, Bert Wheeler, Milada Mladova, Patricia Wymore, Dick Smart, Leni Lynn, Kathryn Mylroie, Milton Frome, Paul Reed, Budd Rogerson, June Graham, Richard D'Arcy.
Director: *Edward Reveaux.*

REVUES. REVUES, REVUES. Here still yet another. It begins to look like a plot against the critics. Having exhausted dulness in our required accounts of so many of them, there is no course left to us but to dismiss them entirely or to write of them brilliantly. As to the former, that is unfortunately impossible in my case, since these annals must be complete or nothing; and, as to the latter, the job is beyond me. Under the circumstances, all I can do is either to figure out how to write dully about this one in some more or less new way or doctor up the review of it with things that have no or very little bearing on it but which may conceivably divert the reader much as he sometimes is diverted by marginal comments which he finds scribbled in a second-rate book picked up in a second-hand shop.

Perhaps combining the two expedients might even work a bit better. It would take some such rough outline and form as the following:

Two of the principal comedians of the revue are the Hartmans. Some people consider them hilarious, or say they do. I do not, and have said I do not, in just such dull terms as this, on several previous occasions. To be a little more polite about it, I might indulge in relative values and say that, after all, they are more amusing than trigeminal neuralgia, but, as with drama, opinion based on relative values has corrupted more theatrical criticism than even the charm and beauty of inferior actresses. In this show, the pair, aided by some bruising material, are more frightening than heretofore. When Mrs. Hartman, for example, offers as comedy the business of pretending to be a Frenchwoman and employs such lingo as "Pâté de foie gras vous moi de chevrolet," I find it even harder to laugh than when Mr. Hartman appears in a baggy white union suit and pretends to be a statue or even when both sing a duet in the course of which Mr. Hartman describes Mrs. Hartman as having been a maid on an old Albany night boat who had been made more often than maid.

One of the production's big features displays the ensemble in ski costumes executing the 1890 chorus pinwheel number and pretending to skate with the assistance of a turntable stage. This is supposed to whet the imagination, and it surely does. One's imagination is whetted to the point of visualizing at least two dozen fresher and more novel versions of the business. One also reflects afield and in a higher direction on the peculiar notion that only first-rate drama is successful in stimulating the imagination. The imagination implicit in such drama is generally so rich and satisfying that it leaves nothing for the auditor further to imagine. His fancy is so fully nourished that no food remains. The dramatist has taken over completely and all that he can do is surrender to his spell. A play like *Lear,* or *Peer Gynt,* or *The Sunken Bell* clogs any supplementary flight of the fancy; it does the job for the person who attends it. And so with most of the world's good plays. It is only the second-rate, third-rate or fourth-rate play that, deficient in imagination, encourages independent imagination in the spectator. It piques his disappointment into fanciful wings of his own. It stimulates imagination by virtue of imagination's very absence. As with a starved man's vision of a banquet, the auditor dreams and, dreaming, finds his imagination kindled. The poor play, as a matter of fact, imposes the necessity of so much imagination upon him that it often completely exhausts him.

Though Milada Mladova is one of the few ballet dancers whom one can look at, apart from technical proficiency, without suffering the impression that one is looking at a pair of oversize bowling pins attached to a keg of white-wash and quivering like custard afflicted by an ague, why is it, my mind wandered, that a play, however poor, if written in verse, whether rhymed or blank and however in turn poor, usually induces a greater sobriety in most dramatic critics than a better play written in prose?

Listening to what was described in the program as the music and that sounded as if its composer were simultaneously recalling to memory the trumpet in an old German street band and Louie, the singing waiter in Weinbasser's old cellar restaurant in Milwaukee, I bemused myself by thinking that the decline of the British Empire is no more perceptible than in the total disappearance from its map of the talented English light operetta and musical comedy composers. Think of those of yesterday like Monckton, Jones, Stuart, Caryll, Rubens, *et al.,* then try to think of one Englishman today who is in any way the equal of any one of them.

One of the blackout sketches shows Hartman as a deep sea diver coming up with a chorus girl dressed as a mermaid. The fault of most such sketches, I decided, is that the blackout comes at the end instead of at the beginning.

Other items in the revue are a male tap dancer, a female tap dancer, a tap dance by the chorus, a sketch in which a woman throws a chunk of green mush into Hartman's face, a skit in which Bert Wheeler sticks two gourds into his sweater in imitation of female breasts, another in which the breasts of a fashion store manikin are nervously draped with a piece of cloth by Mrs. Hartman, and another still in which a butler squirts seltzer into Wheeler's eyes and in which Wheeler seizes the bottle and squirts back at the butler. By this time, my imagination was so stimulated by the thought of the beauty of the outdoor world, be it raining cats and dogs or deep in slush and mud, that I bolted from the theatre, jumped into a cab, came home, and composed this appropriately and, for all my enterprise, still persistently dull review.

FORWARD THE HEART. JANUARY 28, 1949

A play by Bernard Reines. Produced by Theatre Enterprises, Inc., and Leon J. Bronesky for 19 performances in the Forty-Eighth Street Theatre.

PROGRAM

MRS. MARIAN GIBBS	DR. GEORGE WHITING
Natalie Schafer	*Harry Bannister*
DAVID GIBBS *William Prince*	JULIE EVANS *Mildred Joanne Smith*

SYNOPSIS: Act I. Scene 1. *A Monday morning toward the end of May.* Scene 2. *The following day.* Scene 3. *Two days later. Early afternoon.* Act II. Scene 1. *Three weeks later.* Scene 2. *One week later.*
Time: *Spring — not long ago at all.*
Place: *The Gibbs house in a fashionable suburb of Boston.*
Director: *Peter Frye.*

I HAVE NOTED hereinbefore that if a comedian practises a physical indignity of one kind or another on a second comedian, like, for example, poking a finger into his eye, hitting him on the head with a club, or kicking him in the rear, an audience will laugh only if it knows that no slightest pain accrues to the victim. The audience's considerate sympathy in this and other directions is to be challenged at serious expense. It is thus in an obliquely related manner that the picturing of blindness on the stage is at a playwright's peril and that the great majority of plays which have presented it in connection with a leading character have failed at the box-office. Not only does an audience's extra-theatrical pity for the afflicted help to destroy its playgoing mood but it is so sensitive that the very thought and horror of blindness divert what interest in the play it might otherwise possibly have. It suffers pain vicariously, and the evening becomes unpleasant and sometimes even intolerable. This is especially and particularly true when and if the play itself is a good one, since the more the dramatist succeeds in causing his audience to identify itself with his character, the worse it is for his play. Even in make-believe the spectacle of sightlessness is fraught with character and, reflectively, audience pain. We again witness the consequences in the instance of this exhibit, which, however, is scarcely one of merit.

The story here is of the love of a blind, white young war veteran for a girl, an employee in his mother's household; of his confoundment when he learns that she is a Negress; of the opposition to his thought of marriage by his relatives; and of his determination nevertheless to go through with it. Since the main situation, for all the introduction of the blind element, is scarcely new to the drama and has been engaged by audiences, usually in reverse, from the distant day of *The Nigger* to the more recent one of *Strange Fruit,* the arguments pro and con are all too familiar and no longer of any marked theatrical stimulation. And when they are treated to writing repetitive and dramatically supine and to dramaturgy as inexpert and so soon exhausted as in this case, the effect is of replaying an old phonograph record, badly scratched and cracked, of a still older tune.

The play is additionally weakened by the patent facts that its suspense disappears the moment the blind hero realizes his beloved is colored and that, since he is made to realize it very early in the proceedings, the rest of the play has little left but to pursue the duly anticipated course. If the writing were better and the point of view fresher, the drama might possibly hold an audience despite its widowed materials. But since the author has nothing new to contribute in idea, philosophy or panacea and since the general nature of his dialogue is suggested in his elderly doctor's prophylactic prescription for the distraught, sightless protagonist: "Come with me to Maine, where we'll fish and roam the woods, and read Emerson and Thoreau," the play soon languishes. Further contributing to its torpor is the symbolizing of the doctor's wholesome geniality in his jovial embrace of his blind nephew to an accompaniment of such lingo as "Well, you old son-of-a-gun; how are you, fella?"; the scene laid, according to the program, in a "house in a fashionable suburb of Boston" which rather resembles a laborer's house in an unfashionable suburb of Bethlehem, Pa., and which is attended only by a part-time colored maid; such righteous inquiries as "there can't be too much social consciousness in the world today, can there?"; the author's timing of his play in such marked-down Barrie phraseology as "not long ago at all"; and dialogue that lingers lovingly over such concepts as "what does the color of one's skin matter when two people really love each other" and "in a hundred, maybe fifty years, people may come to understand, but not now, not yet."

The performance of Mildred Joanne Smith in the role of the Negress is the highlight of the occasion. As she has proved before, this Smith girl has a simplicity, directness, honesty and feeling that in combination make her one of the valuable younger actresses of our theatre.

DIAMOND LIL. February 5, 1949

*A comedy-melodrama by Mae West. Produced by Albert H.
Rosen and Herbert J. Freezer for an interrupted engagement and resumed performances after the end of the season
in the Coronet Theatre.*

PROGRAM

Jim	Billy Van	Rita	Miriam Goldina
Bill	Jack Howard	Juarez	Steve Cochran
Porter	James Quinn	Mike	James Fallon
Ragtime	Dick Arnold	Diamond Lil	Mae West
Spike	George Warren	Charlie	Peter Chan
Jerry	Harry Warren	Bessie	Buddy Millette
Kitty	Harriet Nelson	Violet	Margaret Magennis
Frances	Sheila Trent	Barbara	Marilyn Lowe
Flo	Sylvia Syms	Captain Cummings	
Maggie	Louise Jenkins		Richard Coogan
Flynn	Charles G. Martin	Pete the Duke	Lester Laurence
Kane	Mike Keene	Doheney	Ralph Chambers
Gus Jordan	Walter Petrie	Jacobson	Louis Nussbaum
Sally	Frances Arons	Chick Clark	Jeff Morrow

*SYNOPSIS: Act I. The back room of Gus Jordan's saloon, the Bow-
ery, New York City, during the Gay Nineties. Act II. Lil's bedroom, late
that evening. Act III. Same as Act I, the following evening.
Director: Charles K. Freeman.*

I F A DOCTOR making the rounds during a smallpox epidemic were to report that his infected patients, while
maybe not exactly in the pink of condition, were suffering
only from minor stomach-aches induced by eating sauerkraut, people with no respect for animals would say that he
should be attending horses. But if a reviewer making the
rounds during such a fatal epidemic as has lately afflicted
the theatre accurately reports that his patients are deathly
ill and doomed, the same people will argue that he must
be a chronic fault-picker and cynical old sourhead who
should himself be attended by horses, to the accompaniment of a certain composition by Wagner. You can not,

however, entirely blame them, witlings though they are,
since it does seem improbable that so many plays and
shows can really be that bad and that their producers can
have had so little sense as to put them on. But, apparently
improbable as it is, it is true, and the result has been a succession of things like *Jenny Kissed Me, Oh, Mr. Meadowbrook!, Don't Listen, Ladies, The Smile Of The World,
Along Fifth Avenue, The Shop At Sly Corner, Leaf And
Bough, Forward The Heart,* and *All For Love* (the worst
revue in thirty years) that had to be smelled to be believed.

In such a situation, the appearance on the scene of even
Mae West and *Diamond Lil* is like the combined appearance in another day and under any situation of Bernhardt,
Coquelin, the Ziegfeld *Follies,* and De Wolf Hopper on
top of an elephant. *Diamond Lil,* surely enough, may not
be an overwhelming example of dramatic art or even a
comedy-melodrama markedly superior to *The Bowery
After Dark,* but it at least has infinitely more life in it than
the torpid junk that has lately been fed us. And, while Mae
may not be the First Lady of the theatre and may not ever
get the gold medal of the American Academy of Arts and
Letters and a free cup of tea and kiss from Henry Seidel
Canby as testimonials to the magnificence of her diction,
she certainly comes as a toothful relief from some of the
more august girls who have recently, to our comprehensive
repose, been giving us their depressingly routine rich vocal
tones, their inert technical proficiency, and their bosom-
less histrionic finesse. Miss Mae, in short, may not be the
kind of actress who inspires the pundits to lengthy, profound, and very dull essays full of such stuff as "subtle nuances," "spiritual undertones" and "radiant inner virtuosity," but she is the kind you never take your eyes off
while she is in action, the kind you attentively listen to
even when she is mouthing rubbish, and the kind you can
not forget — even if you are the most solemn critic this
side of William Winter's grave — half so easily as you can
many such classier actresses as Elisabeth Bergner and
Julian Eltinge. There is something about her, regardless of
authentic quality, that holds and fascinates you and ren-

ders you pleasantly numb, like the hypnosis of a fifteen-cent glass paper-weight with the sun shining on it.

Perhaps I am not being wholly fair to Miss West at that. An actress, after all, can't register any such effect if there isn't more to and in her than meets the superficial eye. At any rate, she certainly can't do it over so long a period as Mae has. They tell me, in example, that our heroine is factually a small, short woman of no particular mammary eminence, of no natural striking personality, and of no especial distinction in physical carriage, glow, or general address. Yet, aided not merely by such obvious artifices as high heels, costumes, and what are slanderously whispered to be a couple of cocoanuts but by something surely approximating real skill, she contrives to present herself to us, and very convincingly, as everything she is not. If that isn't acting, and a very snappy brand of acting to boot, I don't know what acting is.

There have been in every generation girls like Mae who have no end annoyed the professor-critics by impressing audiences. And not only audiences composed of rough-necks, illiterates and other prominent Broadway figures but here and there of the better grade, intelligent theatre-goers. It isn't too hard to understand. Such girls, compared with the actresses of higher standing, are like vacations from school. They are to the stage what a night off from sobriety is, what a light and not particularly well written but entertaining book is, what — in a word — an easy smoking jacket is after formal attire. They may not be anything to take seriously, but they are fun. And, when it comes to me, I am perfectly willing to forget for the time being that I am a critic, to forget also the importance of the miraculous genius of more ceremonial actresses like Eva Le Gallienne, Ilka Chase and Katina Paxinou, and to have a good, uncritical time for a change.

It is much the same with a play like *Diamond Lil*. You either, if you are in that mood, correctly dismiss it as clam stew or let sense, dignity and what your fair companion may think of you go hang and enjoy yourself. It is best, of course, if you care anything for your professional standing,

not to try to defend your lapse from taste in print, since
there are always inconsiderate rats who will dig it up later
on and, just as you are about to be given an honorary degree for the purity of your critical canon by some brewery-
backed college in the Middle West, sorely embarrass you
with it. The only safe procedure is to have your good time
privately and keep it strictly to yourself. Quite a number
of the critics evidently appreciate this, as may be gathered
from their reviews. They are not such fools as freely to admit the good time they had; they pretend that, while the
lower species of playgoing mammals may have it, there
are various qualifications in their cases, which they duly set
down with all the expected piety, since nobody, they realize, is going to trust their opinions on worthwhile drama
if they give themselves away, however honestly, in any such
direction.

Very well. Mae West is not much of an actress by tony
critical standard and *Diamond Lil* by any such standard is
truck. But — let the tumbril come if it must — they are
disgracefully good sport.

BLOOD WEDDING. FEBRUARY 6, 1949

A tragedy (Bodas de Sangre) *by Federico García Lorca, translated by R. L. O'Connell and James Graham-Lujan, with incidental music by Jerome Moross. Produced by New Stages, Inc., for 23 performances in the New Stages Theatre.*

PROGRAM

THE MOTHER	Sarah Cunningham	FOURTH GIRL	Florence Luriea
THE BRIDEGROOM	Louis Hollister	A WOMAN	Gloria Mann
THE NEIGHBOR WOMAN		FIRST YOUNG MAN	Ben Irving
	Nancy R. Pollock	SECOND YOUNG MAN	
LEONARDO'S WIFE	Joan Tompkins		Sidney Walters
THE MOTHER-IN-LAW		THIRD YOUNG MAN	Earl Hammond
	Dorothy Patten	FOURTH YOUNG MAN	Herbert More
LEONARDO	Alexander Scourby	A MAN	Joseph Silver
THE LITTLE GIRL	Jean Gillespie	FIRST WOODCUTTER	Robert Davis
THE SERVANT WOMAN		SECOND WOODCUTTER	
	Peggy Allenby		Mort Neudell
THE BRIDE'S FATHER	Jay Barney	THIRD WOODCUTTER	
THE BRIDE	Inge Adams		Michael Howard
FIRST GIRL	June Prud'homme	DEATH	Sylvia Davis
SECOND GIRL	Shirley Eggleston	THE MOON	Peter Capell
THIRD GIRL	Margaret Owens		

SYNOPSIS: The action takes place in rural Spain. Act I. Scene 1. The Mother's house. Scene 2. Leonardo's house. Scene 3. The Bride's house. Scene 4. Entrance hall of the Bride's house. Act II. Scene 1. Outside the Bride's house. Scene 2. A forest. Scene 3. The Mother's house. Director: *Boris Tumarin.*

THE FAILURE of Spanish tragedy in our theatre has generally been accounted for by the critics on three grounds. The first is that the passions of the Spanish, or Latin, race are so remote from our own feelings in similar situations that they impress an American audience not only as exaggerated and excessive but even as a bit ridiculous. The second is that translation into the English or American idiom presents a problem which translators have usually been unable to surmount. And the third is that, even were the first two not true, American actors find themselves grotesquely out of place in roles which impose upon them the necessity of passing themselves off for Spaniards.

The reasons, though there may occasionally seem to be some warrant for them, are, if I may be so unbrotherly as to say so, most often without much logic or sense. If the passions in these Spanish tragedies are alien to us and unintelligible to our audiences, the same thing might be argued about the passions in various French and Russian tragedies, yet the circumstance has not so regularly spelled failure in their cases. The translation problem in the instance of the Spanish tragedies is, further, certainly no more difficult than in the instance of Spanish lyric comedy, and some of the translations of the latter have been eminently satisfactory. Moreover, there have been some good translations of even the tragedies. There have been more, true enough, that have been poor and it has been these which have evidently persuaded the critics that the translations in sum have been as faulty as Stark Young has aptly pointed out in the case of one such botch: "In many spots the lines . . . sound like a schoolroom version of a passage far removed in every sense from the language we speak; there are, in fact, constant assortments of 'whichs,' verbal structures and high-toned words that, though they may suggest distinction in the translator, compel despair in the actor."

And, finally, though we admittedly have had some absurd performances of the Spanish tragedies, the American actors may hardly be said on that score to be any more permanently out of place and any more naturally grotesque in them than they are in any other Latin or in some of the French, German, Scandinavian, and even British drama.

Lorca's *Blood Wedding* will serve as a general clinical example. Its lyric story of love, lust and sudden death trembles with emotions of a volcanic gaudiness, yet, while such frenzies are not common to the genus Yankee, they surely are not too remote and exotic for his understanding, since his newspapers duplicate them for him day after day in the accounts of native similarly sensational eruptions. The

translation of the play by the Messrs. O'Connell and Graham-Lujan is, I am assured by Spanish scholars, not only
faithful to the dramatist's spirit but, with no outside assurance at all needed, is sufficiently considerate of the English
theatrical idiom to meet the demands of the local audience.
If the actors and the acting leave something to be desired,
the actors and acting in many successful non-Spanish plays
have sometimes left just as much to be desired, so that does
not figure too importantly in the immediate argument.

The tragedy's failure to magnetize an American audience accordingly must lie in different directions. Critically,
it is a play of divers merits. It is clearly the work of one of
the authentic poets of the twentieth century and of one
who, had he not met a murderous Fascist end at the age of
thirty-seven, would surely have added further illumination
to world letters. It has profound feeling, a singing imagination, and much of an artist's sense of selection, simplicity, and reticence. And yet it does not capture and hold the
local audience as plays not one-twentieth so endowed have
done. Why?

In answer, I offer several possible explanations. Apart
from the classics, which the average audience feels itself
bound to admire, that audience has small understanding
and appreciation of, and very small use for, any real poet.
What it best understands and reacts to is the playwright
who goes through the motions of being a poet without any
of a genuine poet's gifts. What it wants and swallows as
poetic inspiration is not that of a Lorca but of playwrights
who palm off in its stead pretty scrim curtains, off-stage
harp music, soothing lighting effects, purple-dyed china
Easter eggs, and Elizabethanized George Barr McCutcheon
dialogue. What it further demands and cherishes is not the
simple, strainless and unsophisticated dramaturgy of such a
Lorca play but dramaturgy full of fancy externals, superficial excitements, be-bop psychology, sizzling curtain lines,
and the drive of a baby carriage propelled by a six-cylinder
engine, preferably very noisy. And what, conversely, it can
not work up much interest and enthusiasm for is a dramatist like this Lorca who concerns himself not so much with

the outer emotions of his actors as with the inner emotions of his characters, who realizes that violence of passion is not necessarily best to be portrayed through violence of language, and who appreciates that even the most tempestuous and tragic of stories of love and lust may be told effectively without recourse to ten-twenty-thirty rape scenes and dialogue that sounds like *Captain Billy's Whiz-Bang* rewritten for the five-dollar trade by Archibald MacLeish in collaboration with Dr. Gregory Zilboorg.

Blood Wedding, which with *Yerma* and *The House of Bernarda Alba* forms a trilogy, was first performed here fourteen years ago under the title *Bitter Oleander* in a translation so awkward, in a performance so generally out of key, and with staging so overdone and raddled that it soon collapsed and thus reinforced the spurious reasons for Spanish tragedy's inevitable local failure.

RICHARD III. February 8, 1949

The tragedy by William Shakespeare. Produced by Herman Levin for 23 performances in the Booth Theatre.

Program

Richard, Duke of Gloucester, Later Richard III	Duke of Buckingham
Richard Whorf	*Philip Bourneuf*
	Stanley *Arrin Redfield*
George, Duke of Clarence	Catesby *William Nichols*
Will Kuluva	Ratcliff *Ray Walston*
Brackenbury *Alan Frost*	Lovel *Charles Nahabedian*
Hastings *Robert H. Harris*	Queen Margaret *Grace Coppin*
Annie, Widow of the Son of	Edward IV *Joseph Foley*
Henry VI, Later Richard's	Lord Mayor of London
Queen *Frances Reid*	*Walter F. Appler*
Tressel *Robert Carricart*	Tyrell, Later Earl of Surrey
Berkeley *Milton Selzer*	*Nehemiah Persoff*
Queen Elizabeth *Polly Rowles*	Richmond, Head of the House of
Rivers *Glenn Wilson*	Lancaster, Later Henry VII
Grey *David Clive*	*Michael Sivy*
Dorset *Douglass Watson*	Citizens { *Connie Lessard*
Vaughan *Warren Burmeister*	*Ed Hoffman*

The scenes of the play take place in and around the Tower of London with the exception of the battle, which was fought at Bosworth Field in 1485.

Director: *Richard Barr.*

As with Maurice Evans and *Hamlet,* Richard Whorf has now come up with the discovery that *Richard III* is essentially a melodrama, a piece of news as startling as the possible revelation that *Macbeth* is not a comedy. Pursuant to his remarkable finding, he has staged the play much as if it were an Alfred Hitchcock film crossed with a Serge Lifar production of *Dracula;* in other words, with such headlong speed that were its equivalent to be visited on *Cradle Song* that might very well also take on the appearance of something by the author of *The Queen Of The Highbinders.* Mr. Whorf has proudly described his intel-

lectual coup as "a good cops-and-robbers show," doubtless
to be followed by "a good guy-meets-broad show" like
Romeo And Juliet or "a hot sex-and-murder show" like
Othello. He has further announced that "we have made
Richard an exciting melodrama," the "we" obviously ex-
cluding any share in the business by Shakespeare. It is all
very interesting and remindful of the old sun-dial story,
not to mention the advertisement of *The Duchess Of Malfi*
by a one-time English provincial theatre manager as "not
a drawing-room comedy."

In speaking of the speed with which Mr. Whorf has
mounted the play, let it be known that I certainly do not
object to speed *per se,* though it seems to me to be more
suitable to baseball pitchers and race horses than to a dramatic poet. I do not, further, object to even a dramatic
poet being staged in a tempo that doesn't suggest, as frequently it has, a dirge played on instruments covered with
layers of congealed tar. But when one like Shakespeare is
made the occasion of something resembling a Madison
Square Garden relay race, when he is drastically cut so the
rapid pace may not be slackened, and when a lot of his dialogue is accordingly made to sound like a Gilbertian patter
song — when the indulgence goes that far I not only object but emit an ear-piercing and blood-curdling yell, to be
heard ten blocks away.

All these producing monkey-tricks, to allow Mr. Whorf
his point, do make for the show he says they do. But the
show is a show not in the sense he seems to imagine but
rather in the sense that throwing a helpless Christian to the
lions in an old Roman arena was one, and it is just about as
endorsable. There can be little doubt that it is impressive
to the type of theatregoer who wishes to enjoy all the sensations except those associated with any critical intelligence
and whose idea of complete satisfaction would be a production of the Bard on *Ben Hur* and *Quo Vadis* treadmills.
But to any other it is best adapted, as actually it first was,
to audiences of GI's largely eager to have it over with as
quickly as possible so that it would not make them miss
what dates they had.

I hope no one will read into these strictures a suspicion
that I am one of those fogies who believe that if a producer or actor does anything to Shakespeare that does not
adhere strictly to the established and conventional he
should be drawn and quartered. Not at all. I am all for
anything, particularly in the case of *Richard,* which Shaw
has observed is at bottom a Punch and Judy show, that will
lend a renewed stage vigor to any one of the plays. But I
nevertheless remain old-fashioned enough not to go wild
with delight when one like this is clearly staged much less
with an eye to Shakespeare than with one to Tom Mix,
minus only the important horse. In view of Whorf's description of his production as a cops-and-robbers show, it
would have been appropriate if he had billed it as *Richard III, Alias Richard K. Fox.*

Richard has been acted in many ways, and Whorf acts
the role in all of them at once. Obviously, therefore, like a
man betting on all the horses in a race, he can not completely miss. But miss he does six-sevenths of the time and,
surrounded by an inferior company, the evening sums up
to no more than a profile of the classic for Class-B little
theatres.

Though it has always seemed to me that, given a vocal
equipment of some range, a patience in the matter of
makeup, and even a faint degree of intelligence, the Richard role does not impose upon an actor's fair account of
himself any need for divine assistance, there has long been
a pro and con critical to-do over its performance almost
equal to that apportioned Hamlet. Hazlitt worked himself
up into a lather over Kean's Richard simply because in the
scene with Lady Anne he did not in leaning against the
pillar "go through exactly the same regular evolution of
graceful attitudes" and because he changed his manner of
resting on the point of his sword before he retires to his
tent. Yet this same critic then worked himself up into such
a state of delight that he reported "the attitude in which
he stands with his hands stretched out after his sword is
taken from him had a preternatural and terrific grandeur."
Forster on the contrary unqualifiedly hailed Kean's "ex-

quisite art" and made the hailing the occasion for a savage assault on Forrest's interpretation of the role, largely because of the "most oppressively gilded dress" with which he adorned his person, because of the "tremendous power of his lungs," which he compared with "the noise of artillery," and because he shook his sword after withdrawing it from Henry's death-wound.

Lewes complained of both Charles Kean's and G. V. Brooke's early performances that "they roared and stamped, and stamped and roared, spluttering and perspiring" and "flew into a passion, and that of the most furious and stentorian kind upon the slightest provocation, indeed without provocation at all." Kean, he observed, "seemed to me the very worst actor, out of a barn, playing great parts," though seeing him some years later he qualified his finding somewhat by allowing that the actor had renounced the stampings, though "he still manifested his abiding fault — that minute and detailed misconception of the meaning of the phrases he has to utter." He concluded, however, that compared with the performance of Brooke, "I must pronounce it great." Leigh Hunt, nevertheless, considered Brooke excellent in the role.

The to-do has not abated in more modern times. Of Irving's Richard, Shaw wrote that he played the scene with Lady Anne "as if he were a Hounsditch salesman cheating a factory girl over a pair of second-hand stockings" and concluded that he should either cast the play to suit his acting or else modify his acting to suit the cast. Of Richard Mansfield, several critics argued that he seemed to think he was playing not Richard but Quasimodo, while several others considered his performance a fairly handsome one. Robert Mantell's Richard was contended by some to be altogether too boisterous and by others altogether too sneakingly *piano*. And so it has been with Hampden, Barrymore, Coulouris and the others who have thrust a bustle up their backs and smeared shoe-blacking on their eyes in their pursuit of classical glory.

What the exact truth of the matter is, I do not presume to say. All I say is what I have said before: that, despite a fury of criticism that has not only matched but surpassed some of Richard's own, it seems to me that, given the minor attributes earlier mentioned, an actor, whether good or bad, can no more entirely fail in being impressive to the majority of lay theatregoers in the role than he can fail in that of Falstaff or Fancourt Babberley.

Of Whorf's support, Philip Bourneuf, as is his wont, declaims Buckingham as if he had not entirely recovered from an attack of lockjaw; and Frances Reid, like many younger actresses unpractised in Shakespeare, gives the impression that she has painstakingly memorized Anne's lines, has then figured out their emotional projection, has not been able to synchronize the two, and as a last resort has fallen back on the device of reciting most of them in italics. And most of the rest seem to have studied their roles on a cinder track.

In view of the speed with which the performance is conducted, the confused picture of the whole that one takes with one out of the theatre is of an extensive genealogical chart rattled off by a joint convention of butchers and high school elocutionists assembled on a Steeplechase Park turntable.

MY NAME IS AQUILON. February 9, 1949

A play by Philip Barry, adapted from L'Empereur de Chine *by Jean Pierre Aumont. Produced by the Theatre Guild for 31 performances in the Lyceum Theatre.*

PROGRAM

PAULETTE	*Phyllis Kirk*	VICTOR BENOIT-BENOIT
PIERRE RENAULT		*Lawrence Fletcher*
	Jean Pierre Aumont	MADELEINE BENOIT-BENOIT
TOTO	*Donald Hanmer*	*Arlene Francis*
CHRISTIANE BENOIT-BENOIT		BASCOUL *Louis Borel*
	Lilli Palmer	RONDET *Richard Hepburn*
DENISE	*Doe Avedon*	

SYNOPSIS: Act I. Scene 1. *An apartment on the Avenue Victor Hugo. Early April.* Scene 2. *Two months later.* Scene 3. *A room in a small hotel on the Quai Des Grand Augustins.* Act II. Scene 1. *The apartment. Late August. Night.* Scene 2. *The hotel room. The following morning.*

The action of the play takes place in Paris between early April and late August last year.

Director: *Robert B. Sinclair.*

Years ago, the Franco-Belgian matinée peach, Lou Tellegen, wrote a play for himself in which five decorative women characters were called upon rapturously to allude to him from time to time as "that handsome devil," "that Greek god," and "that modern Adonis" and longingly to sigh, "Oh, to have such a one take me in his manly arms!" This went on for an hour or so and the audience goodnaturedly and patiently took it in its stride. But when then one of the girls topped matters by exclaiming "and what a brain!", the house, unable longer to contain itself, let out with such howls as had not been heard in a theatre since last the bloodhounds in *Uncle Tom's Cabin* attested to their virtuosity.

Jean Pierre Aumont, a French moving picture star, has now also fashioned a play for himself, hospitality adapted for him for local audiences by Philip Barry, in which he causes four lovely ladies at considerable expense to their humor and sense similarly to lubricate his ego. He is, it seems, according to his self-propaganda not only very good-looking, extremely witty, passionately to be desired as a lover, wholly charming, gifted with a remarkable mentality, and "so different from all other men," but boyishly fascinating, strong, "fearless as the north wind," wise in the ways of the world, disarmingly cherishable, a dreamer of beautiful, captivating, unworldly dreams, and a shrewd philosopher — everything, in short, but a good actor.

The girls whom he makes directly go wild over him are the wife of a wealthy, fashionable French financial wizard, the latter's sex-hungry secretary, his young and beautiful daughter, and the pert young household maid. Indirectly, since they do not appear on the stage in person and are but timidly alluded to by the quartet and, emphatically, by Aumont himself, are and have been enough others to have made the combined mouths of Casanova, Louis XIV and Sacha Guitry water. Since the picture he presents in person is of a chunky young man with mayonnaise hair and feet several sizes too large for his body, it might have been better if they had made a film of the whole thing, as it would more greatly have stimulated the bobby-soxers who are equipped with powers of self-delusion in a such case which a theatre audience finds somewhat beyond its capacity.

The thread of story which permeates the evening's repertory of feminine testimonials to the star is of a man who successfully prevaricates the realistic world about him into a more gratifying one and, if it does nothing else, which it doesn't, indicates that Aumont has seen the plays of Pirandello and has read Max Beerbohm's *The Happy Hypocrite*. Where the author leaves off and the adapter begins, I have no immediate way of knowing, but the dialogue, when it does not consist in quotations of the duller copybook maxims, runs to such lines as "I wasn't in love with you; I was in love with your love for me," "You're quite an odd person, aren't you?," and "I'm full of kisses and they are all for you." Two brief scenes have some mild amusement, notably one during which the obtuse father of the young heroine observes her deeply engrossed in a book, inquires what it is, is assured that it is Beaudelaire's *Flowers Of Evil*, objects to her reading anything with such a title, is told that it is poetry, and remarks, "Oh, if it's poetry, it's all right." But for the rest the play, as recorded, is simply a succession of scenes in which one or another of the women applies herself sedulously to the acquisition of Aumont's person and in which he pleasures himself by remaining grandly impervious to all their overtures.

In this nonsense is cast as the heroine the young Vienna-born actress named Lilli Palmer who with a simplicity of voice, manner and address uncommon to the stage gives such an utterly delightful performance — one of the best in any such ingénue role we have seen — that the play, despite the lines it provides her, takes on interest whenever she figures in its action. In her there is something of the early Ruth Chatterton of *The Rainbow,* of the Marie Doro of the far days of *Clarice,* and of the more recent June Lockhart of *For Love Or Money.* Nor is it simply a matter of personality, physical attraction, and what seems to be a born gentility. She can act. Behind that soft, even, and delicate voice, there is training in register and projection; behind that seemingly natural grace of deportment there is acquired experience in translating it satisfactorily on a stage; and behind the total effect of the created picture there is a technical understanding of such acting attributes as control of expression, timing of pauses, "listening," intermediate pantomime, and the like. All of which, I hope, should embarrass any reader who may too quickly have concluded that this was just another of the usual, exaggerated reviews of a young actress who happens to be charming and very pretty.

I seem to have forgotten to note that the play is further to be identified as the kind which includes, to a romantic end, the little room in the garret overlooking the Seine, the wistful comment on the sad face of a woman in an old painting, and the long, sentimental speech about the loving and gentle mistress to men that Paris has been over the years.

DEATH OF A SALESMAN. February 10, 1949

A tragedy by Arthur Miller, with incidental music by Alex North. Produced by Kermit Bloomgarden and Walter Fried for the rest of the season's performances in the Morosco Theatre.

PROGRAM

WILLY LOMAN	*Lee J. Cobb*	UNCLE BEN	*Thomas Chalmers*
LINDA	*Mildred Duncook*	HOWARD WAGNER	*Alan Hewitt*
HAPPY	*Cameron Mitchell*	JENNY	*Ann Driscoll*
BIFF	*Arthur Kennedy*	STANLEY	*Tom Pedi*
BERNARD	*Don Keefer*	MISS FORSYTHE	*Constance Ford*
THE WOMAN	*Winnifred Cushing*	LETTA	*Hope Cameron*
CHARLEY	*Howard Smith*		

SYNOPSIS: Act I. *The entire action takes place in Willy Loman's house. Its bedrooms, kitchen, basement, front porch and backyard, and in various offices and places he visits in New York City and Boston today.* Act II. *The same.*
Director: *Elia Kazan.*

W. H. AUDEN has thus differentiated between them: "Greek tragedy is the tragedy of necessity; that is, the feeling aroused in the spectator is 'what a pity it had to be this way'; Christian tragedy is the tragedy of possibility, 'what a pity it was this way when it might have been otherwise.' "

The definition again is found to be snugly appropriate to Miller's work and evidently no one appreciates its aptness more than he does. But where other playwrights often have usurped to themselves the Christian pity, he, though doubtless he experiences it himself, prefers to leave it to his audience. Therein lies one of his play's chief merits, for it does succeed in substantially evoking both an immediate and a lingering compassion not alone for the life its protagonist lived but for the life he might have lived in its stead, and with none of the more usual playwright's hard insistence.

There are other merits. The writing is simple; there is

no slightest pretentiousness; and, though the play, because of its basic disorganized expressionistic form, is susceptible of strained effect, little sense of strain is felt by its auditors. There is, moreover, none of the heavy striving for lyric tone common to the plays of prosy writers who seek to conceal their prosiness in something they choose to imagine is poetry, yet something of a poetic tinge nonetheless at times issues from it. And, finally, though it misses the spiritual exaltation that is the requirement of fine tragedy and though its end effect is rather acute depression, it triumphs over itself by virtue of the uncompromising honesty of its emotion.

That the play must have a considerable internal force becomes apparent when one considers that it registers the effect it has registered in spite of several confounding production elements. Though Elia Kazan, aided greatly by Mielziner's imaginative setting, has directed admirably the physical flow of the tragedy, his direction of the vocal is often so bad that its intrinsically gentle spirit has a difficult time in establishing itself. Lines that should be read quietly are so shouted and yelled that it seems at times he is determined to make the play a melodrama in spite of itself. There are moments, indeed, when the melodramatic screaming becomes so loud that it is next to impossible to make out what the father or his two sons are talking about and not to feel that Lincoln J. Carter will pop in at any minute with a scene showing the father in his automobile racing against the tooting New York, New Haven and Hartford on one of his selling trips to Boston.

There is, too, the casting of Lee Cobb as the salesman doomed by false standards and self-deception to humiliation and failure. I can well understand the wisdom of avoiding the conventional in casting the role not with the Donald Meek type of actor but with one of strength and size, since the theatrical effect of tragic decline is thereby heightened. But Cobb is so bullish not merely in physical person but, more disastrously, in elemental grain and spirit that one feels, wrongly to be sure, that the playwright is arbitrarily pulling him into the picture and that, were the character left on its own, his life would have taken a decidedly different course. And there are, as well, several additional points in the staging which take unhappy advantage of the author. The direction resorts to such obvious stuff as indicating the now aged salesman's once younger nature by having him jovially kick up his heels in a gazazka, his love of his elder son by causing him so to overdo camaraderie in pawing embraces and hearty yawping that he seems less the potential figure in a tragedy than a one-time understudy for Sam Bernard in *The Rich Mr. Hoggenheimer,* and his pretence of bravery in the face of consciousness of defeat by such a bellowing as was never equalled by the late Melbourne MacDowell, a booming mountebank if ever there was one, as the Duke de Gonzague. Some of my colleagues, I note, have described Cobb's performance as "tremendous." It is. As a boiler explosion.

That the play is weakened not only by such things but by Kazan's favorite occasional melodramatic emphasis on the box-office's behalf is clear. One periodically gets much the impression one would have got if they had brought in Paul Armstrong and Wilson Mizner to pepper up a play like *Our Town.* But the innate silent power of Miller's script, the reticence of much of his writing, and the intermittent excellent flashes of imagery — such, for one example, as the memory of road drummers "riding on a smile and a shoeshine" — combine to make one sufficiently oblivious of the disturbances and to react to the whole as the author hoped.

Henry Arthur Jones once observed that "unless drama is touched with a sense of eternity, wrapped 'round with the splendor of heroism, and imbedded in what is primary and of everlasting import, the mere reproduction on the stage of the commonplace details of everyday life must always be barren, worthless, and evanescent." There is much to be said for the definition. *Death Of A Salesman,* by it, does not measure up, does not measure up by a very considerable margin, to a tragedy of real artistic stature. Its touch with a sense of eternity is but flicking; there is in it little splendor of heroism; it is imbedded but sketchily in what is primary and of everlasting import; and it reproduces merely the commonplace details of everyday life. But it remains not barren, nor worthless, nor, possibly, evanescent, because it touches these commonplace details with a sense of deep and pitiful recognition, because there is splendor of a sort not in any heroism but in its very human cowardice, and because, at least for the time one is in its presence, what may not be primary and of everlasting import is made out of one's immediate won sympathy to seem so.

Whenever a critic, reviewing a play of some pretensions to quality, employs the word "melodrama" in a derogatory sense, other critics who are extreme in their regard for the play are certain to take him acidly to task with the now familiar remark that, since melodrama is the tone of today's world, it is asinine to use the term in condemnation of it. The gentlemen seem to overlook three small points. First, the fact that melodrama seems to be the present world's chief characteristic does not necessarily justify it as a chief characteristic of dramatic or any other art. Secondly, there are various kinds of melodrama and the melodrama that the critic has in mind in the instance of the play he is considering is the kind which in the interests of theatricalism raises its head at debatable moments. Where, in a word, completely honest characters would comport themselves with some intellectual, psychological and emotional reserve, the characters purely for the sake of theatrical effect are arbitrarily made to dive off the Brooklyn bridge and hold up a mail train. And, thirdly, the melodrama is resorted to in order to lend a surface excitement to what a better dramatist might make even more exciting through emotional and physical reserve.

Sometimes the melodrama, which, incidentally, is the easiest of all dramatic forms to master, is unintentional on the part of a playwright, who confuses it with inner intensity of theme and character. Sometimes, when intentional, it gets out of hand and so supervises character that the latter explodes into nothingness from spontaneous combustion. And, sometimes, of course, it is well considered and completely and properly in key. But much more often in the work of various American playwrights, whether deliberately or not deliberately, it has the air of an exclamation point inserted into what is essentially a passive sentence, the aspect of red-painted fingernails on a small girl child, and the sense of pulling the lever of a street corner fire-box and bringing on the engines, hook-and-ladders and hose carts in a false alarm. It is, in short, frequently a youngster's loud "boo" designed to startle other youngsters, a little boy's Indian whoop hopeful of scaring his quietly amused father. And it also, even when there is nothing intrinsically wrong with it, is sometimes so whimsically out of the immediate surroundings that it sounds something like the major domo of Buckingham Palace elegantly answering the telephone and exclaiming, "Why, yes, of course, Mrs. Greenberg."

This was the kind of melodrama that, among other things, made Miller's widely admired previous play, *All My Sons,* strike me as an inferior performance. I have already in the directly preceding volume of these annals spoken of the dubiety of his character drawing in that play, as well as of other elements in it that were open to skepticism. Since this subsequent play, *Death Of A Salesman,* is clear of all such defects, it is gratifying to hear Miller confess that he himself now sees the faults of *All My Sons* and equally encouraging to observe that some of those critics who were most enthusiastic about it now also see it, belatedly, as having been what they admit was a "contrived job."

As will be remembered, *All My Sons* was a dramaturgically conventional play of the rococo "well-made" species. Commenting on it, Miller says, "The conventional play form forces the writer to siphon everything into a single place at a single time, and squeezes the humanity out of a play. Why shouldn't a play have the depth, the completeness, and the diversity of a novel? I felt I had to perfect conventional technique first and *All My Sons* was an exercise."

Death Of A Salesman is no such exercise; it is the result of profit from trial and error, and not merely in respect to

dramaturgy. There is complete honesty in most of the characters; there is absolute honesty in contemplation of its
theme as against the sense of fabrication one had in the
case of *All My Sons;* and there is, unlike in that play, a
minimum of theatrical compromise. Even in the few instances where one feels that perhaps Miller operates to
avoid a possible monotony by including episodes of some
forced theatrical color, the episodes themselves — as, for
example, the scene in which the sons entertain their father
in a Sixth Avenue corner saloon fabulously equipped with
champagne service — somehow do not seem altogether too
removed from truth. And the point of view throughout, in
its challenge of popular conceptions, is strikingly intelligent. The popular credos that nothing is more valuable to
a man than being liked; that sincere, hard work is bound
to reap its ultimate reward; that children, even if they conceal the fact, have an inborn love for their parents; that
loyalty is always a virtue; and that only the incompetent
fail in this world — such beliefs, with no show of facile
cynicism, Miller punctures. His tragedy of the little man
has in it also, if obliquely, a little something of the tragedy
of much bigger men, whether successes or failures by the
world's standards.

In a preface to the published play, Mr. Miller goes to
considerable lengths to justify his belief that the tragedy of
the little man may be quite as exalted dramatically and
artistically as that of the classic kings and emperors. He
need not have gone to so much trouble. It may be, but
there are two points which, seemingly in the interests of
his own play, he chooses to overlook. Save the little man
have something of a mind, which Mr. Miller's protagonist
has not, his tragedy, while it may be moving, is in finality
without universal size and is like the experience we suffer
in contemplating on the highways a run-over and killed
dog, undeniably affecting but without any profound significance. The tragedy, accordingly, becomes that not of a
full-winged human being but merely that of a mindless
clod, at once pitiful and touching but lost from the outset
in the maelstrom of inevitable circumstance. And his strug-

gle against his surroundings becomes not cumulatively holding but obviously foredoomed, since there is no share of intellect even modestly to assist him. Great tragedy is the tragedy of man's mind in strong conflict with the stronger fates; minor tragedy that of mindless man already beaten by them.

The second point is the language in which tragedy is written. The fall of kings calls for a splendor of prose or poetry, otherwise it may be quite as unimpressive as the fall of little men. But the tragedy of the little man, to be as impressive as that of a king, calls as well for such treatment. It is not the story of and the reasons for a ruler's tragic end that remain in our hearts and memories but the flights of language through which they are related. Commonplace language, though it may be exactly suited to the tragedy of the underdog, may make for first-rate theatre but scarcely for first-rate and overwhelming drama.

In defence of his point of view, Mr. Miller concludes, "It is time, I think, that we who are without kings took up this bright thread of our history and followed it to the only place it can possibly lead in our time — the heart and spirit of the average man."

We are not without kings, though they may not wear the royal purple. We have men of heart and spirit — and also mind. They are or may be the meat of important tragedy. The average man's, the common man's, tragedy, save it be laid over and lifted above itself with the deceptive jewels of English speech, can be no more in the temple of dramatic art than the pathetic picture of a lovable idiot lifting his small voice against the hurricane of the world.

THEY KNEW WHAT THEY WANTED
February 16, 1949

A revival of the play by Sidney Howard. Produced by John Golden for 61 performances in the Music Box.

PROGRAM

JOE	Edward Andrews	HER SON	Joseph Italiano
FATHER MCKEE	Charles Kennedy	SECOND ITALIAN MOTHER	
AH GEE	Francisco Salvacion		Eole Gambarelli
TONY	Paul Muni	HER DAUGHTER	Dolores Brown
THE R. F. D.	John Craven		Jo Van Patten
AMY	Carol Stone	FARM HANDS	Madelon Morka
ANGELO	Danny Leone		Jimmy Moreno
GIORGIO	Victor Rendina		Gerald Teddy
THE DOCTOR	Henry Burk Jones		
FIRST ITALIAN MOTHER			
	Delores Badaloni		

SYNOPSIS: *Tony's farmhouse in the Napa Valley, California.* Act I. *Morning, in early summer.* Act II. *Evening, the same day.* Act III. *Three months later.*

Director: *Robert Perry.*

FIRST PRODUCED in 1924 and revived in 1939, the play, which is still seen to be merely a workmanlike piece of showshop goods, was queerly regarded in its day as one of indubitable quality. Not only was it awarded the Pulitzer prize as a powerful example of superior drama, but its author was endorsed here and there as presently or potentially the equal, if not indeed the superior, of O'Neill. It may therefore be interesting under the circumstances briefly to scrutinize the full body of Howard's work, here viewed chronologically.

Swords (1921). An attempt at the lyric heroic drama since practised so assiduously by Maxwell Anderson. By common critical and popular consent, it amounted mainly to the kind of play written by overly ambitious college boys and girls directly they have completed a course of drama study under a professor of the sort who encourages his students to such lofty flights before they have sprouted wings sufficiently strong to lift them above the ground of even a one-act play in simple prose.

S. S. Tenacity (1922). An adaptation from the French of Charles Vildrac. Howard knew his French and the job was well done.

Casanova (1923). An adaptation from the Spanish, not so ably accomplished and all in all a failure.

Sancho Panza (1923). An adaptation from the Hungarian of Melchior Lengyel. Ditto.

Bewitched (1924). A collaboration with Edward Sheldon and a dramatic zero.

They Knew What They Wanted (1924). A paraphrase of a theme that had previously been handled by several German playwrights. See comment above and following.

Michel Auclair (1925). Another adaptation from the French of Vildrac, as well maneuvered as in the case of *S. S. Tenacity,* but inferior drama.

Lucky Sam McCarver (1925). A fairly interesting performance in shrewd box-office writing, but without critical merit.

The Last Night Of Don Juan (1925). A commendable translation of Rostand's witty, uncompleted play.

Ned McCobb's Daughter (1926). Regarded as one of Howard's best plays and a popular success, it contained flashes of honest character appraisal but little else.

The Silver Cord (1926). Another highly regarded play and also a popular success. Ditto.

Salvation (1928). Written in collaboration with Charles MacArthur. An available dramatic idea, much better managed by Harry Wagstaff Gribble in *Revolt,* and a play which, the authors confessed, did not satisfy even them.

Olympia (1928). An adaptation of one of Ferenc Molnár's poorer plays, and itself very poor.

Half Gods (1929). A somewhat ostentatious excursion into the "thoughtful" drama that got nowhere.

Lute Song (1930). An adaptation of a Chinese classic in collaboration with Will Irwin, it failed of critical and popular approval but was nonetheless an adroitly contrived performance.

One, Two, Three (1930). Another adaptation of a poor play by Molnár and a failure in every respect.

Marseilles (1930). An adaptation of the play by Marcel Pagnol again demonstrating Howard's good ear for French.

The Late Christopher Bean (1932). Still another adaptation from the French, this time René Fauchois. A skilful job and a moderately entertaining minor comedy.

Alien Corn (1933). Third-rate stuff propelled at the box-office by Katharine Cornell.

Dodsworth (1934). A first-rate dramatization of the Sinclair Lewis novel.

Yellow Jack (1934). A documentary play about the Army's battle to conquer yellow fever. A faithful effort, but only intermittently valid drama.

Ode To Liberty (1934). An adaptation from the French of a comedy by Michel Duren and, oddly, an unsatisfactory performance and a failure.

Paths Of Glory (1935). An ineffectual dramatization of a war novel by Humphrey Cobb.

The Ghost Of Yankee Doodle (1937). A poor "social significance" play.

There you have the sum total of Howard's work for the theatre: eleven adaptations, two dramatizations of novels, three collaborations, and ten independently written plays. Of the latter, though several showed an adeptness in dramaturgy, none was of any true merit. Some of the adaptations from the French were tasks well performed, and one of the novel dramatizations (in which, incidentally, Sinclair Lewis assisted) was excellent. Two of the collaborations were failures, one had some quality. A record, in short, of hard work but a record, as well, of relatively small accomplishment. Yet Howard's place in the chronicles of modern American drama is still listed as pretty high. That he had a flair for dramaturgy, as noted, that he could write dialogue acceptable to the popular ear, that he had a certain knack for superficial character delineation, and that he was seldom cheap is to be acknowledged, but that he had in him the qualities of a first-rate dramatist is hard to believe.

The *kudos* carelessly bestowed upon such a playwright leads us to reflect on the indifference to and at times even hostility toward young playwrights who have indicated some material talent and who, unlike Howard, have been denied the encouragement they have stood so badly in need of. There is no room to cover the situation thoroughly, but a few examples may serve.

A new young playwright, Alexander Greendale, not many seasons ago had his first play, *Walk Into My Parlor*, produced in New York. With slight exception, the reviewers fell upon him and gave him an unmerciful beating. They called him bad names, heaped ridicule upon him, derided him as an impostor, and wrote of him generally as if he were an outlaw, guilty of most of the heinous crimes known to man. The poor fellow unquestionably cringed under the bitter stings and it was a wonder that he was not too discouraged to proceed further with any playwriting.

What brought down the wrath on the boy? I will not ironically reply with what happened to be my own personal and contrary critical opinion, to wit, that he had written a play which, for all its unmistakable delinquencies, was an honest, intelligent, propulsive, and here and there even meritorious one. For, after all, as the choicer numskulls frequently contend, that is only one man's opinion, an argument which, if carried to a much loftier level, would logically dismiss as worthless the critical opinions of many such opinionaters as Aristotle, Diderot, Hazlitt, and Shaw. What apparently induced the greater part of that wrath was the youngster's periodic imitation of — or at least patterning his writing after — the work of the then popular and critic-beloved Clifford Odets. That he seemingly and oddly did so admire Odets that his play intermittently took on an Odets flavor was perfectly true. But that this influence, obvious as it was, automatically and logically corrupted his play to its complete undoing was very far from true. Some plays have been similarly inspired by the work of other dramatists and such reasoning would surely not hold that it has hurt them in the least. O'Neill has publicly acknowledged his debt to Strindberg; Synge publicly acknowledged his to Yeats; Gorki privately acknowledged his, though with some reluctance, to Tolstoi. It is not a matter of influence or even of imitation so much as it is a matter of what in paradoxical independence comes out of it. Young Greendale's play, for all its Odetsism, had something of its own.

What I am getting at, however, is the often careless cruelty of many of the critics in the case of beginning playwrights. A sufficient number of the latter deserve all they get, God knows, and full credit to the critics for giving it to them. But there are others who do not deserve it and who in receiving it are discouraged from continuing to try to serve an American drama that might one day conceivably profit from them. If the mere fact of imitation were sufficient permanently to consign a novice playwright to limbo, Robert Sherwood would be there now, and long forgotten, on the score of his imitation of Shaw in *The Road To Rome*. Elmer Rice would properly have been cast aside by the critics in the case of his *The Adding Machine,* an imitation of the German Expressionists, Kaiser and Hasenclever. John Howard Lawson and his similarly inspired *Processional* would very rightly have been flicked into the wastebasket. And the Odets for imitation of whom young Greendale was sent to Coventry would himself have been dispatched to the same place and by the same critics for attempted imitation of Chekhov. (I speak here purely of relative justice, not one way or the other of the playwrights' immediate or subsequent performances.)

And what of Irwin Shaw, whose *Bury The Dead* stemmed from Hans Chlumberg's *Miracle at Verdun*? And young Lynn Riggs, whose *Big Lake* was doubtless inspired by Robinson Jeffers? And of other such beginners? That the critics in some of these instances were unaware of the influences behind the plays or of the imitations and praised the plays only makes the situation more pointed. Perhaps the harsh criticism on the part of the majority of the critics of Saroyan's initial *My Heart's In The Highlands* found its basis in the circumstance that the play was not comfortingly and assuagingly an imitation of anything. The earliest efforts of playwrights often give no, or at best faint, indication of their future competences. Ibsen's *Katilina* did not even vaguely hint at the coming Henrik. Strindberg's *Master Olof* did not remotely suggest the possibilities of the future Strindberg. Echegaray's *Folly Or Saintliness,* Brieux's *Artists' Households,* Hervieu's *Les Paroles Restent,* Shaw's *Widowers' Houses,* Chekhov's *Ivanov,* Wedekind's *The Concert Singer,* Schnitzler's *The Fable,* Hugo von Hofmannsthal's *Yesterday,* Becque's *Michel Pauper,* Heijerman's *Dora Kremer* — none of them was indicative of the high talent to come. O'Neill's five short plays gathered together in the volume called *Thirst,* written in 1913–1914, nowhere in any of them presaged the O'Neill that was one day to bloom.

Young Greendale has abundant company in puppy playwrights whose dawning talents have been sneered into heartbreak by biting and, I allow myself to believe, undiscerning, ill-proportioned and shallow criticism. William Bowers, whose play of life in a little midwestern college was beautifully acute in its observation and collateral humor, was one such. Lucille Prumbs, whose *Five Alarm Waltz,* dealing with the idiosyncrasies of Saroyan, was periodically touched with a resourceful humor, and Francis Swann, whose comedy *Out Of The Frying Pan,* dealing with boys and girls trying to get a start in the theatre, was frequently pungent lampooning, were both abruptly dismissed by most of the critics. Joseph Viertel was treated a bit more kindly in the instance of his *So Proudly We Hail,* but with not enough deserved generosity to keep him from writing me a sincerely modest letter with an awful lot of discouragement and heartache between the lines. And Henry Misrock, with a play, *Bright Honor,* equally commendable at many points for a similar study of life in a boys' military school, did not fare half so well as Viertel.

The list is longer than one would prefer. Raymond Knight's *Run Sheep Run,* a defective comedy but one that nevertheless had a number of points in its favor, was for the greater part treated as if it were a case of typhoid and Knight told off as if he were Typhoid Mary. Dorrance Davis, whose *A Lady In Love* was a witty comedy in the Restoration manner, was sneered into the refuse-can. Louis Bromfield, who ventured into the theatre with *De Luxe,* a weak play but one frequently and independently notable for the accuracy of its character drawing, was killed off on the spot by criticism which confused naturally foul character with foul dramatic purpose. Arthur Wilmurt, though he in *Young Couple Wanted* wrote a better play than Elmer Rice's directly antecedent and similar *Two On An Island,* was made so to suffer for the mere accident of production time and was treated in such fashion that he despairfully took to the woods. Sylvia Regan, whose *Morning Star* contained much of sound character delineation and considerable sound humor, got short shrift from the critics, who permitted the moments of hokum in the play to blind them to its other assets. Margaret Curtis, who in *A Highland Fling* wrote one of the most imaginative and wittiest fantasies of our theatrical time, was lambasted by critics who failed to distinguish between a miserable production and the script. Harry Brown's unusual and often admirable *A Sound Of Hunting* was waved aside by all save three of the reviewers. Theodore Ward, Howard Rigsby, and Dorothy and Howard Baker were excommunicated for *Our Lan'*, *South Pacific,* and *Trio,* all of which were surely far from being beneath contempt. And these are only a few out of the many who in seasons near and far have been inflicted with welts of the whip.

I am not, to repeat, arguing for a blanket tenderness in the critical consideration of beginning playwrights. No one has been tougher than I in dealing with those who very plainly have no competence and no one will continue to be tougher, for only that way may the theatre be served. But it does seem to me that the axe is in other cases a rather injudicious selection of instruments and that — allowing even for difference of critical opinion and allowing even still further that the critics' judgment may not be altogether faulty — some less mortal tool might be more appropriate, more considerate, and certainly a whole lot more called for. When we consider the other side of the picture, the tolerant side, the point I make seems all the more permissible. For it is not easy to figure out just how and why the critics arrive at their occasional dispensations of polite charity. And it is still harder to figure out why they visit them on certain novice playwrights at the expense and pain of others, many of them more deserving of alms. This charity generally takes two forms. One is the allowance that the new playwright shows "promise." The other is that he "should with more experience go far." Let us see how it has worked.

A young writer, Frank Gabrielson, had a play, *The Days Of Our Youth*, produced in New York. Though properly finding fault with it and even roasting it to a turn, some of the critics nevertheless generously let the author down as a playwright of considerable promise. Yet *The Days Of Our Youth* had been written by Gabrielson three years before and since its belated production had — the aforesaid critics apparently overlooked — been preceded by a play written only the year before, to wit, *The More The Merrier*, which these same critics flayed as being utterly worthless. Is that the "promise" they wrote of?

There are all kinds of further confounding and blushful examples. Among many other beginning playwrights peculiarly blessed by the critics with either "unmistakable promise" or the potential ability to "go far" have been such as Charl Armstrong, who followed her meagre *The Happiest Days* with the fribble called *Ring Around Elizabeth;* Edward Chodorov, who progressed from *Wonder Boy,* after the dramatization of another's novel, to the trashy *Cue For Passion* and other such ineptitudes; Albert Bein, who after *Little Ol' Boy* did not get half way 'round the block; and Gretchen Damrosch Finletter, whose plays went progressively from bad to worse. There have been, too, Melvin Levy, who followed up his *Gold Eagle Guy* with the claptrap called *A House In The Country;* and Lynn Starling, who after *Meet The Wife* slowly mounted

to the climactic balderdash called *Beverly Hills;* and
George S. Brooks, who hit the chute on all fours after
Spread Eagle; and Milton Lazarus, who magnificently de-
teriorated to his *Every Man For Himself;* and a fat parcel
of others like Martin Flavin, Reginald Lawrence, Norman
Krasna, Allan Scott, and Lawrence Riley. And, incidentally, what has become of Norman Rosten who — upon the
revelation of his *First Stop To Heaven,* which was not only
a wretchedly bad play but, further and incidentally, a feeble imitation of Saroyan with undertones of Odets — was
excitedly hailed by a number of the critics as being fuller
of rich promise than an actors' agent?

All this gets down, in a way, to the eternal problem that
besets daily journalistic theatrical criticism. That problem
is how safely and inoffensively to shade mere reviewing
into the higher terms of drama criticism. It is, obviously,
a difficult one and the solution is far from easy. Popular
taste, that incubus, must somehow be in the critic's subcon-
scious, yet his conscious mind must deftly pretend that it is
not. The non-journalistic critic may have as his basic operating principle a catholic taste yet a unitarian standard,
but the journalistic critic, while he must because of his
heterogeneous public have the catholic taste, must further
and haplessly convert the unitarian standard into something rather more Swedenborgian and even Mormon. The
newspaper critic who would have, say, the Greeks as his
sole critical standard would be back covering fires within
a week. And rightly. The public may be damned but it
must nevertheless be served and to serve it, its own standards must, however gallingly, be borne steadily in mind.

Is it possible, though, that what I am saying is carrying
coals to Newcastle? Do not the critics in question already
know it? It would seem so from the record. How otherwise
could be explained the fulsome reviews accorded such recent assuredly popular yet critically worthless things as *Edward, My Son* and, on the other hand, the acescent ones
accorded such recent assuredly unpopular yet critically
and relatively reputable plays as Lorca's *Blood Wedding?*

To return, after the long detour, to *They Knew What*

They Wanted. It is, as you may recall, the story of an ageing Italian vintner in the Napa Valley of California who
takes to wife a young San Francisco waitress, who loses her
temporarily to his young overseer, who accepts their illicit
baby in lieu of the one he licitly craved, and who philo-
sophically forgives everybody all around and winds up
happy and contented. It is aimed at the box-office with
the necessary alternate emotions and humors, the former
scarcely more subtle than those of the early Owen Davis
drama and the latter typified by such delicate lines as "My
mother was a Swiss and my father an American, so what
does that make me — a Swiss cheese?," "Her gallstones
turned out to be more like cobblestones," and "Tony's cellar smells like apricots" — "Ours smelled like hell." And
it provides a picnic for what is generally described as a
character actor, that is, with worthy exceptions, an actor
whose years have unhappily advanced beyond the period
when he could prosperously substitute a younger and
handsomer physical person for any real acting ability and
who sagaciously resorts to the makeup box and, if possible,
a foreign accent to prolong his career and the needed
wherewithal that goes with it. Paul Muni presently has the
role originally played by Richard Bennett and, though it
would seem to be hard to fail in view of its sure-fire setup,
accomplishes the apparently impossible with a performance
of such exaggerated vaudeville color that one can not understand how he neglected to include in it a soft shoe
dance, a bird act, and a xylophone solo. Carol Stone misses
entirely the shading that Pauline Lord brought to the for-
lorn waitress part. And the direction only augments the
creaking and tottering of the deeply wrinkled script.

THE BIG KNIFE. FEBRUARY 24, 1949

A play by Clifford Odets. Produced by Dwight Deere Wiman, Lee Strasberg and the author for the rest of the season's performances in the National Theatre.

PROGRAM

RUSSELL	*Frank Wilson*	SMILEY COY	*Paul McGrath*
BUDDY BLISS	*William Terry*	CONNIE BLISS	*Mary Patton*
CHARLIE CASTLE	*John Garfield*	HANK TEAGLE	*Theodore Newton*
PATTY BENEDICT	*Leona Powers*	DIXIE EVANS	*Joan McCracken*
MARION CASTLE	*Nancy Kelly*	DR. FRARY	*John McKee*
NAT DANZIGER	*Reinhold Schunzel*		
MARCUS HOFF			
	J. Edward Bromberg		

SYNOPSIS: *The action takes place in the playroom of Charlie Castle's Beverly Hills house, in the present day. Act I. A summer afternoon. Act II. Late one night, the following week. Act III. Scene 1. Afternoon, four days later. Scene 2. An hour later.*

Director: *Lee Strasberg.*

SEVERAL YEARS AGO, Cedric Hardwicke replied to an interviewer's inquiry as to how he regarded Hollywood: "It gives you everything — blue skies, soft climate, loads of money, a life of ease and luxury, world-wide celebrity, beautiful women — and it takes from you but one thing in return: your talent." Clifford Odets, who deserted the theatre to share in Hollywood's favors and who has now returned, shows evidence of having paid the demanded price.

I am not, however, one of those who saw in Odets before he gave himself to the films the considerable tokens of genius that others seemed to. Aside from his early *Awake And Sing,* which was honestly out of the soil from which he sprang and which had merit, the bulk of his work impressed me as being at bottom largely orthodox melodrama here and there primped up with the then popular theatrical red ribbons of what is called, loudly, "social significance." There was in some of it an unmistakable vigor, but the vigor, as in certain of Edward Sheldon's not entirely dissimilar exhibits of the previous generation, was infinitely less that of sound and reputable drama than of sheer physical lung and muscle. The plays, in short, were like tough featherweight prize fights, at times interesting to watch and at moments even exciting — and of approximately the same profound emotional, intellectual, and artistic value.

But, and this is the point, there was apparent in them, whatever else was not, the passionate and proud desire of a man to lift himself above himself and to write drama that might be of some size and importance.

The Big Knife, Odets' attempt to re-establish himself in the theatre, indicates very clearly that that once proud desire has been infected with the Hollywood virus to be popularly successful at any cost. And it indicates not less clearly that his idea of the recipé for achieving such success closely adheres to the idea he was forcibly impressed with during his years on the movie lots. We accordingly see him resorting to the Hollywood brand of sensationalism, doubly carbonizing his old melodrama, heightening its sex element, and going in wholesale for blackmail, murder, poisoned drinks, fisticuffs, racing motor cars, and other such film delicatessen. And we see him, as well, pathetically trying to palm off such Class-B whoopdedoodle as acceptable theatre drama and to make us think there is some elevated purpose and mind in it by squirting into it some Class-P and under the circumstances boomerang philosophy about the conflict between cheap worldly affluence and decent ideals.

Odets thus follows in the line of various others who, like him, have gained the plump money and tinsel publicity which pass for success in Hollywood circles, who in the process have contaminated the probity and ambition that once were in them, who nervously refuse to admit it to themselves, and who by picturing their bust-ups through fictitious dramatic characters hope to mislead us into believing that they are still the upright men they originally were, that they have all along seen through the Hollywood

sham and evil, and that they have never lost the purity of
their outlook or their honesty and firmness of spirit. They
may fool themselves, but they do not fool us. They have
plainly eaten their cake, and the crumbs are all over their
vests.

Odets' play, as intimated, teems with the kind of melodrama that died the death when they began charging more
than thirty cents for the downstairs seats. A movie star runs
over and kills a child with his automobile. His studio has
news of his connection with the tragedy suppressed and
throws the blame on his press-agent, who goes to jail in his
stead. The studio boss holds it over the actor's head as
blackmail in order to make him do his foul bidding. A
movie trollop who was in the car at the time threatens to
divulge the truth and the villainous studio head's assistant
villain sets about taking her for a ride. The movie actor
gets wind of the plot, confronts the base boss and wallops
him, whereupon the rascally executive proclaims that he
will ruin him. The trollop who was going to betray the actor's part in the death of the child and who was about to
be done away with by the executive's henchman is oppor-
tunely killed by a cruising police car. The actor, stag-
gered by the thought that the studio head, who to boot has
already tried to wreck his marriage, would go so far as murder to safeguard his investment in him, commits suicide.

I am prepared to believe that anything can happen in
Hollywood, except maybe a movie that an intelligent coal-
heaver could look at without belching. But, though probably even worse things than Odets' pictures have happened
there, he doesn't quite convince me. He lays it on too thick
and his tardy indignation against his once beloved old
stamping-ground seems to have led him into a maniacal
raving. Even if what he writes were fact, melodrama is no
good unless it makes fact seem reasonable. Simple fact is
not enough. A play must give it plausibility, and Odets
hasn't mastered the trick. If you were to write a play about
even a case of record like that of the Frenchman who several years ago invited unnumbered people to his house
only to murder them, audiences would not believe it for all

its truth unless you made it believable to them through expert dramaturgical hocus-pocus. They otherwise would consider it fantastic and laugh at it as they did at the deliberately planned *Arsenic And Old Lace,* since it would seem to them, like that play, travesty.

And so it is that we laugh at Odets when he expects us to be serious. Hollywood has robbed him of his sense of dramatic proportion. It has taught him to write with the overintensification necessary to pictures that must be sold to the simple-minded millions. It has driven him to cheap sensationalism and to the blood of stuffed bulls and the thunder of tin-sheets. It has kept him generously, and clothed him fancily, and awarded him the usual handsome swimming-pool, in which to drown himself. And he has now gone down, for the first time, at least.

The confusion which Hollywood has wrought in Odets finds expression in almost every detail of his play. He seems to think that the moral and ethical standards obtaining in the Hollywood picture colony are identical with those in the rest of America and that the nation as a whole is headed for disaster because Americans in the mass are exactly like those in the film industry. His hero and mouthpiece whom he hopes the audience will welcome as a sympathetic, tragic character defeated by his high ideals is a drunk, whoremaster, adulterer with his best friend's wife, and polluter of his own married home. His idea of personal disaster is receiving millions of dollars for not doing a stroke of the kind of work that is odious to one. His concept of dramatic culture is sprinkling a play with irrelevant allusions to the plays of Shakespeare, Russian novels, and celebrated painters. His notion of philosophical utterance is "He died so he could live," and of deep wit "I wish the world would be frivolous again so I could be serious." His idea of the conduct of such national press associations as the A.P. and U.P. is that they would accept as the truth and send out over their wires without further investigation a studio fixer's version of the mysterious death of a famous movie star. And his standard of moral and ethical values embraces the theories that riches are inexorably incompati-

ble with ideals, that a business man who demands that a
contract formally entered into be lived up to is *ipso facto* a
contemptible crook, and that promiscuous outside fornica-
tion should not in itself break up a marriage.

What exactly is it about Hollywood that takes such severe toll of the majority of the writers who go out there?
Most of the reasons have already been set down by various
analysts, all of them in their way convincing. But I think
there is another that is usually overlooked and that is that
most of the writers who respond to the lure of the moving
pictures are inferior men to begin with and are accordingly
unable to preserve what small independence and measure
of quality they may conceivably possess. It is ridiculous to
suppose that any first-rate man and first-rate writer would
inevitably be befouled by Hollywood, save he were to de-
vote himself to it over a considerable period. But first-rate
men and first-rate writers are not in their very natures
tempted by the greasy riches that Hollywood offers and
have preferred to remain this side of that bogus paradise.
It has been and is the intrinsically cheap boys who have
fallen for the mirage and who subsequently have been lost
in trying to get out of the desert wastes.

There is, too, I think, a second reason. Even the most upright of writers can not for long immerse himself in a pulp
mill without having some of the pulp cling to him. This is
every bit as true of New York or anywhere else as it is of
Hollywood, yet Hollywood is always singled out as the sole
culprit. A man can no more, even deliberately and with
tongue in cheek, too long write trash for money and not be
polluted, however strong he may be, than he can sleep in a
contagious disease ward and not be infected. There may be
miraculous exceptions, but they remain exceptions. A
writer in need of funds may undertake a low writing job
to get them. He may even undertake two such jobs. But if
he undertakes three, and in quick succession, he is on the
road to oblivion, since, like narcotics, three are bound to
lead to four, four to five, and so on.

Hollywood is the worst of the dope peddlers because it
sells its opium under a false label. Its customers pull at the

pipe in the belief that it is harmless and, when finally they give it up, find that they are still helplessly dreaming the former delusions. They drop belladonna into their eyes to rid them of their mistiness; they eat oranges to get the arid taste out of their mouths; and they paint their cheeks to hide the yellowish pallor. But they walk stooped and uncertainly the paths they once erectly trod.

It is characteristic of one-time writers for the stage who have hied themselves screenward and, when things have no longer gone well for them, have crawled back to the theatre, to endeavor to re-ingratiate themselves by one means or another. Sometimes they seek to persuade us that all along they were singly devoted to the theatre and went to Hollywood merely out of curiosity, much as one would go to observe the doings in a cancer clinic. To emphasize their contention, they write pieces for the newspapers or give out interviews in which they denounce the place and everything connected with it in virulent terms. Sometimes they take the other tack and hope to convince us that they remain superior to Hollywood by affecting a paternal air of condescension and generously allowing that it has its good points and is usually derogated only by such men as, unlike themselves, have been beaten by it. And at other times they show at least a symptom of some intelligence by remaining mum, otherwise than to state that the big money they got there feels very good in their pockets. But in most of the cases the sound is of a loud whistling in the dark. They are clearly ashamed of themselves and wish to re-establish their pride, that is, if ever they really had any. They are, with few exceptions, Enoch Ardens returned home in rich raiment, but with their talents in tatters.

We pass to the general matter of acting.

Though it would be an unusual critic who would admit it, appraisal of actors and acting is grounded much more on a critic's personal predispositions and prejudices than on any strict technical knowledge. The familiar layman remark, "I may not know much about art, but I know what I like," should, if the critic were entirely truthful, have its counterpart in "I may not know much about acting, but I know what I feel." Since, as everyone is aware, the emotional reactions of the men whose profession is criticism are as different and as variously eccentric as are those of any other men, save alone such as are themselves actors, an actor's performance naturally impresses them in different ways. This, as everyone also knows, accounts for the diversity of opinion in the instances of even the very best actors. So far, platitude.

But on at least one point there should properly be some critical agreement, and that is that, though the actor under review may plainly have mastered all the technical facets of his craft, it is frequently his personal and physical shortcomings that make them go largely for naught. It is thus that an actor who obviously knows much more about his work than some other actor sometimes fails to interest and affect his audience as does a lesser colleague. I am not speaking of physical looks, though they surely have their place also, since that is altogether too facile a comment and one that has small value in critical consideration. What I am referring to is voice that, however ably trained, remains still out of the picture which the actor tries to create, and body which, however also ably trained, yet blemishes the picture further by virtue of its congenital inability fully to accommodate it.

More and more, in another direction, it is body movement, or rather lack of it, that diminishes the effect of so much present day acting. Nor is it entirely the actor's fault. Modern drama consists largely in speech rather than physical action; the emphasis is on the written word rather than, as in the farther past, on movement and "business"; and the result has been the call for acting that stops below the shoulders and confines itself mostly to the area above them. Our stage has accordingly become not a place for acting involving corporeal activity but a place for labial and facial feature, and in the process our actors have helplessly become less and less actors in the old sense than mere ambling reciters. What physical movement they are permitted is not the dispensation of their playwrights but of their directors, and it is consequently an artificial imposition upon them rather than part and parcel of the nature and demands of the plays themselves.

One would think that actors who have had prolonged screen training and who have transferred their activities to the stage would, whatever the nature of the dramatic occasion, be much less constrained in this direction, since the motion pictures by their very name are supposed to be dedicated to physical movement much more than to vocal. But, with the passing of the silent pictures, which necessarily had to rely most greatly on such movement, and with the appearance of the talking films, the screen began to imitate the stage and to make movement secondary to speech. And what ensued was for the most part an exaggeration of stage constriction, with an actor's play of features frozen into what is colloquially known as a "dead pan" and with his body — except maybe for the few minutes when the police chase him or the director inserts a sequence in which he, or more usually his stunt stand-in, jumps on a horse and races after an ingénue being kidnapped in an automobile — compelled into the corpse-like rigidity that movie audiences interpret either as a token of aristocratic birth or of a strong, silent, and often sinister mentality.

John Garfield, who has the role of the protagonist in the Odets' rubbish, is evidently determined to prove that he has retained a degree of acting independent of screen influence and to that end commits himself throughout the evening to such a repertory of face-makings as probably has not been matched hereabout since the late Willie Howard last displayed himself. He additionally, with his director's concurrence, indulges himself in such an excess of irrelevant physical movement, involving almost everything but turning cartwheels, that the role, which if sensibly and logically performed would include no such acrobatics, takes on the appearance of one in a Western film. I appreciate that Mr. Garfield's movie impersonations have been more violently instructed than is the common rule in the films and that, accordingly, there has not in his case been the customary measure of constriction. But when he carries over the rumpus to the dramatic stage, the effect is scarcely conducive to critical comfort. In the cases of such movie alumni appearing with him as J. Edward Bromberg and Theodore Newton and such a screen actress as Nancy Kelly, the congealment, however, is still in full view.

In conclusion, the difference between a playwright who has become a journeyman hack and one who has been and remains essentially an artist is to be observed in a comparison of this play of Odets' with one with much the same theme and with some of the same characters which, though not entirely satisfactory, was everything Odets' is not: the *Get Away, Old Man* of William Saroyan.

ANYBODY HOME. FEBRUARY 25, 1949

A play by Robert Pyzel. Produced by Phyllis Holden for 5 performances in the Golden Theatre.

PROGRAM

FRANKLIN	*Ji my Dutton*	JULIA HENLEY	*Katherine Anderson*
JOAH	*Emory Richardson*	HARRY	*Lloyd Holden*
BILL GORDON	*Roger Clark*	TAYLOR	*Valerie Valaire*
KAY HOWARD	*Phyllis Holden*	JOHN HOWARD	*Donald Curtis*

SYNOPSIS: *The action takes place in John and Kay Howard's country home in Westchester County, N. Y. The time is the present.* Act I. Scene 1. *Late afternoon — a Sunday in August.* Scene 2. *Late afternoon — Tuesday.* Act II. Scene 1. *Early evening — Wednesday.* Scene 2. *Late that night and early Thursday morning.*
Director: *Ralph Forbes.*

MISS HOLDEN made a big mistake in billing herself as the producer of a vehicle in which to display her acting talents. It was bound to prejudice people against her, since it seems to be a conviction that, if any actress aside from Katharine Cornell or any playwright outside the combination known as the Playwrights' Company thus sponsors herself or himself, it signifies that there must surely be something wrong somewhere, that no established producer would undertake the business, and that the actress or playwright in question was driven to the extremity because of apathy on the part of everyone else. The circumstance that no other producer would put on the playwright's play should rather be regarded as a recommendation, since Broadway producers have often indicated their preference for trash as against the plays of such admirable playwrights, to name only one, as O'Casey. And, in the case of actresses, their unmistakable preference for screen performers, whether they have any ability or not, should inspire some hospitality for any legitimate actress who hitherto has been afforded minor opportunity to let us see the nature of her competences. If, after all, years ago a young woman with faith in her abilities had not herself provided the chance to demonstrate them, the theatre might have been denied the delightful Mary Anderson.

It is, however, slightly embarrassing to this splendid good-will and generosity on my part to have to report that Miss Holden, whose previous experience has been confined largely to road companies, the small summer rural theatres and modelling for automobile advertisements, is not only no budding Mary Anderson but scarcely an actress save for the ability to stand on a stage without falling down. Her equipment, so far as anyone can discern, is otherwise limited to a dispensation of the constant implausible smile regarded by its merchant as a symbol of resistless feminine warmth and of the screwing up of the features into something resembling a crunched shredded wheat biscuit at such odd moments as she is called upon to express grief. She has not, further, yet instructed herself how to walk on a stage, or how to sit down without giving the effect that her director is under the back of her skirt tugging her into position, or how to pronounce the word "sandwich," among others.

The antecedent prejudice against the enterprise was perhaps additionally to be understood when it was discovered that it was a strictly family project. The author of the play was Miss Holden's husband, by profession a chemical engineer and one without earlier experience in belles-lettres and the drama other than that associated with weekly reports to the boss. One of the members of the acting company was Miss Holden's brother, who also served as production assistant, assistant stage manager, and distributor in his sister's dressing-room of the flowers sent to her on the opening night by her playwright-husband. Another relative, Kay Holden, was a contributor to the stage setting in the form of a large modernistic painting which adorned the wall above the fireplace. Though it was not confided to the public, it was rumored that one of the other actors was a cousin and that the Negro who had the role of the butler performed extra-theatrical service for the play's author as a valet.

Should there still inconceivably be any curiosity as to the nature of the play, it may be mentioned that it had to do again, and for what must have been the thousandth time, with the husband who devotes himself to his business to the neglect of his poor, little wife, with her attempt to find consolation in the company of a neighbor Lothario, and with the final realization by the husband that he has been sadly inconsiderate and the gladsome reunion of the couple. The dramaturgy consisted mainly in causing one character or another suddenly to appear in a doorway and overhear something he or she was not supposed to hear and in having the butler or woman cook come on and serve tea. At intervals, the author stopped what there was of a play dead in its tracks and had the characters deliver themselves of editorials on capital and labor, Communism, Democracy, free enterprise, or some other such topic, all of which sounded as if they had been clipped out of a minor farm journal of ten years back. The writing *in toto* sounded in turn like a poor paraphrase of the fiction in the same species of publication and was remarkable only for the enthusiastic interest all the characters exhibited in one another's state of health; in the heroine's arch exclamation, "You're hopeless!," whenever the Lothario said anything that privately gratified her; in her elder sister's visually bewildering description of her as "a dear, little child"; in the remark "We live in a modern world" in reproof of whichever other character expressed a conventionally moral view of things; and in the colored butler's mingling among the household like a blood-relative and fellow club member.

I herewith publicly apologize to the author of any play which in the past I may have described as the worst I ever saw. This one, at least up to this hour in my misspent life, enjoys that honor.

TWO BLIND MICE. March 2, 1949

A comedy by Samuel Spewack. Produced by Archer King and Harrison Woodhull for the rest of the season's performances in the Cort Theatre.

Program

Mrs. Letitia Turnbull		Major John Groh, U.S.A.	
	Laura Pierpont		*Raymond Bramley*
Miss Crystal Hower		Lt. Col. Robbins, U.S.A.F.	
	Mabel Paige		*Walter Brooke*
Mr. Murray	*Roland Wood*	Commander Thomas Jellico,	
Miss Johnson	*Jane Hoffman*	U.S.N.	*Robert Pike*
Mailman	*Howard Fischer*	Dr. Henry McGill	
Tommy Thurston			*Richard Kendrick*
	Melvyn Douglas	Sergeant	*Robert Webber*
A Visitor	*Robert P. Lieb*	Charles Brenner	
Simon	*Alonzo Bosan*		*Howard St. John*
Karen Norwood	*Jan Sterling*	Ensign Jamison, U.S.N.	
Wilbur F. Threadwaite, De-			*Elliott Reid*
partment of State	*Geoffrey Lumb*	Senator Kruger	*Frank Tweddell*

SYNOPSIS: Act I. *The Office of Seeds and Standards, Washington, D.C.* Act II. *The same. Several days later.* Act III. *The same. The next morning.*

Director: *Samuel Spewack.*

IF THERE IS ONE THING that scares a Broadway playwright more than anything else — more even than literate English — it is satire. For years, despite sufficient evidence to the contrary, he has been made to believe that the word spells murder at the box-office, just as he has been persuaded, despite more evidence to the contrary, that there isn't a cent in tragedy, religious themes, musical comedies that are not extremely funny, and plays that end with suicides. When and if, accordingly, he is fetched by a satirical idea to the point of not being able to resist it, he casts about him, with the ardor of a man with a five hundred-pound tuna at the end of his line, for ways to land it without breaking his arm, falling out of the boat, and getting soaked.

After much thought and numerous conferences with Broadway lights whose wisdom in such matters has left them owing money to the bank, he arrives at a solution. First, he takes hold of his satirical idea and minimizes it by abstaining from any faintest trace of the wit necessary to promote it. This, it need hardly be remarked, is not difficult for him. Secondly, to make doubly sure, he writes his play in terms of farce approaching burlesque but preserves a little high-toned air for himself by calling it a comedy. And then, safely to bundle up matters all around, he gets himself a director who will see to it that the actors gallop around the stage and make so much noise that, even if a vague suggestion of satire still persists, it will be lost sight of in the general stew.

Mr. Spewack provides the latest example of the technique in this *Two Blind Mice*. The implausible theme of the play is essentially satirical, treating as it does of a fantastic government bureau which was officially abolished some years ago but which continues to flourish with no one the wiser. And not less fundamentally satirical is the eventual investigation, participated in by the State Department, Army, Navy and Air Force, which only further complicates the situation. It is easy, and very pleasant, to imagine what an Irishman like Shaw or some Frenchman like Giraudoux who had never heard about satire being box-office poison would have done with the idea. But it is easier still, under the prevailing local circumstances, to imagine what one like Spewack has done with it. In place of satire, he has given us something vaguely resembling *The Doughgirls*, which was a good show, all too liberally crossed with something vaguely like his own *Woman Bites Dog*, which was a very bad one. Instead of wit, he struggles for what Broadway in its enthusiastic ignorance of anatomy likes to think of as belly-laughs. And by general way of conforming to the principle that, when everything else is in danger of going flat, it is advisable to bring on the equivalent of vaudeville, he trots out a variety of irrelevant acts involving a Negro pants presser, a giddy female dance instructor, a bunch of yodeling darkeys, and similar relics of two-a-day comedy.

The formula has become fairly weather-beaten after acquaintance with it in various such much better plays as *You Can't Take It With You, My Sister Eileen,* and the like. It consists in raising the curtain on several characters who bear some slight resemblance to normal human beings, introducing into their midst others of a consummate eccentricity, embroiling the lot of them in situations that could occur only in one of the more violent wards of one of the more negligently run insane asylums, and ringing down the curtain on a grand splutter of illogical fizgigs which so rattles the audience for the moment that what goes on is mistaken by it for an ending.

After seeing a half dozen or so of the plays one is likely to wake up in the middle of the night from a nightmare in which a household composed of Russian toe dancers, Washington brass-hats, Negro jazz artists, Brazilian sailors, inventors of cellophane spittoons, grand opera bassos, and a menagerie of parrots, poodles, Siamese cats and maybe a orang-utan all cavort on an automatic grand piano that grinds out Rimsky-Korsakoff while seven or eight newspaper reporters chase the distracted maid up and down stairs in pursuit of the facts about a secretly planned amendment to the Magna Charta. The most appalling part of the nightmare is that one recollects on awaking that one laughed loudly at several points in it. And the most confusing part of the waking itself is that one recalls one actually did likewise at its theatrical counterparts. For the truth is that, if these lunatic doings are at all well managed, they can be very amusing at times, since the complete absence of sense in them is much more acceptable than the presence of what so often is made to pass for it in the more straight-faced plays.

Though Spewack's doings are not very well managed and are not anywhere nearly so amusing as they might have been in other hands, the several laughs, as is their wont, nevertheless put in an appearance. They are, however, as is also their wont on these lesser occasions, not the result of any wit but of gags stuck into the proceedings like, in an older day, one Dutch comedian's finger into another's eye. But, so far as the rest of the show goes, the humor, when it does not take the shape of such lines as "It wasn't a marriage; it was a mirage," is the kind that invites the audience to respond to warmed-over stuff like the telephone calls to various government offices out of *John Loves Mary*, the sudden introduction of a group of preposterously incongruous characters out of *My Sister Eileen*, the invitation from the President to come to the White House out of *The Doughgirls*, the two sweet but conniving old ladies out of *Arsenic And Old Lace*, and similar deep-freeze remainders. There is also, in the case of the love interest, a cuckooing of *The Taming Of The Shrew* theme but, unfortunately, without any Cole Porter tunes.

Melvyn Douglas has left the films to preside over the stage as the newspaperman who ravels and unravels the shambles and, though he handles several scenes pretty well, conducts himself for the greater part with an air of smugness that disturbingly implies he is saying to himself, "What a cinch this stage acting is compared with the true virtuosity one has to have to be successful in the pictures." The rest of the company performs ably, and with greater modesty.

I have mentioned the Broadway presumption that certain kinds of plays or certain elements in plays inevitably portend failure at the box-office, or are at least a very dangerous gamble. Let us investigate a few of the prejudices in connection with some later day exhibits.

That tragedy stands little chance has been answered by the success of *Death Of A Salesman, Medea, Anne Of The Thousand Days,* etc.

That satire is risky has been answered by the success of *Man And Superman, The Importance Of Being Earnest,* etc.

That religious themes are risky has been answered by the success of *Shadow And Substance, The White Steed, Father Malachy's Miracle,* etc.

That musical comedies not full of laughs are set for failure has been answered by the success of *Brigadoon, Carousel, Love Life,* etc.

That plays ending in suicides are doomed has been answered by the success of *Death Of A Salesman, Rain,* etc.

That so-called literary plays are certain to collapse at the box-office has been answered by the prosperity of revivals of Wilde, Shaw, etc.

That the word "death" or "dead" in a play's title will keep trade away has been answered by *Death Takes A Holiday, Dead End, Bury The Dead, Death Of A Salesman,* etc.

That death as the theme of a play spells ruin has been answered not only by two of the plays named above but by *Outward Bound, On Borrowed Time,* etc.

That plays which run more than the conventional length are likely to alienate trade has been answered by *Strange Interlude, Mourning Becomes Electra, The Iceman Cometh,* the Evans production of the uncut *Hamlet,* etc.

That long speeches in plays are to be avoided has been ironically answered by O'Neill, among various others.

That plays about very old people are bad investments has been answered by the success of *The Silver Whistle,* etc.

These are but a handful of the ill-founded and senseless prejudices in which Broadway excels. Consider also, in another direction, the nature of its discouragement of those many young women in all parts of the country who have ambitions toward an acting career. No year passes without its numerous published messages to the young 'uns warning them of the pitfalls and hardships ahead and dissuading them from further pursuit of their dream. That some of the warnings are well taken is to be allowed, but that more are open to question is not lost on anyone who knows the theatre.

The most recent caveat issues from Mr. Thomas Weatherly, who has been professionally associated with the theatre for more than twenty years. Seeking to dishearten the girls, he lists a dozen questions and says that if they can answer all of them honestly in the affirmative, then and only then should they even begin to consider the stage as a career. His twelve questions are as follows:

(*1*) Is my physical allure definitely above the average? I mean your worst enemy's opinion, not yours. (*2*) Have I that indefinable, magnetic something known as "personality" which draws people to me in spite of myself? (*3*) Can I project that "personality" across the footlights? (*4*) Have I a good memory? (*5*) Am I forever observing people, watching facial expressions, physical mannerisms and oral colorings? (*6*) Am I a good mimic? (*7*) Have I a sense of chic? (*8*) Do I, at all times, on and off the stage, dramatize my speech and movements? Only very great performers can afford to stop acting when they're off the stage, and, with the exception of Helen Hayes, I never met one who did. (*9*) Am I vain, egotistical and self-centered to the nth degree? (*10*) Can I stand disappointment and failure for a long time without getting bitter and morbid? (*11*) Am I prepared to accept any job, no matter how humble, to get experience and a foothold? (*12*) And, above all, am I prepared to sacrifice everything in the way of home, children, and a normal life, for success in the theatre?

We ponder the questions in order.

1. Physical allure is, of course, always a help, but it is not at all vital to acting success. Many successful actresses of the past lacked it, as, for only a few examples, Ada Rehan, Madge Kendal, Lena Ashwell, Rose Coghlan, Mary Shaw, Henrietta Crosman, Mrs. Fiske, Kathryn Kidder, Amelia Bingham, Beverly Sitgreaves, Olga Nethersole, May Robson, Sarah Cowell LeMoyne, Helena Modjeska, Alison Skipworth, and Nance O'Neil. And at least five of the most successful actresses on the American stage today have a minimum of it.

2. and *3.* Personality, as it is called, is also a great help, but personality in the theatre is sometimes the result and achievement of expert press-agentry and need not necessarily be naturally born in one. Various actresses with very little personality of their own have succeeded as personalities through the stratagems of cunning publicity guidance.

Cora Urquhart (Mrs. James Brown Potter), Bertha Galland, Edith Wynne Matthison, Carlotta Nillson, Marie
Booth Russell, and all kinds of lesser girls like Ruth May-
cliffe, *et al.,* are examples.

4. An actress must be able to remember her lines, but
the celebrated Mrs. Fiske, among others, had a memory not
always what it should have been. And, when it comes to
the men, John Barrymore frequently had a devil of a time
recalling his lines and had to take refuge in copious ad libbing. There are at least three successful actresses on the
present stage whose memory is apparently so poor that they
have to be cued frequently.

5. Forever observing people, watching facial expressions,
physical mannerisms, etc., is more a suitable training for a
police detective than an actress.

6. A good mimic's place is in vaudeville not in the dramatic theatre. Actresses who are merely good mimics will
not get far.

7. If you haven't a sense of chic, do not worry. The majority of the leading actresses on our stage today dress like
frumps in their private lives.

8. Most good actresses do nothing of the kind. For one
Mrs. Pat Campbell or Tallulah Bankhead whose superior
performances have been conducted off stage, there are any
number of prosperous actresses, aside from Helen Hayes,
who reserve theirs solely for the stage. For instance, Edith
Evans, Katharine Cornell, Judith Anderson, Jessica Tandy,
Pamela Brown, Ethel Barrymore, Ina Claire, Margaret
Sullavan, etc., etc. And what of Maude Adams, Eleanor
Robson, and a lot of bygone others?

9. To be vain, egotistical, and self-centered to the nth
degree is to be doomed before you start. Even if you get
the start, you will not last long with impatient producers.

10 and *11.* Correct.

12. It is not at all necessary to sacrifice everything in the
way of home, children, and a normal life for success in the
theatre. All kinds of women who have succeeded have combined such things with their careers. Many of the failures,
on the other hand, have chosen to remain unmarried and

theoretically self-sufficient. The contrary idea is pulp fiction. Study the lives of the leading actresses in the present theatre and verify for yourselves.

In this and most other directions it is usually best to ask the question, "What does Broadway say?," and then pay no attention to the answer.

AT WAR WITH THE ARMY. March 8, 1949

A farce by James B. Allardice. Produced by Henry May and Jerome E. Rosenfeld for the rest of the season's performances in the Booth Theatre.

Program

Captain Ernest Caldwell	Staff Sergeant McVay
William Mendrek	*Mike Kellin*
Second Lieutenant Davenport	A Lost Private *George Mosel*
Kenneth Forbes	Private Jack Edwards
T/5 Corporal Clark	*Bernard Kates*
Mitchell Agruss	First Lieutenant William
Corporal Di Ruccio	Terray *Ty Perry*
Ernest Sarracino	Millie *Maxine Stuart*
Staff Sergeant Krieger	Mrs. Caldwell *Sara Seegar*
Jerry Jarrett	Private First Class Alvin
A Soldier *Alfred Leberfeld*	Hawkins *William Lanteau*
Another Soldier *Joseph Keen*	Colonel Davies *John Shellie*
First Sergeant Robert Johnson	Helen Palmer *Sally Gracie*
Gary Merrill	

SYNOPSIS: *The play takes place in a company orderly room in a training camp in Kentucky. Act I. An afternoon, late 1944. Act II. Scene 1. Early evening, the same day. Scene 2. The following morning. Act III. That afternoon.*

Director: *Ezra Stone.*

I do not wish to pose as the final authority in the matter, but after long experience and meditation I deduce that the net result of each one of the bloody wars of modern times, at least so far as the theatre is concerned, appears most often to have been an illegitimate baby. I have no idea how you feel about it, but to me it all seems to have been an awful waste of lives, time, and money. Some people given to a thoughtless pacifism object to wars on other counts, but my own objection to them is that apparently inevitable illicit brat. My theatrical charity condones many things, yet I now over the years have been confronted with so many of the impromptu offspring that one more and I am going to clap on my bearskin cap, seize hold of my old musket, and go gunning for the playwright who produces another.

There are two kinds of these unconstitutional tots. One, surely against its will, is made to figure in the serious war plays and to be the occasion for more bad acting on the part of its mother than can be found this side of actresses who play the roles of drunks. Mama is usually cast with a young actress equipped with the kind of yelling power that makes the veins in her neck stand out like bluefish. And she is called upon to exercise her vocal horsepower at its fullest when Pop, who ignobly denies the implied proud honor or accepts it with what may over-liberally be described as equanimity, proclaims his suspicion that she has been stepping out in his absence or laments that he can't marry her because he hasn't a dime to his name and, besides, has been told by the psychiatrist that unless he takes five years off in Atlantic City he will go crazy.

The other species of contraband baby shows up in the comedies and farces and is instead made the occasion of an extended debate, nervously engaged in by the Army, Navy, Air Force, and nearby dog-wagon waiters, as to the identity of the male parent. The acting of the mother role in this case does not impose so great a trial, since all that the young actress has to do is to indulge herself in some indelicate wisecracks and run around the stage as if the only babe she had ever heard of was Didrickson.

The most recent improvised infant is in the latter category and figures in this *At War With The Army,* otherwise an often funny slapstick farce. As usual, the suspense, if I may be permitted the rank exaggeration, involves the uncovering of the responsible party who, as is also not unusual in these farcical entertainments, turns out at the last moment to have been O. Henry. Aside from this innutritious business, the evening by way of killing time devotes itself to the hellzapoppin' doings in an Army training camp just prior to the dispatch of the boys overseas. Judging from what goes on, it is a wonder we won the last war, since our GI's training seems to have been centered en-

tirely on vaudeville acts and the art of seduction. The show
in the aggregate accordingly offers the impression of a bill
made up of collops snitched from a diversity of such exhibits as Hoyt's *A Milk-White Flag,* which dealt with the
National Guard, *The Time Of Your Life,* the Byrne brothers' *Eight Bells,* and a dozen or so plays of American school-
boy life and French sex farces.

Some of the performances contribute much to the periodic amusement, notably those of William Lanteau as a
dumb private, Mike Kellin as a tough staff sergeant, Jerry
Jarrett as a Saroyan ditto, and Maxine Stuart as the girl ex-
pecting the spontaneous addition to the population.

The editorial technique of the admired *The New
Yorker* consists in going over an article studiously, painstakingly substituting wherever possible a passive verb for
an active, touching up the whole with adjectives indicating
a tony remoteness and ennui, and sticking in, as a democratic concession, a few cuss-words. The technique of staging these farces, except for the cuss-words, is exactly the
opposite. Where the action is essentially passive it is made
to seem active by loading it with verbs, in the persons of
its actors, which do almost everything short of projecting
the latter over the footlights onto the heads of the audience. And where the adjectives are lethargic, it converts
them into so many physically interpreted, descriptive whiz-
bangs. Unlike *The New Yorker,* the staging is no longer
very successful, since audiences have come to see through
it and decline to be rooked by wooden rocking-horses propelled around a stage like whippets. Nor does the business
of having the actors scream their pica lines as if they were
newspaper scareheads any more work with the clients, who
reflect on the somewhat more resourceful method of the
cop lately described in the periodical prints by a lady
named Alkus.

There was, reports Miss A., a saloon-keeper who esteemed himself as a pretty tough customer but who
couldn't understand how the flatfoot on his beat was able,
unlike himself, to handle the noisiest souses with the greatest ease and efficiency and without the least fuss or rumpus.

Unable to suppress his curiosity, he one day asked the cop how he managed it. "Well, I'll tell y'," the cop confided. "I found out many's th' year ago that whin my wife lets fly with her divilish temper I haven't the voice to drown her out. So I whisper. And bless all the saints if it don't work with th' loud-mouth drunks as well. Not knowin' what I'm gittin' at, every last one of 'em starts t' whisper back at me. Thin I take 'em in."

The yelling, far from taking me in as the directors seem to hope, generally leads me to think I am at a football game instead of a play. I wouldn't be at all surprised, indeed, one night to find myself joining in it and having an usher hustle down, grab me by the collar, eject me from the audience, and push me up onto the stage.

Why is it, we speculate, that no humorous play of definite quality has emanated from any war in our time? Why has there not been even so much as a third-rate *Acharnians,* or *Peace,* or *Lysistrata?* We have had entertaining minor comedies like *The Good Soldier Schweik,* entertaining vaudevilles like *The Better 'Ole* and *Mister Roberts,* and diverting short satires like *O'Flaherty, V.C.* But we have not had one humorous play — even Shaw fell down hard with *Geneva* — which could lay any claim to authentic critical merit. We have had, on the other hand, serious plays of such merit, and also novels and short stories. And we have had some worthy books and stories of a comical nature. But, when it comes to the stage, there has been next to nothing.

The habitual answer that war is not a humorous business makes little sense, since it has been proved otherwise by writers of books since Ludwig Thoma produced his small comic masterpiece on the Franco-Prussian war seen through the eyes of a horse. Death and murder may also not be comical subjects, yet some very amusing plays have been written about them, like *Volpone* and *Arsenic And Old Lace,* to mention but two. What then may the reason be? My guess, which is not too good a one, is that, when a theatre audience sees a play that tries to treat of war and its participants in a humorous manner, it against its will and almost automatically is depressed by the persistent memory of the tragic happenings in the background of the immediate comical stage happenings, that is, by the great picture of the actual misery that stood behind the little snapshot of farcical doings passing before it. And it can not react to the play as the author hoped.

This, however, you say, is no explanation, since it is the playwright and not the audience that is the point of contention. Objection sustained. What the explanation in that direction is, you will not, I fear, be able to learn from me. I can not figure it out in any logical manner. Perhaps playwrights are like the audience, perhaps that thought of war's horrors stubbornly intrudes itself upon them and, without their knowing it, takes its subtle revenge on their hope to be amusing about it. It does not sound likely, but maybe it is nonetheless the fact.

THE SUN AND I. MARCH 20, 1949

*A play by Barrie Stavis. Produced by New Stages, Inc., for
23 performances in the New Stages Theatre.*

PROGRAM

GAD	*Joseph Silver*	THE EXECUTIONER	*Richard Kiley*
ZEBULON	*Maurice Shrog*	MALFI	*Merrill E. Joels*
REUBEN	*Ben Irving*	POTIPHAR	*Martin Tarby*
SIMEON	*Mort Neudell*	THE HARPIST	*Michael Howard*
LEVI	*George Habib*	ASENATH	*Florence Luriea*
DAN	*John Randolph*	RAKAPH	*Mort Neudell*
NAPHTALI	*Jack Manning*	PHARAOH	*Kermit Murdock*
JUDAH	*Richard Kiley*	THE FOOTWASHER	*Louis Hollister*
ISSACHER	*Peter Hobbs*	SHARSHERS	*Willard Swire*
ASHER	*Louis Hollister*	SHITAH	*Michael Howard*
JOSEPH	*Karl Weber*	AN ENGINEER	*William Brower*
AN ISHMAELITE SLAVE TRADER		A WARRIOR	*Frederick de Wilde*
	Salem Ludwig	FIRST GUARD	*Eugene Paul*
VASHNEE	*Nancy R. Pollock*	SECOND GUARD	*Salem Ludwig*
ARRAFI	*Peter Capell*	BIG WORKER	*William Brower*

*SYNOPSIS: The plains of Dotham in Canaan. A few thousand
years ago. Act I. Scene 1. A dungeon in Potiphar's palace in Egypt. Three
years later. Scene 2. A room in Potiphar's palace. Two years later. Act II.
Scene 1. The throne room in Pharaoh's palace. Two years later. Scene 2.
Joseph's office. Three years later. Scene 3. A retaining wall of the dam.
Four weeks later.*

Director: *Boris Tumarin.*

THE NEW STAGES group operates what it likes to announce as an experimental theatre. Its latest experimental
undertaking is the reproduction of a play that was experimentally produced by the experimental Federal Theatre
in 1937. I don't get it. If that is experiment, someone
should start editing a new dictionary at once and put me
down for the first subscriber. Otherwise, one of these days
you may be getting a thesis from me describing as an adventurous experiment the John Golden revival of *They
Knew What They Wanted* or the wrapping of cigarette
packages in cellophane.

The play is Barrie Stavis' *The Sun And I,* which is based on the biblical story of Joseph. I don't quite get the experimental idea there either. How many plays and novels have already been based on the Joseph legend I do not know, but the number must run into the hundreds. I myself have seen, in one language or another, at least twenty-two such plays and have knocked out my eyes on enough of the novels to make the oculists a fancy penny. If there is still an approach to the story that has not been tried, I should like to hear about it. Almost every change that can be rung on it seems already to have been rung.

Stavis has rewritten his opus since it was first produced, has smoothed it out a little, and has improved a bit on the original by cutting out some of the excess oracular baggage, which further and obviously makes the New Stages production a considerably less enterprising experiment than the Federal Theatre's gamble on the rougher script twelve years ago. But, for all his added labor, the play remains substantially what it was, which is to say nothing. Cheap pine, however much polished, does not become mahogany.

I wonder when foolish playwrights like this Stavis will stop trying to write Shaw plays. Since even Shaw himself has found the job impossible in his later years, one would think that they would have sense enough not to tackle it. Nevertheless, they seem to be convinced that all they have to do to turn the trick is to set their scene in a past age and have their characters talk as if they were readers of the *New Republic.* This, they satisfy themselves, constitutes satirical wit of a very high and juicy order. The boys unfortunately overlook a few minor, necessary details. For instance, intellect, original point of view, the ability to write electric English, ingenuity of phrasing, humor, wide education, and several other such trivial attributes. And what they consequently succeed in confecting are not only very bad plays but plays whose hoped for Shavianism begins and ends with the application of some feeble modern revue jokes to a lot of characters dressed up like a *Quo Vadis* troupe.

Stavis' treatment of the biblical tale takes the form of arguing that Joseph's ambitious resolve for the good of the Egyptian state foundered on his inconsiderate attitude toward labor, his disregard of the people's religious beliefs, and his flaunting in general of the masses' personal rights. That, in brief, autocracy which aims to be benevolent may find itself unintentionally the opposite and that force inevitably turns upon and destroys itself. The author very plainly believes as passionately in his theme as I passionately believe in its theatrical dulness if it is not handled with some wit, and since there is not the slightest suggestion of wit in this case, the evening has all the stimulation of flat, warm beer.

I am scarcely alone, I think, in the wish and enthusiastic hope that we have now seen an end of these countless plays that revert to a bygone period in history to draw a parallel commentary on present day conditions. They were once entertaining and now and then even possibly instructive but with repetition have taken their place with the kind of plays in which a family serves as a microcosm of the world at large; in which a woman's frustration is analyzed as having had its inception in the circumstance that, when she was a little girl, she saw the boy she loved kissing a pet goat; and in which a moron with dreams of becoming a Michelangelo or Beethoven gets so upset when he finds he can not realize them that he dives into a bathtub full of vodka and commits suicide.

I fear, however, that our prayer will not be answered, since even should there come a shortage in these political and sociological parables we can count on directors laying hands on the classics and pointing them up in a similar manner. Give a director a Greek or Shakespearean classic these days and what you are pretty sure to get, even if he heroically restrains himself from going to the extreme of dressing the characters in modern clothes, will be a play forced into such contemporary implications that it sounds as if it had been written less by Aristophanes or the Bard than by Freda Kirchwey or Drew Pearson.

I am, as is well known, a man of almost unheard of pa-

tience, but I can't take much more of it. When I go to the
theatre to see Julius Caesar, I don't want to find that what
I am looking at is Oswald Mosley. When I go to listen to
Antigone, I don't want to discover that I am listening instead to Dorothy Thompson. And when and if I have to go
to a biblical play, I don't want to be confronted with a
stage full of Congressmen in Ishmaelite maternity gowns,
carrying spears and talking like Harold Laski and Morey
Amsterdam. Under such conditions, I am like Garbo. I
vant to go home.

As to the performance of the Stavis cherry, I quote from
a prefatory note by William Archer to a book of reminis-
cences by a lay theatregoer named Hibbert published some
thirty years ago: "A piece of bad acting is, after all, such an
ephemeral thing that unless there are aggravating circumstances, such as grave injustice to an unfortunate author, it
is mere cruelty to stick a pin in it and preserve it in a mu-
seum. Let criticism do the little it can to embalm the memory of fine acting and suffer the rest to pass unchronicled
into oblivion." It may be observed in passing, however,
that Archer himself did not always practise what he
preached, and wisely, since there are museums as educa-
tionally devoted to freakish phenomena as are others to
sound and full-blown achievement.

DETECTIVE STORY. March 23, 1949

A melodrama by Sidney Kingsley. Produced by Howard Lindsay and Russel Crouse for the rest of the season's performances in the Hudson Theatre.

Program

Detective Dakis	Robert Strauss	Lt. Monoghan	Horace McMahon
Shoplifter	Lee Grant	Susan Carmichael	Joan Copeland
Detective Gallagher		Patrolman Keogh	
	Edward Binns		Byron C. Halstead
Mrs. Farragut	Jean Adair	Patrolman Baker	Joe Roberts
Joe Feinson	Lou Gilbert	Willy	Carl Griscom
Detective Callahan		Miss Hatch	Maureen Stapleton
	Patrick McVey	Mrs. Feeney	Sarah Grable
Detective O'Brien	John Boyd	Mr. Feeney	Jim Flynn
Detective Brody		Crumb-Bum	Archie Benson
	James Westerfield	Mr. Gallantz	Garney Wilson
Mr. Sims	Les Tremayne	Mr. Pritchett	James Maloney
Detective McLeod	Ralph Bellamy	Mary McLeod	Meg Mundy
Arthur Kindred	Warren Stevens	Tami Giacoppetti	
Patrolman Barnes	Earl Sydnor		Alexander Scourby
1st Burglar (Charlie)		Photographer	Michael Lewin
	Joseph Wiseman	Lady	Ruth Storm
2nd Burglar (Lewis)		Gentleman	John Alberts
	Michael Strong	Mr. Bagatelle	Joseph Ancona
Mrs. Bagatelle		Indignant Citizen	
	Michelette Burani		Jacqueline Paige
Dr. Schneider	Harry Worth		

SYNOPSIS: Act I. *A day in August.* 5:30 p.m. Act II. 7:30 p.m. Act III. 8:30 p.m. Time: *The present. The entire action of the play takes place in the detective squad room of a New York precinct police station.* Director: *Sidney Kingsley.*

WHEN I FIRST BEGAN going to the theatre back in the primeval days when you could get two Martinis for a quarter, with a three-course free lunch, including lobster salad, thrown in, you were always able to pick out the detective in a play ahead of all the other characters because he was the one disguised with a wig and beard that would not have looked natural on any of God's creatures this side of Alexandre Dumas or a buffalo. His prototype was, of course, the celebrated Hawkshaw in *A Ticket-Of-Leave Man,* and his big moment came when he ripped off his barbershop embellishments and, with a triumphant glee shared by him solely with the more backward youngsters in the gallery, proclaimed his identity to the aghast confusion of the villain and the audience's common sense.

The Hawkshaw brand of sleuth persisted for quite a spell, though with the growing sophistication of even the ten-twenty-thirty customers it was found wiser to invest him with more of a comedy flavor. This was accomplished by giving him a brogue and having him end his more emphatic proclamations with an allusion to one B. J. Suss or, if the playwright was uncommonly inventive and witty, disguising him as a Chinaman and causing him at the climactic moment to snatch off his pigtails and kimono and reveal himself in the garb of a United States Secret Service operative which usually looked like a combination of the court dress of the Emperor Franz Josef and the naval uniform of Admiral Farragut.

As my theatrical education progressed, these Hawkshaws were succeeded by a more rational species of gumshoe yet one not less fundamentally romantic, the archetype, obviously, being Sherlock Holmes. For some years, following the vogue of Holmes in the person of William Gillette, the stage could not conceive of a detective without a pipe in his mouth and such a faculty for deduction as was never matched by the most cunning bloodhound or income tax expert. By the simple process of writing their plays backwards, playwrights managed to pose their sleuths as omnipotent clairvoyants who were invariably able to spot the culprits an hour in advance of the plays' ends through traces of evidence that seemed to the more intelligent members of an audience to implicate not so much the criminals as the detectives themselves.

Those were the days when a mere flick of cigar ash studied through a magnifying glass was enough to fasten a crime on the most wily malefactor and when a scoundrel pretending to be a Frenchman was apprehended and rightly sent to the gallows because of his lapse in pronouncing "oui" as "ouch." Those were the gala days, in short, when detectives seemed to have prepared themselves for their profession not by hanging around waterfront saloons and the Bowery but around Harvard or Oxford and the editorial offices of the *Encyclopædia Britannica.*

Came then presently the dawn of a more realistic era, and into the discard went the Sherlocks and their criminologist likes. What followed were detectives who bore some resemblance to the real article and who, indeed, were even at times the collaborative creations of such actual Foxy Quillers as the late William J. Burns. But the theatregoing public was still so under the spell of the romanticized frauds that, when a Burns-instructed dick appeared as one of the characters in Charles Kenyon's *Kindling,* it showed clearly its homesickness for the former spurious brand, and that, when Burns himself took a bow from the stage after the opening performance of *The Argyle Case,* on which he had collaborated, in the Broad Street Theatre in Philadelphia, the audience was audible in its protest that he didn't at all look or act like a detective and was probably a phony.

Nor was it entirely to be blamed. Though some likeness to the factual article had made its appearance in the plays, the stage detective was so glued to a single type that the picture became as standardized as the pictures of newspaper reporters, always with overcoat collars up and half-seas-over; bankers, ever with be-watch-chained bellies protruding from their black cutaways; and prostitutes, always with pink feathered hats, dangling red handbags, and patent leather shoes with six-inch heels. The type, as will be recalled, was the tall, lean, dry-voiced, taciturn fellow with the brim of his soft gray hat pulled down over his eyes who moved about the stage with a chilly languor and confined his acting art chiefly to slitting his eyes and drawling in icy, sarcastic tones at any suspect who opened his mouth, however innocently, in his presence: "Oh, a wise-guy, eh?"

On rare occasions a note of great originality was privileged the character by vouchsafing him a derby in place of the felt number, which provided the critics of the time with the regular opportunity to wax facetious over his habit of never removing it when indoors, particularly if the scene was a fashionable drawing-room or the heroine's Louis XIV boudoir.

I have in my day been permitted the honor of knowing more or less intimately all kinds of detectives and at an early period in my literary life was even closely associated with several of them in the preparation of a lengthy series of magazine treatises on the intricacies of their occult science. But in all my experience I have encountered only one of the profession who resembled Hawkshaw to the faint extent that he wore a toupee, which didn't even fool his new girl; but two who, like Sherlock, could tell the difference between cigar ashes and dandruff; and only one who ever went around with his hat-brim pulled down and talked as if he had just finished sucking a grapefruit. The majority of the boys looked and acted much like a lot of stockbrokers, though better educated and certainly with better manners.

If Sidney Kingsley's new melodrama, *Detective Story*, had nothing else to recommend it, it would at least merit attention on the score of its author's extensive research which has been instrumental in giving the stage what are surely more reasonable facsimiles of the genus sniffhound than it has enjoyed since Burns lent his talents to it. Here are none of the greasepaint humbugs, but various specimens of the genuine article caught from the flesh: the hard, direct, and inexorable type; the tough-fibred but genial; the plodding but restless and impatient; the calmly dutiful; etc., and all, save for a slight compromise with theatricality in one instance, reported with faithful speech and accent.

It is around one of these, the first described, that the melodrama revolves. Possessed by the theory that black is black and white white and that a criminal in the law's eyes, whatever the mitigating circumstances, is a criminal first and last, he sets himself up not only as prosecutor but judge. His especial target is a man charged with criminal abortion and his vindictiveness knows no quarter. It develops presently that one of the young women who have been clients of the abortionist is the girl whom subsequently, without being aware of the fact, the detective has married. When finally he learns the truth, his moral and ethical code remains such that he casts his wife from him. That is the thread of story, a thread embroidered into a complex panorama of the criminal life of a city as seen from the vantage point of a detective squad room in a metropolitan precinct police station, and a thread further spun into the doctrine that no man may arrogate to himself the prerogative of final judgment on others and that in the very errors of police practice as it obtains amongst us lies the core of democratic governmental worth.

Mr. Kingsley has stated in an interview, "The temptation when you are writing is to get up there on the stage and make some great speeches. Those speeches were in there to start with, but now they are in the ashcan. The reporter in this play talks for me, but I had him talking too much; he was preaching. An audience doesn't go to the theatre to be preached to. It goes for a hell of a good time." Though, true enough and to his credit, Kingsley has thrown much of his speechmaking on his theme where he says he threw it, he still has retained a portion of it, not only in the reporter's case but also in the detective's, which might better also have been dispensed with. A melodrama is no place for even the splinter of a soapbox unless its author is able, like Archer in *The Green Goddess,* to dip it into a relieving wit. (I have lately heard, incidentally, that Shaw touched up Archer's sardonic speeches in the play; how far that is true, however, I have been unable so far to verify.) The Kingsley speeches are not at all necessary; his play speaks them in itself.

That play is otherwise for the greater part intelligent and entertaining; and its many minor characters, ranging from thieves and perverts to shoplifters, shyster lawyers, bums, various indignant citizens, and the general ragtag and bobtail which comes under the care or scrutiny of the police, are admirably drawn. The dragging in of love in-

terest in the shape of a young man accused of stealing funds
from his employer and a young woman who believes in
him is, however, much too arbitrary and damages the play's
composition; and the final scene between the protagonist
and his wife does not ring wholly true, probably because
of a brevity calculated to speed up the stage action. But
over-all the melodrama, capitally directed by the author, is
a sound and workmanlike example of the kind of realism
which Kingsley earlier managed in both *Men In White*
and *Dead End*. In other words and in the main, good, practical, popular theatre with some first-rate observation, some
acceptable sentiment, some properly rough humor, and
some gratuitous philosophizing to tickle such playgoers as
are not fully satisfied with entertainment unless it has
something stuck into it to make them, as they put it,
"think."

As a testimonial to the quality of the direction, there is,
among other things, the performance of Ralph Bellamy in
the leading role. This Bellamy in the past has been an actor given to the sort of postures ordered by theatrical photographers in the taking of so-called "stills" and to the kind
of vocal juggling remindful of elocutionary clinics. Here,
for the first time within my experience of him, he has been
converted into an honest and impressive performer. All the
lesser roles have been similarly well instructed. As to Meg
Mundy in the part of the protagonist's wife, I should like,
however, to speak at greater length.

Of this Miss Mundy's directly preceding appearance in
Sartre's meretricious *The Respectful Prostitute*, I allowed
that, though she was probably as talented a beginner as the
stage had discovered in several years and one whose performance of an often ridiculous role was one of the best of
the season, the part of a prostitute, whatever the quality of
a play, is nevertheless one of the easiest and surest in the
entire acting catalogue. Let an actress be as wanting in another kind of role as you will and yet as a fallen sister she
will not only acquit herself very creditably but in all probability will get reviews from the brethren that her scrap-
book has not before remotely matched. The roster of local

actresses who, for all their periodic bad luck in other roles, have been hailed when they appeared as members of the demi-monde would fill a small book. To name only a handful: Frances Starr, Jeanne Eagels, Elsie Ferguson, Willette Kershaw, Mary Nash, Pauline Lord, Lenore Ulric, Constance Cummings, Lillian Gish, Blyth Daly, Marion Waring-Manley, Mary Duncan, Anne Forrest, Mary Ryan, Francine Larrimore, Estelle Winwood, Aline McMahon, June Walker, Dorothy Hall, Hilda Simms and, last but surely not least, Jessica Tandy. Some girls, indeed, have made nigh an entire career out of trollop roles, for just two examples, Dennie Moore and Ann Thomas.

There may be several reasons for the eventuality. Sympathy for the underdog of whatever sort is probably one. Secondly, the fact remains that by and large the role of a daughter of joy has pretty much a ready-made effect. And, thirdly, the character is established much more easily and quickly than most others, almost, indeed, at the first entrance. This is not to say, of course, that any actress can play such a role to complete satisfaction. It is rather to say that, complete satisfaction or not, it is an exceptionally deficient one who can not at least make a passable impression.

I did not — I did not by any means — disparage Miss Mundy's performance. She was for the greater part excellent, and all due credit to her. She was still lacking in the acting experience to give the character minor shadings, which in the dramatic circumstances was not too important; and she had a tendency to repeat the technique of gaining certain points. But over-all she got into the role with voice, comportment, mind, and spirit and managed its execution with an uncommon intelligence.

I concluded by remarking that in looks she suggested an amalgam of Jeanne Eagels and Jessica Tandy, which is not bad looking; that her vocal equipment, considering her one previous brief dramatic appearance in a wholly different kind of part in *How I Wonder,* seemed to have considerable range and flexibility; that both in the earlier play and in this she was personally soothing; and that she appeared to be an actress not only with a present but with a future, if she was sensible enough not to sacrifice her career on the altar of Hollywood gilt.

That her performance on this occasion should be as poor in every respect as it is, accordingly comes as something of a surprise. In voice, shading, carriage and all other directions she misses almost completely. Her acting is forced, artificial, and full of such stereotypes as drooped shoulders to register abashment, drooped head to register humility and grief, and stares into space to register both outraged pride and independent resolve; and her voice employs the same accents whatever her lines' content. Why? No actress who previously has indicated the merit that Miss Mundy has goes so suddenly to pot, particularly when her direction is as competent as Kingsley has proved his to be in the instance of all the other players in the company. The reason, I am reliably informed — I like to have my puzzlement relieved in such a case — is that Miss Mundy, bad girl, made believe to follow the direction until the curtain went up and then elected to forget it and to go it on her own. Her own was not good enough and the result is what I have described. There remains, however, still one other puzzling thing. I had written, from evidence of her earlier performance, that she seemed to be intelligent. How could an intelligent actress allow herself to go so wrong? Maybe the answer is that, when a director is intelligent, it is much better for an actress to be dumb, or obediently pretend to be.

THE BIGGEST THIEF IN TOWN
MARCH 30, 1949

A play by Dalton Trumbo. Produced by Lee Sabinson for 13 performances in the Mansfield Theatre.

PROGRAM

BERT HUTCHINS	*Thomas Mitchell*	SAM WILKINS	*Rhys Williams*
HORTON PAIGE	*Russ Brown*	DR. ROLFE WILLOW	*Brent Sargent*
LAURIE HUTCHINS	*Lois Nettleton*	COL. JARED RUMLEY	*Fay Roope*
BUDDY GWYNNE	*Robert Readick*	JOHN TROYBALT	*William J. Kelly*
DR. JAY STEWART	*Walter Abel*	FIRST NURSE	*Alexander Lockwood*
MISS TIPTON	*Charity Grace*	SECOND NURSE	*Ben Metz*

SYNOPSIS: Act I. Scene: *Bert Hutchins' undertaking parlor, in Shale City, Colorado.* Time: *the present. A spring evening.* Act II. Scene: *same as Act I.* Time: *a half hour later.* Act III. Scene: *same as Act I.* Time: *twenty minutes later.*
Director: *Herman Shumlin.*

THE RULES of criticism, I have been told, specify among other things that a critic must concern himself alone with the work as it is presented to him, not with what it might have been had the author conducted it differently. I fear that once again I shall have to break the particular precept, and so grieve the dons, by telling Mr. Trumbo how he might better have written his play, which will, of course, as usual be of no service whatsoever, since it is too late now for him to do anything about it even assuming that he chose to, which is doubtful.

"The play," he admits in an interview, "started out as a drama of frustration, then the audience . . . changed it into what it is today. We hope it's a comedy." Good plays, Mr. Trumbo should be informed, are not written by audiences but by playwrights. They may profitably be rewritten in part after experimental audience experience, but to cast them in an entirely different mold is not only to toady to the box-office prejudices of such try-out congregations but to sabotage any honesty that the plays may conceivably have possessed. In thus cheaply surrendering, Trumbo has put himself beneath critical consideration by spitting at the original intention of his script and arbitrarily converting it, to money-making ends, into something wholly alien to his initial purpose. That purpose, he has said, was to concern himself with "a modest, decent, honest man badly in need of money for his daughter's education, and who for this most moral of reasons commits an immoral act." What he has now done, in the imaginary interests of the box-office, is to make a joke of his serious purpose and in the doing has concocted a play that does not understandably fall to the ground simply because it tries to sit on two stools but that falls with a thud because it tries to sit on a stool that isn't at all there.

Here is where my advice comes in. His working idea was not a bad one. An undertaker in a small Western community who is down on his luck sets his cap for the body of the town's richest man, presently on his deathbed. When the end is announced, operating in cahoots with a knavish medico he steals the corpse before the family has a chance to get into communication with a rival mortician. Just as everything begins to look rosy for him, the supposed cadaver comes to life, and the rest of the play has to do with his efforts to extricate himself from the situation. It is hard to see how Trumbo could have thought any such plot suitable to solemn drama. That he did indicates a mind peculiarly unfitted for playwriting in the first place. That subsequently he was led to rewrite his play into a comedy shows some progress, but not enough. The materials are purely those of farce and it is as farce that he should have treated them in the beginning. As comedy, or what he believes is comedy, they are ghoulishly objectionable, but as wild farce they might have been acceptable by virtue of their heavier coating of daffy humor.

My advice, however, would have been wasted on Trumbo who, even had he listened to it, is altogether too incompetent a playwright to have followed it to any advantage. His play as it stands is scarcely a play at all. It consists in having his actors tell its story without dramatizing it. Most of the evening is consumed by causing two of the characters, the undertaker and doctor, to sit around swilling whiskey and announce what they are going to do or have done. In order to give the proceedings the sense of a play, the author now and then brings on some other character briefly to interrupt their discourse. And that, except for a few minutes in the last act, is all dramatically there is to it. The theme of the play was held responsible by some of my colleagues for its general depressing quality. I think the theme is not to blame. The onus rests on the treatment. Trumbo's humor is of the most obvious and elementary kind; his imagination and taste are those of the Hollywood movie lots, which are his habitat; and his writing is as dull as an overused lead pencil. But even were things more beneficent, the stage direction would block their way. Mr. Shumlin's forte is assuredly not comedy; he seems quite unable to manipulate direction to prepare the path for it and allow it to spread itself; his handling of it is that of a man who has heard a funny story, tries stutteringly to repeat it, and forgets its point; and his personal discomfort is shared by his auditors.

In the role of the undertaker, Thomas Mitchell, a likeable performer, strains himself to be amusing and finds the task so difficult that he tries to conceal his problem by giving an imitation of the tricks and mannerisms of Victor Moore. Walter Abel, an actor with all the natural repose and humor of a railroad locomotive, adds his dead-weight to the evening's blues; Russ Brown, with musical comedy experience, is more in the picture as the town's scoop-avid newspaper editor; Rhys Williams does what can be done with the heavily contrived part of a boozing evangelist; and the veteran William J. Kelly gives the corpse some life. As the toted-in love interest, Lois Nettleton, when the direction occasionally refrains from making her twirl around on her heels to indicate her fondness for dancing, is pleasant enough, though one might wish that these ingénues would stop jubilantly clasping their hands behind their backs and thrusting out their stomachs to suggest eager, impetuous, adorable youth.

THE TRAITOR. March 31, 1949

A melodrama by Herman Wouk. Produced by Jed Harris for a modest run in the Forty-eighth Street Theatre.

PROGRAM

PROFESSOR TOBIAS EMANUEL		CHIEF MATE WILSON	
	Walter Hampden		*Maurice Manson*
JANE BAILEY	*Louise Platt*	LIEUTENANT SMITH	
MARGARET	*Georgia Simmons*		*James Davidson*
PROFESSOR ALLEN CARR		HAMMONTREE	*Michael Abbott*
	Wesley Addy	FIRST MAN	*Gene Blakely*
EVA MCKEON	*Jean Hagen*	SECOND MAN	*Larry Sherman*
LIEUTENANT HENDERSON		STRICKO	*Michael Dreyfuss*
	Richard Derr	A MAN	*Phillip Coolidge*
MR. FISLINGER	*James Van Dyk*	ANOTHER MAN	*John Wengraf*
CAPTAIN GALLAGHER	*Lee Tracy*	PHARMACIST'S MATE	*Don Doherty*
REYNOLDS			
	William Thunhurst, Jr.		

SYNOPSIS: *The action of the play takes place in the living-room of the ground floor apartment of Professor Tobias Emanuel in upper Manhattan near a University. Time: the present.* Act I. Scene 1. *An afternoon in March.* Scene 2. *Evening.* Act II. Scene 1. *Five minutes later.* Scene 2. *11:05 that same night.*

Director: *Jed Harris.*

MR. WOUK's melodrama persists in being interesting and here and there even exciting in spite of itself. Since that remark does not seem to make much sense, perhaps I had better do a little explaining.

What the author has ventured is an intellectualized thriller, the kind of thing Augustus Thomas used also to attempt. That is to say, a melodrama posed as something a little more high-toned by siphoning into it some thought, or at least what passes for it with an average theatre audience. To illustrate, take a scene from that thumper of more than a half century ago, *Lady Audley's Secret.* Here it is as it was then played:

Lady Audley: "Once I was fool enough to wed for love. Now I have married for wealth. What a change from the wife of George Talboys to the wife of Sir Michael Audley! My fool of a first husband thinks me dead. Oh excellent scheme, oh cunning device, how well you have served me! Where can he be now? Still in India, no doubt. Ha, ha, ha! Why, I have only just begun to live — to taste the sweets of wealth and power. If I am dead to George Talboys, he is dead to me. I am well rid of him, and on this earth we meet no more!" *Enter George Talboys.*

Talboys: "Yes, my proud beauty, we do!!"

And here it is as it probably would be if one of the present day deep thinkers operated on it:

Lady Audley: I was once foolish enough to marry for love, but now I have married for money and belong to the capitalist class so odious to Communism, the champion of an economic determinism that holds it is better to starve on dried herring with Karl Marx than thrive on *escalopes de veau viennoise* with Winthrop Aldrich. My fool of a first husband, who is ignorant of Ouspensky's theory of time, thinks I am dead. But if I am dead to him, he is dead to me in the philosophy of Edmond Louis Antoine Huot de Goncourt which maintains that incompatibility is the incinerator of the ego. I am well rid of him, and we will never meet again." *Enter George Talboys.*

Talboys: "Yes, we do! You forget, my dear, the philosophy of Alphonse Pierre Jean Gaston Bourrique that love is a combination of Communism and Fascism and peremptorily dictates an equal division of property!"

Wouk has written a good, lively spy melodrama and has sought to make it classy by ornamenting it with colloquies on Communism, Democracy, academic freedom, the atom bomb, world peace, the one-world theory, loyalties, errant idealism, etc., which, while they are sometimes intelligent enough, would be better suited to another kind of play and which now and then hold up his thriller's pace and action. But when he leaves his melodrama to itself, things get jumping again and the stage pops with the sort of hullabaloo which that form of entertainment demands. Some of the scenes, as for example when Naval Intelligence officers and their aides, equipped with ticking Geiger counters, dictaphones, flashlights, and the like take over the stage in search of a thorium plate which the atomic traitor is about to hand over to the Russians, have all the nervous pitter-patter in which as kids we used to revel whenever a Civil War or Sikh Rebellion spy hoopdedoodle came to town. And others, like the one in which the traitor at length turned patriot outwits the Russian mastermind and is shot down with a silencer revolver, also don't need a bag of peanuts to make us feel as if we were again in knee pants having the time of our young lives. It is only, in short, when the author confuses his melodrama with the editorial pages of the *Nation* that our boyish hearts sink.

Jed Harris has staged the melodramatic portions of the show admirably. There is only one thing I wish he had edited out of them and that is the frequent loud confidences by the Navy agents that they are secret service men. Somehow, it reminded me of that old revue sketch about the Spanish-American war in which Tom Howard went around with a big sign on his hat reading, "I Am A Spy." Lee Tracy, Walter Hampden, and Wesley Addy have the leading roles. Tracy is amusing as the chief Intelligence officer but would be a lot better if he did not mug as profusely as an 1895 barbershop shelf. Hampden needs only sleigh bells to make the benign college professor a perfect Santa Claus, and Addy only a pocket hypodermic to make the traitorous atomic expert a first-rate dope addict in an old Chinatown or Bowery meller.

With all its sins, however, the show in the aggregate is a sprightly, sublimated dime novel guaranteed innocently to entertain the youngster that endures in even the most venerable of us.

THE IVY GREEN. April 5, 1949

A play by Mervyn Nelson. Produced by Hall Shelton for 7 performances in the Lyceum Theatre.

PROGRAM

MARTIN	Barnard Hughes	CATHERINE DICKENS	
MARTHA TRIPHAM	Ruth White		Judith Evelyn
BARONESS ANGELA BURDETTE-		GEORGINA HOGARTH	
COUTTS	Neva Patterson		Carmen Mathews
DANIEL MACLISE	Oliver Cliff	MARIA BEADNELL	Leta Bonynge
JOHN FORSTER	Hurd Hatfield	HARRIET	Mary Lou Taylor
JOHN DICKENS	Ernest Cossart	ELLEN TERNAN	June Dayton
MARY HOGARTH	Joy Reese	CHARLES DICKENS, JR.	
CHARLES DICKENS			Donald White
	Daniel O'Herlihy		

SYNOPSIS: *The action of play takes place in the drawing-room of Tavistock House, London, England, over a period of years from 1836 to 1870. Act I. Scene 1. A night in spring. Scene 2. Dusk. One year later. Scene 3. An afternoon in summer. Four years later. Scene 4. Christmas Eve. Eight years later. Act II. Scene 1. An afternoon in summer. Ten years later. Scene 2. An evening in early summer. One year later. Scene 3. Sunset. Ten years later (June 16, 1870). Scene 4. 8 a.m. Two days later.*

Directors: *Roy Hargrave and Richard Barr.*

THERE IS a school of biographers, and to a degree playwrights, which seems to be committed to the idea that one of the overwhelmingly important things in the life of an illustrious man was an affair he had with some woman whose name in all probability he didn't remember two days later. Let a celebrated figure have indulged in even his earliest years in what was a negligible relationship with a member of the fair sex and it will be given such implications as would scare the hell out of Ibsen, Strindberg, and the whole French population, or at least that portion of it which didn't laugh itself sick.

What especially enchants the biographer or playwright is to lay hold of a famous man who over the long years has the romantic delusions of biographers who seem to have confused their subjects with themselves, has been a trivial and at times even humorous business. It is true that what they thought was an unloaded pistol occasionally turned out to be loaded and shot off a schnitzel of their ears, but a schnitzel of ear whether on or off has never materially altered the look of a man's face, and theirs, for all the contretemps, remained much the same. Yet what we have got is a repertory of amber-colored biographies that might have been written by Krafft-Ebing in collaboration with Anthony Hope and that would fit very much more snugly the lives of Heliogabalus, Casanova, and movie actors.

And therein lies the paradox. Let a biographer set himself to the composition of a life of such a rake as the aforesaid Casanova and his multiple sexual adventures will occupy him less than the problematical single adventure of someone like, say, Francis Scott Key. Where in a case like the latter we would be persuaded that the solitary alleged and extremely dubious excursion was solely responsible for "The Star Spangled Banner," most of the space in the case of the former will be devoted to his brain exercises in the fields of literature and politics, and what little is left over to his visits and wassail bouts with Voltaire. If I were a public relations counsel and had as a client a man who for his family's sake was worried about the possibility of a post mortem biography, I should advise him to go out forthwith and make a consummate fool of himself with the girls. The chances would be five to one that any future book on him would be devoted exclusively to his professional career and accomplishments, to say nothing of his regular Sunday attendance at church.

Charles Dickens, long the darling of the pure in heart, is the latest theatrical victim of the sex snoopers, and what his playwright-biographer, Mr. Nelson, does to him in this *The Ivy Green* makes some of the most notorious wolves in history look in comparison like so many toy poodles. Since what time I have devoted to Dickens has been confined to his literary performances, I do not know whether what Nelson relates about his various gallivantings and in-

enjoyed an immaculate popular reputation and sh
he was a whited sepulchre. This, to the immense
tion of the chronicler, is conclusively established by
ous research which has dug up the news that the su
the age of sixteen was surprised in the act of k
scullery maid. That he became a renowned scienti
eral, composer, or even archbishop in subsequent ye
never once so much as looked at any other woman
lawfully wedded wife does not seem to count. That
it appears, colored his whole life and being, to say
ing, of course, of the book's jacket.

In his recently published autobiography, Bernard
who has had experience with such biographers and
lucky to be still alive to reproach them, observes: "E
pher, get it into your mind that you can learn n
about your biographies from their sex histories. Th
relation is not a personal relation. It can be irresistib
sired and rapturously consummated between person
could not endure one another for a day in any othei
tion." But, sensible though the words are, they gen
have fallen on deaf ears, and the result is a flood of
formances that sedulously employ their pieces of cha
an elaborate scribbling on the backs of the world's emi
men.

Few of the deceased, big or little, have been spared
nonsense. Presidents from George Washington thro
Abe Lincoln and Grover Cleveland to Harding have l
described as having slept here or there at the expens
considerably more valuable descriptions of what they
while they were awake. Poets, novelists, statesmen, and
diers, some of whom changed the course of the world
their time, are portrayed in terms of rare or casual —
often wholly hypothetical — gallantries, doubtless none
at best very few of which had any more influence on th
careers and psyches than their aunts or valets. Great m
are known to have been wobbled temporarily by lad
with whom they have consorted, but it is principally t
smaller fry whose bewobblement has been extended.

To the majority of the world's illuminati, sex, desp

fidelities is true or not. If true, they would seem to unfit me for the profession of public relations counsel mentioned above. But, fact or not fact, they do not go to constitute an even faintly tolerable play for the simple reason that what the author hoped would impress us as peculiarly salty drama impresses us rather as a paraphrase of Mae West's *Catherine Was Great* with the scene laid in England and with the Russian empress' role played by an actor with whiskers and a British accent. The comic tone is further heightened by portraying Dickens as a nitwit who would have found the writing of even a Lloyd C. Douglas novel far beyond his abilities and who comports himself even when senile like a character in a Tristan Bernard bedroom farce, yet who is presented as such an irresistible magnet that every woman who comes into contact with him has to grab hold of a chair to keep from swooning with passionate desire of him. Mr. Nelson can possibly support his picture with the necessary evidence, but I still do not believe that Dickens was so complete and entire an ass. What is more, even if he was, I still think that, as in other such biographical cases, the picture at best is just one of those candid camera snapshots of a notable man caught in his off and wholly immaterial and irrelevant moments.

Though Stewart Chaney provides a handsome setting for the play, the acting scarcely adds to its credibility, and the direction further assists incredulity by having most of the female characters conduct themselves with a continuous gliding, pit-a-patting, hopping and jumping about the stage that gives the scene the appearance of a ballet rehearsal. In the Dickens role, Daniel O'Herlihy, imported from Dublin, makes matters a little more difficult by playing the eminent literatus as if he were a pretty Hollywood screen actor in a revival of *Brown Of Harvard*. As his sorely tried yet unfaltering wife, Judith Evelyn, burdened with a Scotch accent that sounds like Harry Lauder with tonsilitis, does a bit better but accompanies her lines and silent brooding with face-makings of a fecundity and range exceeded only by Carmen Mathews in the role of her sister. I have beheld some remarkable physiognomy gymnastics in

my day, but I doubt if any actress I have ever seen has surpassed this Miss Mathews in the art of screwing her features into such a variety of unearthly patterns. Hurd Hat-
field, as John Forster, Dickens' friend and biographer,
comports himself on the contrary with a frigidity of expression and a rigidity of carriage, an inheritance from the
movie cameras, that suggest he has dropped into the proceedings from the nearby *The Biggest Thief In Town* and
is still playing the corpse. Only Neva Patterson in the minor part of Angela and Ernest Cossart as John Dickens
seem to remember that actors and actresses, despite their
profession, may be members of the human race.

It is Cedric Hardwicke's theory that an actor really acts
only when he is not speaking. In other words, that his fullest resources are called upon when he is acting independently of his provided lines; when, in brief, he is left largely
on his own. There is much, it strikes me, in the contention
and it gains considerable support from watching most of
the actors and actresses in this Nelson exhibit. When they
haven't lines to fall back on, they are completely lost and
become so many sticks. The lines they have, true, do not
much help them to conceal their acting infirmities, but
those infirmities become life-size whenever they are de-
prived of them and have to rely on pauses, silences, byplay,
and incidental physical comportment. In such circumstances, the effect they provide is of a lot of dummies at sea.

RINGLING BROTHERS' CIRCUS. April 6, 1949

The annual sawdust-ring show, produced by the Ringling Brothers for four and one-half weeks in Madison Square Garden.

PRINCIPALS

Martine, the Ugo troupe, the Justino Loyals, the Bostocks, the Geraldos, Francis Brunn, Lola Dobritch, the Joanidies, Alma Piaia, Jean Sleeter, Czeslan Mroczkowski, the Three Margas, Swanson, the Mandos Sisters, Unus, Del Morals, Los Onas, the Flying Artonys, Concellos, Harolds and Comets, Claude Valois, Lilian Wittmack, the Great Bokaros, Lou Jacobs, Emmett Kelly, Felix Adler, the Alzanas, *et al.*

Director: *John Murray Anderson.*

EVEN AT the tender age of six I was such an objectionably precocious heel that, when my father took me to the Barnum and Bailey circus, I outraged his patience and geniality by my open suspicion that not only wasn't it Julius Caesar himself, as advertised, who was driving one of the chariots in the big Kiralfy spectacle but that the Queen of Sheba looked to me very much like our last year's cook. It is possible that in the intervening years I have become more acquiescently imaginative and that my public manners have seen some slight improvement, but it is nonetheless obvious from the record that I am not the man to write about any circus with critical fairness. I accordingly ask you to read what follows about the Ringling Brothers' with your fingers crossed or, perhaps better still, with one of them adjusted to the tip of your nose.

That the show is a fine one to the great majority of folk, I do not for a moment question. And, as circuses go, I suppose it is up at the top. But, though I have been looking at circuses almost since Forepaugh and P. T. began operating them, I wouldn't know, since what is called "the greatest show on earth," for all its million dollars' worth of elephants, jugglers, and trapeze performers, has never impressed me one-tenth so much as even an economical stock production of a Somerset Maugham comedy.

I don't doubt that the sight of a man or woman hanging by one foot from a trapeze is considerably more thrilling to many people than *Hamlet.* I don't doubt that the spectacle of a dozen elephants standing with one paw on one another's backs, even if they look extremely skeptical of the people who regard the feat as remarkable, is more inspiring to most folk than the spectacle of Romeo placing his hand in Juliet's. Nor do I doubt that there are some people who get more satisfaction looking at a gorilla than at Patricia Morison. It's simply that I am not one of them.

I don't pose as an aloof and superior fellow; I am probably just a bore. But I didn't hire myself for this critical job to put Baron Munchausen out of business and I am not going to start losing it by pretending that nothing excites me more than a jaguar standing on its hind legs or a Chinaman balancing himself on a pole. What is more, if you want the real lowdown, I can get a heap more pleasure watching the undulations of Mae West than those of a giraffe and am entertained considerably less by Lola Dobritch toe-dancing on a tight-wire than by Bernard Shaw doing the same thing on the English language.

There is, I think, a lot of hypocrisy in connection with the circus, and the newspapers are not the least offenders. Just why, I do not know, but for innumerable years now a paper that wouldn't think of giving more than a couple of sticks of advance reading matter to, say, a visiting Old Vic company will spread itself with columns and pictures whenever the circus is due. It may be on the peculiar theory that the circus is a public institution and the theatre is not; it may be on the even more peculiar theory that the bulk of the paper's readers are children. But, whatever it is, the notion seems to be ingrained that it is only proper to treat the circus with the reverence with which Americans speak of the King of England and the dead.

Do not get the idea that I am blasé, an epithet usually bestowed on anyone who, among other things, can no longer get very excited over a cage full of elderly tigers whose understandable annoyance at being poked in their rears with a sharp stick is mistaken for a man-eating ferociousness. I am far from blasé. I am, in fact, so little blasé that I still get a kick from boiled beef with horseradish sauce, spy melodramas, pay telephones that accidentally return my nickel, and love. But, impeach me if you will. I can not get all worked up over Mother Goose pageants, acrobats who dress as monkeys to conceal the essential routine nature of their act, ladies in pink tights riding docile nags bareback, and wenches who climb up ropes and twirl around on them while the band toots "I'm In Love With A Girl In The Moon." I am a little more cordial, however, to the act called "Bostock's Erudite Mules." The erudition of Mr. Bostock's protégé's may, true enough, not be any more notable than Dr. Harlow Shapley's, but I admire them for their greater wisdom in keeping their mouths shut.

Moreover, far from being blasé, I am still a pigeon for clowns. Give me one look at Ilya Ehrenburg, Father Divine or Bobby Clark and it takes someone to hit me over the head with a club to make me stop laughing. But, aside from the old reliable Emmett Kelly, the circus this year hasn't any who can in any way equal them. What is more, they have not thought up any new tricks and repeat the same old chestnuts. I can still, innocent at heart as I am, be amused by the clown's nose that lights up with a red bulb, by the clown who parades solemnly around the ring gazing dreamily at a jonquil, and by the one who cracks a peanut with a sledge-hammer and is reduced to tears when he finds it smashed beyond eating possibility. But I fear that my features remain unconvulsed when one or another of the buffoons for the hundredth time blows bubbles out of a trombone, or mimics Charlie Chaplin, or minces around dressed in women's clothes.

When Kelly tries to saw a piece of wood, can't make any progress and uses the saw puzzledly to scratch the back of his neck, I am right there chuckling with the rest of the kids. But for the larger part of the evening the great privilege of getting all stuck up with spun candy, having the man behind me explode a bottle of soda pop down my collar, and eating a hot dog with a small cobblestone in it does not entirely compensate me for the stiff neck I get looking up at three dozen successive wire-walkers, trapeze performers and flying ring adagio duos or for the doubtful enchantment I experience when, in the grand finale, they unveil a huge picture of Harry Truman.

SOUTH PACIFIC. April 7, 1949

A musical play with music by Richard Rodgers, lyrics by Oscar Hammerstein II, and book by the latter and Joshua Logan, adapted from James A. Michener's Tales Of The South Pacific. *Produced by the Messrs. Rodgers and Hammerstein in association with Leland Hayward and Joshua Logan for far beyond the season performances in the Majestic Theatre.*

Program

Ngana	*Barbara Luna*
Jerome	
Michael Deleon or *Noel DeLeon*	
Henry	*Richard Silvera*
Ensign Nellie Forbush	
	Mary Martin
Emile De Becque	*Ezio Pinza*
Bloody Mary	*Juanita Hall*
Bloody Mary's Assistant	
	Musa Williams
Abner	*Archie Savage*
Stewpot	*Henry Slate*
Luther Billis	*Myron McCormick*
Professor	*Fred Sadoff*
Lt. Joseph Cable	*William Tabbert*
Capt. George Brackett, USN	
	Martin Wolfson
Cmdr. William Harbison, USN	
	Harvey Stephens
Yeoman Herbert Quale	
	Alan Gilbert
Sgt. Kenneth Johnson	
	Thomas Gleason
Seabee Richard West	
	Dickinson Eastham
Seabee Morton Wise	
	Henry Michel
Seaman Tom O'Brien	*Bill Dwyer*
Radio Operator Bob McCaffrey	
	Biff McGuire
Marine Cpl. Hamilton Steeves	
	Jim Hawthorne

Staff Sgt. Thomas Hassinger	
	Jack Fontan
Seaman James Hayes	*Beau Tilden*
Lt. Genevieve Marshall	
	Jacqueline Fisher
Ensign Dinah Murphy	
	Roslyn Lowe
Ensign Janet MacGregor	
	Sandra Deel
Ensign Cora MacRae	
	Bernice Saunders
Ensign Sue Yaeger	*Pat Northrop*
Ensign Lisa Minelli	*Gloria Meli*
Ensign Connie Walewska	
	Mardi Bayne
Ensign Pamela Whitmore	
	Evelyn Colby
Ensign Bessie Noonan	
	Helena Schurgot
Liat	*Betta St. John*
Marcel, Henry's Assistant	
	Richard Loo
Lt. Buzz Adams	*Don Fellows*

	Mary Ann Reeve
Islanders	*Chin Yu*
Sailors	*Alex Nicol*
Marines	*Eugene Smith*
Officers	*Richard Loo*
	William Ferguson

The action of the play takes place on two islands in the South Pacific during the recent war. There is a week's lapse of time between the two acts.

Director: *Joshua Logan.*

LITTLE IS MORE DANGEROUS to the prosperity of women and musical shows than crediting them openly with too much intelligence. Some time ago, Elsa Maxwell paid that doubtful compliment in her syndicated newspaper column to the charming actress, Lilli Palmer, and was subsequently told by the latter that it had succeeded in depriving her of a job for a full year and a half. To say of a musical show that it is intelligent is similarly to scare people away from it, since to speak of intelligence in connection with any such exhibit is like touting a drama for its stupidity. There is, moreover, often some reason in the people's fright. A musical show, as I have noted in the past, is in its very nature properly a holiday from the mind; it is, or should be, a pleasant lunacy in the midst of the world's struggle for rationalism; and the intrusion into it of too much sense spoils the party.

Do not be unduly alarmed, however, when I describe this *South Pacific* as an infinitely more intelligent musical than most. Though its story line and many other things about it have been contrived with more brains than we are accustomed to in such cases, its creators have warily seen to it that its savvy does not get out of control and throw a wrench into the works, and the consequence is an unusually satisfying evening. Almost everything connected with the occasion indicates an uncommon taste, expertness, and quality of theatrical mind. The book, derived from two of the Michener stories and ingeniously combined and edited, concurrently narrates two love stories: one, that of an American wartime nurse and a French exile planter with two children by a Polynesian woman, the other of a young American marine aviator and a Tonkinese girl, and employs both for a glance at inborn or acquired prejudice against race and color. But the theme is not pointed up and stressed; the idea is allowed to develop quietly, gently and very naturally from the acted story. The music is close to Rodgers' best; the songs dramatize character and action and are part and parcel of the play and, above all, are independent of the common musical psychology described some years ago by the late composer and producing musical director of Broadway shows, Herbert Stothart.

"Musical scoring," he observed, with both motion pictures and their Broadway stage counterparts in mind, "is, I believe, largely a matter of psychology. The composer, through experience, learns what elements generate certain moods. Anger can be generated by what I call 'red' tones, which slightly clash in orchestration and so mentally irritate. A tranquil mood can be inspired by quiet, gently flowing melody. Alarm can be created by clashing harmonies; unrest by the montonous beat of tom-toms, and by effects strange in musical principle, hence played to unaccustomed ears. Sonorous bells and deep tones of the organ inspire reverence. These are all matters of elemental psychology. By deciding to what extent to use them, one gets the shades in between the basic classifications."

No such nursery nonsense for Rodgers. He writes a score not, as do various of his colleagues, for the *table d'hôte* but, with some slight respect, for the *à la carte* ear. Most of his songs are delightful: "Dites-Moi Pourquoi," "Some Enchanted Evening" (with a hint of Lehár) , "There Is Nothing Like A Dame," "I'm In Love With A Wonderful Guy," "Younger Than Springtime," "Happy Talk" (with its delicately lovely pantomime by Betta St. John as the Tonkinese girl) , "I'm Gonna Wash That Man Right Outa My Hair," and "This Nearly Was Mine." Nothing, to be sure, to threaten the reputation of Franz Schubert or Arthur Sullivan, but delightful none the less. And all set to the kind of words — simple, unaffected, tender, humorous, and never strainfully sophisticated — which Hammerstein alone in our musical theatre seems to be able to write.

Logan's staging of the show is exceptional, even down to the matter of the actors' facial expressions, and the performances of most of the roles could scarcely be bettered.

Ezio Pinza, recruited from the Metropolitan Opera, in voice, acting and bearing takes chief honors; his is by far the best performance the local musical stage has seen in some time. Mary Martin, who has never been one of my passionate enthusiasms, for the most part is excellent as the Arkansas nurse; she has developed her comedy in a notable manner; but her occasional tendency to blacksmith over-emphasis calls for the rod. Others like Juanita Hall, as a native peddler of grass skirts, shrunken human heads and girls of saleable virtue; Myron McCormick, William Tab-bert and Martin Wolfson as part of the United States mili-tary personnel; and the earlier mentioned prehensile Betta St. John as the secondary love interest are in every way ex-actly what they should be.

If these impress the reader as pretty big words and ones he has not been often accustomed to in the critical vocabu-lary of the present recorder, he should read for relative size those of most of that recorder's confrères. As with *Death Of A Salesman,* the press reviews of the show bordered on an ecstasy that in the former case would have seemed more fitting to something like *Electra* and in this to *Lohengrin.* But, since daily journalistic criticism is conducted largely on a basis of comparative Broadway values, they were in the present instance justified, even if some of the more ex-treme raptures obliquely reminded us of the time-honored Broadway view of theatre criticism in general, to wit, that it too frequently is tragically deficient in such theoretically contagious warmth and excitement which sends customers rushing post-haste to the ticket-window. It thus has been that in the last quarter of a century not more than four out of the many practitioners of the craft — the four given to an irradiation of heat exceeded only by a like number of Pittsburgh blast furnaces — have been esteemed as authen-tic, A1, white-headed boys. These four were members, respectively, of the Oh-What-A-Genius! school, the Hor-ticulture-And-Hat-Removing school, the Dancing-In-The-Streets-And-Hat-Tossing-In-Air school, and the Glauber's-Salts-or-Self-Purgative school, all closely affiliated.

The first of the tropical quartet was Acton Davies, of the

Oh-What-A-Genius! school. When Davies wound himself
up, the heat was such that one had to wrap a cold towel
around one's head to read him. His especial fanaticism was
the late Belasco, and herewith a sample of the pyrexia induced in and spread by him: "When we take stock of true
genius, the kind associated with the names of such immor-
tals as Michelangelo, Mozart and Dostoievski, where can
we find a truer, more beautiful and complete flowering of
it than in the superb art of David Belasco's magnificent
production of *The Darling Of The Gods?* The answer,
plainly, is nowhere! It makes your pulse bounce with renewed life and your brain buzz with such visions of grandeur as are rarely the gift to us mortals. It makes you shout
for supreme joy and, seeing it, it is all you can do to keep
from rushing up to the nearest stranger on the street and
hugging him while you cry out in happiness over such
stunning mastery."

Following Davies, came Clayton Hamilton, a member of
the Horticulture-And-Hat-Removing school. It was sometimes impossible, reading him, to know whether you were
looking at a seed catalogue, a Stetson advertisement, or a
theatre review. When he got up full steam, you had to turn
on the mechanical piano with the mandolin attachment for
an accompaniment. Did J. M. Barrie come forth with a
play in which little babies were mentioned so much as
even once and Clayton wept into his beer, "Art has here
sprung alive into the world with the music of a million
Easter-lilies leaping from the grave and laughing with a
silver singing." And as to the hat motif, a typical morsel:
"In this particular part *(Boys Will Be Boys,* by Irvin S.
Cobb) Harry Beresford reaches greatness; and whenever
greatness is achieved, all lovers of the arts should rise to
their feet and stand reverently, hats off, with uncovered
heads!"

Hamilton's successor in the Broadway affection was Alexander Woollcott, a member of the Dancing-In-The-
Streets-And-Hat-Tossing-In-Air school. As a street dancer,
Alec rivalled Carmen Amaya in her youth, and as a hat
tosser he was the theatre's William Jennings Bryan. Let

Mrs. Fiske or Ethel Barrymore or any one of two or three dozen older actresses appear and, whatever her vehicle, Alec's review would contain enough hoofing on the boulevards and projection of his beanie into the ether to make the Fourteenth of July in Paris look like Black Friday. The dancing in the streets and hat-tossing were also occasionally supplemented by reverential crawling, as in the instance of an actor named Jacob Ben-Ami, of whom Alec rhapsodized, "See him by all means, even if you have to crawl on your very hands and knees to get to the theatre where he is playing!" But when it came to the mimic Elsie Janis, he got really hot: "When she danced her moonlight dance . . . when she sang her moonlight song . . . when, above all, when she stood there in the uniform of a French chasseur and sang 'Madelon' . . . well, these were great moments not to be forgotten . . . All of which is solemnly reported by one who finds it difficult to keep from growing incoherent in the process!"

There was no stopping the boy once he started to unbosom himself. "Perhaps," he would write, "it does not choke you up a little when, from some high-walled schoolyard, you hear suddenly the shrill clamor of children at recess. If it does not, the play *Five O'Clock* would have no particular call upon your sympathies." Or, "A little of the real flame is in Edward Robinson. You have only to see his performance as Satin (*Night Refuge*) to realize it and to realize, too, how all-compensating is the real fire. Here is a young actor seemingly without an atom of what is feebly called 'personal distinction.' His speech, and Satin was supposed to be a man of education, is what dear Mrs. Sanders used to call 'barbareous.' He takes the keynote speech of the play, wherein Satin cries out: 'What is truth? Human beings — that's the truth,' and devastates it by saying 'You-man beans.' *Yet he is still worth his weight in gold!*"

If the late lamented Woollcott may be said to have had a successor, it was probably my old friend Burton Rascoe, a member of the Glauber's-Salts-or-Self-Purgative school, with further matriculation in the Great-Stuff academy. In the single season that he substituted on the *World-Telegram* for John Mason Brown, absent in the armed services, Burton managed to find more great plays and great actors than even Davies, Hamilton and Woollcott in their combined long and eager careers. In all kinds of exhibits that aroused a remarkable lack of enthusiasm elsewhere, he discovered all kinds of rich and notable art, and his tributes to actors ranging from John Philliber, who had a bit in *Mr. Sycamore,* to George Coulouris, who in everybody else's opinion was pretty bad as Richard III, were so voluptuous that you had to look twice to make certain that he was not writing about somebody like Lillian Russell. But the castor oil got into full operation in the case of the movie actress, Geraldine Fitzgerald, whose performance left most of his colleagues constipated. "But let me tell you," he declared, "that on Saturday afternoon I dropped in at the Morosco and stood in the back to catch a part of *Sons And Soldiers* again. I wanted to see if my first impression of Geraldine Fitzgerald, as she appears in this play, was correct — that she is one of the greatest actresses of our time. I caught her in that party scene in which she is the middle-aged mother getting a little tipsy at the celebration of her son's twenty-fifth birthday. My physical sensations were these: tinglings ran up and down my spine; my heart seemed suddenly to fill up and almost to stop; tears trickled down my cheeks. I was in the presence of perfection, of magic, of beauty!"

It was this brand of jive criticism that originally gave birth to movie criticism, with its "epics," "colossals," "supers," "peerless artists," "triumphs," "masterpieces," "director geniuses," and the like. Nevertheless, I somehow still perversely believe, Broadway notwithstanding, that so-called "cold" criticism like Hazlitt's "Miss O'Neill's Lady Teazle appears to us to be a complete failure . . . the only thing that had an air of fashion about her was the feather in her hat," or Shaw's "I think something better could be done with Réjane's talents than this business (*Madame Sans-Gêne*) of playing the washerwoman like a real duchess and the duchess like a stage washerwoman," or, better still, his "Sardou's *Delia Harding* is the worst play I have ever seen; the whole business was so stale, so obviously factitious, so barrenly inept, that at last the gallery broke out into open derision" — nevertheless, as I say, I somehow still perversely believe that such criticism in the long run helps the theatre a thousandfold more than the kind that sounds less as if it were written by reviewers than blown by Louis Prima.

MAGNOLIA ALLEY. April 18, 1949

A comedy by George Batson. Produced by Lester Cole for 8 performances in the Mansfield Theatre.

Program

Angel Tuttle	*Julie Harris*	Miss Eels	*Frances Bavier*
Laura Beaumont		Nita	*Anne Jackson*
	Jessie Royce Landis	Cravin	*Brad Dexter*
Andy Hamill	*Jackie Cooper*	Colonel Stacey	*Fred Stewart*
Maybelle	*Bibi Osterwald*	The Doctor	*Don Kennedy*
Tom	*Robert White*	Mr. Albus	*Douglas Rutherford*
Joadie	*Hildy Parks*		

SYNOPSIS: *The action takes place in the living-room of Laura's home, in a small Southern town. Act I. Mid-afternoon, early summer. Act II. Scene 1. Late afternoon, a week later. Scene 2. Two weeks later. Act III. Scene 1. Early the next afternoon. Scene 2. The following afternoon.*

Director: *Carl Shain.*

THE PREMIÈRE of the play was accompanied by unprecedently early swarms of mosquitoes. The premature appearance of the beasts, which sorely puzzled the management, was, however, in spite of its startling nature readily explained. The play was an immigrant from one of last summer's little rural theatres and when it traveled to the city the mosquitoes naturally became confused in thinking that summer had begun again and came along with it. Hardly more difficult to explain was the sound of cows mooing during the performance. Some contended that it was the actors. It may have been. But I will swear it was cows I heard and, at one time, crickets, to say nothing of a screech owl.

There was also clearly the powerful smell of manure, which would have emanated from the play even if it had never got anywhere near the country. For two and a half hours the stage was given over mainly to cheap sex smut retailed by a variety of trollops both lay and professional

and, when momentarily they let up, to odorous jocosities
on religion, the marriage relation, and kindred topics. Of
anything remotely resembling coherent dramaturgy there
was not a trace. The only thing that could be fairly said to
the credit of the play was that the remarks of the audience
in the intermissions were dirtier than those of Batson's actors, though the dirt in that case obviously had much
stronger justification.

The scene of the bilge was a Southern boarding-house
peopled and visited largely by males and females in quest
of sexual intercourse, and presided over by a middle-aged
woman of similar bent. Mixed in was a former young pugi-
list hopeful of a comeback who was used as the tool of a
crooked fight promoter. The dialogue smirked with double meanings and, more often, single; and the actors, with
one or two exceptions, dawdled about the stage painfully
mouthing the guano as if to kill time until the storehouse
wagon arrived to cart them away. They did not have to
wait long.

The performance in general was as bad as the play itself,
and the stage direction worse. Jessie Royce Landis evidently viewed the role of the boarding-house keeper as an
opportunity to seize the laurels of the late Laurette Taylor,
but her contributions to that lofty end began and finished
with a Southern accent, some funny dresses, and a few
Glass Menagerie rhumba steps. Jackie Cooper, as the trou-
bled prize-fighter, rambled about the stage like a dejected
bloodhound looking for a lost collar-button. And, of the
rest, only Julie Harris as a young religious fanatic and
Frances Bavier in the bit role of a shyly concupiscent in-
surance agent, managed to subdue their material into audience acceptance.

The conventional question asked on occasions like this
is how anyone could possibly be so dumb as to venture the
production of any such play in New York. Though dumb-
ness of such amplitude evades my powers of comprehension, a guess may be hazarded. Every season, someone concludes that a play which has gone well in one of the hot
weather, bucolic barn theatres will repeat its success in

the city and, in the conviction, confidently invests money
in it and brings it to town. The result in most instances is
the same, since what seems a likely play in the remitted
judgment of summer audiences proves to be nothing of the
kind in the less hospitable judgment of the Broadway species. Theatregoing in the country, like summertime reading, is a casual and off-hand business; a play is idly picked
up like a light book or magazine and almost any kind
serves to kill a couple of monotonous nighttime hours. In
the city, matters are different. Theatregoing is a planned,
carefully considered and more serious enterprise; and the
goods have to be better. A play like *Magnolia Alley* thus
may pass with cocktail-filled vacationers taking a few hours
off before going back to highballs and in the distracting
hubbub of flitting moths, croaking frogs and the rustle of
palm-leaf fans, but hardly with audiences who go to a theatre primarily to see something approaching a reputable
play reputably staged and acted.

THE HAPPIEST YEARS. April 25, 1949

A comedy by Thomas Coley and William Roerick. Produced by Gertrude Macy at the close of the season for 8 performances in the Lyceum Theatre.

PROGRAM

Martha Johnson	Judy Parrish	Roger Littlefield	
Richard Johnson	Douglas Watson		James Goodwin
Alida Wentworth	Jessie Busley	Joan Miller	Louisa Horton
Clara Graves	Peggy Wood	Florence Graves	June Walker
Bertram Graves	Richard Bishop	Morton Graves	Loring Smith

SYNOPSIS: *The living-room of the Graves' home in a small mid-Western college town. Act I. Ten o'clock of a Friday evening in late January. Act II Scene 1. 7:45 a.m. the next morning. Scene 2. Nine o'clock the same evening. Act III. Noon the next day.*

Director: *James Neilson.*

LIKE THE FOREGOING *Magnolia Alley*, this was also an issue of the previous summer's backwoods playhouses and little better than its predecessor, even though less given to the French postcard view of human existence. The sex aspect was, however, sufficiently present, for if there is one thing more than another that fetches the hot weather pastoral impresario it is a newly found script that indulges stagewise in matters more usually reserved in the cold weather for bed. This is in a manner understandable, since it remains a popular conviction that, whereas sex activities are likely to be of a relatively moral and circumspect nature and largely the result of an imposed connubial or friendly duty in winter and hence not particularly interesting, they become something of an illicit pleasure and possessed of an inordinate, carefree gusto and interest the moment the temperature goes up and the grass turns green.

While it is not my province or purpose to encroach upon the field of mortal conduct staked out by the Indiana Havelock Ellises and while my conclusions are of course based purely on hearsay, I may timidly hazard the opinion that there is possibly something in the theory. But, since it is my province to treat of the theatre, I may present as my observation that there is no more reason to think that peo- ple who go to it in summer are therefore arbitrarily fasci- nated by sex than to think that the same people who go to it in winter are arbitrarily fascinated by plays that avoid the topic. The one or two sex plays that were real successes on the 1948 summer circuit were not new plays but plays like *The Voice Of The Turtle* that had scored heavily with New York cold season audiences. Not a single new sex play tried out in the rural theatres achieved any noticeable pros- perity. The biggest popular success in those theatres, inci- dentally, was the venerable and immaculate *Peg o' My Heart*. The situation may conceivably change, but as this volume goes to press it seems that, however the summer audiences may feel privately, they are not any more espe- cially interested in dramatically demonstrated anatomy than they are in any other subject, if indeed as much.

The sex element in the present play is introduced, heav- ily, by a meddlesome mother-in-law's suspicions that her son-in-law, a biology student, is up to no good with a fe- male student who is collaborating with him on a thesis. Everything the two do and every move they make provide her with the opportunity to titillate herself with suggestive comment. That they are innocent of any wrongdoing she refuses to permit herself to believe and, driven by the au- thors' apparent idea that an audience will react lubri- ciously to her doubts, she belabors her apprehensions until the evening's end when, for added Minsky measure, she is given a double-meaning line to the effect that, if the col- laborating student had been a man, there would not have been any trouble.

The people the play mainly deals with — the principal character of the mother-in-law is the most tedious of the lot — are deliberately and intentionally presented by the authors as whining, bickering, dull-witted and irritating bores. Since the authors haven't the dramaturgical skill to make them properly intolerable only to one another, the result is a play about bores that, instead of confining their irksomeness to the plot, realistically projects it into the audience. It takes something like genius to write a play about a woman who bores her family, a family that bores her, and relatives who bore both which will convert the general dreariness into amusing theatre. The present authors have simply added themselves to their boresome characters.

Though Peggy Wood contributes to the role of the officious mother-in-law nothing at all in the way of acting but merely reads her lines under the peculiar notion that her performance will thus seem a winningly natural one, some of the other players do moderately well. Loring Smith, as a relative who tortures the other characters, including his sore-footed wife, with endless such jokes as — in answer to the latter's question as to where her mules are — observing that they are probably in the stable, is as passable as the dreadful circumstances permit, and so is June Walker as his tolerant spouse. Richard Bishop, as the stellar pest's husband, Louisa Horton as the suspected female, and Jessie Busley as a shy boarder in the household, also manage to bear up under the handicaps imposed upon them. But it is all wasted effort.

The stage setting, supposed to be the living-room of a house in a small mid-Western college town, fascinated me. I may be wrong, but I seem to have seen that same set at least a dozen times in other plays where it was supposed to be everything from the music-room in a château to the drawing-room in an English country house. In view of the economical look of the whole production, my suspicion was encouraged by the undoubtedly written-in remark of one of the characters that the walls needed repainting but that the job had been interrupted.

❖　　❖　　❖

Até a vista.

Especially Interesting Performances

HOPE'S THE THING
  Dan Reed
BALLET BALLADS
  Paul Godkin
S. S. GLENCAIRN
  Kenneth Treseder
  George Mathews
THE VIGIL
  King Donovan
MAGDALENA
  Irra Petina
EDWARD, MY SON
  Robert Morley
  Torin Thatcher
  Leueen MacGrath
SUMMER AND SMOKE
  Margaret Phillips
  Tod Andrews
LIFE WITH MOTHER
  Robert Emhardt
BRAVO!
  Oscar Homolka
  Lili Darvas
GOODBYE, MY FANCY
  Madeleine Carroll
LIGHT UP THE SKY
  Audrey Christie
THE SILVER WHISTLE
  José Ferrer
RED GLOVES
  Charles Boyer
ANNE OF THE THOU-
  SAND DAYS
  Rex Harrison
LEND AN EAR
  William Eythe

  Dorothy Babbs
  Carol Channing
MAKE WAY FOR LUCIA
  Cyril Ritchard
KISS ME, KATE
  Patricia Morison
THE SMILE OF THE
  WORLD
  Warren Stevens
  Laura Pierpont
LEAF AND BOUGH
  Alice Reinheart
FORWARD THE
  HEART
  Mildred Joanne Smith
MY NAME IS AQUILON
  Lilli Palmer
DEATH OF A SALES-
  MAN
  Mildred Dunnock
AT WAR WITH THE
  ARMY
  William Lanteau
DETECTIVE STORY
  Ralph Bellamy
  Lou Gilbert
  Joseph Wiseman
  Michael Strong
  Horace McMahon
SOUTH PACIFIC
  Ezio Pinza
  Mary Martin
  Betta St. John
  Myron McCormick
  Juanita Hall

Index of Plays

Index of Authors and Composers

A NOTE ON THE TYPE USED IN THIS BOOK

The text of this book has been set on the Linotype in a typeface called "Baskerville." The face is a facsimile reproduction of types cast from molds made for John Baskerville (1706–1775) from his designs. The punches for the revived Linotype Baskerville were cut under the supervision of the English printer George W. Jones.

John Baskerville's original face was one of the forerunners of the type-style known as "modern face" to printers: a "modern" of the period A.D. 1800.

The typographic scheme and the binding design are by W. A. Dwiggins. The book was composed, printed, and bound by The Plimpton Press, Norwood, Massachusetts.

WAD